The Global Economy

in the 90s

The Global Economy in the 90s

A User's Guide

Bill Orr

NEW YORK UNIVERSITY PRESS
New York & London

Library of Congress Cataloging-in-Publication Data
Orr, Bill
The global economy in the 90s / Bill Orr.
p.   cm.
Includes bibliographical references.
ISBN 0–8147–6176–3
1. International finance.   2. International trade.   I. Title.
HG3881.0772   1992
330.9 ′049—dc20   91–36551
CIP

New York University Press books are printed on acid-free paper,
and their binding materials are chosen for strength and durability.

c 10 9 8 7 6 5 4 3 2 1

Book design by Catherine Broucek Orr

To Catherine

whose loving support,
creative contributions,
and hard work
made it happen

Sources

Asian Development Bank
Bank for International Settlements
Deutsche Bank
European Community
General Agreement on Tariffs and Trade (GATT)
Inter-American Development Bank
International Finance Corporation
International Monetary Fund
Institute of International Finance
J. P. Morgan & Co., Incorporated
New York Clearing House Association
Organization for Economic Cooperation and Development (OECD)
Twentieth Century Fund
US Bureau of Labor Statistics
US Central Intelligence Agency
US Council of Economic Advisers
US Department of Agriculture
US Department of Commerce
US Federal Reserve System
United Nations
World Bank

Contents

2 Output   25

The undeveloped world

5 Trade geography   121

6 Trade in services   157

7 Foreign Exchange

8 Balance of Payments

9 Capital Markets

10 Bond Markets 195

11 Stock Markets 209

12 Banking 219

13 External Debt   233

14 Development Aid   249

15 Prices and Wages 257

16 Saving & Investment 271

17 Fiscal Management 281

18 Energy   297

19 Human Capital   307

References   329

Special terms

Bank for International Settlements (BIS). The central bank for central banks of 18 reporting countries and 7 offshore banking centers. Reporting countries are Austria, Belgium-Luxembourg, Canada, Denmark, Finland, France, Germany, Ireland, Italy, Japan, Netherlands, Norway, Spain, Sweden, Switzerland, United Kingdom, United States. Offshore banking centers: Bahamas, Bahrain, Cayman Islands, Hong Kong, Netherlands Antilles, Singapore, US branches in Panama.

CEE. Central and Eastern Europe. Always: Bulgaria, Czechoslovakia, the former East Germany (German Democratic Republic), Hungary, Poland, Romania. Sometimes includes Yugoslavia.

Developed economies. Used in place of *industrialized economies*. In most cases, the OECD economies less Turkey. In a few cases, economies with annual per-capita incomes of $6000 or more, thus adding Cyprus, Czechoslovakia, East Germany, Hong Kong, Hungary, Israel, Singapore, Taiwan, USSR.

Developing economies. High-income: Bahamas, Bahrain, Cyprus, Hong Kong, Ireland, Israel, Kuwait, Qatar, Saudi Arabia, Singapore, Taiwan, United Arab Emirates. (Note that some of these economies are sometimes counted in the developed class.) **Upper middle income:** Algeria, Antigua & Barbuda, Argentina, Barbados, Gabon, Hungary, Libya, Malta, Oman, Seychelles, South Africa, South Korea, St Kitts & Nevis, Suriname, Trinidad & Tobago, Uruguay, Venezuela, Yugoslavia.
Lower middle income: Belize, Bolivia, Botswana, Brazil, Cameroon, Cape Verde, Chile, Colombia, Congo, Costa Rica, Cote d'Ivoire, Dominica, Dominican Republic, Ecuador, Egypt, El Salvador, Fiji, Grenada, Guatemala, Honduras, Iran, Iraq, Jamaica, Jordan, Malaysia, Mauritius, Mexico, Morocco, Nicaragua, Panama, Papua New Guinea, Paraguay, Peru, Philippines, Poland, Senegal, Solomon Islands, St Lucia, St Vincent, Swaziland, Syria, Thailand, Tonga, Tunisia, Turkey, Vanuatu, Western Samoa, Yemen Arab Republic, Zimbabwe.

European Community (EC). Belgium, Denmark, France, Germany, Greece, Ireland, Italy, Japan, Luxembourg, Netherlands, Portugal, Spain, United Kingdom.

European Free Trade Association (EFTA). Austria, Finland, Iceland, Norway, Sweden, Switzerland.

G–7. Group of seven main economies: Canada, France, Germany, Italy, Japan, United Kingdom, United States.

General Agreement on Tariffs and Trade (GATT). As of 1 October 1990, 100 contracting parties subscribing to the organization's set of principles governing world trade. Antigua & Barbuda, Argentina, Australia, Austria, Bangladesh, Barbados, Belgium, Belize, Benin, Bolivia, Botswana, Brazil, Burkina Faso, Burundi, Cameroon, Canada, Central African Republic, Chad, Chile, Colombia, Congo, Costa Rica, Cote d'Ivoire, Cuba, Cyprus, Czechoslovakia, Denmark, Dominican Republic, Egypt, Finland, France, Gabon, Gambia, Germany, Ghana, Greece, Guyana, Haiti, Hong Kong, Hungary, Iceland, India, Indonesia, Ireland, Israel, Italy, Jamaica, Japan, Kenya, Kuwait, Lesotho, Luxembourg, Madagascar, Malawi, Malaysia, Maldives, Malta, Mauritania, Mauritius, Mexico, Morocco, Myanmar, Netherlands, New Zealand, Nicaragua, Niger, Nigeria, Norway, Pakistan, Peru, Philippines, Poland, Portugal, Romania, Rwanda, Senegal, Sierra Leone, Singapore, South Africa, South Korea, Spain, Sri Lanka, Suriname, Sweden, Switzerland, Tanzania, Thailand, Togo, Trinidad & Tobago, Tunisia, Turkey, Uganda, United Kingdom, United States, Uruguay, Venezuela, Yugoslavia, Zaire, Zambia, Zimbabwe.

Germany. Usually indicated as (W) or (E). When not, signifies unified Germany after June 1990.

Gross domestic product (GDP). The total output of goods and services of an economy, with no deductions for depreciation, and not counting the earnings of assets owned abroad. The more commonly used measure of total output.

Gross national product (GNP). Same as GDP, except that earnings of assets owned abroad are counted.

Myanmar. Formerly Burma.

Organization for Economic Cooperation and Development (OECD). Australia, Austria, Belgium, Canada, Denmark, Finland, France, Germany, Greece, Iceland, Ireland, Italy, Japan, Luxembourg, Netherlands, New Zealand, Norway, Portugal, Spain, Sweden, Switzerland, Turkey, United Kingdom, United States.

Transitioning economies. Those in the process of moving from the centrally-planned socialist model toward free markets. USSR and CEE economies.

Undeveloped economies. Bangladesh, Benin, Bhutan, Burkina Faso, Burundi, Central African Republic, Chad, China, Comoros, Equitorial Guinea, Ethiopia, Gambia, Ghana, Guinea, Guinea-Bissau, Guyana, Haiti, India, Indonesia, Kenya, Laos, Lesotho, Liberia, Madagascar, Malawi, Maldives, Mali, Mauritania, Mozambique, Myanmar, Nepal, Niger, Nigeria, Pakistan, Rwanda, Sao Tome & Principe, Sierra Leone, Somalia, Sri Lanka, Sudan, Tanzania, Togo, Uganda, Viet Nam, Yemen PDR, Zaire, Zambia.

USSR, the former Union of Soviet Socialist Republics. Armenia, Azerbaijan, Belorussia, Estonia, Georgia, Kazakhstan, Kirghizia, Latvia, Lithuania, Moldavia, Russia, Tadzhikistan, Turkmenistan, Ukraine, Uzbekistan.

Western Europe. In almost all cases, the EC plus EFTA.

Introduction

This book describes, mostly in facts and figures, the global economy as it moves into the decade of the 90s. The term "global economy" is an increasingly fashionable but still elusive one. Surely the global economy is more than the simple sum of the economic statistics of 160 or so national economies. And just as surely it does not imply a supranational governing entity — or an economic elite who pull strings behind the scenes.

We treat the global economy as a set of markets where private and public players from anywhere on the globe meet — usually electronically — to make mutually beneficial deals. In this view, governments can be players, but they don't really "govern" much of the action. The global markets are, predominately, arenas for private players. The markets live by their own rules of supply and demand . . . and information.

In this global economy, is there, then, any role for "sovereign" national governments to play? Yes. However, populist rhetoric aside, that role is not to control raw market forces. To attempt that, Canute-like, is as futile as trying to hold back the tides or declaring it illegal for Canadian winds to cross a sovereign border and bring an early winter to my Vermont woods. Rather than controlling cross-border actions, the main economic mission of national governments is to organize domestic resources — human capital, social harmony, infrastructures — so they can function effectively in the ever-changing global environment.

Even if we wished it otherwise, current history emphatically tells us that it's not possible to opt out of the global economy. The huge, resource-rich economy of the Soviet Union tried that and ended up with products not even their own people wanted. Global markets set quality standards for domestic products as well as traded ones.

So when we cite national economies in this book, our purpose is to pinpoint the locations of economic activity, not to imply any sovereign control over it.

We present the global economy in the language of facts in order to provide tools for researchers, teachers, students, business persons, and journalists to use creatively in their work. Graphs show trends and relationships. Tables give users discrete numbers to work with. Analyses put each subject in its global context. In most cases, we present each graph with the table of data from which it is derived: we call this combination a figure. In some cases, the figure number follows a series of graphs and their related table. When a table is not associated with a graph, we call it a table.

For our facts, we have turned mostly to official sources, the designated collectors of primary economic data. The facts we present are as timely as was possible at publication time. But since the contents of any book begin to age from the moment they roll off the press, we have emphasized, along with the best possible timeliness, other attributes of the facts: comprehensiveness, integrity, and context.

We have not edited nor altered the data from our sources, but we do reorganize it and add columns (such as shares and ratios) to make the information more useful. We have used our judgment in selecting what data to include. But we have not undertaken to fashion our own integrated model of the global economy; that's the Herculean labor of econometricians. So this book is not a seamless fabric; the reader must expect to find gaps and overlaps where we have stitched together data from different sources, each with its own slant on its subject. These sources speak for themselves, and we identify each one in the text and in an appendix on references. I take this opportunity to praise them whole-heartedly for the increasing sophistication of their reports. I have leaned heavily on their analyses as background for my own. I have frequently called on individual specialists for clarifications and always found them knowledgeable and cooperative. For their crucial contribution to this book, I extend my sincere thanks. Of course, I am responsible for any errors that may have occurred in using their data.

In some areas, notably output and trade, it takes many months for official agencies to gather and compile final data from 100–160 primary sources of varying sophistication. For most researchers, we trust, that delay doesn't detract much from the usefulness of the data, since trends and relationships change slowly. We hope our book will be useful as background even for those who also rely on the raw, up-to-the-minute numbers available in computer databases.

The opening chapter, Macro Trends, is an overview of current and forecast changes in macroeconomic performance, with emphasis on trends in the main developed economies.

The next two chapters cover the world's output of goods, presented by geography (nations) and products. Three chapters cover trade: what products (merchandise) are traded and where they are traded, and trade in services.

A chapter on foreign exchange shows the turbulence of the 1980s and lays out the European Community's plan for monetary union by 2000.

The next five chapters treat capital markets, starting with capital flows as measured in balance-of-payments accounts. This part contains an overview of capital markets, followed by chapters on international bond and stock markets and one on banking.

Two chapters on external debt and development aid treat the plight of developing economies as they struggle to emerge from the crises of debt and poverty.

The chapter on prices and wages treats the most fundamental factor in market economics. The chapter on saving and investment provides background for considering a vital current issue: is a global capital shortage pushing up interest rates and squeezing developing countries out of contention for investment funds?

We next treat the fiscal management tools, spending and taxing, that government policymakers use to adapt their macroeconomies to the global environment. Energy gets its own chapter because of its critical influence on so much of economic life. Finally, we look at the main factors in developing and maintaining human capital — beyond doubt the most important aspect of the global economy that individual governments have any control over.

As in most reference works, readers don't have to use our book in any particular order to get the most out of it.

Fall 1991

BILL
ORR
Waterbury Center, Vermont
USA

1 Macro Trends

The global economy is the synergistic interplay of some 160 national economies, dominated by the group of seven main economies (G–7) that produce nearly 60% of the gross world output. A few supranational organizations rise above the hustle of the world's work, but their function is to monitor the action, not to guide it. What guidance there is comes from the G–7, who control the policies of the world bodies and in fact have set up their own shop to fashion modest policies for coordinating their own macroeconomics.

In the first half of the 1980s, policymakers in the United States and Japan held fast to the doctrine of floating foreign-exchange rates, while the European Community (conspicuously absent the United Kingdom) set to the task of fashioning what eventually is to become a fixed-rate system. After five years of fluctuating exchange rates and a soaring US dollar, the G–7 abruptly changed its policy in 1985 at the now-famous Plaza meeting. Intervention has been commonplace since.

Following that first major attempt at policy coordination, economic performance improved: current-account imbalances narrowed, the G–7's fiscal policies were more harmonious, and exchange rates calmed down. With that success in hand, some global economists now advocate building up the structure of coordination, hoping to achieve new successes. Others aren't so sure that coordination works — after all, wasn't the dollar already poised to go down in 1985? And, they say, when coordinated policies are wrong, they can do far more harm than uncoordinated ones.

The prevailing doctrine of minimal intervention doesn't produce only good results. One corollary is that it is essentially futile to try to reduce unemployment. Thus, joblessness in the OECD economies didn't fall below 6% throughout the long expansion of the 1980s — or below 8% in the European Community.

Another corollary of the minimalist doctrine is that policymakers must accept low growth, if that's the hand that free markets deal out. Thus, even in the expansionary 1980s, world economic growth was a modest 2.6%, well below its postwar average. It was 1% in 1990, forecast to be zero in 1991, and projected to hover between 2%–3% as far out as the eye can see.

This modest rate of expansion is slower than the global economy's growth potential, in terms of population growth and feasible gains in productivity.

A clear triumph of free-market doctrine is the stunning progress of the European Community toward its goal of creating a borderless internal market within which goods, services, capital, and people can move freely. Before the century ends, the EC will surely have enlarged itself to include all of western Europe and probably much of central Europe. The same integrating spirit is moving North American economies toward a free-trade area. Japan is consolidating its economic leadership in Asia. Thus the global economy is shaping up as a more or less integrated system with three closely integrated centers: Europe, North America, and Asia.

In theory, the minimalist approach should advocate the freest possible forms of world trade. And spokesmen for international organizations tirelessly preach that doctrine. Yet the growth rate of world trade is slowing down, and populist sentiment in leading countries builds up pressures for ever more restrictions in the form of subsidies, "voluntary" export restraints, nontariff barriers, and unilateral retaliations outside the pale of the global trade organization. The Uruguay Round of talks, aimed at lowering tariffs and improving the efficiency of world trade, was thwarted (temporarily, it is hoped) by inability to compromise on the issue of agriculture subsidies. Indeed, the OECD's chief economist recently threw cold water on any tendency to overconfidence: "Despite all that has happened since 1945, the world economy in April 1991 is clearly less integrated than it was in April 1914."

On balance, though, G–7 policymakers seem pleased with the minimalist approach and are clearly disposed to continue it and even extend it to the developing world. The shining success stories in that world are the newly-industrializing of Asia: Hong Kong, Singapore, Taiwan, and South Korea. The economies of Thailand and Malaysia seem to have set the same course. And in Latin America — almost written off as hopeless — Mexico, Chile, and Venezuela are on their way to sustained growth and full participation in the global financial markets.

Surely the biggest emotional, if not yet an economic, triumph for free-market doctrine was the astonishingly sudden rejection of communism in central and eastern Europe. The former socialist economies are taking different tortured paths toward their versions of free markets.

This chapter presents these trends in macroeconomics from a coordinator's perspective. That view focuses on year-to-year changes and on forecasts for the next few years out. Whether or not the forecasts turn out to be accurate, they inform the decisions that coordinators make and are therefore important.

Among the G–7, only Japan is growing faster than the developed world as a whole. Germany's growth is being attenuated by the demands of unification.

Economic growth in the Middle East, set back by the Gulf War, recovers as the region rebuilds and the world economy picks up after recession.

The developing economies of Europe, including those now transitioning from socialism, continue to contract, although at a slowing rate.

In these IMF forecasts, the world economy recovers to a 2.9% rate of growth in 1992.

Output

Growth of world output

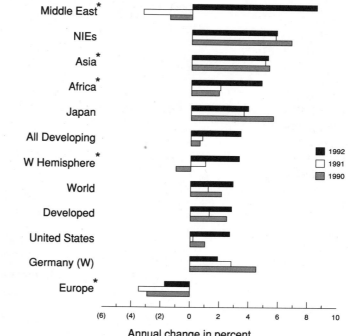

Annual change in percent

*Developing economies only

	1973-82	1990	1991	1992
DEVELOPED				
United States	2.0	1.0	0.2	2.7
Japan	3.9	5.6	3.6	3.9
Germany (W)	1.9	4.5	2.8	1.9
NIEs	8.1	6.8	5.7	5.8
Total	**2.4**	**2.5**	**1.3**	**2.8**
DEVELOPING				
Middle East	4.9	-1.5	-3.3	8.5
Asia	5.7	5.3	5.0	5.2
Africa	2.9	1.9	2.0	4.8
Western Hemisphere	4.3	-1.0	1.0	3.3
Europe	4.3	-2.9	-3.5	-1.7
Total	**4.5**	**0.6**	**0.8**	**3.4**
World	**3.0**	**2.1**	**1.2**	**2.9**

Figure 1–1

Average is compound annual rates of change. Excludes China.
Annual changes in percent.
Figures for 1991 and 1992 are forecasts.
NIEs = newly industrializing economies of Asia.
Source: International Monetary Fund (10).

The 24 developed economies of the OECD produce 78% of global output.

The United States, the European Community, and Japan produce 90% of OECD's total output. The G–7 produce 86%; smaller OECD economies produce the remaining 14%.

The OECD forecast, more recent than IMF's by a few months, gives Japan slightly higher growth. The United States turns negative in 1991 before recovering. The OECD, EC, and G–7 all continue modest growth.

Industrial production in the G–7 and the total OECD snaps back in 1992 after near-zero growth the previous year.

Distribution of OECD output

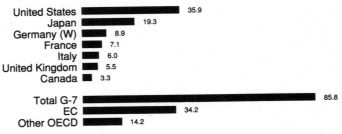

Source: Organization for Economic Cooperation and Development (9).

Figure1–2

Growth of output in OECD economies

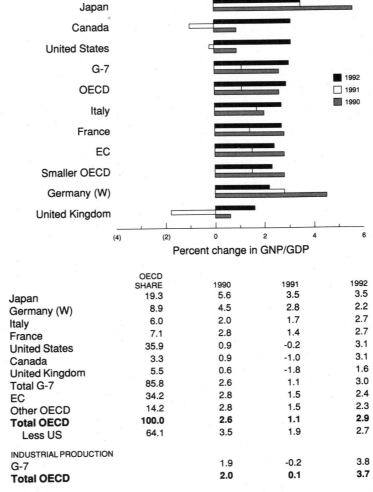

Percent change in GNP/GDP

	OECD SHARE	1990	1991	1992
Japan	19.3	5.6	3.5	3.5
Germany (W)	8.9	4.5	2.8	2.2
Italy	6.0	2.0	1.7	2.7
France	7.1	2.8	1.4	2.7
United States	35.9	0.9	-0.2	3.1
Canada	3.3	0.9	-1.0	3.1
United Kingdom	5.5	0.6	-1.8	1.6
Total G-7	85.8	2.6	1.1	3.0
EC	34.2	2.8	1.5	2.4
Other OECD	14.2	2.8	1.5	2.3
Total OECD	**100.0**	**2.6**	**1.1**	**2.9**
Less US	64.1	3.5	1.9	2.7
INDUSTRIAL PRODUCTION				
G-7		1.9	-0.2	3.8
Total OECD		**2.0**	**0.1**	**3.7**

Figure 1–3

Percent change, seasonally adjusted at annual rates. Figures for 1991 and 1992 are forecasts.
Source: Organization for Economic Cooperation and Development (9).

Turkey leads the smaller OECD economies in growth, despite the setbacks suffered in the Gulf war. In all, these smaller economies copy the modest growth pattern of the OECD as a whole.

Finland recovers from difficulties related to the loss of barter trade with the former Soviet Union.

Sweden recovers from recession.

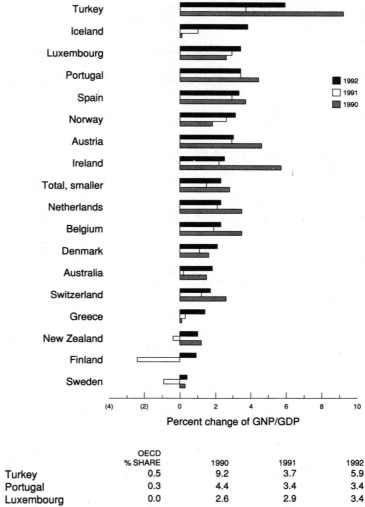

Growth of real output in smaller OECD economies

Percent change of GNP/GDP

	OECD % SHARE	1990	1991	1992
Turkey	0.5	9.2	3.7	5.9
Portugal	0.3	4.4	3.4	3.4
Luxembourg	0.0	2.6	2.9	3.4
Austria	0.9	4.6	2.9	3.0
Spain	2.3	3.7	2.9	3.3
Norway	0.7	1.8	2.6	3.1
Ireland	0.2	5.7	2.2	2.5
Netherlands	1.7	3.5	2.1	2.3
Belgium	1.1	3.5	1.9	2.3
Total, smaller	14.2	2.8	1.5	2.3
Switzerland	1.4	2.6	1.2	1.7
Denmark	0.8	1.6	1.1	2.1
Iceland	0.0	0.1	1.0	3.8
Greece	0.4	0.1	0.3	1.4
Australia	1.6	1.5	0.2	1.8
New Zealand	0.3	1.2	-0.4	1.0
Sweden	1.3	0.3	-0.9	0.4
Finland	0.7	0.0	-2.4	0.9

Figure 1–4

Percentage change, seasonally adjusted at annual rates.
Source: Organization for Economic Cooperation and Development (9).

Exports of the developed economies maintain the strong growth pattern of the 1970s. Exports of developing economies are erratic, but turn strongly positive by 1992. Fuel exporters continue a zig-zag pattern, while other developing economies resume their decade-earlier export growth.

The pattern of imports is similar for all developed and developing economies, except for the much more erratic pattern of oil exporters.

Export prices remain fairly constant for the developed economies — growing far less than they did in the 1970s. Export prices of all developing economies are nearly constant after rising hugely in the 1970s.

Trade

Trends in world exports

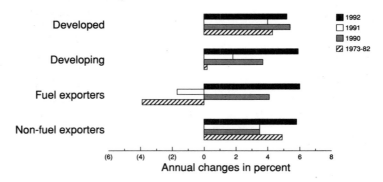

Trends in world imports

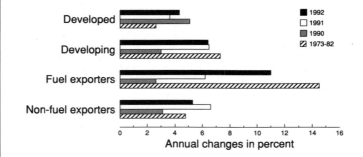

Trends in unit value of exports

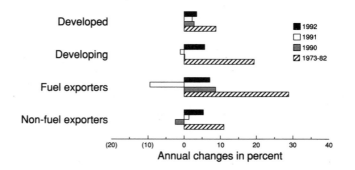

Import prices come down sharply in all economies, compared with the experience of the 1970s.

Terms of trade remain neutral for the developed economies. For non-fuel exporters, they turn slightly positive after more than a decade in the negative. Again fuel exporters show erratic swings of relatively large amplitudes. In 1986, their terms of trade changed 47% negative as oil prices fell precipitously.

Trends in unit value of imports

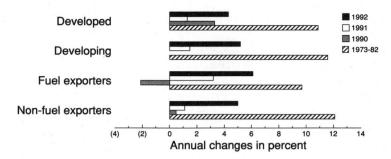

Annual changes in percent

Trends in terms of trade

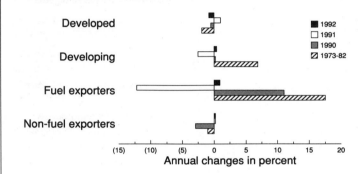

Annual changes in percent

Trends of world trade volumes and prices

	1973-82	1990	1991	1992
VOLUME				
Exports				
Developed	4.3	5.4	4.0	5.2
Developing	0.2	3.7	1.8	5.9
Fuel exporters	-3.9	4.1	-1.7	6.0
Non-fuel exporters	4.9	3.5	3.5	5.8
Imports				
Developed	2.6	5.1	3.6	4.3
Developing	7.3	3.0	6.5	6.4
Fuel exporters	14.5	2.6	6.2	11.0
Non-fuel exporters	4.8	3.1	6.6	5.3
UNIT VALUE				
Exports				
Developed	8.8	2.8	2.2	3.5
Developing	19.3	0.2	-1.0	5.6
Fuel exporters	28.9	8.7	-9.4	7.1
Non-fuel exporters	11.0	-2.4	1.4	5.3
Imports				
Developed	10.9	3.3	1.3	4.3
Developing	11.6		1.5	5.2
Fuel exporters	9.7	-2.1	3.2	6.1
Non-fuel exporters	12.1	0.5	1.1	5.0
				(MORE)

The United States continues its strong export growth, leading all other groups of economies.

The United Kingdom and Canada show the slowest growth, with Canada's export volume actually turning negative in 1991.

Trends of world trade volumes and prices, cont'd

	1973-82	1990	1991	1992
TERMS OF TRADE				
Developed	-1.9	-0.5	1.0	-0.8
Developing	6.9	0.2	-2.5	0.4
Fuel exporters	17.5	11.0	-12.2	0.9
Non-fuel exporters	-1.0	-2.9	0.2	0.2
PRICES				
Manufactures	9.0	9.6	8.3	3.6
Oil		28.3	-22.1	4.0
Non-fuel commodities	7.6	-7.9	-2.7	3.2

Figure 1–5

Annual changes in percent.
Averages = compound annual rates, excluding China.
Source: International Monetary Fund (10).

Growth of export volumes in developed economies

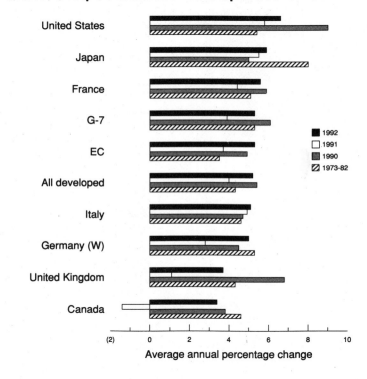

Japan, striving to reduce its trade surpluses, steadily increases its import growth; the United States, needing to reduce its deficits, moderates its imports.

Japan's terms of trade switch abruptly from negative to positive as inflation picks up. The European Community's terms of trade move close to zero, after being moderately negative in the 1970s.

The G–7 and the United States show similar patterns of mostly-negative terms of trade.

Growth of import volumes in developed economies

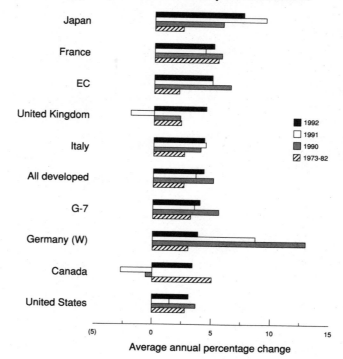

Average annual percentage change

Trends in terms of trade in developed economies

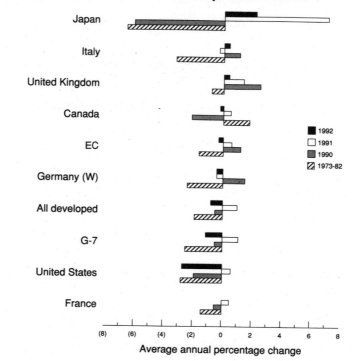

Average annual percentage change

Prices of traded manufactures continue to grow, although at a slower rate in 1992 than in the previous two years or in the 1970s.

The price of oil turned down in most years of the 1980s, then swung up sharply during the Gulf war and sharply back down after it. In 1992, prices turn up a little.

Prices of non-fuel commodities resume a moderately upward course after falling for a couple of years.

Growth of trade in developed economies

	1973-82	1990	1991	1992
EXPORT VOLUMES				
United States	5.4	9.0	5.8	6.6
Japan	8.0	5.0	5.5	5.9
France	5.1	5.9	4.4	5.6
G-7	5.3	6.1	3.9	5.3
EC	3.5	4.9	3.7	5.3
All developed	4.3	5.4	4.0	5.2
Italy	4.6	4.7	4.9	5.1
Germany*	5.3	4.5	2.8	5.0
United Kingdom	4.3	6.8	1.1	3.7
Canada	4.6	3.8	-1.4	3.4
IMPORT VOLUMES				
Japan	2.4	5.8	9.4	7.5
France	5.4	5.7	4.3	5.0
EC	2.1	6.5	4.9	4.9
United Kingdom	2.3	2.2	-2.0	4.4
Italy	2.6	4.0	4.4	4.3
All developed	2.6	5.1	3.6	4.3
G-7	3.2	5.6	3.5	4.0
Germany*	3.0	13.0	8.7	3.8
Canada	5.0	-0.6	-2.7	3.4
United States	2.8	3.7	1.5	3.1
TERMS OF TRADE				
Japan	-6.6	-6.1	7.1	2.2
Italy	-3.2	1.1	-0.3	0.4
United Kingdom	-0.8	2.5	1.4	0.4
Canada	1.8	-2.1	0.5	-0.2
EC	-1.6	1.2	0.6	-0.3
Germany*	-2.4	1.5	-0.4	-0.4
All developed	-1.9	-0.5	1.0	-0.8
G-7	-2.5	-0.5	1.1	-1.1
United States	-2.8	-1.9	0.6	-2.7
France	-1.4	-0.5	0.5	

Figure 1–6

Annual changes in percent, for goods only. Averages = compound annual rates of change.
*For West Germany only through 1990.
Source: International Monetary Fund (10).

Trends in prices of traded commodities

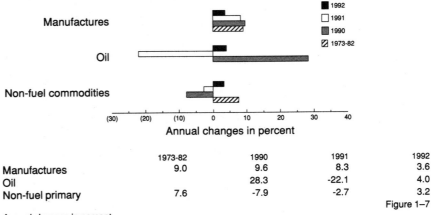

	1973-82	1990	1991	1992
Manufactures	9.0	9.6	8.3	3.6
Oil		28.3	-22.1	4.0
Non-fuel primary	7.6	-7.9	-2.7	3.2

Figure 1–7

Annual changes in percent
Source: International Monetary Fund (10).

The imbalances in the current accounts of the main economies narrowed in the late 1980s and, with the exception of Japan, continue that trend. Analysts generally agree that the present levels of current-account balances are manageable and are no longer the threat to the global economy that they were in the 1980s.

Germany's surplus falls the most dramatically in the early 1990s as suddenly-increased demand in the eastern states draws in imports and the stimulated economy pushes up interest and exchange rates.

The current-account deficit of the United States nears zero in 1991, thanks to the inflow of contributions to the Gulf war. While it is still shrinking, analysts see it vulnerable to swings in exchange rates.

The US deficit jumps back to its 1990 track after the Gulf war windfall.

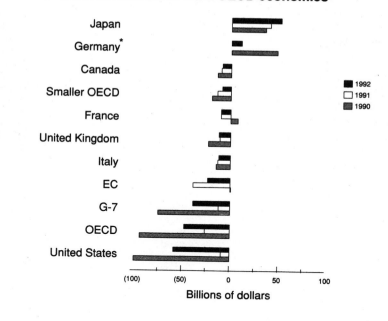

Current-account balances in main OECD economies

Billions of dollars

1992 · 1991 · 1990

	1990	1991	1992
Germany*	47.9	0	11
Japan	35.8	41	52
France	7.8	-10	-10
Canada	-13.7	-10	-9
Italy	-14.4	-13	-12
United Kingdom	-22.7	-11	-12
United States	-99.3	-9	-58
Total G-7	-74.3	-12	-38
EC	0.9	-38	-23
Other OECD	-19.2	-14	-9
Total OECD	**-93.5**	**-26**	**-47**
Less US	5.8	-17	11

Billions of dollars, seasonally adjusted at annual rates.
Figures for 1991 and 1992 are forecasts.
*Figures are for unified Germany from 1991 onward.
Source: Organization for Economic Cooperation and Development (9).

Figure 1–8

The current-account balances of the smaller OECD economies as a whole imitate the pattern of the larger economies, with steadily shrinking deficits.

However, surpluses increase in Switzerland and the Netherlands. And the large deficits of Australia and Spain persist.

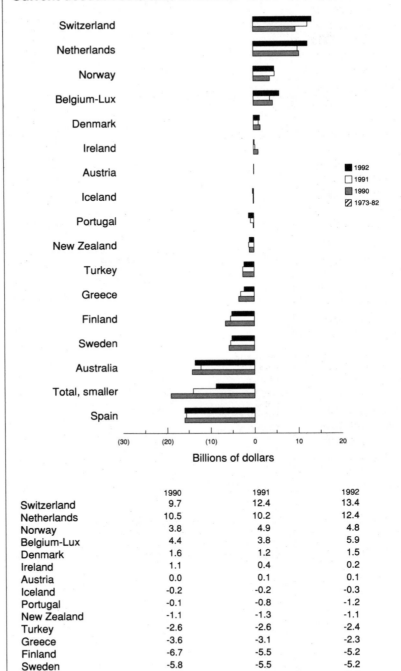

Current-account balances in smaller OECD economies

Billions of dollars

	1990	1991	1992
Switzerland	9.7	12.4	13.4
Netherlands	10.5	10.2	12.4
Norway	3.8	4.9	4.8
Belgium-Lux	4.4	3.8	5.9
Denmark	1.6	1.2	1.5
Ireland	1.1	0.4	0.2
Austria	0.0	0.1	0.1
Iceland	-0.2	-0.2	-0.3
Portugal	-0.1	-0.8	-1.2
New Zealand	-1.1	-1.3	-1.1
Turkey	-2.6	-2.6	-2.4
Greece	-3.6	-3.1	-2.3
Finland	-6.7	-5.5	-5.2
Sweden	-5.8	-5.5	-5.2
Australia	-14.3	-12.3	-13.6
Total, smaller	-19.2	-14.0	-8.9
Spain	-16.0	-15.6	-16.0

Figure 1–9

Billions of dollars, seasonally adjusted at annual rates.
Source: Organization for Economic Cooperation and Development (9).

The fiscal balances of G–7 governments show no trend in the early 1990s, although Italy's large deficit and France's small one shrink a little. Japan's surpluses grow slightly.

The huge deficit of the United States hovers just below 3% of GNP. Based on more-recent forecasts, it's likely that the US deficit is understated in the data shown. US fiscal management is confounded by exposure to very large off-budget liabilities. Most prominent of these are repaying investors in failed savings-and-loan institutions, building up the deposit-insurance fund for a troubled banking industry, and trade guarantees — which could become substantial in the case of the former Soviet Union.

Growth of "narrow money" — cash and demand deposits — was modest in all G–7 economies in 1990, contracting dramatically in the United Kingdom and moderately in Canada.

Fiscal/monetary

Fiscal balances of G–7 general governments

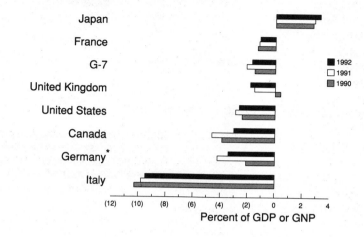

	1990	1991	1992
Japan	2.8	2.9	3.3
France	-1.3	-1.2	-1.1
G-7	-1.5	-2.1	-1.7
United Kingdom	0.4	-1.5	-1.8
United States	-2.4	-2.9	-2.6
Canada	-3.9	-4.6	-3.0
Germany*	-2.1	-4.2	-3.4
Italy	-10.3	-9.8	-9.5

Percent of GDP or GNP.
* For West Germany only through 1990.
Source: International Monetary Fund (10).

Figure 1–10

Growth of narrow money in G–7 economies

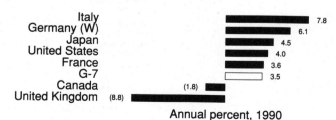

Annual percent, 1990

Narrow money or M1 = currency in circulation plus private demand deposits.
Source: International Monetary Fund (10).

Figure 1–11

Growth of "broad money" — cash plus some term deposits — was moderate in the G–7 economies as a whole.

It grew fastest in the United Kingdom and slowest in France. The small growth of broad money in the United States reflected concern for inflation and a focus on medium-term effects, even as the economy was falling into recession.

Shortterm interest rates in Germany reflected an economy that was heating up. Rates in the United States were below Germany's but still above Japan's.

Inflation is on a declining trend in the OECD economies as a whole, although the European Community shows a slight increase. Inflation grows robustly in Germany, reversing longterm trends and policy dogma.

Growth of broad money in G–7 economies

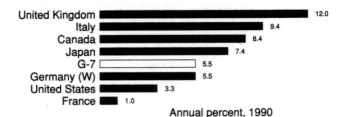

Annual percent, 1990

Figure 1–12

Broad money = M1 plus quasi-money: private term deposits and other noticed deposits.
Source: International Monetary Fund (10).

Shortterm interest rates

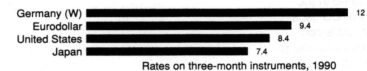

Rates on three-month instruments, 1990

Figure 1–13

Percent of GDP or GNP.
Eurodollar rate = London interbank offered rate on six-month US dollar deposits.
Source: International Monetary Fund (10).

Inflation in main OECD economies

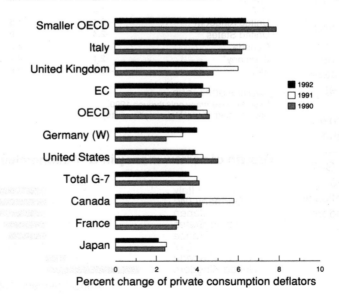

Percent change of private consumption deflators

Inflation in the smaller OECD economies as a whole is on a declining trend, which holds for every economy except Norway, Austria, the Netherlands, and Denmark. Turkey's rate remains at the threshhold of hyperinflation.

Inflation in OECD economies

	1990	1991	1992
Italy	6.2	6.4	5.5
United Kingdom	4.8	6.0	4.5
Canada	4.2	5.8	3.4
United States	5.0	4.3	3.9
Germany (W)	2.5	3.3	4.0
France	3.0	3.1	3.0
Japan	2.4	2.5	2.1
Total G-7	4.1	4.0	3.6
EC	4.2	4.6	4.3
Other OECD	7.9	7.5	6.4
Total OECD	**4.6**	**4.5**	**4.0**
Less US	4.3	4.6	4.0

Figure 1–14

Percent change in private consumption deflators, seasonally adjusted at annual rates.
Figures for 1991 and 1992 are forecasts.
Source: Organization for Economic Cooperation and Development (9).

Inflation in smaller OECD economies

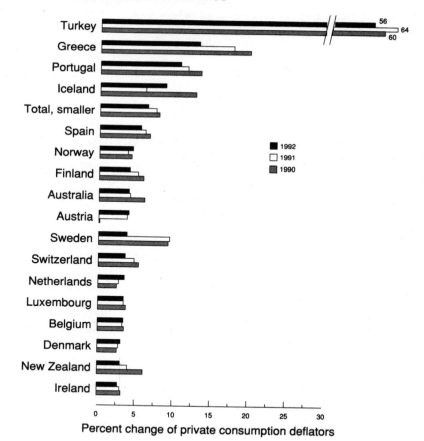

Percent change of private consumption deflators

Labor productivity in the G–7 economies as a whole, as in all developed economies, grows at about the same rate that did in the 1970s.

Japan's productivity growth remains strongest of all economies.

Productivity growth in the European Community recovers to about half of its rate in the 1970s.

Growth in the United Kingdom recovers some of the ground it lost in the 1980s, and then some.

In the United States, productivity growth moves well ahead of its pace in the 1970s.

Growth in Germany is on a steadily declining path. Canada and Italy show patternless growth.

Inflation in smaller OECD economies

	1990	1991	1992
Turkey	60.3	64.0	56.0
Greece	20.0	17.8	13.2
Portugal	13.4	11.7	10.7
Sweden	9.3	9.5	3.8
Total, smaller	7.9	7.5	6.4
Iceland	12.8	6.1	8.8
Spain	6.7	6.1	5.5
Finland	5.9	5.2	4.1
Switzerland	5.4	4.8	3.6
Australia	6.1	4.2	4.0
New Zealand	6.1	4.0	3.0
Norway	4.3	3.8	4.5
Austria	0.1	3.8	4.0
Luxembourg	3.7	3.4	3.4
Belgium	3.5	3.3	3.4
Ireland	3.2	3.0	2.7
Denmark	2.6	2.8	3.1
Netherlands	2.5	2.7	3.5

Figure 1–15

Percent change in private consumption deflators, seasonally adjusted at annual rates.
Source: Organization for Economic Cooperation and Development (9).

Labor

Growth of productivity in G–7 economies

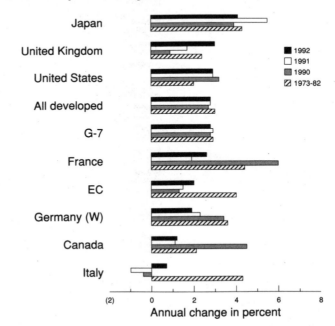

Annual change in percent

Wages continue to grow only moderately in the G–7, as in all developed economies, in contrast to rapid growth in the 1970s.

In Italy and France, the change from the 1970s is even more dramatic.

Wage growth in the United States and Canada is the slowest among the G–7 and all developed economies. The US rates are well below those of the 1970s; even in that decade wage growth was below that of all the other developed economies.

Growth of productivity in G–7 economies

	1973-82	1990	1991	1992
Japan	4.3	3.9	5.5	4.1
United Kingdom	2.4	0.9	1.7	3.0
United States	2.0	3.2	2.9	2.9
All developed	3.0	2.7	2.8	2.8
G-7	2.9	2.8	2.9	2.8
France	4.4	6.0	1.9	2.6
EC	4.0	1.3	1.5	2.0
Germany (W)	3.6	3.4	2.3	1.9
Canada	2.1	4.5	1.1	1.2
Italy	4.3	-0.4	-1.0	0.7

Annual changes in percent. Figures for 1991 and 1992 are forecasts.
Source: International Monetary Fund (10).

Figure 1–16

Growth of hourly earnings in G–7 economies

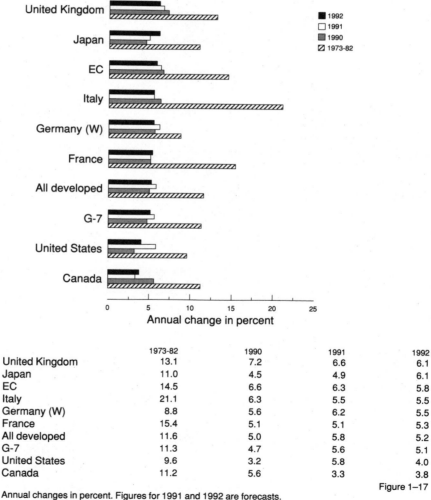

	1973-82	1990	1991	1992
United Kingdom	13.1	7.2	6.6	6.1
Japan	11.0	4.5	4.9	6.1
EC	14.5	6.6	6.3	5.8
Italy	21.1	6.3	5.5	5.5
Germany (W)	8.8	5.6	6.2	5.5
France	15.4	5.1	5.1	5.3
All developed	11.6	5.0	5.8	5.2
G-7	11.3	4.7	5.6	5.1
United States	9.6	3.2	5.8	4.0
Canada	11.2	5.6	3.3	3.8

Annual changes in percent. Figures for 1991 and 1992 are forecasts.
Source: International Monetary Fund (10).

Figure 1–17

Unit labor costs, an inverse measure of productivity, grow at rates well below those of the 1970s in every developed economy.

Growth of labor costs in the United States and Japan was below the G–7 and developed-economy average in the 1970s and remains so into the early 1990s.

Growth of unit labor costs in G–7 economies

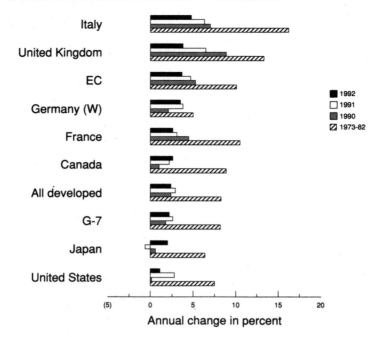

Annual change in percent

	1973-82	1990	1991	1992
.taly	16.2	7.0	6.3	4.8
United Kingdom	13.3	8.9	6.5	3.8
EC	10.1	5.3	4.7	3.7
Germany (W)	5.0	2.1	3.8	3.5
France	0.5	4.5	3.1	2.6
Canada	8.9	1.0	2.2	2.6
All developed	8.3	2.4	2.9	2.4
G-7	8.2	1.8	2.6	2.2
Japan	6.4	0.6	-0.6	2.0
United States	7.5	0.1	2.8	1.1

Figure 1–18

Annual changes in percent. Figures for 1991 and 1992 are forecasts.
Source: International Monetary Fund (10).

Unemployment rates remain high in the European Community and throughout the OECD economies — most notably in Italy, Canada, France, and the United Kingdom.

Unemployment remains lowest in Japan.

In Germany, the rate hovers around 5%, despite massive unemployment in the eastern states.

Unemployment in the United States remains relatively low. In 1992 the rate falls a little as the recession wanes.

Unemployment in main OECD economies

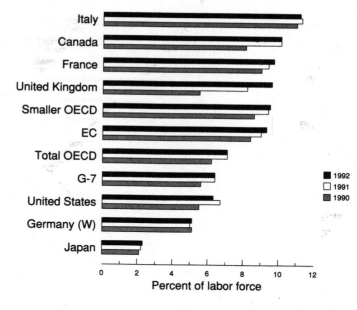

Percent of labor force

■ 1992
□ 1991
▨ 1990

	1990	1991	1992
Italy	11.0	11.3	11.2
Canada	8.1	10.1	10.1
France	9.0	9.4	9.7
United Kingdom	5.5	8.2	9.6
United States	5.5	6.7	6.3
Germany (W)	5.1	5.0	5.1
Japan	2.1	2.2	2.3
Total G–7	5.6	6.4	6.4
EC	8.4	9.0	9.3
Other OECD	8.6	9.4	9.5
Total OECD	**6.2**	**7.1**	**7.1**
Less US	6.6	7.2	7.5

Figure 1–19

Percent change, seasonally adjusted at annual rates. Figures for 1991 and 1992 are forecasts.
Source: Organization for Economic Cooperation and Development (9).

Unemployment in the smaller OECD economies varies more than it does in the larger ones.

Spain's unemployment remains the highest, although it declines slightly in the early 1990s.

Rates in Ireland, Turkey, Greece, and Australia increase at a relatively high level.

Rates in Austria and Sweden remain relatively low, but increase in the early 1990s.

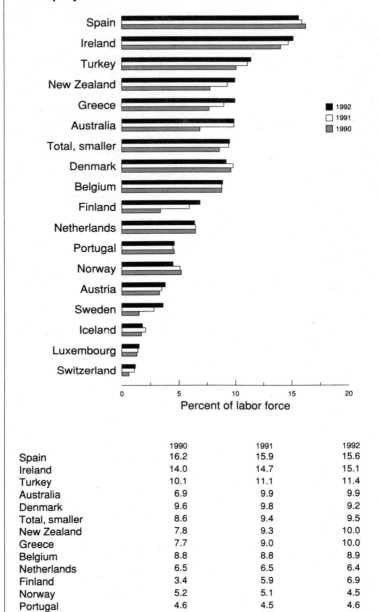

Unemployment in smaller OECD economies

Percent of labor force

	1990	1991	1992
Spain	16.2	15.9	15.6
Ireland	14.0	14.7	15.1
Turkey	10.1	11.1	11.4
Australia	6.9	9.9	9.9
Denmark	9.6	9.8	9.2
Total, smaller	8.6	9.4	9.5
New Zealand	7.8	9.3	10.0
Greece	7.7	9.0	10.0
Belgium	8.8	8.8	8.9
Netherlands	6.5	6.5	6.4
Finland	3.4	5.9	6.9
Norway	5.2	5.1	4.5
Portugal	4.6	4.5	4.6
Austria	3.3	3.5	3.8
Sweden	1.5	2.8	3.6
Iceland	1.7	2.1	1.8
Luxembourg	1.3	1.4	1.5
Switzerland	0.6	1.1	1.2

Figure 1–20

Percent of labor force per national definitions.
Source: Organization for Economic Cooperation and Development (9).

The economies that are transitioning from socialism turn sharply down in the 1990s, as the tasks of privatization, wage and price liberalization, and meeting world quality standards prove to be far more difficult than expected.

Projections beyond 1990 for the former USSR are all but impossible to make, as the economy — or sovereign economies — seem to give political organization a higher priority than economic policies.

Transitioning economies

Growth in transitioning economies

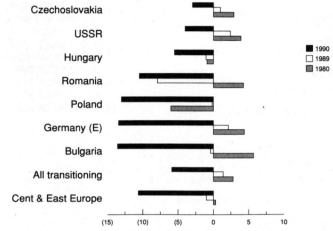

Percent annual change of net material product

	1980	1989	1990
Czechoslovakia	2.9	1.0	-3.0
USSR	3.9	2.4	-4.0
Hungary	-0.9	-1.1	-5.5
Romania	4.2	-7.9	-10.5
Poland	-6.0	-0.2	-13.0
Germany (E)	4.4	2.1	-13.4
Bulgaria	5.7	-0.4	-13.6
All transitioning	2.8	1.4	-5.9
Central & Eastern Europe	0.3	-1.0	-10.6

Figure 1–21

Annual percentage change of net material product. Figures for 1990 are estimates.
Source: World Bank (6).

In the former Soviet Union, out-of-control political events render all forecast data virtually meaningless. Severe depression throughout the former union now seems inevitable, with or without massive external aid. Trade patterns among the republics, fixed by fiat during the years of central planning, will surely be disrupted, but to what extent remains unforeseeable.

Prospects are bleak for most of the republics, should they try to make it on their own. Only the Ukraine, the three Baltic republics, Russia, and possibly Georgia are judged to have a high economic potential, based on their own resources and business culture.

Economic potential of former Soviet republics

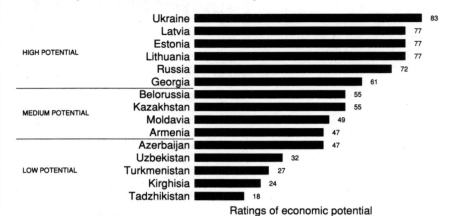

Ratings of economic potential

Figure 1–22

Ranking based on quantification of 12 criteria indicating economic potential: degree of industrialization, hard-currency-earning potential of industrial goods, agricultural production, hard-currency-earning potential of agricultural products, degree of self-sufficiency in industrial goods, mineral resources, hard-currency-earning capacity of raw materials, business-mindedness, proximity to Europe, level of education, homogeneity of population, and infrastructure.
Source: Deutsche Bank (3).

East and South Asian economies continue a longterm growth pattern through the 1990s, although growth doesn't match the high rates of the 1980s.

In Latin America and Sub-Saharan Africa, growth resumes after the "lost decade" of the 1980s.

The differences in rates of growth for gross domestic product (GDP) and per-capita GDP are due to the high birth rates.

Developing economies

Growth of per-capita GDP in developing economies

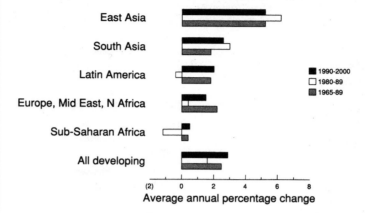

Average annual percentage change

- ■ 1990-2000
- □ 1980-89
- ▨ 1965-89

Growth of GDP in developing economies

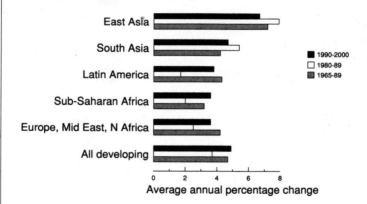

Average annual percentage change

- ■ 1990-2000
- □ 1980-89
- ▨ 1965-89

GROSS DOMESTIC PRODUCT	1965-89	1980-89	1990-2000
East Asia	7.2	7.9	6.7
South Asia	4.2	5.4	4.7
Latin America	4.3	1.7	3.8
Sub-Saharan Africa	3.2	2.0	3.6
Europe, Mid East, N Africa	4.2	2.5	3.6
All developing	4.7	3.7	4.9

(MORE)

The volume of exports from developing economies continues to grow in the early 1990s at an encouraging rate compared with the 1970s. Imports grow at about the same rate as they did in the 1970s.

The unit values of both exports and imports grow, but at declining rates.

Terms of trade hover around zero change in the early 1990s, a sharp setback from their rates in the 1970s.

Purchasing power continues to grow at about the same rate in the early 1990s as it did in the 1970s, though in 1991 it dropped a little in the aftermath of oil-price increases at the outset of the Gulf War.

Growth of GDP and per-capita GDP in developing economies, cont'd

PER-CAPITA GDP	1965-89	1980-89	1990-2000
East Asia	5.2	6.2	5.2
South Asia	1.8	3.0	2.6
Latin America	1.8	-0.4	2.0
Europe, Mid East, N Africa	2.2	0.4	1.5
Sub-Saharan Africa	0.4	-1.2	0.5
All developing	2.5	1.6	2.9

Figure 1-23

Average annual percentage change.
Projections for the 1990s per the World Bank's baseline scenarios.
Source: World Bank (6).

Merchandise trade in developing economies

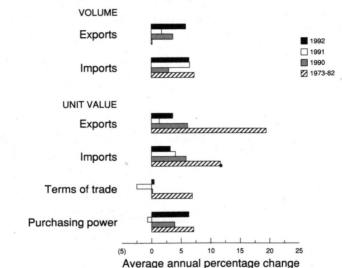

	1973-82	1990	1991	1992
Volume				
Exports	0.2	3.7	1.8	5.9
Imports	7.3	3.0	6.5	6.4
Unit value				
Exports	19.5	6.1	1.4	3.6
Imports	11.7	5.9	4.1	3.2
Terms of trade	6.9	0.2	-2.5	0.4
Purchasing power	7.1	3.9	-0.7	6.3

Figure 1-24

Annual changes in percent, excluding China.
Averages = compound annual rates of change.
Purchasing power = export earnings deflated by import prices.
Figures for 1991 and 1992 are forecasts.
Source: International Monetary Fund (10).

2 Output

Gross world product (GWP) ended the decade at $20.2 trillion, recording a modest growth of 2.5% that took its position on a growth path that has been declining since 1970. Most forecasters expected declines in growth rates in 1990 and 1991, followed by a resumption of moderate growth through 1994.

West Germany, Belgium, and the Netherlands recorded real growth rates of 4%–4.5% in 1989, their best year of the decade. In the English-speaking countries — mainly the United States, the United Kingdom, and Canada — growth slowed from the earlier pace, as planned by policymakers. Growth in Japan, Australia, and several main European economies fell below their rates of the two previous years.

Growth in the developed economies, setting the pace for GWP, is expected to continue its decline in 1991 and turn around in 1992. Exceptions to this pattern are Japan and Germany, which will grow a little faster than average, and the United States, Canada, and the United Kingdom, which will grow more slowly than average.

At the decade's end, growth also slowed in China and the newly-industrializing economies of Asia. In the USSR, growth was

Growth of gross world product (GWP)

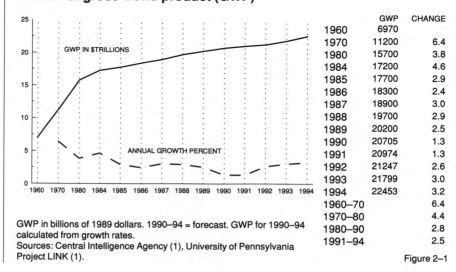

Year	GWP	CHANGE
1960	6970	
1970	11200	6.4
1980	15700	3.8
1984	17200	4.6
1985	17700	2.9
1986	18300	2.4
1987	18900	3.0
1988	19700	2.9
1989	20200	2.5
1990	20705	1.3
1991	20974	1.3
1992	21247	2.6
1993	21799	3.0
1994	22453	3.2
1960–70		6.4
1970–80		4.4
1980–90		2.8
1991–94		2.5

GWP in billions of 1989 dollars. 1990–94 = forecast. GWP for 1990–94 calculated from growth rates.
Sources: Central Intelligence Agency (1), University of Pennsylvania Project LINK (1).

Figure 2–1

slight in 1989, and it was negative in the socialist economies of Central and Eastern Europe (CEE). The USSR and CEE economies are expected to contract in 1991 and '92 — and probably beyond that as their painful transitions stretch out longer than expected.

In the developing world, growth slowed in 1990 and was expected to pick up appreciably in 1991.

The size of GDPs shows the distribution of output throughout the world. Relative levels of output change slowly over years. Most analysts say that output in the former USSR is dropping so rapidly that it has now fallen below Japan's GDP.

Outputs of biggest economies

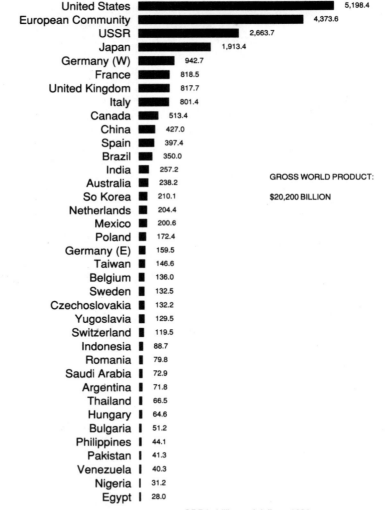

	GDP
United States	5,198.4
European Community	4,373.6
USSR	2,663.7
Japan	1,913.4
Germany (W)	942.7
France	818.5
United Kingdom	817.7
Italy	801.4
Canada	513.4
China	427.0
Spain	397.4
Brazil	350.0
India	257.2
Australia	238.2
So Korea	210.1
Netherlands	204.4
Mexico	200.6
Poland	172.4
Germany (E)	159.5
Taiwan	146.6
Belgium	136.0
Sweden	132.5
Czechoslovakia	132.2
Yugoslavia	129.5
Switzerland	119.5
Indonesia	88.7
Romania	79.8
Saudi Arabia	72.9
Argentina	71.8
Thailand	66.5
Hungary	64.6
Bulgaria	51.2
Philippines	44.1
Pakistan	41.3
Venezuela	40.3
Nigeria	31.2
Egypt	28.0

GROSS WORLD PRODUCT:

$20,200 BILLION

GDP in billions of dollars, 1989

Figure 2–2

Source: Central Intelligence Agency (1).

Per-capita GNP (or GDP) measures how much output is available, on average, for every person in an economy.

Using currency conversions based on purchasing power parities, the United States was the world's most-affluent economy in 1989. The European Community's per-capita GNP was two-thirds of that of the US.

East Germany, the USSR, Czechoslovakia, and Hungary all had figures above $6000, which is used in this publication as the minimum income in defining a developed economy.

The world's average per-capita GNP was $3865 in 1989.

The three economic superpowers — the US, EC, and Japan — produced 57% of the gross world product with 13% of the world's population. The average per-capita GNP in these economies was well over four times the world average.

A spectrum of economies

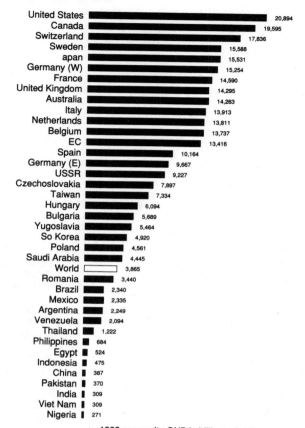

1989 per-capita GNP in billions of dollars

	POP	GNP	GNPPC
World	**5227**	**20200**	**3865**
US, EC, Japan, USSR	**987**	**14149**	**14340**
Percent of world	19	70	371
US, EC, Japan	**698**	**11485**	**16455**
Percent of world	13	57	426

Figure 2–3

Population in millions, 1989. GNP in billions of dollars, 1989. Figures for developed economies based on purchasing power parities. Figures for developing economies based on market rates. Figures for transitioning (former communist) economies based on geometric mean method.
Source: Central Intelligence Agency (1).

Growth trends of main economies

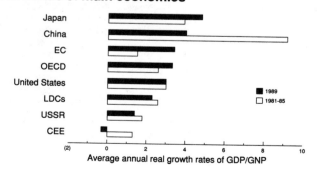

Average annual real growth rates of GDP/GNP

Japan's economy outgrew all others in 1989, climaxing three decades of exceptionally strong growth. The European Community had the greatest growth turnaround when compared with its own early-decade performance. China's growth slowed dramatically during this period, as did those of the central and eastern European economies. As a group, lesser-developed economies grew more slowly in 1989 than in earlier years.

World trade increased 45% during the 1980s — compared with a 29% increase in gross world product, a 17% increase in population, and a 16% increase in agriculture production.

The production of crude steel, crude oil, and some metals declined during the decade.

Growth trends of main economies

	1960s	1970s	1981-85	1988	1989
Japan	10.6	4.6	3.9	5.7	4.8
China		5.8	9.2	11.2	4.0
European Community	4.8	3.0	1.5	3.8	3.4
OECD	4.9	3.2	2.6	4.4	3.3
United States	3.8	2.8	3.0	4.5	3.0
Less developed countries	5.2	5.5	2.6	4.3	2.3
USSR	4.9	2.4	1.8	2.2	1.4
CEE	3.8	3.4	1.3	1.5	-0.3

Figure 2–4

Average annual real growth rates of GDP/GNP.
CEE = Central & Eastern Europe: Bulgaria, Czechoslovakia, E Germany, Hungary, Poland, Romania.
Rates for USSR are at factor costs.
Source: Central Intelligence Agency (1).

Trends in world outputs

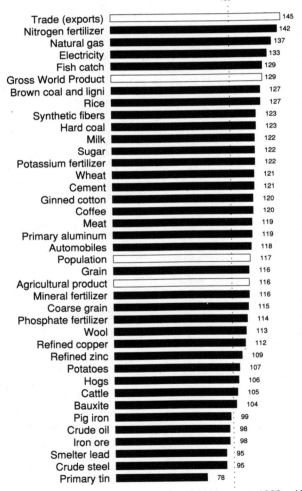

Index of 1989 output; 1980 = 100

Figure 2–5

Source: Central Intelligence Agency (1).

For most of the post-World War II era, analysts and lay persons have referred to developing economies as the Third World. By implication, the developed (or industrialized) economies are the First World. Until 1989, the Second World comprised the socialist economies of central and eastern Europe (CEE).

Today, the CEE socialist economies have embarked on a long and difficult transition to becoming mixed economies with more free-market content and less centralized management.

Three-fourths of humanity now live in economies normally called "developing." Yet those economies at the bottom of this group are much poorer than those in the upper tier. In this presentation, those poorest economies — in which more than half of all humanity labors to produce 5% of the world's output — are grouped together as "undeveloped." The cutoff point for this group is per-capita income less than $500 per year.

Four economic worlds

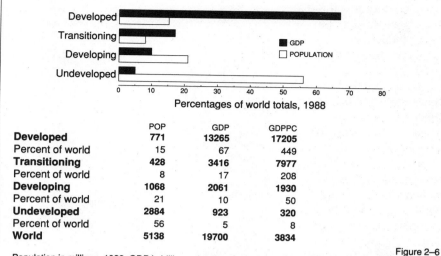

Percentages of world totals, 1988

	POP	GDP	GDPPC
Developed	771	13265	17205
Percent of world	15	67	449
Transitioning	428	3416	7977
Percent of world	8	17	208
Developing	1068	2061	1930
Percent of world	21	10	50
Undeveloped	2884	923	320
Percent of world	56	5	8
World	5138	19700	3834

Figure 2–6

Population in millions, 1988. GDP in billions of dollars, 1988. GDP per capita in dollars, 1988. Source: World Bank (1).

Structure of production of selected economies

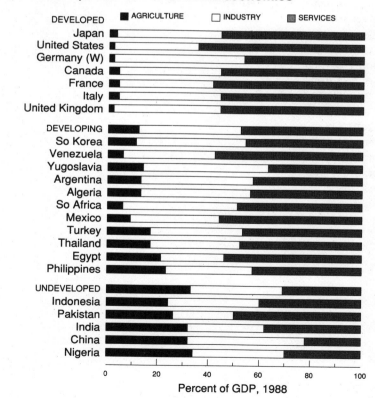

Percent of GDP, 1988

Selected economies in descending order of per-capita GDP.

The world's people produce output in three main sectors: agricultures, industrial products (including manufactures), and services. The pattern of this output varies strikingly among economies, in accordance with affluence.

In developed economies, agricultures are only a tiny percent of total output, and the services sector is a bigger share of GNP than industry. (West Germany is a notable exception.) The United States has the biggest services sector and the smallest agriculture sector.

In the developing world, agricultures are a bigger share of GNP, as are manufactures.

In the undeveloped world, the three sectors are approximately equal — except for China, with more industrial output, and Pakistan, with a large services sector.

Structure of production in selected economies

	AGRICULTURE		INDUSTRY		SERVICES	
	1965	1988	1965	1988	1965	1988
DEVELOPED						
Japan	9	3	43	41	48	56
United States	3	2	38	33	59	65
Germany (W)	4	2	53	51	43	47
Canada	6	4	41	40	53	56
France	8	4	38	37	54	59
Italy	10	4	37	40	53	56
United Kingdom	3	2	46	42	51	56
DEVELOPING	20	12	33	40	46	48
So Korea	38	11	25	43	37	46
Venezuela	6	6	40	36	55	58
Yugoslavia	23	14	42	49	35	37
Argentina	17	13	42	44	42	43
Algeria	15	13	34	43	51	44
So Africa	10	6	42	45	48	49
Mexico	14	9	27	35	59	56
Turkey	34	17	25	36	41	47
Thailand	32	17	23	35	45	48
Egypt	29	21	27	25	45	54
Philippines	26	23	28	34	46	43
UNDEVELOPED	44	33	28	36	28	31
Indonesia	56	24	13	36	31	40
Pakistan	40	26	20	24	40	50
India	44	32	22	30	34	38
China	44	32	39	46	17	22
Nigeria	54	34	13	36	33	30

Figure 2–7

Percent of GDP.
In descending order of per-capita GDP, 1988.
Source: World Bank (1).

The people of North America, 7% of the world's population, produce 28% of its annual output. This region's per-capita gross domestic product is about four times the world average — five times if Mexico is not included.

Western Europe is on a par: the same share of the world's people produce almost exactly the same share of its output.

The people of the USSR and central and eastern Europe produce well more than twice the average per-capita GDP.

All other regions, except tiny Oceana, produce much less than the average output per capita. Nearly half of humanity labor in the economies of East and South Asia; they produce 18% of the gross world product — most of which (13%) is generated in Japan. This areas's per-capita output is 40% of the world's average. In Sub-Saharan Africa, the average per-capita GDP is only 12% of the world's average.

Among the rich economies of Western Europe, all but Portugal produce more than the world's average per-capita GNP.

Geography of production

Gross regional products

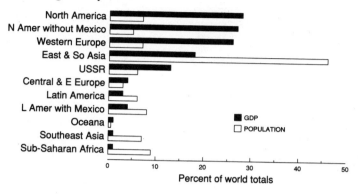

Percent of world totals

	POP	GDP	GDPPC	POP SHARE	GDP SHARE	GDPPC RATIO
North America	356	5476	15383	7	28	401
without Mexico	272	5329	19564	5	27	510
Western Europe	357	5046	14155	7	26	369
East & So Asia	2379	3627	1525	46	18	40
USSR	289	2626	9097	6	13	237
Central & E Europe	140	789	5659	3	4	148
Latin America	303	671	2215	6	3	58
with Mexico	388	835	2153	8	4	56
Oceana	25	242	9622	0.5	1	251
Southeast Asia	376	239	636	7	1	17
Sub-Saharan Africa	483	220	456	9	1	12

Figure 2–8

Population in millions, 1988. GDP in billions of dollars, 1988. GDP per capita in dollars, 1988.
Share = percent of world total or average.
Sources: World Bank (1) and Central Intelligence Agency (1).

Western Europe

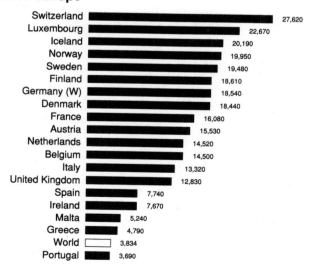

Per-capita GDP, 1988

In North America, the people of the United States and Canada recently took steps to integrate their economies in a free-trade area, which now produces a per-capita output more than five times the world's average.

The region is in the process of extending the free-trade area to include Mexico, a developing economy with strong economic ties to the United States. If and when this common market comes into being, it will be the world's largest, surpassing the European Community in both size and affluence.

Western Europe

RANK		POP	GDP	GDPPC
1	Switzerland	6.545	180.773	27620
2	Luxembourg	0.371	8.399	22670
3	Iceland	0.249	5.027	20190
4	Norway	4.205	83.890	19950
5	Sweden	8.357	162.794	19480
6	Finland	4.944	92.008	18610
7	Germany (W)	61.049	1131.849	18540
8	Denmark	5.133	94.653	18440
9	France	55.873	898.438	16080
10	Austria	7.563	117.450	15530
11	Netherlands	14.760	214.315	14520
12	Belgium	9.867	143.072	14500
13	Italy	57.470	765.500	13320
14	United Kingdom	57.019	731.554	12830
15	Spain	38.997	301.837	7740
16	Ireland	3.574	27.413	7670
17	Malta	0.345	1.808	5240
18	Greece	10.030	48.044	4790
19	Portugal	10.162	37.498	3690
	Western Europe	**357**	**5046**	**14155**
	World	**5138**	**19700**	**3834**
	Percent of world	7	26	369

Figure 2–9

Population in millions, 1988. GDP in billions of dollars, 1988. GDP per capita in dollars, 1988. Source: World Bank (1).

North America

United States	19,840
Canada	16,960
World	3,834
Mexico	1,935

Per-capita GDP, 1988

RANK		POP	GDP	GDPPC
1	United States	246.300	4886.592	19840
2	Canada	26.104	442.724	16960
3	Mexico	84.886	164.267	1935
	North America	**357**	**5494**	**15376**
	World	**5138**	**19700**	**3834**
	Percent of world	7	28	401
	N Amer without Mexico	**272**	**5329**	**19564**
	Percent of world	5	27	510

Figure 2–10

Population in millions, 1988. GDP in billions of dollars, 1988. GDP per capita in dollars, 1988. Source: World Bank (1) and Inter-American Development Bank (1).

Output

The transitioning economies of the USSR and central and eastern Europe (CEE) lie close to the boundary dividing developed from developing status. Together, their per-capita GDP is twice the world's average. The huge economy of the USSR dominates the region, but the former East Germany produces a higher per-capita output.

Within the USSR, the Russian republic has half the population and produces an even greater share of the Union's total output. The Ukraine, with 18% of the population, produces 16% of total output.

USSR and Central & Eastern Europe

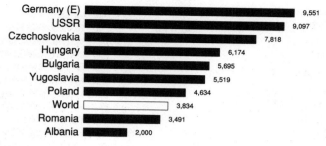

Per-capita GDP, 1988

RANK		POP	GDP	GDPPC
1	Germany (E)	16.5	157.6	9551
2	USSR	288.7	2626.4	9097
3	Czechoslovakia	15.6	122.0	7818
4	Hungary	10.6	65.4	6174
5	Bulgaria	9.0	51.3	5695
6	Yugoslavia	23.7	130.8	5519
7	Poland	37.8	175.2	4634
8	Romania	23.2	81.0	3491
9	Albania	3.1	6.2	2000
	USSR & CEE	**428**	**3416**	**7977**
	CEE	**140**	**789**	**5659**
	World	**5138**	**19700**	**3834**
	Percent of world:			
	USSR & CEE	8	17	208
	USSR	6	13	237
	CEE	3	4	148

Figure 2–11

Population in millions, 1989. GDP in billions of dollars, 1988. GDP per capita in dollars, 1988. GDP figure for Albania is for 1987.
NMP = Net Material Product, a measure of national income produced, which excludes some accounts that are included in GNP.
Source: Central Intelligence Agency (1) and (for Albania) United Nations (1).

Population and Net Material Product of Soviet republics

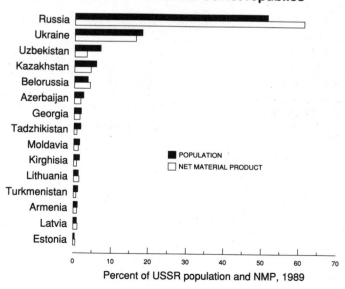

Percent of USSR population and NMP, 1989

In mid–1991, the union of 15 socialist republics that then made up the USSR was on the threshhold of an historic reconstitution of their political and legal relationships. However that turns out, the various republics will for some time at least be bound together in assigned commercial relationships that were set in place during the era of central planning.

Russia — the largest, richest, and best-endowed republic — is the most economically independent: only 18% of its output goes to other republics. At the other extreme, almost 70% of the output of Belorussia is traded with other republics. The three Baltic republics also have strong trading links with the others.

Russia, Uzbekistan, and Estonia lead the other republics in foreign trade outside the union. But none of the 15 republics have strong trading relationships with the outside world.

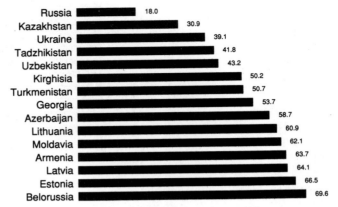

Inter-republic commerce in the USSR

Percent of deliveries to other republics

| | POPULATION | | GNP | GNPPC | NMP | PCT TO OTHER | PERCENT EXPORTS |
	1989	PERCENT	1989	1989	PERCENT	REPUBS	ABROAD
Russia	148.4	51.4	1627.5	10968	61.1	18.0	8.6
Ukraine	51.8	18.0	434.2	8375	16.3	39.1	6.7
Uzbekistan	19.9	6.9	87.9	4423	3.3	43.2	7.4
Kazakhstan	16.7	5.8	114.5	6857	4.3	30.9	3.0
Belorussia	10.4	3.6	111.9	10790	4.2	69.6	6.5
Azerbaijan	7.2	2.5	45.3	6289	1.7	58.7	3.7
Georgia	5.5	1.9	42.6	7789	1.6	53.7	3.9
Tadzhikistan	5.2	1.8	21.3	4111	0.8	41.8	6.9
Moldavia	4.3	1.5	32.0	7399	1.2	62.1	3.4
Kirghisia	4.3	1.5	21.3	4933	0.8	50.2	1.2
Lithuania	3.7	1.3	37.3	9960	1.4	60.9	5.9
Turkmenistan	3.5	1.2	18.6	5395	0.7	50.7	4.2
Armenia	3.2	1.1	24.0	7567	0.9	63.7	1.4
Latvia	2.6	0.9	29.3	11304	1.1	64.1	5.7
Estonia	1.4	0.5	16.0	11099	0.6	66.5	7.4
USSR	**289**	**100**	**2664**	**9230**			
World	**5227**		**20200**	**3865**			
Percent of world	6		13	239			

Figure 2–12

Population in millions, 1989. GNP in billions of dollars, 1989. GNPPC in dollars, 1989.
GNP and GNPPC calculated from share of net material product (NMP), based on CIA estimates of GNP using purchasing power parities.
Percent of republican NMP in current domestic prices.
NMP = Net Material Product, a measure of national income produced, which excludes some accounts that are included in GNP.
Sources: Internation Monetary Fund (6) and Central Intelligence Agency (1).

Output

The economies of Latin America, with 7% of the world's population, produce 3% of its output — a little over half the world's average per-capita GDP. All of the region's main economies fall below the world average. The main economies are usually classified as "middle income developing;" Haiti's is an undeveloped economy.

Brazil's and Argentina's economies, the region's largest, ranked among the top ten in per-capita GDP. Venezuela's economy, the third-largest, led the major economies in per-capita GDP.

If Mexico is included in Latin America rather than North America, its GDP ranks 2nd and its per-capita GDP 12th.

Latin America

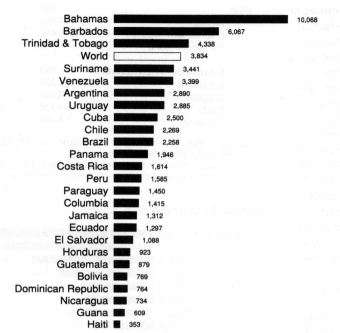

Per-capita GDP in dollars, 1988

RANK		POP	GDP	GDPPC
1	Bahamas	0.234	2.356	10068
2	Barbados	0.254	1.541	6067
3	Trinidad & Tobago	1.157	5.077	4338
4	Suriname	0.359	1.235	3441
5	Venezuela	18.757	63.752	3399
6	Argentina	31.534	91.142	2890
7	Uruguay	3.060	8.827	2885
8	Cuba	10.400	26.000	2500
9	Chile	12.748	28.925	2269
10	Brazil	144.428	326.073	2258
11	Panama	2.322	4.518	1946
12	Costa Rica	2.866	4.625	1614
13	Peru	21.256	33.694	1585
14	Paraguay	4.039	5.856	1450
15	Columbia	30.568	43.250	1415
16	Jamaica	2.427	3.185	1312
17	Ecuador	10.070	13.065	1297
18	El Salvador	5.032	5.473	1088
19	Honduras	4.829	4.457	923
20	Guatemala	8.681	7.628	879
21	Bolivia	6.918	5.321	769
22	Dominican Republic	6.867	5.244	764
23	Nicaragua	3.622	2.659	734
24	Guana	0.755	0.460	609
25	Haiti	6.263	2.210	353
	Latin America	**335**	**673**	**2006**
	World	**5138**	**19700**	**3834**
	Percent of world	7	3	52

(MORE)

The fabled oil wealth of Middle East countries is more fable than fact. If the gross regional product were distributed equally among the twenty economies, their average per-capita GDP would be less than half the world average. Three very small economies, with only one percent of the region's total population, have per-capita GDPs that put them in the class of rich developed economies; they are United Arab Emirates, Kuwait, and Qatar.

Eight of the thirteen members of OPEC are in the Middle East; five of them are above and three below the world average per-capita GDP.

Oilless Israel has a higher per-capita GDP than all oil producers but the United Arab Emirates and Kuwait.

Latin America, cont'd

RANK	POP	GDP	GDPPC
Mexico	84.886	164.267	1935
L Amer with Mexico	**414**	**835**	**2017**
Percent of world	8	4	53
L Amer Common Market	**183**	**432**	**2359**
Argentina	31.534	91.142	2890
Uruguay	3.060	8.827	2885
Brazil	144.428	326.073	2258
Paraguay	4.039	5.856	1450

Figure 2–13

Population in millions, 1988. GDP in billions of dollars, 1988. GDP per capita in dollars, 1988.
Figures for Cuba are for 1987.
The four-nation common market is scheduled to begin Jan 1, 1995.
Sources: Inter-American Development Bank (1), United Nations (1).

Middle East and North Africa

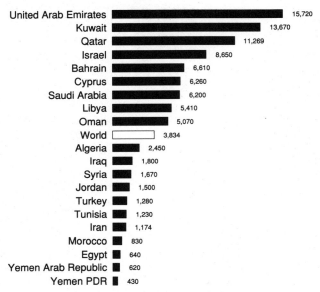

Per-capita GDP, 1988

RANK		POP	GDP	GDPPC
1	United Arab Emirates	1.500	23.580	15720
2	Kuwait	1.919	26.233	13670
3	Qatar	0.500	5.6	11269
4	Israel	4.444	38.441	8650
5	Bahrain	0.458	3.027	6610
6	Cyprus	0.686	4.294	6260
7	Saudi Arabia	14.016	86.899	6200
8	Libya	4.249	22.984	5410
9	Oman	1.402	7.108	5070
10	Algeria	23.805	58.322	2450
11	Iraq	18.100	32.6	1800
12	Syria	11.667	19.484	1670
13	Jordan	3.937	5.906	1500
14	Turkey	53.772	68.828	1280

(MORE)

Output

Close to half of the world's people live in east and south Asian countries. They produce 16% of the world's output.

The region's share of world production drops spectacularly when its high-income economies — Japan, Hong Kong, Taiwan, and South Korea — are not counted. Then the region still has 43% of the world's people but produces only 4% of its output, and its per-capita GDP is about 8% of the world average.

Middle East and North Africa, cont'd

RANK		POP	GDP	GDPPC
15	Tunisia	7.796	9.589	1230
16	Iran	53.900	63.3	1174
17	Morocco	23.920	19.854	830
18	Egypt	51.447	32.926	640
19	Yemen Arab Republic	2.339	1.450	620
20	Yemen, PDR	8.742	3.759	430
	Middle East & No Africa	**289**	**534**	**1851**
	World	**5138**	**19700**	**3834**
	Percent of world	6	3	48

Figure 2–14

Population in millions, 1988. GDP in billions of dollars, 1988. GDP per capita in dollars, 1988.
Figures for Bahrain are for 1987.
Sources: World Bank (1) and Central Intelligence Agency (1).

East and South Asia

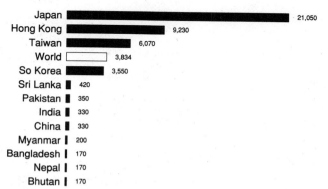

Per-capita GDP, 1988

RANK		POP	GDP	GDPPC
1	Japan	122.433	2577.215	21050
2	Hong Kong	5.674	52.371	9230
3	Taiwan	20.300	146.600	6070
4	So Korea	42.593	151.205	3550
5	Sri Lanka	16.6000	6.972	420
6	Pakistan	105.677	36.987	350
7	India	813.990	268.617	330
8	China	1083.889	357.683	330
9	Myanmar (Burma)	40.000	8.000	200
10	Bangladesh	108.851	18.505	170
11	Nepal	18.053	3.069	170
12	Bhutan	1.373	0.233	170
	East & South Asia	**2379**	**3627**	**1525**
	World	**5138**	**19700**	**3834**
	Percent of world	46	18	40
	Without top 4	**2188**	**700**	**320**
	Percent of world	43	4	8.3

Figure 2–15

No data for: Afghanistan, Maldives, Mongolia, No Korea.
Population in millions, 1988. GDP in billions, 1988. GDP per capita in dollars, 1988.
Figures for Myanmar are for 1986.
Source: World Bank (1).

Singosad stands out as the high-income economy of southeast Asia, with Malaysia and Thailand also far above the region's average per-capita GDP.

Singapore stands out as the high-income economy of southeast Asia, with Malaysia and Thailand also far above the region's average per-capita GDP.

Similarly, Australia and New Zealand stand out among the other tiny economies of Oceana.

Southeast Asia

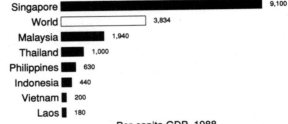

Per-capita GDP, 1988

RANK		POP	GDP	GDPPC
1	Singapore	2.639	24.015	9100
2	Malaysia	16.921	32.827	1940
3	Thailand	54.469	54.469	1000
4	Philippines	59.686	37.602	630
5	Indonesia	174.832	76.926	440
6	Viet Nam	63.550	12.710	200
7	Laos	3.940	0.709	180
	Southeast Asia	**376**	**239**	**636**
	World	**5138**	**19700**	**3834**
	Percent of world	7	1	17

Figure 2–16

No data for: Brunei, Kampuchea.
Population in millions, 1988. GDP in billions of dollars, 1988. GDP per capita in dollars, 1988.
Source: World Bank (1).

Oceana

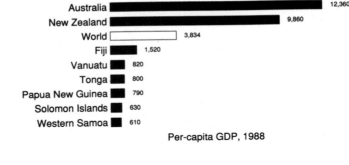

Per-capita GDP, 1988

RANK		POP	GDP	GDPPC
1	Australia	16.506	204.014	12360
2	New Zealand	3.339	32.923	9860
3	Fiji	0.732	1.113	1520
4	Vanuatu	0.151	0.124	820
5	Tonga	0.101	0.081	800
6	Papua New Guinea	3.804	3.005	790
7	Solomon Islands	0.304	0.192	630
8	Western Samoa	0.168	0.102	610
	Oceana	**25**	**242**	**9622**
	World	**5138**	**19700**	**3834**
	Percent of world	0.5	1	251

Figure 2–17

No data for: Kiribati, New Caledonia, Tuvalu.
Population in millions, 1988. GDP in billions, 1988. GDP per capita in dollars, 1988.
Source: World Bank (1).

All of the 41 economies of Sub-Saharan Africa have per-capita GDPs below the world average — most of them far below it.

Sub-Saharan Africa

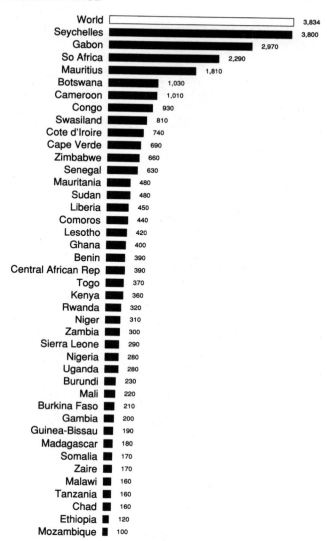

Per-capita GDP, 1988

World	3,834
Seychelles	3,800
Gabon	2,970
So Africa	2,290
Mauritius	1,810
Botswana	1,030
Cameroon	1,010
Congo	930
Swasiland	810
Cote d'Iroire	740
Cape Verde	690
Zimbabwe	660
Senegal	630
Mauritania	480
Sudan	480
Liberia	450
Comoros	440
Lesotho	420
Ghana	400
Benin	390
Central African Rep	390
Togo	370
Kenya	360
Rwanda	320
Niger	310
Zambia	300
Sierra Leone	290
Nigeria	280
Uganda	280
Burundi	230
Mali	220
Burkina Faso	210
Gambia	200
Guinea-Bissau	190
Madagascar	180
Somalia	170
Zaire	170
Malawi	160
Tanzania	160
Chad	160
Ethiopia	120
Mozambique	100

Output

In this region, nearly 500 million people, 9% of the world's total, produce only 1% of its output.

All but the top twelve economies in the region fall in the category of undeveloped.

If the higher-income top four economies of the region are not counted, the average per-capita GDP drops by a third, to 8% of the world average.

Sub-Saharan Africa

RANK		POP	GDP	GDPPC
1	Seychelles	0.068	0.257	3800
2	Gabon	1.077	3.199	2970
3	So Africa	33.938	77.718	2290
4	Mauritius	1.048	1.897	1810
5	Botswana	1.164	1.199	1030
6	Cameroon	11.213	11.325	1010
7	Congo	2.100	1.953	930
8	Swaziland	0.737	0.597	810
9	Cote d'Ivoire	11.587	8.574	740
10	Cape Verde	0.352	0.243	690
11	Zimbabwe	9.257	6.110	660
12	Senegal	7.154	4.507	630
13	Mauritania	1.907	0.915	480
14	Sudan	23.776	11.412	480
15	Liberia	2.401	1.080	450
16	Comoros	0.442	0.194	440
17	Lesotho	1.673	0.703	420
18	Ghana	14.040	5.616	400
19	Benin	4.454	1.737	390
20	Central African Rep	2.794	1.090	390
21	Togo	3.362	1.244	370
22	Kenya	23.021	8.288	360
23	Rwanda	6.657	2.130	320
24	Niger	6.998	2.169	310
25	Zambia	7.486	2.246	300
26	Sierra Leone	3.938	1.142	290
27	Nigeria	110.131	30.837	280
28	Uganda	16.195	4.535	280
29	Burundi	5.149	1.184	230
30	Mali	7.989	1.758	220
31	Burkina Faso	8.546	1.795	210
32	Gambia	0.822	0.164	200
33	Guinea-Bissau	0.940	0.179	190
34	Madagascar	11.259	2.027	180
35	Somalia	5.882	1.000	170
36	Zaire	33.615	5.715	170
37	Malawi	8.155	1.305	160
38	Tanzania	24.739	3.958	160
39	Chad	5.399	0.864	160
40	Ethiopia	46.144	5.537	120
41	Mozambique	14.967	1.497	100
	Sub-Saharan Africa	**483**	**220**	**456**
	World	**5138**	**19700**	**3834**
	Percent of world	9	1	12
	Without top 4	**446**	**137**	**306**
	Percent of world	8.7	0.7	8

Figure 2–18

No data for: Namibia
Population in millions, 1988. GDP in billions of dollars, 1988. GDP per capita in dollars, 1988.
All figures for Liberia and Sierra Leone are for 1987.
Source: World Bank (1).

In this analysis, economies are divided, largely by per-capita GDP, into four economic "worlds" — developed, transitioning, developing, and undeveloped.

The developed world includes economies that are largely industrialized and have a per-capita GDP of at least $6000 per year. These are the world's richest economies, with average incomes almost four times the world average.

The OECD economies lead the list. Four transitioning economies — East Germany, USSR, Czechoslovakia, and Hungary — also meet the criteria for "developed," although their instability during the transition makes comparative figures very unreliable.

Three newly-industrializing economies — Hong Kong, Singapore, and Taiwan — also meet this publication's definition of developed.

Israel, too, meets the definition, although it is not always included in the developed class.

The developed world

Developed economies

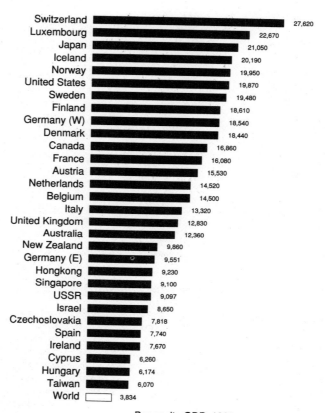

Per-capita GDP, 1988

RANK		POP	GDP	GDPPC
1	Switzerland	6.545	180.773	27620
2	Luxembourg	0.371	8.399	22670
3	Japan	122.433	2577.215	21050
4	Iceland	0.249	5.027	20190
5	Norway	4.205	83.890	19950
6	United States	245.871	4885.457	19870
7	Sweden	8.357	162.794	19480
8	Finland	4.944	92.008	18610
9	Germany (W)	61.049	1131.849	18540
10	Denmark	5.133	94.653	18440
11	Canada	26.104	440.113	16860
12	France	55.873	898.438	16080
13	Austria	7.563	117.450	15530
14	Netherlands	14.760	214.315	14520
15	Belgium	9.867	143.072	14500

(MORE)

Comparative measures of GDP must, in one way or another, translate prices and incomes from local currencies into a common one, most often the US dollar. Using official or market exchange rates does not accurately reflect relative purchasing powers in different economies. So over several years, the OECD developed an alternative measure based on purchasing power parities (PPPs). This method provides an international conversion factor that transforms prices in any currency into the equivalent prices in US dollars.

Using current prices in local currencies, Switzerland's is the most-affluent economy, followed by Iceland, Japan, and the other Nordic economies. Using a PPP basis, the United States and Canada have the highest per-capita GDP, with Switzerland third. Japan, which ranks third using exchange rates, ranks eighth on a PPP basis.

All but the least-affluent economies rank lower using PPPs than they do using exchange rates.

Developed economies, cont'd

RANK		POP	GDP	GDPPC
16	Italy	57.470	765.500	13320
17	United Kingdom	57.019	731.554	12830
18	Australia	16.506	204.014	12360
19	New Zealand	3.339	32.923	9860
20	Germany (E)[1]	16.500	159.500	9551
21	Hong Kong[2]	5.6740	52.3710	9230
22	Singapore[2]	2.6390	24.0150	9100
23	USSR[1]	288.700	2663.700	9097
24	Israel	4.444	38.441	8650
25	Czechoslovakia[1]	15.600	123.200	7818
26	Spain	38.997	301.837	7740
27	Ireland	3.574	27.413	7670
28	Cyprus	0.686	4.294	6260
29	Hungary[1]	10.600	64.600	6174
30	Taiwan[2]	20.300	146.600	6070
	Developed economies	**1115**	**16375**	**14682**
	World	**5138**	**19700**	**3834**
	Percent of world	22	83	383
	Without TRE[1] and NIE[2]	**771**	**13265**	**17205**
	Percent of world	15	67	449

Figure 2–19

Population in millions, 1988. GDP in billions of dollars, 1988. GDP per capita in dollars, 1988.
Developed economies = industrialized with per-capita GDP more than $6000.
Figures for Transitioning Economies based on purchasing power parities.
[1]Transitioning economies.
[2]Newly-industrializing economies.
Sources: Central Intelligence Agency (1) and World Bank (1).

Relative per-capita GDP in OECD economies

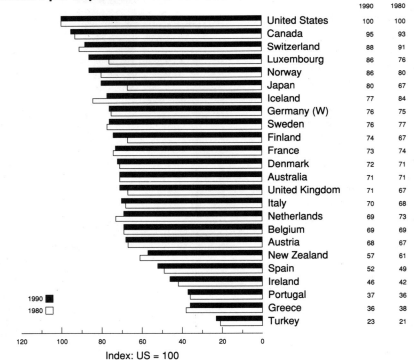

	1990	1980
United States	100	100
Canada	95	93
Switzerland	88	91
Luxembourg	86	76
Norway	86	80
Japan	80	67
Iceland	77	84
Germany (W)	76	75
Sweden	76	77
Finland	74	67
France	73	74
Denmark	72	71
Australia	71	71
United Kingdom	71	67
Italy	70	68
Netherlands	69	73
Belgium	69	69
Austria	68	67
New Zealand	57	61
Spain	52	49
Ireland	46	42
Portugal	37	36
Greece	36	38
Turkey	23	21

1990 ■
1980 □

Index: US = 100

The United States has OECD's largest economy, followed by Japan, West Germany, France, and Italy.

Norway's economy grew the most in 1989, followed by those of Spain, Portugal, Finland, and Japan. Only Iceland's economy contracted in that year, although New Zealand's growth was barely positive.

In general, more-affluent economies are characterized by large service sectors and small agriculture sectors. The notable exceptions are West Germany and Japan, with smaller service sectors and larger industrial sectors than other rich economies. Their industrial sectors were one-third larger than that of the United States.

GDP in OECD economies

	GDP 1989	1989 RANK	GDP 1988	CHANGE 1989	CHANGE 1988	PER CAPITA, 1988 CURRENT	RANK	PPP	RANK
US	5165.8	1	4817.8	2.9	2.7	19558	9	19558	1
Canada	545.6	7	484.6	2.8	3.2	18675	10	18446	2
Switzerland	174.4	12	183.7	3.1	2.2	27581	1	16700	3
Norway	93.1	17	91.2	5.7	3.5	21654	4	16322	4
Iceland	5.2	24	5.9	-2.7	3.5	23936	2	16068	5
Luxembourg	6.6	23	6.6	4.2	2.7	17592	11	15558	6
Sweden	189.3	11	181.9	1.9	2.3	21546	5	14772	7
Japan	2812.1	2	2843.4	4.7	4.2	23190	3	14288	8
Germany (W)	1200.2	3	1201.8	4.2	1.9	19581	8	14161	9
Finland	114.7	15	105.2	4.8	3.8	21266	6	13792	10
France	948.5	4	949.9	3.4	2.0	17002	12	13603	11
Denmark	105.3	16	107.5	1.7	1.8	20912	7	13555	12
UK	831.6	6	822.8	2.5	2.2	14413	18	13428	13
Australia	282.9	9	247.1	4.2	3.3	14940	16	13412	14
Italy	864.0	5	828.9	3.2	2.8	14430	17	12985	15
Netherlands	225.0	10	228.3	4.2	1.4	15461	14	12832	16
Belgium	151.4	13	150.0	4.2	1.8	15180	15	12623	17
Austria	126.7	14	127.2	4.0	2.1	16748	13	12506	18
New Zealand	40.5	21	41.8	0.8	1.7	12555	19	11028	19
Spain	376.3	8	340.1	4.9	2.2	8722	21	9343	20
Ireland	32.7	22	32.5	4.5	2.6	9182	20	8146	21
Greece	53.8	19	52.5	2.3	1.7	5244	22	6799	22
Portugal	45.2	20	41.7	4.8	2.8	4265	23	6750	23
Turkey	81.6	18	70.6	1.8	4.1	1303	24	4353	24

Figure 2–20

GDP in billions of dollars at current market prices and exchange rates.
Change = average annual volume change from previous year.
PPP = current prices using purchasing power parity.
Source: Organization for Economic Cooperation and Development (1).

Structure of production in OECD economies

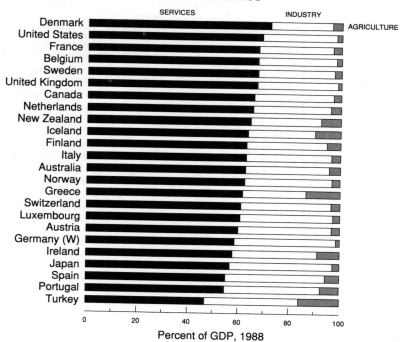

Percent of GDP, 1988

Growth in industrial output was fairly uniform in the OECD economies, especially in the output of chemicals and machinery. For all economies but the United States, Canada, and Italy, textile output (including apparel) declined between 1985 and 1988.

Structure of production in OECD economies

	SERVICES	INDUSTRY	AGRICULTURE
Denmark	71.9	24.4	3.7
United States	68.8	29.2	2.0
France	67.3	29.3	3.3
Belgium	67.1	30.9	2.1
Sweden	67.0	30.3	2.7
United Kingdom	66.8	31.8	1.4
Canada	65.7	31.3	3.0
Netherlands	65.3	30.7	4.0
New Zealand	64.5	27.7	7.9
Iceland	63.5	26.5	10.0
Finland	63.0	31.5	5.5
Italy	62.7	33.7	3.7
Australia	62.6	32.9	4.5
Norway	62.3	34.5	3.1
Greece	61.6	24.9	13.5
Switzerland	60.9	35.5	3.6
Luxembourg	60.7	36.6	2.7
Austria	59.8	37.0	3.2
Germany (W)	58.4	40.1	1.5
Ireland	57.8	33.4	8.8
Japan	56.7	40.6	2.8
Spain	55.0	39.3	5.7
Portugal	54.7	37.8	7.4
Turkey	46.9	37.0	16.1

Figure 2–21

Percent of GDP.
Source: Organization for Economic Cooperation and Development (1).

Trends in industrial output in main OECD economies

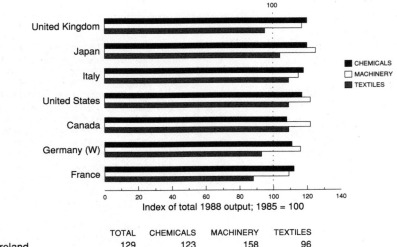

Index of total 1988 output; 1985 = 100

CHEMICALS
MACHINERY
TEXTILES

	TOTAL	CHEMICALS	MACHINERY	TEXTILES
Ireland	129	123	158	96
United Kingdom	120	121	122	99
Japan	120	115	117	95
Italy	118	116	125	104
United States	117	119	115	109
Portugal	116	123	110	107
Finland	115	110	113	81
Canada	113	108	122	109
Germany (W)	113	111	116	93
Netherlands	113	113	104	92

(MORE)

Output

While all of the developed OECD economies have large service sectors, there are large differences in share of GDP and in the structure of component services. The United States and Belgium have the largest service sectors and Iceland and Turkey the smallest. West Germany's is the smallest of the main economies.

Trends in industrial output in OECD economies, cont'd

	TOTAL	CHEMICALS	MACHINERY	TEXTILES
Spain	113	107	133	97
Belgium	112	121	109	98
Switzerland	112	119	112	94
Luxembourg	109	129	107	112
Austria	108	111	107	93
France	108	112	109	88
Sweden	107	116	110	81
Denmark	107	114	109	87
Australia	104	113	98	93
Norway	103	108	102	69
Greece	102		94	105

Figure 2–22

Index of 1988 output; 1985 = 100.
Machinery = metal, machinery, and equipment.
Textiles = textiles, apparel, and leather.
Source: Organization for Economic Cooperation and Development (1).

Structure of services sector in OECD economies

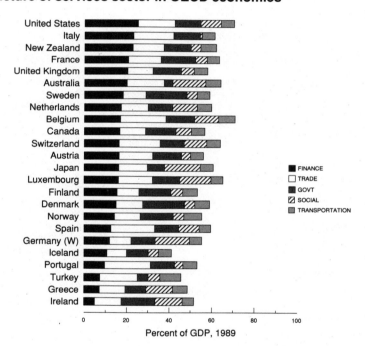

Percent of GDP, 1989

Financial services range from 25% of the Unites States' GDP to only 5% of Ireland's. Finance is less than half as important to West Germany's economy as it is to the US's.

Commercial trade bulks largest in the GDPs of Portugal and Belgium and smallest in Iceland's. The trade sectors of Japan and West Germany are much smaller than that of the United States.

Government services take the greatest share of Denmark's GDP and the smallest share of Australia's. Government services are about the same share of GDP in the United States and West Germany, and a smaller share in Japan.

Social services take the largest share of Japan's and West Germany's GDP and the smallest share of Italy's.

Transportation services take similar shares of GDP in all of the OECD economies — most in Belgium, New Zealand, and Australia. Among the main economies, West Germany's transportation sector is the smallest share of GDP.

Structure of services sector in OECD economies

	FINANCE	TRADE	GOVT	SOCIAL	TRANS
United States	25.1	17.2	12.0	9.7	6.1
Italy	22.9	18.8	12.4	0.9	6.0
New Zealand	22.5	14.7	12.6	4.4	7.5
France	20.5	15.3	16.1	5.4	5.9
United Kingdom	20.3	11.8	13.1	6.1	6.3
Australia	19.9	17.4	4.0	15.4	7.3
Sweden	18.0	10.8	19.3	4.7	5.9
Netherlands	17.1	12.7	11.6	11.3	6.9
Belgium	16.8	21.4	13.3	11.4	7.8
Canada	16.7	12.0	14.3	7.2	6.3
Switzerland	16.2	19.3	11.4	10.4	6.5
Austria	16.2	15.9	13.4	4.4	6.0
Japan	16.1	13.3	8.2	16.7	6.2
Luxembourg	16.0	16.0	12.6	14.8	5.7
Finland	15.5	10.2	14.9	5.5	7.0
Denmark	14.9	12.5	19.6	5.0	6.8
Norway	14.2	12.1	15.5	4.9	8.6
Spain	12.5	20.7	11.1	9.6	5.6
Germany (W)	11.9	10.2	11.3	16.2	5.7
Iceland	10.7	9.1	10.4	4.8	6.1
Portugal	9.7	21.5	11.3	4.0	6.7
Turkey	7.5	17.4	5.3	5.5	9.8
Greece	7.3	11.9	9.9	12.6	7.0
Ireland	5.1	12.3	16.1	12.6	5.5

Figure 2–23

Value added as percent of GDP.
In descending order of financial services.
Finance = insurance, real estate and business services.
Trade = wholesale and retail trade, restaurants and hotels.
Trans = transport, storage, and communication.
Source: Organization for Economic Cooperation and Development (1).

Output

Estimating the GDPs of transitioning socialist economies is clouded by basic differences in national accounting methods. Further, the transitions from social-ist to mixed economies are creating large, rapid swings in every sector. These factors make data on these econo-mies very unreliable and useful mainly for making comparisons.

If China is included, 31% of the world's people live in transition-ing economies, produc-ing 22% of the world's output. Average per-capita GDP is 71% of the world average. Without China, this group is only 10% of world population; their average per-capita GDP is nearly two times the world aver-age. The USSR, by far the largest transitioning economy, is the most-affluent, except for the former East Germany.

Transitioning economies produce large shares of some the world's basic in-dustrial output: almost one-third of electricity (their proportional share by population); half the output of crude steel; and 45% of the world output of cement. The USSR alone produces one-fourth of the world's crude steel.

The transitioning world

Transitioning economies

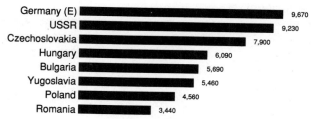

Per-capita GNP in dollars, 1989

	POP	GNP	GNPPC	ELECTRICAL PRODUCTS	CRUDE STEEL	CEMENT
Germany (E)	16.5	159.5	9670	119.0	7.8	12.3
USSR	288.7	2663.7	9230	1722.0	160.0	140.0
Czechoslovakia	15.6	123.2	7900	89.6	15.5	11.0
Hungary	10.6	64.6	6090	29.9	3.3	3.8
Bulgaria	112.6	650.7	5780	506.0	60.9	62.2
Yugoslavia	23.7	129.5	5460	82.8	4.5	9.0
Poland	37.8	172.4	4560	147.0	17.0	17.1
Romania	23.2	79.8	3440	76.2	14.4	13.6
China	1102.4	427.0	390	579.6	61.2	204.4
Total/average	**1631**	**4470**	**2741**	**3352**	**345**	**473**
World	**5227**	**20200**	**3865**	**11000**	**676**	**1050**
Percent of world	31	22	71	30	51	45
Without China	**529**	**4043**	**7648**	**2773**	**283**	**269**
Percent of world	10	20	198	25	42	26
Czech, Hungary, Poland, Yugoslavia	**88**	**490**	**5584**	**349**	**40**	**41**
Percent of world	1.68	2.42	144	3.18	5.96	3.90
USSR						
Percent of world	6	13	239	16	24	13

Figure 2–24

All figures are for 1989.
Population in millions.
GDP in billions of dollars, based on US purchasing power equivalents. GDP per capita in dollars.
Electricity production in billions of kilowatt-hrs.
Crude steel and cement production in millions of metric tons.
Source: Central Intelligence Agency (1).

The developing world, with 21% of the world's population, produces 10% of its output, a per-capita GDP just half of the world average. (Note: The International Monetary Fund includes as "developing" the economies classified in this publication as "undeveloped.")

Using the IMF's broader classification, the developing world is analyzed in several overlapping groupings.

Viewed by region, developing economies in Asia and the Western Hemisphere generate almost two-thirds of the total output and trade of the developing world — and close to the same share of its debt.

Classifying developing economies by their principal exports, those who export mostly manufactures lead the other groupings, accounting for half the GDP and half the exports of the developing world. Fuel-exporting economies are the second-biggest producers of output and trade.

Almost four-fifths of developing economies are net debtors; they owe 95% of the developing world's total debt.

The developing world

Developing world's GDP by type of exports

Percent of developing economies' GDP, 1985-87

Overview of the developing world

	GDP	XGS	DEBT
By Region	**100**	**100**	**100**
Asia	34.0	41.9	25.8
Western Hemisphere	29.5	17.3	35.4
Middle East	15.7	19.8	13.5
Africa	11.9	11.0	15.3
Europe	8.9	10.0	10.0
By Predominant Export	**100**	**100**	**100**
Fuel	28.9	28.8	27.1
Non-fuel products	71.1	71.2	72.9
Manufactures	49.0	49.4	36.4
Primary products	11.9	8.1	18.8
Agricultures	10.0	5.6	13.5
Minerals	1.9	2.5	5.3
Services,private transfers	3.6	4.7	7.9
Diversified	6.6	9.0	9.8
By Finance	**100**	**100**	**100**
Net creditors	13.5	21.0	5.3
Net debtors	86.5	79.0	94.7
Market borrowers	37.9	41.7	43.4
Diversified borrowers	38.1	28.9	31.9
Official borrowers	10.5	8.4	19.4
Debt-service problems	48.2	34.0	61.1
No debt-service problems	38.3	45.0	33.6
Miscellaneous	**100**	**100**	**100**
Sub-Saharan Africa	4.0	3.9	7.2
12 major oil exporters	21.7	23.4	16.9
Net-debtor fuel exporters	17.8	14.8	22.7
Newly-industrializing, Asia	7.5	24.6	5.4
Small, low-income	6.0	3.5	9.4
15 heavily indebted	33.8	20.4	41.0

Figure 2–25

Percent of each category, 1985-87, within developing world.
XGS = exports of goods and services.
Fuel = economies of which fuel exports constitute more than 50% of total exports. Similar for other categories in group.
Source: International Monetary Fund (1).

The IMF also analyzes developing economies in terms of their levels of affluence — that is, per-capita GDP.

All of the twelve high-income developing economies have per-capita outputs large enough to place them in the class of developed economies. Indeed, if they are sufficiently "industrialized," these economies are classed as developed in this publication. That is the case with Hong Kong, Singapore, Israel, Ireland, and Taiwan.

Five economies in this group are primarily oil exporters.

All have per-capita outputs several times greater than the world average.

Eighteen developing economies are classed as upper middle income, most of them with per-capita outputs below the world average.

High-income developing economies

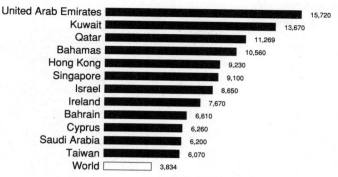

Per-capita GDP in dollars, 1988

Upper-middle income developing economies

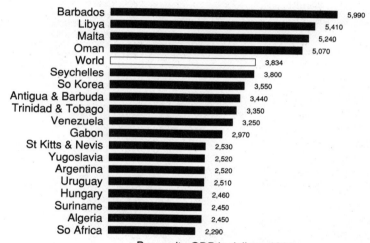

Per-capita GDP in dollars, 1988

Forty-nine developing economies are classed as lower middle income, all of them well below the world average per-capita GDP.

Eleven of the 15 "heavily indebted" economies fall in this group, among them the biggest Latin American debtors: Brazil and Mexico.

A wide difference of nearly 4:1 in per-capita output separates Brazil at the top of this class from Bolivia at the bottom.

By a wide margin, Singapore leads newly-industrializing economies in per-capita value added by manufacturing. Taiwan and Hong Kong are also much stronger than other NIEs in this economic sector — a vital one for rapidly growing, export-led economies.

Of seven newly-industrializing economies, four are Asian and three Latin American. Together, Brazil, Argentina, and Mexico produce 70% of Latin America's GDP.

Lower-middle income developing economies

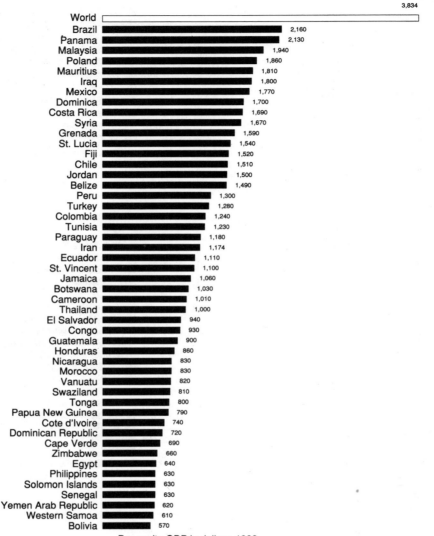

Per-capita GDP in dollars, 1988

Manufacturing output of newly industrializing economies (NIEs)

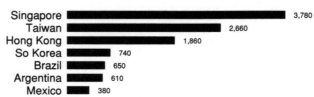

Per-capita value added by manufacturing, 1989

The 13 members of OPEC produce 36% of the world's oil. The top four producers — and the 7th and 11th — are Persian Gulf economies. Saudi Arabia, the world's biggest producer, accounts for 23% of OPEC's output but only 8% of the world's.

Saudi Arabia's economy is more dependent on oil than any other OPEC producer, although Iraq, the United Arab Emirates, and Gabon come close. Libya also depends heavily on its oil output.

Manufacturing output of NIEs

	POP	GDP	GDPPC	GDP GROWTH	INDUS GROWTH	MFRPC VALADD	ELECT PROD
Singapore	2.7	27.7	10260	9.2	9.9	3780	14.0
Taiwan	20.3	146.6	7220	7.2	4.6	2660	49.2
Hong Kong	5.7	63.0	11050	2.5	5.9	1860	24.5
So Korea	42.7	210.1	4920	6.7	2.9	740	94.5
Brazil	149.6	350.0	2340	3.6	3.2	650	214.1
Argentina	31.9	71.8	2250	-6.0	-8.0	610	46.3
Mexico	85.9	200.6	2340	2.5	5.6	380	114.3

Figure 2–26

Argentina is included because its economy closely resembles the NIEs.
Population in millions. GDP in billions of dollars. GDP per capita in dollars. GDP growth in percent.
Industrial growth = percent growth of production.
Manufacturing per capita = value added in US$.
Electricity production in billions of kilowatt-hrs.
All figures are for 1989, except: per-capita manufacturing for Argentina and Mexico is for 1986, and for Brazil and So Korea is for 1988; electricity production for Brazil is for 1988.
Source: Central Intelligence Agency (1).

Organization of Petroleum Exporting Countries (OPEC)

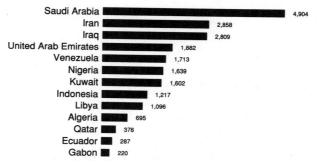

Crude oil production in thousands of barrels/day, 1989

	POP	GDP	GDPPC	CRUDE OIL PROD	OPEC SHARE	WORLD SHARE	GNP SHARE
Saudi Arabia	16.4	72.9	4450	4904	23	8	54
Iran	53.9	63.6	1180	2858	13	5	10
Iraq	18.1	36.0	1990	2809	13	5	50
United Arab Emirates	2.1	24.8	11810	1882	9	3	40
Venezuela	19.2	40.3	2100	1713	8	3	15
Nigeria	115.3	31.2	270	1639	8	3	26
Kuwait	2.0	19.5	9750	1602	8	3	34
Indonesia	186.7	88.7	480	1217	6	2	9
Libya	4.1	21.4	5220	1096	5	2	45
Algeria	24.9	58.5	2350	695	3	1	25
Qatar	0.5	5.9	11800	378	2	1	30
Ecuador	10.3	11.5	1170	287	1	0.5	10
Gabon	1.1	3.2	2910	220	1	0.4	50
Total/average	**455**	**932**	**2050**	**21300**	**100**	**36**	

Figure 2–27

All figures are for 1989.
Population in millions. GDP in billions of dollars. GDP per capita in 1989 US dollars.
Crude oil production in thousands of barrels per day.
Share = percent of OPEC production, world production, and GNP.
Total world production = 58,600 thousand barrels per day.
Source: Central Intelligence Agency (1).

Output

China's industry sector is the largest by far among Asian developing economies. A large industry sector characterizes Asia's stronger economies, except for Hong Kong's, where financial services predominate.

Services make up larger shares of GDP in Hong Kong and Singapore than they do in any other economies in this group. The economies of Taiwan, Thailand, Sri Lanka, and Pakistan all have service sectors near half of GDP.

Agriculture is a tiny sector of GDP in Hong Kong and Singapore, and a larger but still comparatively small sector of Taiwan's economy. All of the newly-industrializing economies, along with Thailand's, have reduced their agriculture sectors by at least half over the past twenty years. China reduced its agriculture sector by nearly as much over that period. But Myanmar (formerly Burma), alone among the Asian developing economies according to available data, increased this sector.

Industry's share of GDP in Asian developing economies

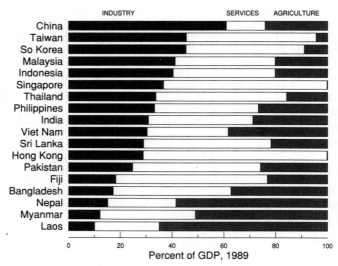

	AGRICULTURE --------------		INDUSTRY--------------------		SERVICES --------------------	
	1970	1989	1970	1989	1970	1989
NIEs						
Taiwan	16.9	4.4	35.5	45.4	47.7	50.1
So Korea	28.0	9.0	22.4	45.2	49.6	45.8
Singapore	2.3	0.4	29.8	36.6	67.9	63.0
Hong Kong	2.2	0.4	36.5	28.8	61.4	70.9
Southeast Asia						
Malaysia	32.0	20.2	24.7	41.0	43.3	38.7
Indonesia	46.0	20.5	20.9	40.3	33.1	39.3
Thailand	30.2	15.9	25.7	33.7	44.1	50.5
Philippines	28.8	26.9	29.4	33.1	41.8	40.0
Viet Nam		38.4		30.2		31.4
Laos		65.0		10.0		25.0
South Asia						
India	44.5	30.9	24.0	30.8	31.5	40.3
Sri Lanka	31.8	22.0	16.0	28.9	52.2	49.1
Pakistan	38.9	26.0	22.7	24.7	38.4	49.3
Bangladesh		37.4		17.1		45.5
Nepal	67.5	58.6	11.4	15.0	21.0	26.4
Myanmar (Burma)	38.3	51.1	14.7	12.2	47.0	36.7
China	41.2	24.3	35.9	60.7	22.9	15.0
South Pacific						
Fiji	26.8	23.4	19.8	18.1	53.4	58.6

Figure 2–28

Percent of GDP.
NIEs = newly industrializing economies.
Source: Asian Development Bank (1).

Manufacturing adds the most value to GDP in Latin America's biggest economies: Brazil, Mexico, and Argentina. But Peru has the region's largest manufacturing sector, as a percent of GDP.

Commercial trade is a significant sector of Mexico's big economy, but does not bulk large in the other major economies.

In Brazil's huge economy, finance adds almost as much value to its GDP as does manufacturing, making its finance sector larger by far than that of any other Latin American developing economy.

Agriculture is a small sector in the region's biggest economies, though larger in Argentina's. Some of the smaller economies have small agriculture sectors because they specialize in financial services.

Structure of production in Latin American economies

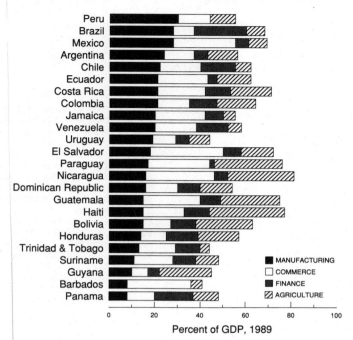

Percent of GDP, 1989

	MANUFACTURING		COMMERCE --------		FINANCE -------------		AGRICULTURE-----	
	VALADD	GDPPCT	VALADD	GDPPCT	VALADD	GDPPCT	VALADD	GDPPCT
Peru	8.7	30	4.1	14			3.2	11
Brazil	94.9	28	29.9	9	76.4	23	26.4	8
Mexico	46.9	28	46.4	27	10.5	6	13.7	8
Argentina	20.9	24	10.9	13	4.8	6	11.3	13
Chile	7.1	22	5.8	18	4.9	15	2.3	7
Ecuador	2.8	21	2.9	22	0.5	4	1.9	15
Costa Rica	1.0	21	1.0	21	0.5	11	0.9	18
Colombia	9.3	21	6.2	14	5.2	12	7.7	17
Jamaica	0.7	20	0.8	22	0.3	8	0.2	5
Venezuela	11.6	20	10.5	18	8.5	14	3.8	6
Uruguay	1.7	19	0.9	10	0.5	6	0.8	9
El Salvador	1.0	18	1.8	32	0.5	8	0.7	14
Paraguay	1.0	17	1.7	27	0.1	2	1.9	30
Nicaragua	0.4	16	0.8	30	0.2	6	0.8	29
Dominican Rep	0.9	16	0.8	14	0.5	10	0.8	14
Guatemala	1.2	15	1.9	25	0.7	9	2.0	26
Haiti	0.3	15	0.4	18	0.2	11	0.7	33
Bolivia	0.8	15	0.6	12	0.6	11	1.3	25
Honduras	0.6	14	0.5	11	0.6	14	0.8	18
Trinidad&Tobago	0.6	13	0.8	16	0.5	11	0.2	4
Suriname	0.1	11	0.2	17	0.1	10	0.1	10
Guyana	0.0	10	0.0	7	0.0	5	0.1	23
Barbados	0.1	8	0.4	28			0.1	5
Panama	0.3	8	0.5	12	0.8	17	0.5	11
Latin America	**213.1**	**25**	**129.7**	**15**	**116.9**	**14**	**82.2**	**10**

Figure 2–29

Value added in billions of dollars and percent of GDP, 1989.
In descending order of manufacturing percent of GDP.
Commerce = wholesale and retail trade, restaurants and hotels.
Source: Inter-American Development Bank (1).

Output

53

The world's average per-capita GDP is seven times that of the highest-income economy in the undeveloped world. The 47 economies in this class are so far below the development level of even typical "Third World" countries that their ability to develop at all is in doubt. Indeed, most of the people living in these countries have seen their living standards fall during the last decade.

China's economy, which has grown robustly for a decade, seems to be an exception. Most analysts believe it is only a matter of time — perhaps another generation, or more — before China develops into a modern world-class economy.

Many analysts think that the huge economies of India and Indonesia may be taking the next steps up the development ladder.

While more Asians live in undeveloped economies than people from any other continent, 32 of the 47 undeveloped national economies are in Africa. Twelve are in Asia, two are in Latin America, and one is in the Middle East.

The undeveloped world

Undeveloped economies

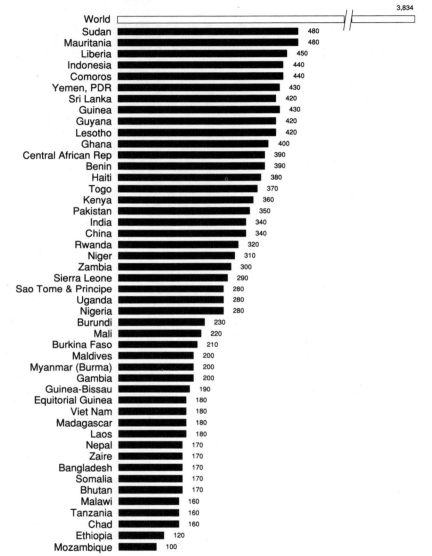

Country	Per-capita GDP (dollars)
World	3,834
Sudan	480
Mauritania	480
Liberia	450
Indonesia	440
Comoros	440
Yemen, PDR	430
Sri Lanka	420
Guinea	430
Guyana	420
Lesotho	420
Ghana	400
Central African Rep	390
Benin	390
Haiti	380
Togo	370
Kenya	360
Pakistan	350
India	340
China	340
Rwanda	320
Niger	310
Zambia	300
Sierra Leone	290
Sao Tome & Principe	280
Uganda	280
Nigeria	280
Burundi	230
Mali	220
Burkina Faso	210
Maldives	200
Myanmar (Burma)	200
Gambia	200
Guinea-Bissau	190
Equitorial Guinea	180
Viet Nam	180
Madagascar	180
Laos	180
Nepal	170
Zaire	170
Bangladesh	170
Somalia	170
Bhutan	170
Malawi	160
Tanzania	160
Chad	160
Ethiopia	120
Mozambique	100

Per-capita GDP in dollars, 1988

Figure 2–30

No data for: Afghanistan, Kampuchea (Cambodia).
1987 data for Equitorial Guinea, Maldives, Myanmar, and Sao Tome & Principe.
Source: World Bank (1).

3 Products

The structure of the output of any national economy is related to the global economy in crucial ways: it provides a base of national income and welfare; it shapes and reflects comparative advantages; it yields products for export; and it determines what products must be imported.

The global economy of the 1990s does not correspond well with "classic" ideas of imperialistic relations in which undeveloped "satellite" economies provide raw materials to service wealthy economies, which in turn produce and export high-value-added manufactures.

This relationship does indeed hold in much of the developing world today, but it is a waning condition. The world's richest economy, that of the United States, produces a lion's share of raw materials. The world's second-largest economy, that of the USSR, vies with the US as a producer of raw materials. China, a huge economy still in an undeveloped status, is a top raw materials producer — and its manufacturing sector is a larger percent of output than it is in any Asian developing economy. Japan, the world's third-largest economy, must import nearly all of its raw materials.

The more-aggressive developing economies resist their classic role by diversifying outputs and producing world-class manufactures. The newly-industrializing economies of Asia have become envied models for the developing economies of Latin America and the transitioning economies of Central and Eastern Europe.

Only in Africa do the old relationships seem to persist.

Three national economies — those of the USSR, the United States, and China — dominate the world output of commodities, a classification that includes basic manufactured products.

The three economies rank 1–2–3 in the output of primary energy, the aggregate of energy sources: coal, petroleum, natural gas, and hydronuclear facilities. In the actual production of energy, the United States leads all others, with the USSR either second or third. China drops back to fourth, fifth, and eighth in these categories.

In total grain production, the three economies also dominate, with China first. China leads in the world output of wheat and rice. The United States produces the most coarse grains and soybeans. The USSR is the world's top sugar producer.

In mining products, the USSR leads in the output of iron, with China close behind.

In metal products, The USSR leads in the output of steel, and the United States produces the most copper and aluminum. China follows close behind. The US and USSR are leading producers of platinum and gold.

In the output of manufactured commodities (those that are essentially interchangeable within product type), the USSR produces the most chemical fertilizers and synthetic rubber. The United States leads in the output of synthetic fibers, rubber tires, and trucks and buses. The US is the second-biggest producer of passenger automobiles.

The USSR and the United States produced almost exactly the same amount of primary energy products in 1989. The USSR's production grew by 24% during the 1980s, while the US's remained flat. The European Community's energy production increased by 16%.

China increased its output by more than 50% during the decade; Canada increased output by almost as much.

France's output grew the most, almost doubling in the decade, while the energy output of the Netherlands declined by one-fifth.

Energy products

Primary energy production

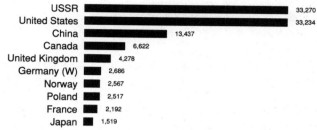

USSR 33,270
United States 33,234
China 13,437
Canada 6,622
United Kingdom 4,278
Germany (W) 2,686
Norway 2,567
Poland 2,517
France 2,192
Japan 1,519

Thousands of barrels of oil equivalent per day, 1989

	1980	1989	INDEX
USSR	26740	33270	124
United States	32567	33234	102
China	8628	13437	156
Canada	4741	6622	140
United Kingdom	4242	4278	101
Germany (W)	2523	2686	106
Norway	1424	2567	180
Poland	2446	2517	103
France	1129	2192	194
Japan	1178	1519	129
Germany (E)	1239	1440	116
Netherlands	1713	1365	80
Romania	1102	1175	107
Czechoslovakia	963	1053	109
Yugoslavia	528	690	131
Hungary	278	337	121
Bulgaria	172	231	134
EC	10913	12697	116
Top 5, percent	84	84	118
Top 10, percent	93	94	120

Figure 3–1

Thousands of barrels per day of oil equivalent.
Index of 1989 production; 1980 = 100.
Covers coal, crude oil, natural gas, and hydronuclear energy.
Excludes minor fuels such as peat, shale, and fuelwood.
Source: Central Intelligence Agency (1).

Coal production

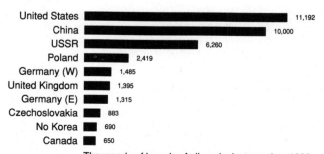

United States 11,192
China 10,000
USSR 6,260
Poland 2,419
Germany (W) 1,485
United Kingdom 1,395
Germany (E) 1,315
Czechoslovakia 883
No Korea 690
Canada 650

Thousands of barrels of oil equivalent per day, 1989

The United States and China lead the world in coal production, followed by the USSR.

In the 1980s, coal output of the United States increased at close to the average of the top ten producers. China's output grew by two-thirds during the period, while the USSR's fell slightly.

Canada's coal output grew the most, almost doubling in the decade.

The USSR and United States produced most of the world's crude oil and natural gas liquids. During the 1980s, output remained flat in the USSR and declined in the US.

The second-tier producers in 1989 — China, Canada, and the United Kingdom — all increased output during the decade.

Coal production

	1980	1989	INDEX
United States	9785	11192	114
China	5932	10000	169
USSR	6370	6260	98
Poland	2318	2419	104
Germany (W)	1789	1485	83
United Kingdom	1762	1395	79
Germany (E)	1104	1315	119
Czechoslovakia	899	883	98
No Korea	580	690	119
Canada	338	650	192
Yugoslavia	259	390	151
Romania	164	250	152
France	284	170	60
Japan	244	135	55
Bulgaria	111	125	113
Hungary	138	116	84
Top 5, percent	82	84	120
Top 10, percent	96	97	118

Figure 3–2

Thousands of barrels per day of oil equivalent. Index of 1989 production; 1980 = 100.
Source: Central Intelligence Agency (1).

Production of crude oil and natural gas liquids

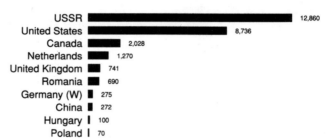

Thousands of barrels of oil equivalent per day, 1989

	1980	1989	INDEX
USSR	12030	12140	101
United States	10170	9094	89
China	2113	2780	132
Canada	1754	1937	110
United Kingdom	1639	1750	107
Romania	242	180	74
Netherlands	35	75	214
France	51	75	147
Yugoslavia	85	68	80
Poland	7	40	571
Hungary	41	40	98
Japan	10	10	100
Bulgaria	5	6	120
Czechoslovakia	2	3	150
Germany (E)	1	1	100
Top 5, percent	98	98	100
Top 10, percent	100	100	100

Figure 3–3

Thousands of barrels per day of oil equivalent. Index of 1989 production; 1980 = 100.
Source: Central Intelligence Agency (1).

The USSR produces more crude oil than any other economy, followed by the United States and Saudi Arabia. Output by all three producers fell during the 1980s — by almost half in Saudi Arabia.

Among the main producers, Iran increased output the most during the decade — by 72%. Mexico and China also increased output substantially.

Output of the top ten producers declined a little over the 1980s.

Crude oil production

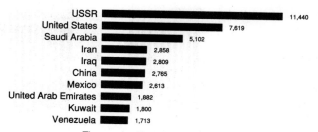

Thousands of barrels of oil equivalent per day, 1989

	1980	1989	INDEX
USSR	11700	11440	98
United States	8597	7619	89
Saudi Arabia	9903	5102	52
Iran	1662	2858	172
Iraq	2514	2809	112
China	2113	2765	131
Mexico	1936	2613	135
United Arab Emirates	1702	1882	111
Kuwait	1661	1800	108
Venezuela	2165	1713	79
United Kingdom	1619	1640	101
Nigeria	2058	1639	80
Canada	1424	1557	109
Norway	528	1447	274
Indonesia	1576	1217	77
Libya	1830	1096	60
Algeria	1020	695	68
Romania	242	180	74
Yugoslavia	85	68	80
Hungary	41	40	98
Albania	41	39	95
Cuba	5	13	260
Bulgaria	3	6	200
Czechoslovakia	2	3	150
Poland	7	3	43
Germany (E)	1	1	100
EC	1837	2099	114
Top 5, percent	63	59	87
Top 10, percent	87	81	92

Figure 3–4

Thousands of barrels per day.
Excludes natural gas liquids, shale oil (except for US and Canada), natural gasoline, and synthetic crude oil.
Index of 1989 production; 1980 = 100.
Source: Central Intelligence Agency (1).

Products

The USSR and the United States produce most of the world's natural gas. Output increased substantially in the USSR over the decade and fell a little in the US.

Output also increased substantially in Canada, the number three producer.

Worldwide, output of natural gas increased by about one-fourth.

The United States leads in the production of hydronuclear energy, and its output increased by about half during the 1980s.

Second-tier producers in 1989 were Canada, USSR, France, and Japan. All of these economies increased output sharply in the 1980s; France's output nearly tripled.

Worldwide, output increased by two-thirds during the decade.

Natural gas production

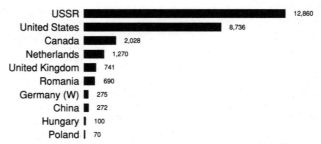

Thousands of barrels of oil equivalent per day, 1989

	1980	1989	INDEX
USSR	7170	12860	179
United States	9838	8736	89
Canada	1202	2028	169
Netherlands	1657	1270	77
United Kingdom	629	741	118
Romania	639	690	108
Germany (W)	327	275	84
China	254	272	107
Hungary	99	100	101
Poland	104	70	67
Yugoslavia	33	60	182
France	129	54	42
Germany (E)	50	40	80
Japan	39	37	95
Czechoslovakia	9	12	133
Top 5, percent	92	94	125
Top 10, percent	99	99	123

Figure 3–5

Thousands of barrels per day of oil equivalent.
Index of 1989 production; 1980 = 100.
Source: Central Intelligence Agency (1).

Hydronuclear energy production

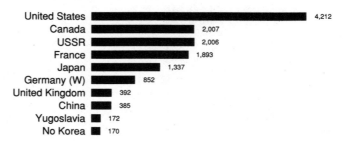

Thousands of barrels of oil equivalent per day, 1989

	1980	1989	INDEX
United States	2774	4212	152
Canada	1447	2007	139
USSR	1170	2006	171
France	665	1893	285
Japan	885	1337	151
Germany (W)	314	852	271
United Kingdom	212	392	185
China	329	385	117

(MORE)

The United States and the USSR together have 40% of the world's total crude oil refining capacity. The European Community has 18% of the world's capacity.

Refining capacity is more concentrated than production: the top ten refiners have 69% of the world's total, while the top ten producers account for 92% of the total.

Hydronuclear energy production, cont'd

	1980	1989	INDEX
Yugoslavia	152	172	113
No Korea	145	170	117
Czechoslovakia	53	155	292
Bulgaria	53	100	189
Germany (E)	84	84	100
Hungary	1	81	8100
Romania	57	55	96
Poland	17	25	147
Netherlands	21	20	95
Top 5, percent	83	82	165
Top 10, percent	97	96	166

Thousands of barrels per day of oil equivalent.
Index of 1989 production; 1980 = 100.
Source: Central Intelligence Agency (1).

Figure 3–6

Crude oil refining capacity

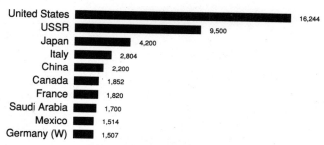

United States	16,244
USSR	9,500
Japan	4,200
Italy	2,804
China	2,200
Canada	1,852
France	1,820
Saudi Arabia	1,700
Mexico	1,514
Germany (W)	1,507

Thousands of barrels per day, January 1, 1990

United States	16244	Yugoslavia	484
USSR	9500	Germany (E)	470
Japan	4200	Algeria	465
Italy	2804	Czechoslovakia	455
China	2200	Nigeria	433
Canada	1852	Poland	397
France	1820	Libya	329
Saudi Arabia	1700	Netherlands Antilles	320
Mexico	1514	Iraq	318
Germany (W)	1507	Bulgaria	300
Brazil	1397	Trinidad & Tobago	300
Netherlands	1381	Hungary	242
Spain	1293	OECD	36681
United Kingdom	1253	USSR & CEE	12468
Venezuela	1201	EC	11612
India	1080	OPEC	7140
Singapore	830	**World**	**62817**
Kuwait	819	Top 5, percent	56
Iran	750	Top 10, percent	69
Indonesia	714		
Argentina	689		
Australia	675		
Romania	620		
Belgium	614		
Virgin Islands	545		
Egypt	489		

Figure 3–7
Thousands of barrels per day, 1 January 1990.
CEE = Central and Eastern Europe, including Yugoslavia.
Source: Central Intelligence Agency (1).

The United States leads the world in installed electricity-generating capacity, with twice as much as the USSR. But during the 1980s, the US increased its capacity less than the average of the top ten producers.

China increased its capacity by 71% during the decade. The United Kingdom was the only main economy to reduce capacity in the 1980s.

Installed electricity-generating capacity

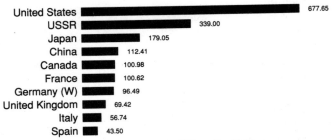

Millions of kilowatts, 1988

	1980	1988	INDEX
United States	630.94	677.65	107
USSR	266.71	339.00	127
Japan	137.94	179.05	130
China	65.87	112.41	171
Canada	81.64	100.98	124
France	63.66	100.62	158
Germany (W)	82.55	96.49	117
United Kingdom	73.64	69.42	94
Italy	46.82	56.74	121
Spain	29.92	43.50	145
Sweden	27.42	33.17	121
Poland	24.77	30.97	125
Norway	20.01	25.70	128
Germany (E)	20.45	23.59	115
Romania	16.11	21.73	135
Czechoslovakia	16.65	21.70	130
Yugoslavia	14.51	20.18	139
Netherlands	17.29	17.43	101
Bulgaria	8.20	11.31	138
Hungary	5.25	7.09	135
No Korea	5.04	6.90	137
Cuba	2.62	3.50	134
Top 5, percent	71	70	119
Top 10, percent	89	89	120

Figure 3–8

Millions of kilowatts.
Index of 1988 production; 1980 = 100.
Figures for Romania and Yugoslavia are for 1987.
Source: Central Intelligence Agency (1).

The European Community had the most installed nuclear-electric generating capacity in 1989. But the United States, with about the same capacity, had more than any single national economy.

During the 1980s, France increased its capacity more than did any other main economy, while the European Community was tripling its capacity. Of the leading users of nuclear power, the United Kingdom and the United States increased their capacities the least during the decade.

Installed nuclear-electric generating capacity

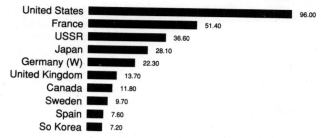

Thousands of megawatts, 1989

	1980	1989	INDEX
United States	51.70	96.00	186
France	12.90	51.40	398
USSR	12.50	36.60	293
Japan	14.50	28.10	194
Germany (W)	8.60	22.30	259
United Kingdom	8.00	13.70	171
Canada	5.10	11.80	231
Sweden	4.70	9.70	206
Spain	1.10	7.60	691
So Korea	0.60	7.20	1200
Belgium	1.70	5.50	324
Taiwan	1.20	4.90	408
Czechoslovakia	0.90	3.30	367
Switzerland	1.90	2.90	153
Bulgaria	0.90	2.70	300
Finland	1.20	2.30	192
Germany (E)	1.80	1.80	100
Hungary	0.00	1.80	inf
So Africa	0.00	1.80	inf
India	0.60	1.20	200
Italy	0.40	1.10	275
Argentina	0.30	0.90	300
Yugoslavia	0.00	0.70	inf
Brazil	0.00	0.60	inf
Netherlands	0.50	0.50	100
Pakistan	0.10	0.10	100
OECD	112.30	252.90	225
EC	33.20	102.10	308
Top 5, percent	76	74	234
Top 10, percent	91	90	238

Figure 3–9

Thousands of megawatts.
Index of 1989 production; 1980 = 100.
Net production (i.e., less station and transmission losses), except for USSR and Central & Eastern European economies.
Source: Central Intelligence Agency (1).

The United States leads the USSR and the rest of the world by large margins in the production of electricity. US production is 1.7 times that of the European Community.

During the 1980s, the United States increased production at a little less than the average of the top ten producers, while the USSR increased at that average.

India and China made the biggest gains in production during the decade and the United Kingdom made the smallest.

Electricity production

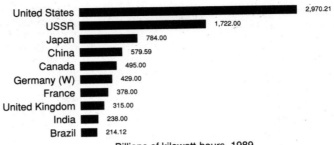

Billions of kilowatt-hours, 1989

	1980	1989	INDEX
United States	2437.82	2970.21	122
USSR	1293.88	1722.00	133
Japan	577.52	784.00	136
China	300.62	579.59	193
Canada	376.05	495.00	132
Germany (W)	368.77	429.00	116
France	243.29	378.00	155
United Kingdom	284.94	315.00	111
India	119.15	238.00	200
Brazil	139.49	214.12	154
Italy	185.74	210.00	113
Australia	96.32	149.00	155
Poland	121.87	146.96	121
Spain	110.32	145.00	131
Sweden	93.43	137.00	147
Germany (E)	98.81	119.00	120
Czechoslovakia	72.73	89.64	123
Yugoslavia	59.44	82.78	139
Romania	67.49	76.25	113
Bulgaria	34.83	44.20	127
No Korea	23.00	30.00	130
Hungary	23.87	29.90	125
Cuba	9.90	15.24	154
OECD	5227.33	6602.64	126
EC	1386.58	1711.85	123
Top 5, percent	70	70	131
Top 10, percent	86	86	132

Figure 3–10

Billions of kilowatt-hours.
Index of 1989 production; 1980 = 100.
Gross production, including station and transmission losses.
Figure for Brazil is for 1988.
Source: Central Intelligence Agency (1).

Products

China and the United States led the USSR and India in total grain production in 1989.

Among the top ten producers, Poland, Indonesia, and India made the biggest gains during the 1980s.

The European Community's total grain production was less than that of any of the four leading national economies.

Agriculture products

Total grain production

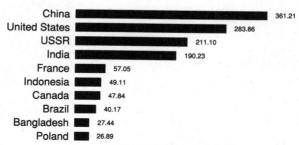

Millions of metric tons, 1989

	1980	1989	INDEX
China	320.56	361.21	113
United States	269.68	283.86	105
USSR	189.09	211.10	112
India	131.15	190.23	145
France	47.36	57.05	120
Indonesia	33.65	49.11	146
Canada	39.81	47.84	120
Brazil	33.19	40.17	121
Bangladesh	21.66	27.44	127
Poland	18.34	26.89	147
Germany (W)	22.41	26.11	117
Thailand	20.60	25.20	122
United Kingdom	19.42	22.79	117
Australia	16.36	22.38	137
Pakistan	16.86	21.07	125
Argentina	18.27	19.25	105
Turkey	24.21	19.15	79
Spain	18.64	18.64	100
Viet Nam	14.40	18.60	129
Mexico	21.11	18.58	88
Romania	20.20	18.38	91
Italy	17.99	17.07	95
Yugoslavia	15.66	16.02	102
Hungary	14.01	15.20	108
Japan	13.17	14.30	109
Czechoslovakia	10.70	12.00	112
So Africa	13.02	11.53	89
No Korea	4.60	11.16	243
Egypt	7.52	10.98	146
Germany (E)	9.63	10.81	112
Bulgaria	7.81	9.79	125
Colombia	3.24	3.83	118
Zimbabwe	1.88	2.53	135
Peru	1.14	2.18	191
Kampuchea	1.60	2.14	134
Venezuela	1.55	1.72	111
Laos	1.10	1.42	129
New Zealand	0.75	0.74	99
Cuba	0.50	0.63	126
EC	144.52	162.20	112
Top 5, percent	66	66	115
Top 10, percent	77	78	117

Figure 3–11

Millions of metric tons. Index of 1989 production; 1980 = 100.
For these products, where produced: barley, corn, oats, rice, rye, sorghum, wheat.
Figures for Kampuchea are for rice only. For Cuba, corn and rice only.
Source: Central Intelligence Agency (1).

China and the USSR led the United States and India in wheat production in 1989. Over the decade, India and China made large gains, while the United States and the USSR both produced less.

The European Community outproduced the US in 1989 after increasing output substantially during the 1980s.

Wheat production

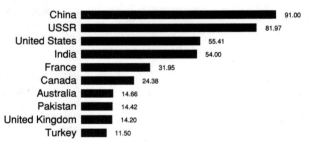

Millions of metric tons, 1989

	1980	1989	INDEX
China	55.21	91.00	165
USSR	87.38	81.97	94
United States	64.62	55.41	86
India	31.83	54.00	170
France	23.68	31.95	135
Canada	19.29	24.38	126
Australia	10.86	14.66	135
Pakistan	10.86	14.42	133
United Kingdom	8.47	14.20	168
Turkey	16.55	11.50	69
Germany (W)	8.16	11.03	135
Argentina	7.78	10.15	130
Poland	4.18	8.50	203
Italy	9.16	7.40	81
Romania	6.47	7.00	108
Iran	6.00	6.80	113
Hungary	6.08	6.60	109
Czechoslovakia	5.39	6.20	115
Yugoslavia	5.09	5.40	106
Spain	6.04	5.20	86
Bulgaria	3.85	4.45	116
Germany (E)	3.10	3.45	111
EC	61.58	78.58	128
Top 5, percent	66	66	120
Top 10, percent	82	83	120

Millions of metric tons.
Index of 1989 production; 1980 = 100.
Source: Central Intelligence Agency (1).

Figure 3–12

In coarse grains, the United States outproduced the European Community and all national economies by wide margins in 1989. During the 1980s, the US increased output less than most of the other top ten producers.

Mexico's was the only top producer to reduce output over the decade.

The European Community ended the decade at the same level of production that it had in 1980.

Coarse grain production

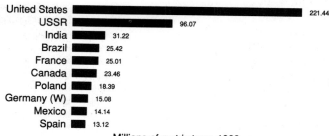

Millions of metric tons, 1989

	1980	1989	INDEX
United States	198.43	221.44	112
USSR	72.77	96.07	132
India	19.01	31.22	164
Brazil	20.71	25.42	123
France	23.65	25.01	106
Canada	20.51	23.46	114
Poland	14.16	18.39	130
Germany (W)	14.25	15.08	106
Mexico	17.86	14.14	79
Spain	12.17	13.12	108
Romania	13.69	12.62	92
Yugoslavia	10.52	10.40	99
So Africa	11.55	9.35	81
Argentina	10.23	8.61	84
United Kingdom	10.95	8.59	78
Italy	7.87	8.38	106
Hungary	7.86	8.33	106
Turkey	7.42	7.42	100
Germany (E)	6.53	7.36	113
Denmark	6.40	5.59	87
Czechoslovakia	5.31	5.53	104
Bulgaria	3.89	3.53	91
EC	81.64	81.26	100
Top 5, percent	65	69	119
Top 10, percent	80	83	117

Figure 3–13

Millions of metric tons.
These products, where produced: barley, corn, oats, rye, sorghum.
Index of 1989 production; 1980 = 100.
Source: Central Intelligence Agency (1).

In rice production, China greatly leads India, Indonesia, the European Community, and all national economies. At the decade's end, China was producing 4.5 times as much rice as it did in 1980 — by far the greatest increase of any economy.

Among the top ten producers, Myanmar (formerly Burma) and Japan did not increase rice production during the 1980s; Brazil was the only main producer to reduce output over the decade.

Rice production

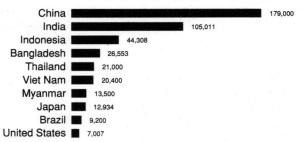

Millions of metric tons, 1989

	1980	1989	INDEX
China	39910	179000	449
India	80312	105011	131
Indonesia	29652	44308	149
Bangladesh	20821	26553	128
Thailand	17368	21000	121
Viet Nam	11700	20400	174
Myanmar (Burma)	13317	13500	101
Japan	12824	12934	101
Brazil	9776	9200	94
United States	6629	7007	106
So Korea	3550	5897	166
USSR	2791	2256	81
Kampuchea	1600	2200	138
Laos	1100	1417	129
Italy	968	1287	133
Cuba	479	467	97
Bulgaria	67	76	113
Romania	39	70	179
Hungary	24	34	142
Yugoslavia	42	18	43
EC	1667	1955	117
Top 5, percent	74	83	200
Top 10, percent	96	97	181

Millions of metric tons.
Index of 1989 production; 1980 = 100.
Source: Central Intelligence Agency (1).

Figure 3–14

Products

In soybean production, the United States leads Brazil, China, and all national economies by wide margins.

However, during the 1980s, all other main producers increased output more than the United States did. India's increase over the decade was far greater than was that of any other economy.

Soybean production is a highly concentrated business: the top five producers account for over 90% of the world's output.

Soybean production

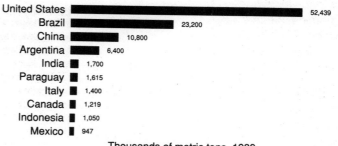

Thousands of metric tons, 1989

	1980	1989	INDEX
United States	48921	52439	107
Brazil	15156	23200	153
China	7966	10800	136
Argentina	3600	6400	178
India	442	1700	385
Paraguay	595	1615	271
Italy	0	1400	inf
Canada	690	1219	177
Indonesia	653	1050	161
Mexico	280	947	338
USSR	525	900	171
Thailand	100	575	575
Romania	448	450	100
No Korea	340	440	129
Japan	174	272	156
So Korea	216	260	120
Yugoslavia	34	204	600
Viet Nam	32	107	334
Bulgaria	107	40	37
Top 5, percent	95	91	124
Top 10, percent	98	97	129

Figure 3–15

Thousands of metric tons.
Index of 1989 production; 1980 = 100.
Source: Central Intelligence Agency (1).

The European Community leads all national economies in sugar production. The USSR leads India by a moderate margin; Cuba and Brazil follow.

Among the top producers, India and China more than doubled production over the 1980s, while Brazil and France produced less.

Sugar production

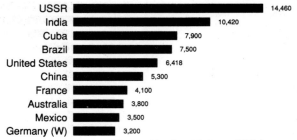

Thousands of metric tons, 1989

	1980	1989	INDEX
USSR	10978	14460	132
India	4528	10420	230
Cuba	6665	7900	119
Brazil	8270	7500	91
United States	5313	6418	121
China	2570	5300	206
France	4253	4100	96
Australia	3415	3800	111
Mexico	2719	3500	129
Germany (W)	2994	3200	107
So Africa	1780	2400	135
Italy	1934	1830	95
Poland	1160	1820	157
Philippines	2332	1750	75
United Kingdom	1202	1345	112
Czechoslovakia	847	878	104
Yugoslavia	709	800	113
Romania	553	692	125
Germany (E)	797	670	84
Hungary	509	500	98
Bulgaria	371	351	95
EC	14015	14708	105
Top 5, percent	56	59	131
Top 10, percent	81	84	129

Figure 3–16

Thousands of metric tons.
Beet sugar, except for Australia and European countries, which include cane sugar.
Index of 1989 production; 1980 = 100.
Source: Central Intelligence Agency (1).

In coffee production, Brazil leads Columbia and other national economies.

Brazil's increase in production over the 1980s was about as great as that of any of the top ten producers except Uganda.

Coffee production is relatively well dispersed throughout the world and among economies. Output of the top ten producers is only 82% of the world's output.

Malaysia, Indonesia, and Thailand produce almost all of the world's natural rubber.

Over the 1980s, Malaysia's output declined a little, Indonesia's increased substantially, and Thailand's more than doubled.

Coffee production

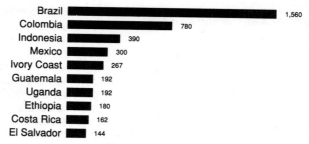

Thousands of metric tons, 1989

	1980	1989	INDEX
Brazil	1061	1560	147
Colombia	724	780	108
Indonesia	295	390	132
Mexico	208	300	144
Ivory Coast	250	267	107
Guatemala	163	192	118
Uganda	110	192	175
Ethiopia	187	180	96
Costa Rica	109	162	149
El Salvador	165	144	87
India	150	135	90
Ecuador	69	132	191
Kenya	91	119	131
Zaire	88	96	109
Honduras	76	93	122
Philippines	145	87	60
Peru	95	84	88
Cameroon	102	78	76
Madagascar	85	69	81
Dominican Republic	60	50	83
Top 5, percent	60	65	130
Top 10, percent	77	82	127

Figure 3–17

Thousands of metric tons. Index of 1989 production; 1980 = 100.
Source: Central Intelligence Agency (1).

Natural rubber production

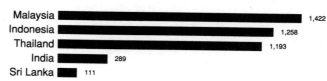

Thousands of metric tons, 1989

	1980	1989	INDEX
Malaysia	1530	1422	93
Indonesia	1010	1258	125
Thailand	501	1193	238
India	155	289	186
Sri Lanka	133	111	83

Figure 3–18

Thousands of metric tons.
Figures for Malaysia include: Malaya and Singapore, Sarawak, and Sabah.
Source: Central Intelligence Agency (1).

In the production of iron ore, the USSR leads China, Brazil, and all other national economies.

While the USSR's production was declining during the 1980s, that of China and Brazil was increasing substantially.

Among the top ten producers, outputs of the United States, Canada, and Sweden declined during the decade.

The top ten producers account for 94% of the world's output.

Mining products

Iron ore production

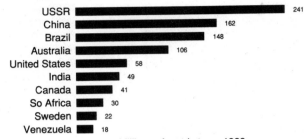

Millions of metric tons, 1989

	1980	1989	INDEX
USSR	245	241	98
China	120	162	135
Brazil	115	148	129
Australia	96	106	111
United States	71	58	82
India	42	49	118
Canada	49	41	84
So Africa	26	30	114
Sweden	27	22	79
Venezuela	16	18	112
Liberia	18	12	64
France	29	11	36
No Korea	9	10	112
Mexico	8	8	101
Yugoslavia	5	5	112
Spain	9	5	52
Romania	2	2	106
Czechoslovakia	2	2	88
Bulgaria	2	2	85
Albania	1	1	160
EC	43	17	39
Top 5, percent	73	77	111
Top 10, percent	91	94	109

Millions of metric tons.
Index of 1989 production; 1980 = 100.
Source: Central Intelligence Agency (1).

Figure 3–19

Australia dominates the world's output of bauxite, and during the 1980s increased its production more than did any other economy.

Among the top ten producers, half reduced outputs during the decade.

The top ten producers account for virtually all of the world's output.

Bauxite production

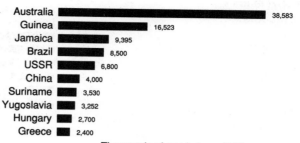

Thousands of metric tons, 1989

	1980	1989	INDEX
Australia	27178	38583	142
Guinea	11862	16523	139
Jamaica	12054	9395	78
Brazil	6688	8500	127
USSR	9100	6800	75
China	3300	4000	121
Suriname	4696	3530	75
Yugoslavia	3138	3252	104
Hungary	2950	2700	92
Greece	3286	2400	73
Guyana	2471	1281	52
France	1921	800	42
United States	1559	588	38
Romania	470	313	67
EC	5230	3200	61
Top 5, percent	74	81	119
Top 10, percent	93	97	114

Figure 3–20

Thousands of metric tons.
Index of 1989 production; 1980 = 100.
US figure is for 1988.
Source: Central Intelligence Agency (1).

In the production of pig iron, the USSR leads Japan by a moderate margin.

During the 1980s, substantial increases in output were achieved by South Korea, the United Kingdom, Brazil, and China. Other leaders either reduced output or held it flat.

Pig iron production

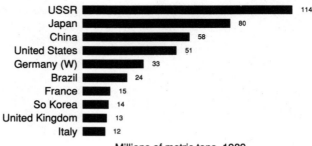

Millions of metric tons, 1989

	1980	1989	INDEX
USSR	107	114	106
Japan	87	80	92
China	38	58	152
United States	62	51	81
Germany (W)	34	33	97
Brazil	13	24	185
France	19	15	79
So Korea	6	14	250
United Kingdom	6	13	197
Italy	12	12	97
India	9	11	129
Poland	12	11	88
Canada	11	11	94
Czechoslovakia	10	10	100
Belgium	11	9	86
Romania	9	8	91
No Korea	4	7	186
So Africa	8	6	85
Australia	7	6	87
Spain	7	6	85
Mexico	5	3	60
Yugoslavia	2	3	121
Germany (E)	3	3	108
Hungary	2	2	91
Bulgaria	2	2	100
Top 5, percent	68	66	102
Top 10, percent	79	81	107

Figure 3–21

Millions of metric tons.
Index of 1989 production; 1980 = 100.
Source: Central Intelligence Agency (1).

The production of crude steel, once the hallmark of an industrialized economy, is now widely dispersed throughout the world, among developed and developing economies.

The USSR leads in crude steel production, followed by the leading developed economies — and China.

Production in the European Community, second only to that of the USSR, ended the decade at almost exactly the same level of output as the EC produced in 1980.

Among the top ten producers, South Korea, China, the United Kingdom, and Brazil increased production the most during the 1980s.

Metal products

Crude steel production

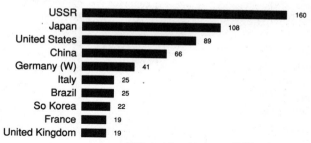

Millions of metric tons, 1989

	1980	1989	INDEX
USSR	148	160	108
Japan	111	108	97
United States	102	89	88
China	37	66	178
Germany (W)	44	41	94
Italy	27	25	95
Brazil	15	25	163
So Korea	9	22	253
France	23	19	83
United Kingdom	11	19	166
Poland	20	17	87
Czechoslovakia	15	16	101
Canada	16	16	97
India	9	14	153
Romania	13	14	109
Spain	13	13	101
Belgium	12	11	89
So Africa	9	9	98
No Korea	4	8	222
Mexico	7	8	110
Germany (E)	7	8	107
Australia	8	7	87
Yugoslavia	4	5	125
Hungary	4	3	87
Bulgaria	3	3	112
Cuba	0.3	0.4	133
EC	142	140	99
Top 5, percent	66	64	105
Top 10, percent	79	79	109

Millions of metric tons.
Figures are for ingots and steel for castings.
Index of 1989 production; 1980 = 100.
Source: Central Intelligence Agency (1).

Figure 3–22

The top producers of rolled steel were the same leading producers of crude steel, except for the absence of South Korea and Brazil.

The European Community was the leading producer of rolled steel in 1980 and maintained that level through the decade. In 1989, the EC's output was slightly below that of the USSR.

Among the leaders, West Germany and China increased output sharply over the decade. The United Kingdom increased output substantially. Output declined in France and Japan.

Rolled steel production

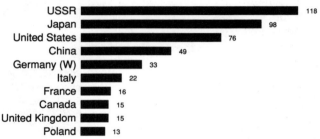

Millions of metric tons, 1989

	1980	1989	INDEX
USSR	103	118	115
Japan	102	98	96
United States	76	76	100
China	27	49	179
Germany (W)	17	33	190
Italy	20	22	112
France	21	16	77
Canada	12	15	122
United Kingdom	10	15	149
Poland	14	13	96
Czechoslovakia	11	12	107
Spain	10	11	106
Romania	9	11	113
Belgium	11	9	83
Yugolslavia	4	8	179
Germany (E)	5	6	107
Bulgaria	3	4	112
Hungary	3	3	99
EC	119	116	97
Top 5, percent	71	72	115
Top 10, percent	88	88	113

Figure 3–23

Millions of metric tons.
Figures are for ingots and steel for castings.
Index of 1989 production; 1980 = 100.
Source: Central Intelligence Agency (1).

By a wide margin, the United States is the leading producer of refined copper. The European Community, second-biggest producer, increased output substantially over the 1980s.

Japan, the third-biggest in 1980, did not increase output over the decade and dropped to fifth place. All other top producers except Zambia substantially increased output over the decade.

Refined copper production

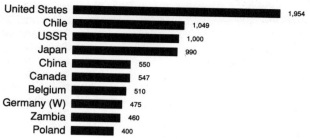

Thousands of metric tons, 1989

	1980	1989	INDEX
United States	1730	1954	113
Chile	811	1049	129
USSR	855	1000	117
Japan	1014	990	98
China	295	550	186
Canada	549	547	100
Belgium	374	510	136
Germany (W)	374	475	127
Zambia	608	460	76
Poland	357	400	112
Australia	166	255	154
Peru	230	225	98
Zaire	144	182	126
Spain	154	166	108
Yugoslavia	131	151	115
United Kingdom	161	125	78
Bulgaria	63	90	143
Germany (E)	51	80	157
Romania	65	45	69
Czechoslovakia	26	27	104
Hungary	12	19	158
Albania	8	13	163
Cuba	3	3	100
EC	1130	1404	124
Top 5, percent	58	59	118
Top 10, percent	85	85	114

Figure 3–24

Thousands of metric tons.
Figures are for primary and secondary refined copper produced from domestic and imported ores and scrap.
Index of 1989 production; 1980 = 100.
Source: Central Intelligence Agency (1).

The United States is the leading producer of primary aluminum. The USSR and European Community follow, at about each other's level of output. Over the decade, output declined in all three economies.

Australia and Brazil increased output over the decade to levels about four times those of 1980.

India and China also increased output sharply over the decade. Production was about flat in West Germany, which dropped from fourth to eighth place. Spain also maintained about the same level of production through the 1980s.

Primary aluminum production

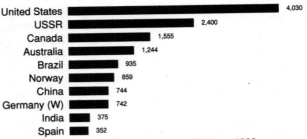

Thousands of metric tons, 1989

	1980	1989	INDEX
United States	4654	4030	87
USSR	2705	2400	89
Canada	1068	1555	146
Australia	303	1244	411
Brazil	260	935	360
Norway	653	859	132
China	415	744	179
Germany (W)	731	742	102
India	185	375	203
Spain	386	352	91
France	432	335	78
United Kingdom	374	297	79
Netherlands	259	274	106
Yugoslavia	185	260	141
Romania	241	250	104
Italy	271	220	81
Ghana	188	169	90
Greece	146	145	99
Hungary	73	75	103
Germany (E)	62	60	97
Poland	95	47	49
Japan	1091	35	3
Czechoslovakia	38	30	79
EC	2600	2365	91
Top 5, percent	61	66	113
Top 10, percent	77	86	117

Figure 3–25

Thousands of metric tons.
Index of 1989 production; 1980 = 100.
Source: Central Intelligence Agency (1).

Cobalt production is dominated by Zaire, which sharply widened its lead over the 1980s.

The top five producers account for virtually all of the world's output of cobalt.

Almost all of the world's platinum is produced by South Africa and the USSR.

Although the United States dramatically increased output over the last decade, it is still a minor player.

Cobalt production

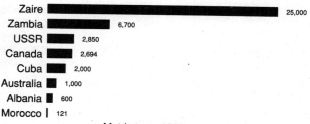

Metric tons, 1989

	1980	1989	INDEX
Zaire	15422	25000	162
Zambia	4400	6700	152
USSR	6000	2850	48
Canada	1603	2694	168
Cuba	1613	2000	124
Australia	1975	1000	51
Albania	326	600	184
Morocco	838	121	14
Finland	1035	0	0
Top 5, percent	87	96	135

Figure 3–26

Metric tons.
Recoverable cobalt content of ores mined.
Index of 1989 production; 1980 = 100.
Source: Central Intelligence Agency (1).

Platinum-group metals production

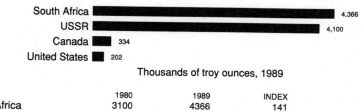

Thousands of troy ounces, 1989

	1980	1989	INDEX
South Africa	3100	4366	141
USSR	3700	4100	111
Canada	411	334	81
United States	3	202	6733

Figure 3–27

Thousands of troy ounces.
Recoverable cobalt content of ores mined.
Index of 1989 production; 1980 = 100.
Source: Central Intelligence Agency (1).

South Africa, the world's leading producer of gold, was the only producer to reduce its output during the 1980s.

Australia increased its output tenfold during the 1980s. The United States also increased output by a large multiple.

Gold production

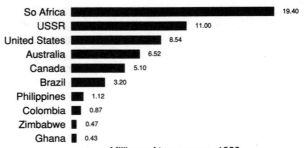

Millions of troy ounces, 1989

	1980	1989	INDEX
So Africa	21.67	19.40	90
USSR	9.45	11.00	116
United States	0.97	8.54	880
Australia	0.55	6.52	1185
Canada	1.63	5.10	313
Brazil	1.30	3.20	246
Philippines	0.64	1.12	175
Colombia	0.51	0.87	171
Zimbabwe	0.37	0.47	127
Ghana	0.35	0.43	123
Mexico	0.20	0.27	135
Japan	0.10	0.20	200
Top 5, percent	91	89	148

Millions of troy ounces.
Index of 1989 production; 1980 = 100.
Source: Central Intelligence Agency (1).

Figure 3–28

In production of chemical fertilizer, the USSR leads the United States, the European Community, China, and Canada.

The USSR and China sharply increased production over the 1980s, while output of the United States, the European Community, West Germany, and France fell a little.

The USSR and the United States lead in the production of synthetic rubber. The European Community produces a little less than the US.

Every major producer except Canada increased output over the 1980s, the United Kingdom by the most.

Manufactured products

Chemical fertilizer production

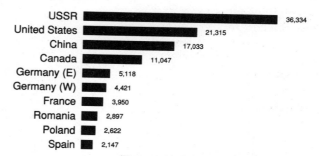

Thousands of metric tons, 1989

	1980	1987	INDEX
USSR	24767	36334	147
United States	23377	21315	91
China	12321	17033	138
Canada	9816	11047	113
Germany (E)	4735	5118	108
Germany (W)	4824	4421	92
France	4924	3950	80
Romania	2451	2897	118
Poland	2237	2622	117
Spain	2148	2147	100
Italy	1837	1880	102
Japan	1850	1533	83
Czechoslovakia	1182	984	83
Bulgaria	947	933	99
Hungary	847	895	106
Yugoslavia	439	592	135
EC	20089	18822	94
Top 5, percent	76	80	121
Top 10, percent	93	94	117

Thousands of metric tons.
Nitrogen, phosphorus, and potassium based fertilizers.
Index of 1987 production; 1980 = 100.
Source: Central Intelligence Agency (1).

Figure 3–29

Synthetic rubber production

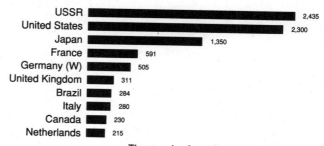

Thousands of metric tons, 1989

The United States dominates production of synthetic fibers, leading the European Community and Japan by wide margins.

Every main producer except France and the United Kingdom increased output substantially over the 1980s. Among the top four, the USSR increased output the most. South Korea, fifth biggest producer, increased output sharply during the decade. Romania doubled its output from a smaller base.

Synthetic rubber production

	1980	1989	INDEX
USSR	2040	2435	119
United States	2215	2300	104
Japan	1094	1350	123
France	511	591	116
Germany (W)	390	505	129
United Kingdom	212	311	147
Brazil	249	284	114
Italy	250	280	112
Canada	253	230	91
Netherlands	212	215	101
Germany (E)	150	160	107
Mexico	91	150	165
Romania	150	150	100
Poland	118	125	106
Czechoslovakia	60	75	125
Bulgaria	30	25	83
EC	1771	2114	119
Top 5, percent	78	78	115
Top 10, percent	93	93	114

Figure 3–30

Thousands of metric tons. Index of 1989 production; 1980 = 100.
Source: Central Intelligence Agency (1).

Synthetic fibers production

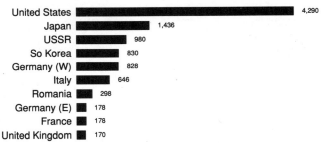

United States 4,290
Japan 1,436
USSR 980
So Korea 830
Germany (W) 828
Italy 646
Romania 298
Germany (E) 178
France 178
United Kingdom 170

Thousands of metric tons, 1989

	1980	1989	INDEX
United States	3571	4290	120
Japan	1400	1436	103
USSR	570	980	172
So Korea	538	830	154
Germany (W)	721	828	115
Italy	400	646	162
Romania	141	298	211
Germany (E)	139	178	129
France	224	178	79
United Kingdom	288	170	59
Poland	168	166	99
Czechoslovakia	110	144	131
Yugoslavia	50	101	202
Bulgaria	56	59	106
Hungary	21	32	154
EC	2030	2360	116
Top 5, percent	81	81	123
Top 10, percent	95	95	123

Figure 3–31

Thousands of metric tons. Excludes waste, glass fibers, and rubber fibers.
Figures for Germany (E), Romania, and Yugoslavia are for 1988. Index of 1989 production; 1980 = 100.
Source: Central Intelligence Agency (1).

Products

The European Community produces more passenger automobiles than any single national economy. Japan, the United States, and West Germany maintained their relative positions over the 1980s. All of the top three producers increased output over the decade, the United States less than the others.

South Korea, now the tenth-biggest national producer, increased output much more than tenfold over the decade — from a position behind Malaysia in 1980.

Only the USSR and France decreased output during the decade.

Passenger automobile production

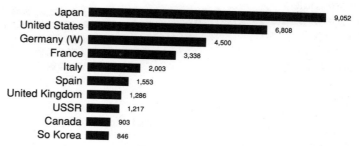

Thousands of units, 1989

	1980	1989	INDEX
Japan	7038	9052	129
United States	6400	6808	106
Germany (W)	3512	4500	128
France	3487	3338	96
Italy	1445	2003	139
Spain	1048	1553	148
United Kingdom	924	1286	139
USSR	1327	1217	92
Canada	847	903	107
So Korea	58	846	1459
Yugoslavia	255	312	122
Brazil	652	308	47
Poland	351	285	81
Mexico	316	228	72
Germany (E)	177	218	123
Czechoslovakia	184	189	103
Romania	88	129	147
Malaysia	79	77	97
Bulgaria	15	15	100
EC	10500	13147	125
Top 5, percent	78	77	117
Top 10, percent	92	95	121

Thousands of units.
Figures for Mexico and Romania are for 1987.
Index of 1989 production; 1980 = 100.
Source: Central Intelligence Agency (1).

Figure 3–32

The United States and Japan dominated production of trucks and buses throughout the 1980s. The European Community was the third-biggest producer over the period.

The United States extended its lead during the decade by more than doubling its output, while Japan's remained flat.

China, Spain, and Canada also increased output sharply over the decade, while that of West Germany and the United Kingdom fell substantially.

Truck and bus production

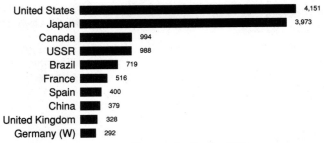

Thousands of units, 1989

	1980	1989	INDEX
United States	1667	4151	249
Japan	4006	3973	99
Canada	528	994	188
USSR	872	988	113
Brazil	516	719	139
France	505	516	102
Spain	146	400	274
China	136	379	279
United Kingdom	389	328	84
Germany (W)	380	292	77
Italy	167	256	153
Poland	74	52	70
Czechoslovakia	49	51	104
Germany (E)	40	38	95
Hungary	14	13	93
Bulgaria	7	10	143
Yugoslavia	21	4	19
EC	1620	1930	119
Top 5, percent	80	82	143
Top 10, percent	96	97	139

Figure 3–33

Thousands of units.
Figure for Yugoslavia is for 1987.
Index of 1989 production; 1980 = 100.
Source: Central Intelligence Agency (1).

Products

In production of rubber tires, the United States and Japan led the rest of the world by wide margins. Both economies increased output substantially during the 1980s, as did the other main producers — except the United Kingdom and Italy.

Rubber tire production

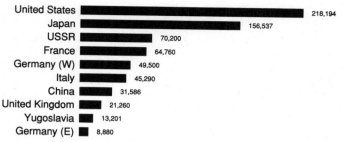

Thousands of units, 1989

	1980	1989	INDEX
United States	159263	218194	137
Japan	113004	156537	139
USSR	60100	70200	117
France	50544	64760	128
Germany (W)	37800	49500	131
Italy	52320	45290	87
China	11000	31586	287
United Kingdom	26346	21260	81
Yugoslavia	9584	13201	138
Germany (E)	7067	8880	126
Romania	5046	6487	129
Poland	8020	6039	75
Czechoslovakia	6740	5297	79
Bulgaria	2117	1884	89
Hungary	840	967	115
Cuba	387	228	59
Top 5, percent	76	80	133
Top 10, percent	96	97	129

Figure 3–34

Thousands of units.
Excludes aircraft and bicycle tires, and, for OECD countries, motorcycle tires.
Figure for Romania is for 1987, not 1989.
Index of 1989 production; 1980 = 100.
Source: Central Intelligence Agency (1).

Products

4 Merchandise Trade

The annual value of world merchandise trade began the new decade at $3.3 trillion, up 14.6% from the previous year, 1989. Merchandise trade is 80% of total trade, which also includes services.

After the deep recession of the early '80s, **exports** of goods grew 50% faster than the **output** of goods. This divergence implies that the global economy continued to become more integrated; that is, driven more by the comparative economic advantages of national economies than by their political identities. The United States Trade Representative attributed 40% of her country's growth in GNP over the past several years to a robust increase in exports.

The three main components of merchandise trade — manufactures, agricultures, and mining products — did not perform uniformly well during the decade.

In 1989, manufactures were 70% of the **value** of merchandise trade and contributed almost all of the increase in its **volume** (i.e., discounting price effects). Exports of manufactures grew more slowly than in the previous year. After 1983, trade in manufactures grew to a little over half of total world trade, including services. Over the decade, mostly in its later years, the volume of trade in manufactures grew about 20% more than did the world's production of manufactures.

Growth of world merchandise trade vs world output

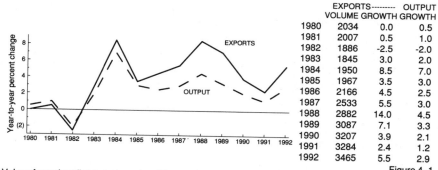

	EXPORTS		OUTPUT
	VOLUME	GROWTH	GROWTH
1980	2034	0.0	0.5
1981	2007	0.5	1.0
1982	1886	-2.5	-2.0
1983	1845	3.0	2.0
1984	1950	8.5	7.0
1985	1967	3.5	3.0
1986	2166	4.5	2.5
1987	2533	5.5	3.0
1988	2882	14.0	4.5
1989	3087	7.1	3.3
1990	3207	3.9	2.1
1991	3284	2.4	1.2
1992	3465	5.5	2.9

Figure 4–1

Value of merchandise exports and world output in billions of dollars. Year-to-year percent change. 1991 and 1992 figures are estimates.
Sources: General Agreement on Tariffs & Trade (2) and (3), International Monetary Fund (11).

Overall, the 1980s were a decade of continuing economic changes and surprises, some more welcome than others, which affected world trade. One surprise, coming off two jolting shocks in the 1970s, was the decline in the price and traded volume of petroleum products. Monetary authorities brought double-digit inflation under control with unexpected swiftness, causing major disruptions in trade patterns, especially those of developing economies.

During the decade, imports to the United States surged as that economy's consumption increased faster than its production. The resulting trade deficits moved the US from its 70-year position as the world's largest creditor to that of its largest debtor. Japan, its trade surpluses mirroring US deficits, became the largest creditor. However, as the decade closed, these trade imbalances began to dwindle. Comparing the first nine months of 1990 and 1989, Japan's surplus declined by 16%, and the US deficit declined by over 8%. West Germany's surplus also declined by about 8%. For this period, Japan's exports grew at the slowest rate of all of the main industrial economies; Germany's imports grew at the fastest rate.

Very serious debt problems emerged in the developing economies after 1982, leading to a sudden contraction of their trade with the developed world.

The world's trading-policy forum, the General Agreement on Tariffs and Trade (GATT), increased its membership to 100 by early 1991. In 1986, GATT launched the Uruguay round of multilateral trade negotiations. This eighth and most ambitious round aimed at liberalizing trade in agricultures and bringing commercial services into the system. But by mid–1991, the contracting parties had missed their goal for completing the negotiations and were stalled on the issue of agriculture subsidies.

Many analysts worried that the parallel growth of regional free-trade areas, most importantly in Europe and North America, might be leading the world into becoming a hostile field of self-centered trade fortresses. Advocates of free-trade areas deny such an intention, and some early evidence suggests that these areas are not inhibiting cross-regional trade. GATT officials and other observers also express concern over the persistence of non-tariff trade barriers and the growing practice, especially in the United States, of superimposing unilateral trade restrictions on trading partners without going through the global multilateral system.

The value of total world trade reached $3.8 trillion in 1989, a growth of about 8% over the previous year, in which it grew 13%. The values of trade in merchandise and commercial services increased, but not as fast as they did in 1988. Trade in commercial services was close to the combined totals of agricultures and mining products.

Greatest growth came in mining products, due mostly to rising prices of crude petroleum. Trade in "Other" private services, including financial services, also grew faster than the year before.

The developed world dominated world trade with a 73% share of it. Trade of the transitioning socialist economies of the USSR and central and eastern Europe was a negligible part of the global total.

Overview of merchandise trade

Value of world exports

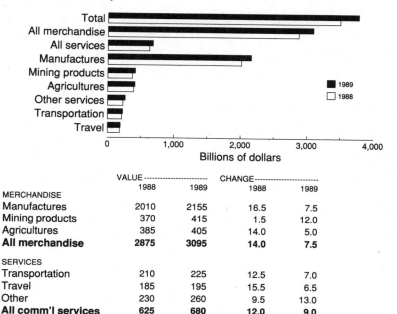

	VALUE		CHANGE	
	1988	1989	1988	1989
MERCHANDISE				
Manufactures	2010	2155	16.5	7.5
Mining products	370	415	1.5	12.0
Agricultures	385	405	14.0	5.0
All merchandise	**2875**	**3095**	**14.0**	**7.5**
SERVICES				
Transportation	210	225	12.5	7.0
Travel	185	195	15.5	6.5
Other	230	260	9.5	13.0
All comm'l services	**625**	**680**	**12.0**	**9.0**
Total	**3500**	**3775**	**13.3**	**7.9**

Figure 4–2

Billions of dollars and percent change.
A discrepancy of about $31.5 billion in 1989 exports of services has been added to the figure for transportation services. Discrepancies between the figures for 1988 and comparable figures shown elsewhere are presented as published.
Source: General Agreement on Tariffs & Trade (4).

Participation in world trade

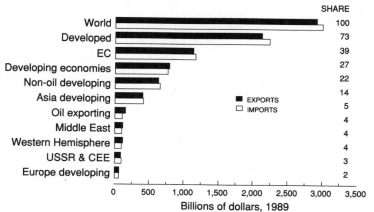

Source: International Monetary Fund (2)).

Figure 4–3

In the developed world, the growth of both exports and imports dropped significantly in 1989. Because these economies dominate global trade, their slowing also slowed growth in the rest of the world.

In the developing world, export growth fell slightly, while import growth dropped by more than half. This in turn reduced exports from the developed economies.

Merchandise balances of the three main economies converged during the later 1980s.

Germany's trade surpluses (theretofore the world's largest) declined steadily after 1989, as the economy accommodated a massively increased demand for goods in the newly integrated eastern provinces. By mid–1991, Germany's trade account was actually in deficit.

Japan's trade surpluses appeared to be on the verge of resuming an upward trend, after declining steadily since 1988.

The huge deficits of the United States declined steadily after 1987. But analysts expect the US deficits to begin growing again in the next few years.

Merchandise trade by development status

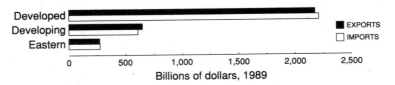

Billions of dollars, 1989

	EXPORTS			IMPORTS		
	1989 VALUE	1988 CHANGE	1989 CHANGE	1989 VALUE	1988 CHANGE	1989 CHANGE
Developed	2175	14.5	7.0	2210	13.0	8.0
Developing	650	15.0	13.0	610	21.0	9.0
Eastern	270	7.5	0.0	275	11.5	2.0
World	**3095**	**14.0**	**7.5**	**3095**	**14.0**	**7.5**

Figure 4–4

Billions of dollars and year-to-year percent change. Eastern economies = Central and East European countries, USSR, China, and other centrally-planned economies in Asia.
Source: General Agreement on Tariffs & Trade (4).

Merchandise trade balances of three main economies

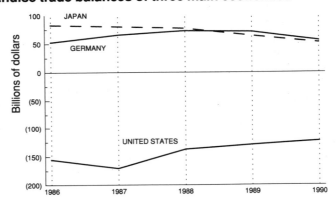

Merchandise trade balances of G–7 economies

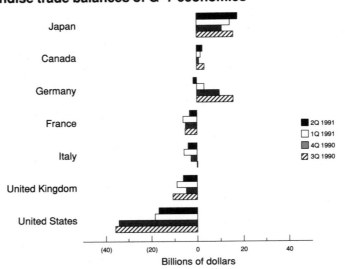

Billions of dollars

Merchandise trade was 81% of total trade in 1989, maintaining a share it has held for 20 years.

Trade in manufactures dominated merchandise trade and was 57% of total trade, recovering all and a little more of the share it had in 1970, before the oil shocks sent up the share of mining products.

Through the decade of the 1980s, the price (unit value) of traded merchandise grew hardly at all. Prices of manufactured goods grew robustly during the 1980s; prices of agricultural exports grew a little less; prices of mining products dropped by nearly a third.

The **volume** of all traded merchandise (i.e., adjusted for price changes) grew much more than **value** at current prices.

Growth in the volume of traded manufactures outpaced that of other merchandise. The volume of traded agricultures increased moderately. The volume of mining products grew about half as much as that of agricultures, even as exporters received sharply lower prices.

Merchandise trade balances of main developed economies

	1986	1987	1988	1989	1990	1990 3Q	1990 4Q	1991 1Q	1991 2Q
Germany	52.5	65.9	72.9	71.5	55.8	15.8	9.8	3.20	-1.50
Japan	83.2	80.3	77.5	64.2	52.2	15.9	11	14.40	17.80
Canada	4.8	5.6	3.9	0.5	6.8	3.3	0.8	1.60	2.50
Italy	-2.2	-8.7	-10.7	-12.5	-11.6	0.2	-2.8	-5.70	-4.00
France	-4.5	-10.1	-11.1	-13.6	-18.0	-5.3	-5.1	-6.10	-3.30
United Kingdom	-19.1	-23.1	-44.2	-45.4	-37.6	-10.8	-4.9	-8.90	-6.20
United States	-155.1	-170.3	-137.1	-129.1	-122.7	-35.9	-34.2	-18.50	-16.80

Billions of dollars. Exports f.o.b. and imports c.i.f. Unified Germany after June 1990.
Source: International Monetary Fund (12).

Figure 4–5

Trends in merchandise exports

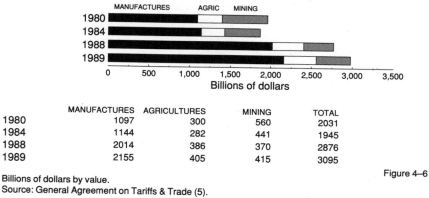

	MANUFACTURES	AGRICULTURES	MINING	TOTAL
1980	1097	300	560	2031
1984	1144	282	441	1945
1988	2014	386	370	2876
1989	2155	405	415	3095

Billions of dollars by value.
Source: General Agreement on Tariffs & Trade (5).

Figure 4–6

Trends in world exports and output

Unit value	121	117	69	102
Volume	165	118	107	142
Output	137	122	100	128

Index 1989; 1980 = 100.
Source: General Agreement on Tariffs & Trade (5).

Table 4–1

Trends in product trading

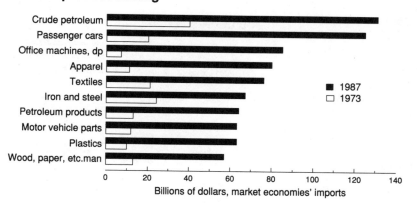

Crude petroleum continued to be the world's most-traded product in 1987, and passenger motor cars moved up to second place from fourth in 1973. Over those 14 years, other products on the most-traded roster moved up in rank, signalling important changes in modern industry and lifestyles.

Office machines (and computers) jumped from 20th to 2nd place over the period, and transistors from 38th to 13th. Interestingly, fish and preparations also made a big jump in rank.

In broader product groupings, machinery and transport equipment dominated world trade in manufactures in 1988. In that year, iron and steel products moved ahead of textiles.

Germany led the top ten traders in manufactures in 1988, followed closely by Japan. Both leaders showed strong trade surpluses. The number three trader, the United States, imported much more than it exported as, to a lesser degree, did France and the United Kingdom.

Trends in product trading

	1973			1987		
	RANK	VALUE	SHARE	RANK	VALUE	SHARE
Crude petroleum	1	39541	7.4	1	130945	5.6
Passenger motor cars	4	19740	3.7	2	125022	5.4
Office machines/dataprocessing equip	20	7201	1.3	3	85037	3.6
Apparel	9	11479	2.2	4	80178	3.4
Textiles	3	21263	4	5	76426	3.3
Iron and steel	2	23866	4.5	6	66726	2.9
Petroleum products	7	12528	2.3	7	63994	2.7
Motor vehicle parts	8	11598	2.2	8	63176	2.7
Plastics	15	9976	1.9	9	62527	2.7
Wood, cork, and paper manufactures	6	12753	2.4	10	56548	2.4
Organic chemicals	18	8341	1.6	11	50224	2.2
Fruits and vegetables	11	11392	2.1	12	41064	1.8
Transistors, valves, etc.	38	3517	0.7	13	37703	1.6
Telecom equip and accessories	17	8453	1.6	14	36351	1.6
Fish and preparations	32	4313	0.8	15	29093	1.2
Total of market economies		**533545**	**100**		**2332530**	**100**
1987 Top 15		205961	39		1005014	43
1987 Top 10		169945	32		810579	35
1987 Top 5		99224	19		497608	21

Figure 4–7

Millions of dollars and percentages.
Source: General Agreement on Tariffs & Trade (2).

Manufactures

Trade in manufactures

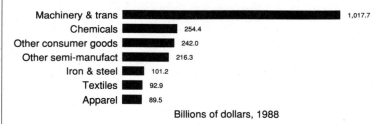

Billions of dollars, 1988

Figure 4–8

Top traders in manufactures

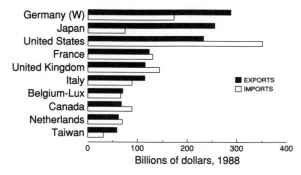

Billions of dollars, 1988

The USSR, the world's second- (now third-) biggest economy, has never been a major trader. From 1973 through the 1980s, the value of its trade quadrupled, but its share of world trade never rose above 2%.

Over the past two decades, the concentration of trade among the top five exporters declined a little, while the top five importers increased their world share.

Main traders in manufactures

1988 RANK	EXPORTERS	1973 VALUE	1973 SHARE	1980 VALUE	1980 SHARE	1988 VALUE	1988 SHARE
1	Germany (W)	59	17	162	15	287	14
2	Japan	35	10	123	11	255	13
3	United States	45	13	146	13	232	11
4	France	25	7	81	7	123	6
5	United Kingdom	24	7	82	7	115	6
6	Italy	18	5	65	6	114	6
7	Belgium-Lux	17	5	44	4	70	3
8	Canada	12	3	30	3	67	3
9	Netherlands	13	4	37	3	62	3
10	Taiwan	4	1	17	2	58	3
11	Hong Kong	5	1	18	2	57	3
12	So Korea	3	1	16	1	56	3
13	Switzerland	9	2	27	2	47	2
14	Sweden	9	3	24	2	42	2
15	USSR	8	2	20	2	32	2
16	Spain	3	1	15	1	29	1
17	Singapore	2	1	8	1	27	1
18	Austria	4	1	15	1	24	1
19	China	1	0	3	0	24	1
20	Czechoslovakia	5	2	18	2	22	1
	World	**351**	**100**	**1110**	**100**	**2045**	**100**
	Top 20	301	85	949	86	1744	85
	Top 15	286	81	891	80	1617	79
	Top 10	253	72	787	71	1383	67
	Top 5	189	54	594	54	1012	49
	IMPORTERS						
1	United States	43	12	125	11	351	17
2	Germany (W)	29	8	98	9	173	8
3	United Kingdom	20	6	72	6	144	7
4	France	23	6	73	6	130	6
5	Italy	13	4	44	4	89	4
6	Canada	18	5	41	4	89	4
7	Japan	10	3	26	2	75	4
8	USSR	13	4	41	4	70	3
9	Netherlands	14	4	41	4	69	3
10	Belgium-Lux	14	4	41	4	66	3
11	Hong Kong	4	1	17	2	54	3
12	Switzerland	8	2	26	2	47	2
13	Spain	5	1	13	1	42	2
14	China					37	2
15	Sweden	8	2	21	2	36	2
16	So Korea	2	1	10	1	35	
17	Singapore	3	1	13	1	31	2
18	Taiwan	2	1	10	1	31	2
19	Austria	5	1	17	2	30	1
20	Australia	6	2	15	1	28	1
	World	**360**	**100**	**1136**	**100**	**2115**	**100**
	Top 20	240	67	741	65	1627	77
	Top 15	221	61	677	60	1473	70
	Top 10	196	55	601	53	1256	59
	Top 5	127	35	411	36	888	42

Figure 4–9

Billions of dollars and percentages
Share = percent of total world exports/imports of manufactures.
Figures for Hong Kong and Singapore include substantial reexports.
Source: General Agreement on Tariffs & Trade (2).

Machinery and transport equipment accounted for one-third of merchandise exports and half of all exports in manufactures — over $1 trillion in 1988. Trade in this group of products grew twice as fast that year as it had, on average, over the previous years of the decade.

About three-fourths of this trade involved developed economies. Most of the rest involved developing economies, with eastern socialist economies trading less than one-tenth of the total.

Passenger motor cars and their parts and accessories ranked first and third on the list of traded products in this category. In between were office machines and computers, which since 1973 jumped 17 places on the larger list of all traded merchandise.

The building of ships and boats, along with metalworking tools, lost rank over that period.

Machinery and transport equipment

World trade in machinery and transport equipment

Value	1016
Share in world merchandise exports	34.5
Share in world exports of manufactures	49.5
Annual change, 1988	16.0
Average annual change, 1980-88	8.5

Table 4–2

Billions of dollars and percentages, 1988.
Source: General Agreement on Tariffs & Trade (2).

Distribution of trade in machinery and transport equipment

\ DESTINATION ORIGIN \	DEVELOPED VALUE	DEVELOPED SHARE	DEVELOPING VALUE	DEVELOPING SHARE	EASTERN VALUE	EASTERN SHARE	WORLD VALUE	WORLD SHARE
Developed	568	90	135	82	24	29	727	83
Developing	58	9	20	12	4	5	82	9
Eastern	5	1	10	6	54	66	68	8
World	**631**	**100**	**164**	**100**	**82**	**100**	**876**	**100**
World share		72		19		9		100

Table 4–3

Billions of dollars and percentages, 1987.
Eastern economies = USSR and Central Europe plus China and centrally-planned Asian economies.
Source: General Agreement on Tariffs & Trade (2).

Main trade in machinery and transport equipment

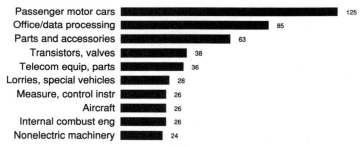

Passenger motor cars		125
Office/data processing		85
Parts and accessories		63
Transistors, valves		38
Telecom equip, parts		36
Lorries, special vehicles		28
Measure, control instr		26
Aircraft		26
Internal combust eng		26
Nonelectric machinery		24

Billions of dollars, 1987

1973 RANK	1987 RANK		1987 VALUE	1987 SHARE
4	2	Passenger motor cars	125	5.4
20	3	Office/data processing equip, parts	85	3.6
8	8	Parts and accessories, motor vehicles	63	2.7
38	13	Transistors, valves	38	1.6
17	14	Telecom equip, parts, accessories	36	1.6
27	16	Lorries, special vehicles	28	1.2
46	19	Measuring, controlling instruments	26	1.1
25	20	Aircraft	26	1.1
24	22	Internal combustion piston engines	26	1.1
29	26	Nonelectric machinery parts, accessories	24	1.0
39	29	Electrical apparatus	23	1.0
14	34	Ships and boats	19	0.8
45	40	Photo apparatus, cinema supplies	16	0.7
34	41	Metalworking machine tools	14	0.6
40	42	Civil engineering equipment	14	0.6

(MORE)

Japan and West Germany were the leading traders in machinery and transport equipment. Both had trade surpluses; Japan's was a huge $163 billion and Germany's about half as much. During the 1980s, Japan overtook the United States and Germany to achieve the rank of top exporter in these products.

Main trade in machinery & transport equipment, cont'd

1973 RANK	1987 RANK		1987 VALUE	1987 SHARE
23	43	Other engines and motors	13	0.6
43	44	Heating, cooling equipment	13	0.6
		Total of above	**588**	**25**

Figure 4–10

Billions of dollars.
Source: General Agreement on Tariffs & Trade (2).

Main traders in machinery and transport equipment

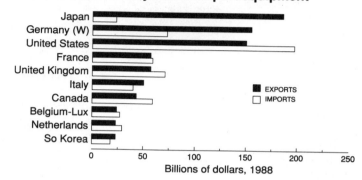

EXPORTS
IMPORTS

Billions of dollars, 1988

1988 RANK		1980 VALUE	1988 VALUE	1980 SHARE	1988 SHARE	1980–87 CHANGE	1988 CHANGE	1980 DEPEND	1988 DEPEND
	EXPORTERS								
1	Japan	76	186	14	19	12	15	58	70
2	Germany (W)	85	155	16	16	8	9	45	48
3	United States	89	150	17	15	5	24	40	47
4	France	37	57	7	6	5	12	32	34
5	United Kingdom	40	57	8	6	3	21	36	39
6	Italy	25	50	5	5	7	13	32	36
7	Canada	17	43	3	4	12	20	25	38
8	Belgium-Lux	14	24	3	3	7	7	22	26
9	Netherlands	13	23	3	2	7	17	17	22
10	So Korea	4	23	1	2	25	35	20	38
11	Sweden	12	21	3	2	7	12	40	43
12	Taiwan	5	21	1	2	20	24	25	36
13	Singapore	5	19	1	2	14	51	27	48
14	USSR	12	18	3	2	5	7	16	16
15	Hong Kong	4	17	1	2	17	50	20	27
	Top 15	438	864	82	85				
	Top 10	400	768	74	75				
	Top 5	327	605	61	60				
	IMPORTERS								
1	United States	64	197			16	8	25	43
2	Germany (W)	35	73			9	14	19	30
3	United Kingdom	30	71			9	32	26	38
4	France	29	59			8	18	21	33
5	Canada	27	59			9	23	43	55
6	USSR	23	44			8	11	34	41
7	Italy	20	40			8	18	20	29
8	Netherlands	15	29			8	11	20	29
9	Belgium-Lux	16	27			6	9	22	29
10	Spain	6	24			16	39	18	39

(MORE)

The top ten exporters of automotive products all substantially increased their trade during the 1980s. Among the top five exporters, Japan replaced West Germany in the number one position; France slid from fourth to fifth place; Canada increased exports by the greatest percentage. South Korea, the 12th-biggest exporter, increased exports by 59% during the decade.

Exports of automotive products accounted for a full one-quarter of Canada's merchandise exports and virtually the same share of Japan's. During the decade, dependence on exports of automotive products increased substantially in Canada, Japan, and Germany, less in the US, and close to none at all in France.

Spain's dependence on these exports also increased substantially during the 1980s, and by 1988 their annual value approached that of Sweden and the United Kingdom.

Main traders in machinery & transport equipment, cont'd

1988 RANK	1980 VALUE	1988 VALUE	1980 SHARE	1988 SHARE	1980–87 CHANGE	1988 CHANGE	1980 DEPEND	1988 DEPEND
11 Japan	8	23			10	39	6	12
12 Singapore	7	19			9	45	30	43
13 Hong Kong	5	18			14	46	23	29
14 So Korea	5	18			16	29	22	35
15 Switzerland	9	18			9	14	24	35
Top 15	299	719						
Top 10	265	623						
Top 5	185	459						

Figure 4–11

Billions of dollars and percentages. Share = percent of world exports.
1980–87 change = average annual change.
Depend(ency) = share of product in economy's merchandise exports or imports.
Figures for Singapore and Hong Kong include substantial reexports and imports for reexport.
Source: General Agreement on Tariffs & Trade (2).

Automotive

Top exporters of automotive products

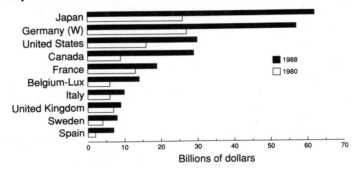

1988 RANK	1980 VALUE	1988 VALUE	1980 SHARE	1988 SHARE	1980–87 CHANGE	1988 CHANGE	1980 DEPEND	1988 DEPEND
1 Japan	26	62	21	24	13	6	20	24
2 Germany (W)	27	57	22	22	10	7	14	18
3 United States	16	30	14	12	7	17	8	10
4 Canada	9	29	8	11	15	23	14	25
5 France	13	19	11	8	5	11	11	12
6 Belgium-Lux	6	14	5	5	10	8	10	15
7 Italy	6	10	5	4	6	12	8	8
8 United Kingdom	7	9	6	4	1	16	7	7
9 Sweden	4	8	3	3	10	6	12	15
10 Spain	2	7	2	3	15	27	11	19
11 USSR	3	5	2	2	10		4	5
12 So Korea	0	4	0	2	59	18	1	6
13 Netherlands	2	3	1	2	10	21	2	4
14 Mexico	0	3	1	2	35	8	3	16
15 Brazil	1	3	1	1	10	19	7	10
Top 15	122	263	100	100				
Top 10	116	244	95	93				
Top 5	91	197	75	75				

Figure 4–12

Billions of dollars and percentages. Share = share in top 15 exporters.
1980–87 change = average annual change.
Depend(ency) = share of product in economy's merchandise exports or imports.
US figures adjusted for undocumented exports to Canada (about $3 billion in 1988).
Mexico's exports include shipments from trade processing zones (which exceeded $1 billion in 1988).
For USSR, 1988 figures are estimates.
Source: General Agreement on Tariffs & Trade (2).

Imports of Japanese passenger cars into the United States nearly doubled their market share in the decade of the 1970s, but because of voluntary export restraints (VERs), that share remained constant throughout the 1980s. The share of foreign cars in the Japanese market remains negligible.

Developed economies accounted for nearly all of the world's exports of chemicals, and an even greater share of that trade was between developed economies.

Market shares of Japanese passenger cars

	1977	1980	1987
United States	12	21	21
Canada		13	19
Germany (W)	3	10	15
United Kingdom	11	12	10
France	3	3	3
Share of foreign cars in Japanese market	2	2	3

Table 4–4

Percentages based on numbers sold.
Figures exclude locally assembled or produced Japanese passenger cars.
Source: General Agreement on Tariffs & Trade (2).

Chemicals

World trade in chemicals

Value	253
Share in world merchandise exports	9.0
Share in world exports of manufactures	12.5
Annual change, 1988	17.0
Average annual change, 1980-88	7.5

Table 4–5

Billions of dollars and percentages, 1988.
Source: General Agreement on Tariffs & Trade (2).

Distribution of trade in chemicals

DESTINATION ORIGIN	DEVELOPED VALUE	DEVELOPED SHARE	DEVELOPING VALUE	DEVELOPING SHARE	EASTERN VALUE	EASTERN SHARE	WORLD VALUE	WORLD SHARE
Developed	138	92	37	79	10	53	185	86
Developing	7	5	7	15	2	11	16	7
Eastern	5	3	3	6	8	42	15	7
World	**150**	**100**	**47**	**100**	**19**	**100**	**216**	**100**
World share		69		22		9		100

Table 4–6

Billions of dollars and percentages, 1988.
Eastern economies = USSR and Central Europe plus China and centrally-planned Asian economies.
Source: General Agreement on Tariffs & Trade (2).

Top traders in chemicals

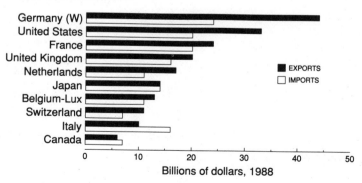

Billions of dollars, 1988

West Germany and the United States were the top exporters and importers of chemicals. For Switzerland, the eighth-largest trader in chemicals, exports amounted to more than one-fifth of all merchandise exports. Canada increased exports by over one-third in 1988.

China nearly doubled imports in 1988, while Taiwan and South Korea increased imports by about one-third.

Top traders in chemicals

1988 RANK		1980 VALUE	1988 VALUE	1980 SHARE	1988 SHARE	1980–87 CHANGE	1988 CHANGE	1980 DEPEND	1988 DEPEND
	EXPORTERS								
1	Germany (W)	24	44	17	18	7	14	13	14
2	United States	21	33	15	13	4	22	10	10
3	France	13	24	10	10	7	16	12	14
4	United Kingdom	12	20	9	8	5	17	11	14
5	Netherlands	11	17	8	7	6	14	16	17
6	Japan	7	14	5	6	9	18	5	5
7	Belgium-Lux	7	13	5	5	5	25	12	14
8	Switzerland	6	11	4	5	9	10	19	22
9	Italy	5	10	4	4	7	12	7	8
10	Canada	3	6	3	3	5	34	5	6
11	Hong Kong	1	4	1	2	19	7	4	6
12	Spain	2	4	1	2	10	20	8	9
13	Germany (E)	2	4	2	2	8	16	11	12
14	Sweden	2	4	1	2	9	15	6	7
15	USSR	2	3	2	2	7	11	3	3
	Top 15	118	211	84	84				
	Top 10	109	192	78	77				
	Top 5	81	138	58	55				
	IMPORTERS								
1	Germany (W)	13	24			7	13	7	10
2	United States	9	20			10	22	4	5
3	France	12	20			5	16	9	4
4	United Kingdom	7	16			10	21	7	9
5	Italy	8	16			8	17	8	12
6	Japan	6	14			10	24	4	8
7	Belgium-Lux	6	11			6	22	9	12
8	Netherlands	6	11			6	9	8	11
9	China	3	9			8	83	15	17
10	USSR	2	8			19	8	3	7
11	Canada	3	7			8	24	5	6
12	Switzerland	4	7			7	15	10	12
13	Taiwan	2	6			14	35	10	13
14	So Korea	2	6			15	35	8	12
15	Spain	3	6			11	17	8	10

Figure 4–13

Billions of dollars and percentages.
1980–87 change = average annual change.
Depend(ency) = share of product in economy's merchandise exports or imports.
Exports for Hong Kong include substantial reexports.
Source: General Agreement on Tariffs & Trade (2).

Merchandise Trade

In microelectronics, market shares of Japan and the United States were about the same, Japan having gained share since 1980. Singapore's share dropped by nearly half during the decade.

The United States and Japan also dominated the world market in computers. The US lost much of its share through the 1980s, and Japan gained as much. Most other traders also lost share during the decade.

In telecommunications equipment, Japan was the clear leader in 1989, rising from fourth place in 1980.

The United States dominated the world's aerospace market throughout the decade, losing only a small share in that period. The United Kingdom lost nearly half of its 1980 market share.

High technologies

Top exporters of high-technology products

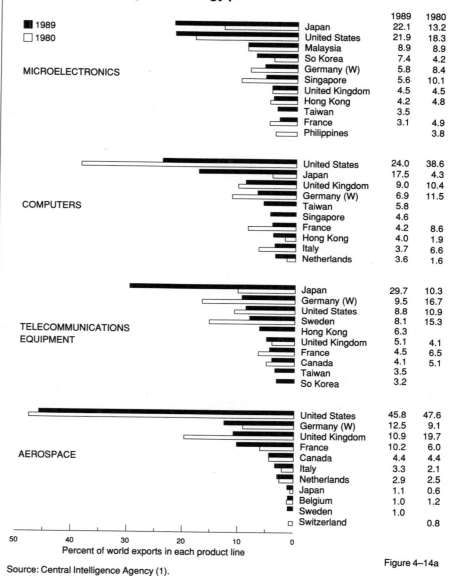

■ 1989
□ 1980

	1989	1980
MICROELECTRONICS		
Japan	22.1	13.2
United States	21.9	18.3
Malaysia	8.9	8.9
So Korea	7.4	4.2
Germany (W)	5.8	8.4
Singapore	5.6	10.1
United Kingdom	4.5	4.5
Hong Kong	4.2	4.8
Taiwan	3.5	
France	3.1	4.9
Philippines		3.8
COMPUTERS		
United States	24.0	38.6
Japan	17.5	4.3
United Kingdom	9.0	10.4
Germany (W)	6.9	11.5
Taiwan	5.8	
Singapore	4.6	
France	4.2	8.6
Hong Kong	4.0	1.9
Italy	3.7	6.6
Netherlands	3.6	1.6
TELECOMMUNICATIONS EQUIPMENT		
Japan	29.7	10.3
Germany (W)	9.5	16.7
United States	8.8	10.9
Sweden	8.1	15.3
Hong Kong	6.3	
United Kingdom	5.1	4.1
France	4.5	6.5
Canada	4.1	5.1
Taiwan	3.5	
So Korea	3.2	
AEROSPACE		
United States	45.8	47.6
Germany (W)	12.5	9.1
United Kingdom	10.9	19.7
France	10.2	6.0
Canada	4.4	4.4
Italy	3.3	2.1
Netherlands	2.9	2.5
Japan	1.1	0.6
Belgium	1.0	1.2
Sweden	1.0	
Switzerland		0.8

50 40 30 20 10 0
Percent of world exports in each product line

Source: Central Intelligence Agency (1).

Figure 4–14a

Japan and West Germany led exporters of machine tools and robotics. Japan gained market share during the 1980s, while Germany and the United States, a distant third, lost share.

In the market for scientific equipment, the United States held the largest share throughout the decade, giving up a little of it during that period. Japan was the only trader to appreciably increase its share during the 1980s.

In medicine and biologicals, West Germany, Switzerland, the United States, the United Kingdom, and France competed for market leadership throughout the decade.

West Germany and the United States led in market shares of organic chemicals during the 1980s. The US and sixth-ranked Japan were the only top traders to gain market share.

Analysts commonly use the ratio of exports to imports as a measure of international competitiveness. Applying this measure to high technology, Japan became the unchallenged champion competitor by 1984.

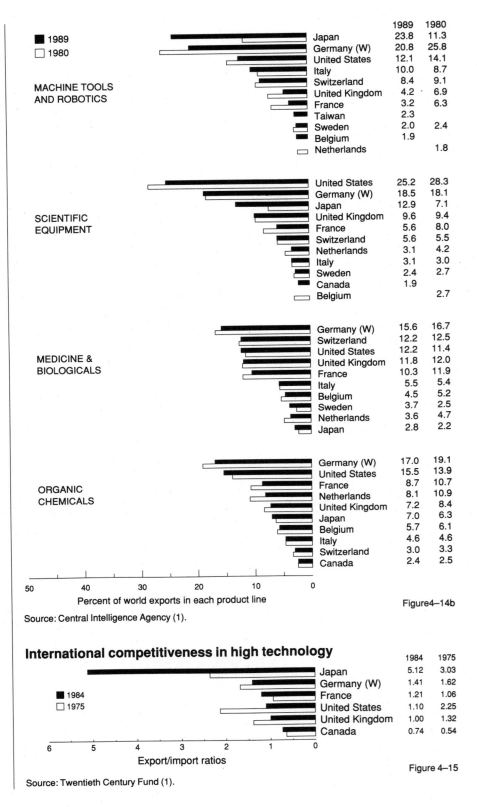

■ 1989
□ 1980

	1989	1980
MACHINE TOOLS AND ROBOTICS		
Japan	23.8	11.3
Germany (W)	20.8	25.8
United States	12.1	14.1
Italy	10.0	8.7
Switzerland	8.4	9.1
United Kingdom	4.2	6.9
France	3.2	6.3
Taiwan	2.3	
Sweden	2.0	2.4
Belgium	1.9	
Netherlands		1.8
SCIENTIFIC EQUIPMENT		
United States	25.2	28.3
Germany (W)	18.5	18.1
Japan	12.9	7.1
United Kingdom	9.6	9.4
France	5.6	8.0
Switzerland	5.6	5.5
Netherlands	3.1	4.2
Italy	3.1	3.0
Sweden	2.4	2.7
Canada	1.9	
Belgium		2.7
MEDICINE & BIOLOGICALS		
Germany (W)	15.6	16.7
Switzerland	12.2	12.5
United States	12.2	11.4
United Kingdom	11.8	12.0
France	10.3	11.9
Italy	5.5	5.4
Belgium	4.5	5.2
Sweden	3.7	2.5
Netherlands	3.6	4.7
Japan	2.8	2.2
ORGANIC CHEMICALS		
Germany (W)	17.0	19.1
United States	15.5	13.9
France	8.7	10.7
Netherlands	8.1	10.9
United Kingdom	7.2	8.4
Japan	7.0	6.3
Belgium	5.7	6.1
Italy	4.6	4.6
Switzerland	3.0	3.3
Canada	2.4	2.5

50 40 30 20 10 0
Percent of world exports in each product line

Figure4—14b

Source: Central Intelligence Agency (1).

International competitiveness in high technology

■ 1984
□ 1975

	1984	1975
Japan	5.12	3.03
Germany (W)	1.41	1.62
France	1.21	1.06
United States	1.10	2.25
United Kingdom	1.00	1.32
Canada	0.74	0.54

6 5 4 3 2 1 0
Export/import ratios

Figure 4—15

Source: Twentieth Century Fund (1).

The United States and Japan have shared most of the world semiconductor market since 1978. At the beginning of the decade, the US share was double Japan's; by 1986 the two shares were equal. Europe's share has remained steady at about 10 percent.

In the market for sophisticated DRAM memory chips, the United States lost 80% of the monopoly it had in 1974.

The European Community is a net importer in its high-tech trade with other developed economies (except EFTA). It is a net exporter to developing and state-trading economies.

World semiconductor market

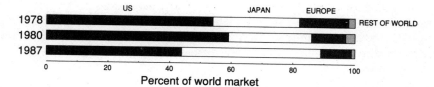

Percent of world market

	US	JAPAN	EUROPE	REST OF WORLD
1978	54	28	16	2
1980	59	27	11	3
1986	44	45	10	1

Percentages of world market.
Source: Twentieth Century Fund (1).

Figure 4–16

Shares of world DRAM market

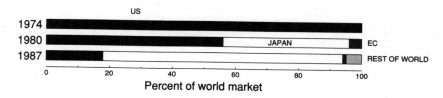

Percent of world market

	US	JAPAN	EC	REST OF WORLD
1974	100	0	0	0
1980	56	40	4	0
1987	18	76	1	5

Percentage shares.
DRAM is dynamic random access memory.
Source: Twentieth Century Fund (1).

Figure 4–17

EC's main trading partners in high-tech products

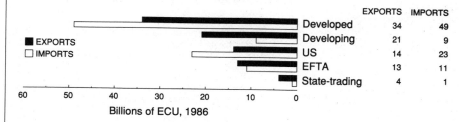

	EXPORTS	IMPORTS
Developed	34	49
Developing	21	9
US	14	23
EFTA	13	11
State-trading	4	1

Billions of ECU, 1986

Figure 4–18

EFTA = European Free Trade Association: Switzerland, Sweden, Austria, Norway, Finland, Iceland.
Source: Eurostat (1).

Japan and the United States held about equal shares of the rich OECD market for high-tech products in 1988. West Germany had the largest share of the overall technology markets.

In competitiveness, as measured by the export/import ratio, Japan led Germany by a wide margin in high-tech and mid-tech products, while Germany led slightly in the low-tech field. By this measure, the United Kingdom, Switzerland, Sweden, Ireland, and Denmark were more competitive than the United States at all levels of technology. The US measured least-competitive of all OECD economies in low-tech products.

OECD trade in technology

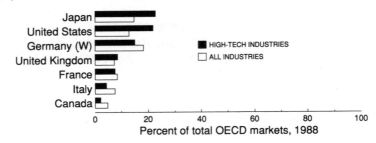

Percent of total OECD markets, 1988

	EXPORTS/IMPORTS			EXPORT MARKET SHARES	
	HITECH	MIDTECH	LOWTECH	ALL INDUS	HITECH INDUS
Japan	5.15	4.23	0.92	14.71	22.66
United States	0.86	0.52	0.35	12.81	21.76
Germany (W)	1.26	2.30	0.93	18.18	14.95
United Kingdom	0.93	0.93	0.67	7.25	8.47
France	0.96	1.05	0.85	8.43	7.51
Italy	0.77	1.18	1.33	7.43	4.34
Switzerland	1.46	1.10	0.52	2.85	3.83
Netherlands	0.83	1.04	1.19	5.16	3.74
Canada	0.47	0.90	1.45	4.83	2.19
Luxembourg	0.83	1.06	1.18	4.76	2.13
Belgium	0.83	1.06	1.18	4.76	2.13
Sweden	0.89	1.18	1.41	2.80	2.06
Ireland	1.59	0.78	1.27	0.95	1.63
Austria	0.74	0.82	1.08	1.72	1.23
Denmark	0.88	0.73	1.19	1.39	1.07
Spain	0.36	0.73	1.29	1.97	0.90
Finland	0.58	0.68	2.18	1.26	0.60
Norway	0.28	0.62	0.66	0.78	0.33
Portugal	0.43	0.28	1.66	0.59	0.24
Australia	0.09	0.49	0.95	0.84	0.18
Turkey	0.19	0.34	1.96	0.53	0.10
New Zealand	0.10	0.28	2.27	0.37	0.05
Greece	0.13	0.17	0.78	0.33	0.05
Iceland	0.04	0.27	0.68	0.04	0.00
Yugoslavia	0.76	0.84	1.73		

Figure 4–19

Ratios and percentages, 1988.
Hi-tech/high R&D intensity industries: aerospace; office machinery, computer electronic components; drugs, medicines; instruments; electrical machinery.
Medium-tech industries: motor vehicles; chemicals; other manufacturing; nonelectrical machinery; rubber, plastics; nonferrous metals, other transportation.
Low-tech: all other industries.
Yugoslavia is a special-status country in the OECD.
Payment figure for Belgium includes Luxembourg.
Export market shares = percent of total OECD markets.
Source: Organization for Economic Cooperation and Development (1).

Merchandise Trade

Trade in textiles and apparel is a small but steadily growing segment of world exports.

The developed economies dominate this "classic" global commerce, often associated with developing economies, with 67% of total textiles exports and 85% in apparel. The developed world trades textiles mostly within itself, but trades apparel products equally with the developing world. The Eastern economies do their heaviest trading in textiles with developing economies, and they trade apparel products mainly among themselves.

West Germany's domestic market imports a greater share of both textiles and apparel than any other economy. This penetration is especially acute in apparel, where nearly four-fifths of consumption is imported. All the main developed economies have increased the import share of their domestic markets.

Textiles & apparel

World trade in textiles and apparel

	TEXTILES	APPAREL
Value	89	88
Share in world merchandise exports	3.0	3.0
Share in world exports of manufactures	4.5	4.5
Annual change, 1988	8.0	9.0
Average annual change, 1980-88	6.0	9.5

Billions of dollars and percentages, 1988.
Source: General Agreement on Tariffs & Trade (2).

Table 4–7

Distribution of trade in textiles and apparel

DESTINATION ORIGIN	DEVELOPED VALUE	DEVELOPED SHARE	DEVELOPING VALUE	DEVELOPING SHARE	EASTERN VALUE	EASTERN SHARE	WORLD VALUE	WORLD SHARE
TEXTILES								
Developed	41	73	9	39	2	29	51	62
Developing	9	17	9	42	4	47	22	27
Eastern	3	6	4	20	2	25	9	11
World	**55**	**100**	**22**	**100**	**8**	**100**	**83**	**100**
World share		67		27		9		100
APPAREL								
Developed	32	46	2	32	1	17	35	43
Developing	31	45	3	42	1	15	35	43
Eastern	6	8	2	26	3	70	11	13
World	**69**	**100**	**7**	**100**	**5**	**100**	**81**	**100**
World share		85		9		6		100

Table 4–8

Billions of dollars and percentages, 1987.
Eastern economies = USSR and Central Europe plus China and centrally-planned Asian economies.
Source: General Agreement on Tariffs & Trade (2).

Trends in textile and apparel imports

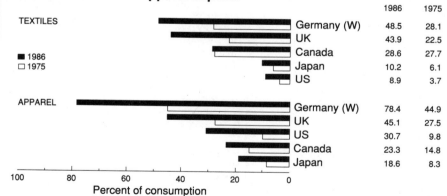

	1986	1975
TEXTILES		
Germany (W)	48.5	28.1
UK	43.9	22.5
Canada	28.6	27.7
Japan	10.2	6.1
US	8.9	3.7
APPAREL		
Germany (W)	78.4	44.9
UK	45.1	27.5
US	30.7	9.8
Canada	23.3	14.8
Japan	18.6	8.3

■ 1986
□ 1975

Percent of consumption

Figure 4–20

West Germany was both the top exporter and top importer of textiles in a very competitive field of traders. All traders recorded strong growth between 1980–87. The exception was Japan, which had flat growth and lost a third of its market share in the period. The United States showed the largest one-year (1988) growth in exports.

Hong Kong, France, and the United States imported more textiles than they exported. South Korea, Italy, and Belgium-Luxembourg had large textile-trade surpluses; Germany's surplus was moderate. In 1988, Japan and China greatly increased their imports, while the US decreased its imports a little.

Top traders in textiles

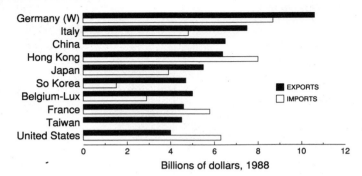

Billions of dollars, 1988

China is not among the top 15 importers.

1988 RANK		1988 VALUE	1980 SHARE	1988 SHARE	1980-87 CHANGE	1988 CHANGE	1980 DEPEND	1988 DEPEND
	EXPORTERS							
1	Germany (W)	11	12	12	20	9	4	4
2	Italy	8	8	9	22	3	6	6
3	China	7	5	8	37	12	14	14
4	Hong Kong	6	3	7	43	13	9	10
5	Japan	6	9	6	2	-1	4	2
6	So Korea	5	4	6	27	15	13	8
7	Belgium-Lux	5	7	6	20	8	6	6
8	France	5	6	5	17	10	3	3
9	Taiwan	5	3	5	34	11	9	8
10	United States	4	7	5	10	28	2	1
11	United Kingdom	3	6	4	24	15	3	3
12	Netherlands	3	4	4	18	4	3	3
13	Switzerland	2	3	3	12	4	5	5
14	Pakistan	2	2	2	47	-3	34	40
15	India	2	2	2	47		14	15
	Top 15	71	78	81				
	Top 10	59	62	67				
	Top 5	37	36	41				
	IMPORTERS							
1	Germany (W)	9			3	8	4	4
2	Hong Kong	8			14	10	13	13
3	United Kingdom	7			7	14	3	4
4	United States	6			15	-4	1	2
5	France	6			5	6	3	4
6	Italy	5			8	9	3	4
7	Japan	4			9	32	1	2
8	Netherlands	3			4	3	3	3
9	Belgium-Lux	3			2	3	3	29
10	China	2			9	29	5	5
11	Canada	2			7	9	2	2
12	USSR	2			-1		3	2
13	Switzerland	2			4	7	3	3
14	Austria	2			4	2	5	4
15	So Korea	2			20	6	2	3

Figure 4–21

Billions of dollars and percentages.
1980-87 change = average annual change.
Depend(ency) = share of product in economy's merchandise exports or imports.
Figures for Hong Kong include substantial reexports and imports for reexport.
Figures for USSR are 1987 rather than 1988.
Source: General Agreement on Tariffs & Trade (2).

The leading traders in apparel — Hong Kong, Italy, and South Korea — all had large trade surpluses in 1988, South Korea's being the largest. West Germany, France, and the United Kingdom had trade deficits, Germany's being the largest by far.

During the 1980s, Hong Kong's trade in apparel dropped from 25% (largest among the leading traders) to 19% of total exports. The export earnings of South Korea and China also depended on the apparel trade to a greater degree than other main traders. Turkey, Portugal, Thailand, India, and Greece also depended heavily on exports of apparel.

Top traders in apparel

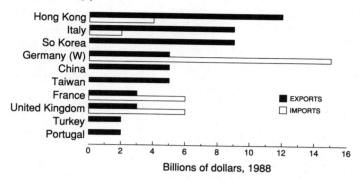

Billions of dollars, 1988

South Korea, China, Taiwan, Turkey, and Portugal are not among the top 15 importers.

1988 RANK		1988 VALUE	1980 SHARE	1988 SHARE	1980-87 CHANGE	1988 CHANGE	1980 DEPEND	1988 DEPEND
	EXPORTERS							
1	Hong Kong	12	12	14	12	10	25	19
2	Italy	9	11	11	10	1	6	7
3	So Korea	9	7	10	15	16	17	15
4	Germany (W)	5	7	6	8	7	2	2
5	China	5	4	6	12	30	10	10
6	Taiwan	5	6	6	11	-6	13	8
7	France	3	6	4	4	9	2	2
8	United Kingdom	3	5	3	3	8	2	2
9	Turkey	2	1	3	50	9	5	21
10	Portugal	2	2	3	19	8	14	21
11	Thailand	2	1	2	28	23	4	12
12	United States	2	3	2	-1	35	1	1
13	India	2	2	2	15		7	14
14	Netherlands	2	2	2	7	9	1	2
15	Greece	1	1	2	20		8	22
	Top 15	63	67	73				
	Top 10	55	59	63				
	Top 5	40	41	46				
	IMPORTERS							
1	United States	23			18	5	3	5
2	Germany (W)	15			8	3	5	6
3	Japan	7			17	44	1	4
4	France	6			12	8	2	4
5	United Kingdom	6			7	22	3	3
6	Hong Kong	4			25	23	3	7
7	USSR	4			6		4	4
8	Netherlands	4			4	-2	4	4
9	Switzerland	3			10	3	4	5
10	Belgium-Lux	3			5	6	3	3
11	Sweden	2			6	3	4	5
12	Canada	2			14	8	1	2
13	Italy	2			11	13	1	2
14	Austria	2			9	1	4	5
15	Norway	1			9	-10	4	5

Figure 4–22

Billions of dollars and percentages.
1980-87 change = average annual change.
Depend(ency) = share of product in economy's merchandise exports or imports.
Figures for Hong Kong include substantial reexports and imports for reexport.
Source: General Agreement on Tariffs & Trade (2).

Bilateral restrictions — the Multi-Fiber Agreements — severely limit the amount of textile and apparel products that the main developed economies admit into their domestic markets. These restrictions affect half of all textile imports and nearly two-thirds of apparel imports.

On average, the percent of restricted imports of both kinds increased slightly during the 1980s. Most of this increase came from the United States; restricted shares decreased substantially in Sweden and moderately in the European Community.

Many developing economies depend heavily on earnings from textile exports, Egypt and Pakistan far more than all others. Neither of these economies reduced their dependencies during the 1980s, but Bangladesh and China made spectacular reductions. Turkey reduced its dependency by more than half. Peru nearly doubled its dependency.

Growth in the world trade in iron and steel products jumped sixfold in 1988, compared with its decade average.

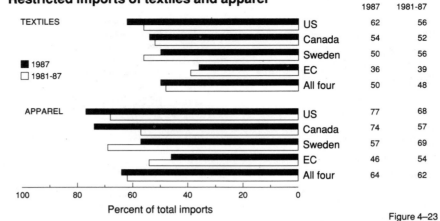

Restricted imports of textiles and apparel

	1987	1981-87
TEXTILES		
US	62	56
Canada	54	52
Sweden	50	56
EC	36	39
All four	50	48
APPAREL		
US	77	68
Canada	74	57
Sweden	57	69
EC	46	54
All four	64	62

Percent of total imports

Figure 4–23

Percent of restricted imports to total imports from developing countries.
Restricted imports are those subject to bilateral quotas.
Source: World Bank (3).

Economies most dependent on textile exports

	1980 SHARE	1988 SHARE
Egypt	78	79
Pakistan	69	61
Peru	28	43
Bangladesh	83	35
China	86	28
India	26	21
Greece	20	19
Turkey	44	17
Indonesia	9	12
Portugal	19	12

Table 4–9

Percentages of manufacturing exports. Figure for Egypt is 1987, not 1988.
Source: General Agreement on Tariffs & Trade (2).

Iron & steel

World trade in iron and steel

Value	100
Share in world merchandise exports	3.5
Share in world exports of manufactures	5.0
Annual change, 1988	22.0
Average annual change, 1980–87	3.5

Table 4–10

Billions of dollars and percentages, 1988.
Source: General Agreement on Tariffs & Trade (2).

Distribution of trade in iron and steel

DESTINATION ORIGIN	DEVELOPED VALUE	DEVELOPED SHARE	DEVELOPING VALUE	DEVELOPING SHARE	EASTERN VALUE	EASTERN SHARE	WORLD VALUE	WORLD SHARE
Developed	43	87	13	74	8	51	63.4	78
Developing	5	9	3	16	1	3	7.8	10
Eastern	2	4	2	11	7	45	10.5	13
World	**50**	**100**	**17**	**100**	**15**	**100**	**81.7**	**100**
World share		61		21		18		100

Table 4–11

Billions of dollars and percentages, 1987.
Eastern economies = USSR and Central Europe plus China and centrally-planned Asian economies.
Source: General Agreement on Tariffs & Trade (2).

The developed world did most of the trading in iron and steel products, and almost all of their trade was within the developed world. Developing economies also did most of their trading with the developed world. Japan and West Germany are the top exporters of iron and steel products. All of the top ten traders exported more of these products than they imported.

During the 1980s, none of the leading traders, except for Brazil, increased their exports substantially. Several reduced exports a little; the United States reduced exports by 12%.

The top exporters were also the top importers, reflecting increasing intra-industry specialization. The United States, the 11th-ranked exporter, was top importer in 1988. Japan, China, and South Korea increased imports throughout the 1980s. Except for China, which reduced imports in 1988, all of the main traders substantially increased imports in that year.

Top traders in iron and steel

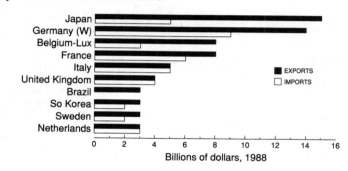

Billions of dollars, 1988

1988 RANK		1980 VALUE	1988 VALUE	1980 SHARE	1988 SHARE	1980-87 CHANGE	1988 CHANGE	1980 DEPEND	1988 DEPEND
	EXPORTERS								
1	Japan	16	15	21	16	-3	22	12	6
2	Germany (W)	12	14	15	14	1	15	6	4
3	Belgium-Lux	6	8	9	8	-1	34	10	9
4	France	7	8	10	8	-2	18	7	5
5	Italy	4	5	5	5	1	10	5	4
6	United Kingdom	2	4	3	5	7	19	2	3
7	Brazil	1	3	1	4	13	61	5	10
8	So Korea	2	3	2	3	5	38	10	6
9	Sweden	2	3	3	3	2	24	8	7
10	Netherlands	2	3	3	3	2	21	3	3
11	United States	3	3	4	3	-12	68	2	1
12	Spain	2	2	3	2	0	16	10	6
13	Austria	2	2	2	2	3	9	10	7
14	Canada	2	2	3	2	2	-3	3	2
15	Finland	1	1	1	1	9	15	4	5
	Top 15	63	76	83	76				
	Top 10	54	66	71	67				
	Top 5	45	49	59	50				
	IMPORTERS								
1	United States	8	12			3	26	3	3
2	Germany (W)	7	9			2	24	4	4
3	France	5	6			-1	20	4	4
4	Italy	4	5			1	27	4	4
5	Japan	1	5			16	36	1	3
6	China	2	5			10	-4	12	9
7	United Kingdom	3	4			-1	36	2	2
8	Netherlands	2	3			1	29	3	3
9	Belgium-Lux	2	3			4	30	3	4
10	Taiwan	1	3			9	43	6	6
11	Canada	1	3			4	50	2	2
12	So Korea	1	2			10	26	5	5
13	Switzerland	1	2			2	24	4	3
14	Spain	1	2			9	23	3	3
15	Sweden	1	2			-1	24	4	4

Figure 4–24

Billions of dollars and percentages, 1988.
Depend(ency) = share of product in economy's merchandise exports or imports.
Source: General Agreement on Tariffs & Trade (2).

The value of all traded primary products fell by over $100 billion in the 1980s, all of the drop due to the halving of the price of crude petroleum. During the decade, the price of the total primary-products group fell slightly.

World trade in food, accounting for 10% of world merchandise exports, grew hardly at all through most of the 1980s, then surged in 1987.

The developed economies were either the origin or destination of the overwhelming majority of world trade in food products.

Among the top traders in food products, the United States, France, Netherlands, and Canada all exported much more than they imported. West Germany, Italy, and the United Kingdom imported much more food than they exported.

Primary products

Trade in primary products

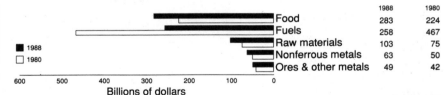

	1988	1980
Food	283	224
Fuels	258	467
Raw materials	103	75
Nonferrous metals	63	50
Ores & other metals	49	42

■ 1988
□ 1980

Billions of dollars

Figure 4–25

Agriculture

World trade in food

Value	252
Share in world merchandise exports	10.0
Share in world exports of manufactures	35.5
Annual change, 1987	11.0
Average annual change, 1980-87	1.5

Table 4–12

Billions of dollars and percentages, 1987.
Source: General Agreement on Tariffs & Trade (2).

Distribution of trade in food

DESTINATION ORIGIN	DEVELOPED VALUE	DEVELOPED SHARE	DEVELOPING VALUE	DEVELOPING SHARE	EASTERN VALUE	EASTERN SHARE	WORLD VALUE	WORLD SHARE
Developed	128	70	30	63	6	27	165	65
Developing	48	26	13	27	8	36	69	27
Eastern	6	3	5	10	7	32	18	7
World	**182**	**100**	**48**	**100**	**22**	**100**	**252**	**100**
World share		72		19		9		100

Table 4–13

Billions of dollars and percentages, 1987.
Eastern economies = USSR and Central Europe plus China and centrally planned Asian economies.
Source: General Agreement on Tariffs & Trade (2).

Top traders in food

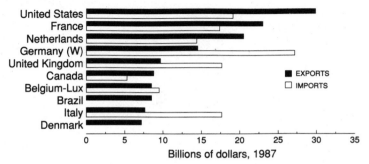

■ EXPORTS
□ IMPORTS

Billions of dollars, 1987

Brazil and Denmark are not among the top 15 importers.

Food exports from the United States and Brazil fell during most of the 1980s, but both picked up in 1987. Food imports into Japan and Western Europe increased sharply in 1987, after years of little change. Imports into the US barely changed in 1987, after years of growth.

Led by Brazil, the top developing-world traders in agricultures all exported more than they imported in the 1986–88 period. Except for Mexico and India, these trade surpluses were very large earners of foreign exchange.

Top traders in food

1987 RANK		1980 VALUE	1987 VALUE	1980 SHARE	1987 SHARE	1980-86 CHANGE	1987 CHANGE	1980 DEPEND	1987 DEPEND
	EXPORTERS								
1	United States	40	30	18	12	-7	11	18	12
2	France	18	23	8	9	2	19	16	16
3	Netherlands	15	21	7	8	3	19	20	22
4	Germany (W)	10	15	5	6	4	16	6	5
5	United Kingdom	8	10	4	4	1	16	7	8
6	Canada	8	9	4	4	0	12	12	9
7	Belgium-Lux	6	9	3	4	4	11	10	10
8	Brazil	9	9	4	4	-5	19	47	32
9	Italy	6	8	3	3	3	16	7	7
10	Denmark	6	7	3	3	3	14	33	28
11	Spain	4	6	2	3	3	35	18	18
12	Cuba	5	6	2	3	2	11		
13	China	3	6	2	3	12	3	16	15
14	Australia	7	6	3	2	-4	-6	33	21
15	Ireland	3	4	2	2	1	33	37	28
	Top 15	146	166	66	66				
	Top 10	125	138	55	55				
	Top 5	90	98	40	39				
	IMPORTERS								
1	Germany (W)	23	27			1	13	12	12
2	United States	19	25			5	1	8	6
3	Japan	17	25			4	16	12	17
4	United Kingdom	16	18			1	13	14	12
5	Italy	13	18			3	18	13	14
6	France	14	17			2	16	10	11
7	USSR	17	15			-3	3	24	16
8	Netherlands	12	14			1	22	15	16
9	Belgium-Lux	8	10			1	18	11	12
10	Spain	4	6			1	22	13	12
11	Canada	4	5			2	8	7	6
12	Hong Kong	3	4			4	21	26	33
13	Switzerland	3	4			2	17	8	8
14	Saudi Arabia	4	4			-3	3	14	19
15	Egypt	2	4			8	1	48	31

Figure 4–26

Billions of dollars and percentages.
1980-86 change = average annual change.
Source: General Agreement on Tariffs & Trade (2).

Main developing-economy traders in agricultures

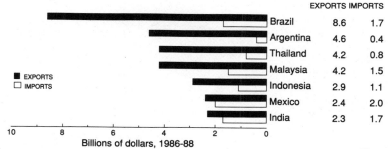

	EXPORTS	IMPORTS
Brazil	8.6	1.7
Argentina	4.6	0.4
Thailand	4.2	0.8
Malaysia	4.2	1.5
Indonesia	2.9	1.1
Mexico	2.4	2.0
India	2.3	1.7

■ EXPORTS
□ IMPORTS

Billions of dollars, 1986-88

Source: Federal Reserve Bank of Boston (1).

Figure 4–27

By a wide margin, the United States led OECD economies in both exports and imports of agriculture products. West Germany and Japan were net importers by a wide margin.

Denmark increased its exports by 75% and Turkey had a threefold increase in imports.

OECD trade in agriculture products

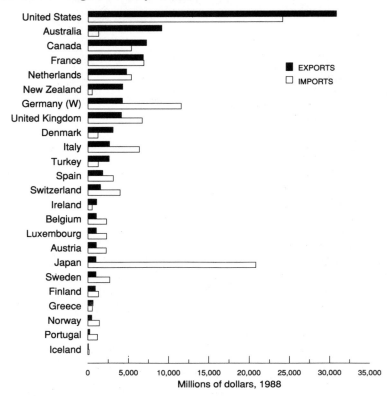

	EXPORTS		IMPORTS	
	VALUE	CHANGE	VALUE	CHANGE
United States	30806	-18.5	24090	30.7
Australia	9096	9.5	1315	33.2
Canada	7181	-10.5	5351	23.3
France	6836	11.9	6889	15.1
Netherlands	4719	25.5	5337	7.3
New Zealand	4265	21.3	498	21.5
Germany (W)	4228	22.0	11549	16.9
United Kingdom	4106	17.2	6723	-0.6
Denmark	3100	74.8	1196	2.0
Italy	2663	16.2	6365	15.0
Turkey	2593	0.3	1219	288.4
Spain	1781	37.2	3119	-3.7
Switzerland	1548	56.7	3976	43.6
Ireland	1051	42.6	468	23.6
Belgium	1034	-5.6	2250	-1.3
Luxembourg	1034	-5.6	2250	-1.3
Austria	1012	32.2	2236	47.9
Japan	941	16.7	20814	28.8
Sweden	940	16.5	2670	41.3
Finland	869	29.5	1259	18.5
Greece	601	-9.0	508	15.1
Norway	424	31.8	1378	34.5
Portugal	235	22.0	1146	-10.5
Iceland	29	41.6	134	33.4

Figure 4–28

Millions of dollars, 1988. Change = since 1982.
Source: Organization for Economic Cooperation and Development (1).

Merchandise Trade

In the trading of forest products, the OECD economies as a whole had an almost exact balance of exports and imports. Canada had the most exports and the least imports. Japan, the United Kingdom, and the United States had the largest deficits of net imports.

By a very wide margin, Japan was the biggest customer of the United States in agricultures, taking one-fifth of its total exports.

Liberalization of trade in agricultures was one of the goals of the Uruguay Round of negotiations among GATT parties. Indeed, the talks broke down at the end of 1990 for lack of agreement on how to reduce or eliminate altogether the tangle of subsidies, quotas, and tariffs that now distort trade in agricultures.

A United Nations study modeled the effects of various Uruguay Round proposals on prices, export earnings, and benefits to producers, consumers, and taxpayers. As the accompanying graph clearly shows, in the policymaking countries, there were different gainers and losers in the various proposals.

OECD trade in forest products

	EXPORTS	IMPORTS
Canada	21.1	1.8
United States	10.9	17.3
Germany (W)	6.2	10.0
France	3.3	5.7
Japan	1.7	10.2
Italy	1.6	5.2
United Kingdom	1.5	9.7
North America	32.1	19.1
OECD Europe	44.2	47.6
OECD	79.1	78.4
World	**100.0**	**100.0**

Table 4–14

Percent of world exports of forest products. Figures for latest available year. Published 1990.
Source: Organization for Economic Cooperation and Development (1).

Main US trading partners in agricultures

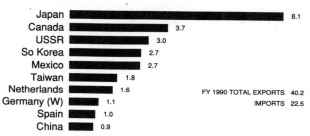

Billions of dollars, 1990

Source: US Department of Agriculture (4).

Figure 4–29

Gainers and losers in agriculture trade liberalization

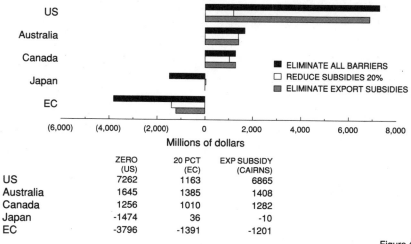

Millions of dollars

	ZERO (US)	20 PCT (EC)	EXP SUBSIDY (CAIRNS)
US	7262	1163	6865
Australia	1645	1385	1408
Canada	1256	1010	1282
Japan	-1474	36	-10
EC	-3796	-1391	-1201

Figure 4–30

Millions of dollars. Combined effects from net export earnings and benefits to consumers and producers from price changes.
Columns refer to proposals made at Uruguay negotiations: Zero option supported by the US eliminates all subsidies, tariffs, quotas, and internal taxes on tropical products. A 20% reduction in producer price supports corresponds to the EC's proposal. Elimination of export subsidies corresponds to the minimum proposal of the Cairns Group of agriculture exporters.
Source: United Nations (1).

Producer Subsidy Equivalents (PSEs) are a measure of the cost of agriculture subsidies; they estimate the value of transfers from consumers and taxpayers to producers. PSEs are defended as an appropriate social cost of maintaining food security and a rural way of life. Detractors see PSEs as unjustifiable costs that distort trade flows. Each country claims that its own use of subsidies is purely defensive.

PSEs make up 45% of the value of all agricultures produced by OECD economies. These subsidies result in nearly doubling the price of crops in Japan, the OECD's heaviest user of PSEs. In the United States, producer subsidies make up about a third of the price of all agriculture products. The European Community would be hardest hit by removing all subsidies.

Consumer Subsidy Equivalents (CSEs) are similar to PSEs, but they measure the cost to consumers of transfers to producers and taxpayers — hence they are a "negative" subsidy. CSEs make up about 37% of the cost of agriculture production in the OECD economies.

Agriculture producer subsidies

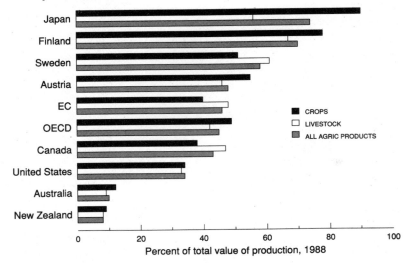

Percent of total value of production, 1988

	PRODUCER SUBSIDIES			CONSUMER SUBSIDIES		
	CROPS	LIVESTK	ALL	CROPS	LIVESTK	ALL
Japan	90	56	74	-57	-47	-53
Finland	78	67	70	-65	-73	-70
Sweden	51	61	58	-60	-57	-5
Austria	55	46	48	-52	-51	-51
EC	40	48	46	-39	-44	-42
OECD	49	42	45			-37
Canada	38	47	43	-13	-39	-31
United States	34	33	34	-4	-7	-7
Australia	12	9	10	-7	-6	-6
New Zealand	9	8	8	0	-7	-6

Figure 4–31

Percent of total value of production, 1988.
Producer Subsidy Equivalents (PSE) = value of transfers from domestic consumers and taxpayers to agricultural producers.
Consumer Subsidy Equivalents (CSE) = value of transfers from domestic consumers to agricultural producers and taxpayers.
PSE and CSE are not calculated individually for members of the EC.
Source: Organization for Economic Cooperation and Development (1).

World trade in fuels rose in 1987, after falling moderately in the earlier years of the decade. Two-thirds of the traded fuels went to developed economies, and two-thirds of fuel imports came from developing and eastern economies.

At the decade's end, the USSR was the world's top trader in fuels and the only trader to increase exports in that period. Saudi Arabia's exports dropped 87% during the 1980s; exports of other traders also dropped, though not as drastically.

The United States and Japan both reduced imports sharply in the 1980s; lesser importers also reduced imports by comparable percentages.

Fuels

World trade in fuels

Value	284
Share in world merchandise exports	11.0
Share in world exports of primary products	40.0
Annual change, 1987	8.5
Average annual change, 1980-87	-7.0

Billions of dollars and percentages.
Source: General Agreement on Tariffs & Trade (2).

Table 4–15

Distribution of trade in fuels

\DESTINATION ORIGIN\	DEVELOPED VALUE	DEVELOPED SHARE	DEVELOPING VALUE	DEVELOPING SHARE	EASTERN VALUE	EASTERN SHARE	WORLD VALUE	WORLD SHARE
Developed	68	36	7	12	1	3	76	27
Developing	101	53	43	75	4	11	148	52
Eastern	22	12	7	12	32	89	60	21
World	191	100	57	100	36	100	284	100
World share		67		20		13		100

Billions of dollars and percentages, 1987.
Eastern economies = USSR and Central Europe plus China and centrally-planned Asian economies.
Source: General Agreement on Tariffs & Trade (2).

Table 4–16

Top traders in fuels

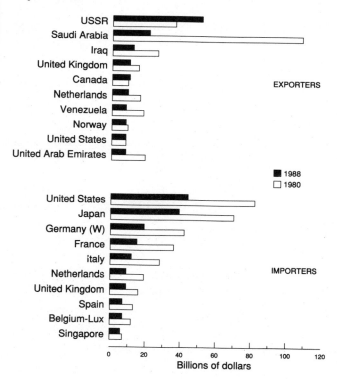

EXPORTERS

■ 1988
□ 1980

IMPORTERS

Billions of dollars

Throughout the decade, petroleum exports approached 100% of the total exports of many traders. Several exporters — notably Mexico, Algeria, the United Arab Emirates, and Iran — reduced their dependency on oil for foreign-exchange earnings. Only Kuwait increased its dependency.

World trade in raw materials jumped sharply in 1988, after a modest average rise in previous years of the decade.

Top traders in fuels

1988 RANK		1980 VALUE	1988 VALUE	1980 SHARE	1987 SHARE	1980-87 CHANGE	1988 CHANGE	1980 DEPEND	1987 DEPEND
	EXPORTERS								
1	USSR	36	51	8	18	5	3	47	47
2	Saudi Arabia	108	21	23	8	-20	-9	99	86
3	Iraq	26	12	6	4	-12	5	100	96
4	United Kingdom	15	10	3	5	-1	-28	14	7
5	Canada	9	10	2	4	2	6	14	9
6	Netherlands	16	9	4	4	-7	-14	22	9
7	Venezuela	18	8	4	3	-10	-8	95	83
8	Norway	9	8	2	3	0	-6	48	37
9	United States	8	8	2	3	0	6	4	3
10	United Arab Emir	19	8	4	3	-10	-11	92	64
11	Iran	13	8	3	4	-4	-20	100	82
12	Nigeria	25	7	6	3	-15	-13	98	97
13	Kuwait	18	7	4	3	-13	0	89	98
14	Mexico	10	7	2	3	-2	-22	63	24
15	Algeria	13	5	3	2	-13	0	91	58
	Top 15	343	179	73	67				
	Top 10	264	145	56	53				
	Top 5	194	104	41	38				
	IMPORTERS								
1	United States	82	44			-8	-6	33	10
2	Japan	70	39			-8	-2	50	21
3	Germany (W)	42	19			-9	-13	23	8
4	France	36	15			-10	-14	27	8
5	Italy	28	12			-7	-31	28	9
6	Netherlands	19	9			-9	-9	24	10
7	United Kingdom	16	9			-7	-10	14	5
8	Spain	13	7			-7	-14	39	12
9	Belgium-Lux	12	7			-6	-14	17	7
10	Singapore	7	6			-2	4	29	14
11	So Korea	7	6			-2	0	30	12
12	Brazil	11	4			-11	-23	43	26
13	Taiwan	5	4			-3	7	26	8
14	Thailand	3	2			-6	-15	31	8
15	Hong Kong	1	1			0	0	6	2

Figure 4–32

Billions of dollars and percentages.
Depend(ency) = share of product in economy's merchandise exports or imports.
1980-87 change = average annual change.
Exports from the Netherlands includes reexports.
Source: General Agreement on Tariffs & Trade (2).

Raw materials

World trade in raw materials

Value	103
Share in world merchandise exports	3.5
Share in world exports of manufactures	13.5
Annual change, 1988	16.0
Average annual change, 1980-88	4.0

Table 4–17

Billions of dollars and percentages, 1988.
Source: General Agreement on Tariffs & Trade (2).

Two-thirds of the world's imports of raw materials came from developed economies; most of those imports were received by other developed economies.

The United States and Canada were the top exporters of raw materials throughout the 1980s. Both had surpluses of exports over imports, Canada's being very much larger. West Germany, France, and China, also top exporters, imported more than they exported.

New Zealand and Malaysia had the highest dependency on exports. Malaysia reduced its dependency appreciably during the 1980s.

Distribution of trade in raw materials

\DESTINATION ORIGIN\	DEVELOPED VALUE	SHARE	DEVELOPING VALUE	SHARE	EASTERN VALUE	SHARE	WORLD VALUE	SHARE
Developed	46	73	9	54	3	38	58	66
Developing	13	20	5	31	2	26	20	22
Eastern	5	8	3	15	3	38	11	12
World	**63**	**100**	**17**	**100**	**9**	**100**	**89**	**100**
World share		72		19		10		100

Table 4–18

Billions of dollars and percentages, 1987.
Eastern economies = USSR and Central Europe plus China and centrally-planned Asian economies.
Source: General Agreement on Tariffs & Trade (2).

Top traders in raw materials

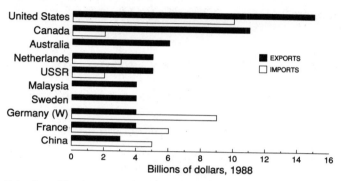

Billions of dollars, 1988

Australia, Malaysia, and Sweden are not among the top 15 importers.

1988 RANK		1988 VALUE	1980 SHARE	1988 SHARE	1980-87 CHANGE	1988 CHANGE	1980 DEPEND	1988 DEPEND
	EXPORTERS							
1	United States	15	15	15	1	25	5	5
2	Canada	11	10	11	6	11	11	10
3	Australia	6	4	6	7	47	12	18
4	Netherlands	5	4	5	8	11	4	5
5	USSR	5	6	5	2		6	4
6	Malaysia	4	6	4	0	8	31	21
7	Sweden	4	4	4	2	14	10	8
8	Germany (W)	4	3	4	5	11	1	1
9	France	4	4	4	4	11	3	2
10	China	3	2	3	9	16	7	6
11	Finland	3	4	3	-1	4	19	12
12	New Zealand	2	2	2	3	29	26	25
13	Indonesia	2	4	2	-9	26	14	10
14	United Kingdom	2	2	2	2	5	2	2
15	Singapore	2	3	2	-7	41	11	5
	Top 15	71	69	69				
	Top 10	60	55	59				
	Top 5	42	37	41				
	IMPORTERS							
1	Japan	17			1	22	9	9
2	United States	10			5	10	3	2
3	Germany (W)	9			2	12	4	4
4	Italy	9			2	16	7	7
5	United Kingdom	7			3	16	4	4
6	France	6			0	12	4	3
7	So Korea	5			7	30	11	10
8	China	5			-1	66	15	8

(MORE)

Trade in ores, minerals, and nonferrous metals jumped sharply in 1987, after dropping slightly in the previous years of the decade.

Most of the top exporters of these products were developed economies which were even heavier importers Canada and the USSR were net exporters.

Top traders in raw materials, cont'd

1988 RANK		1988 VALUE	1980 SHARE	1988 SHARE	1980-87 CHANGE	1988 CHANGE	1980 DEPEND	1988 DEPEND
9	Taiwan	3			8	12	9	7
10	Belgium-Lux	3			2	12	3	3
11	Netherlands	3			2	10	3	3
12	Spain	3			5	13	5	4
13	Hong Kong	2			9	13	5	3
14	Canada	2			4	15	2	2
15	USSR	2			0		3	2

Figure 4-33

Billions of dollars and percentages.
Depend(ency) = share of product in economy's merchandise exports or imports.
1980-87 change = average annual change.
Excludes leading traders from the USSR and Eastern Europe.
Figures for Hong Kong and Singapore include substantial imports for reexport.
Source: General Agreement on Tariffs & Trade (2).

Ores, minerals, and nonferrous metals

World trade in ores, minerals, and nonferrous metals

Value	87
Share in world merchandise exports	3.5
Share in world exports of manufactures	12.5
Annual change, 1987	14.0
Average annual change, 1980-87	-1.5

Table 4-19

Billions of dollars and percentages, 1987.
Source: General Agreement on Tariffs & Trade (2).

Distribution of trade in ores, minerals, and nonferrous metals

\DESTINATION ORIGIN\	DEVELOPED VALUE	SHARE	DEVELOPING VALUE	SHARE	EASTERN VALUE	SHARE	WORLD VALUE	SHARE
Developed	47	72	9	61	2	22	57	66
Developing	15	24	4	28	1	19	21	24
Eastern	3	5	2	11	4	60	9	10
World	**65**	**100**	**15**	**7**	**7**	**100**	**87**	**100**
World share		75		17		8		100

Table 4-20

Billions of dollars and percentages, 1987.
Eastern economies = USSR and Central Europe plus China and centrally-planned Asian economies.
Source: General Agreement on Tariffs & Trade (2).

Top traders in ores, minerals, and nonferrous metals

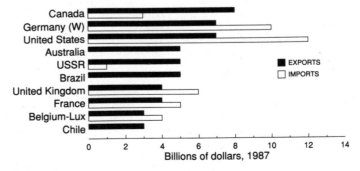

Australia, Brazil, and Chile are not among the top 15 importers.

The big jump in exports of ores, minerals, and nonferrous metals, after years of flat or declining trade, affected all of the top exporters. Brazil's exports increased 56%, Chile's 31%, and Norway's 27%. Chile depended on such exports for over half of its total export earnings, down a little from its level of dependence in 1980.

Japan, the United States, and West Germany were the top importers throughout the decade. In 1987, Taiwan increased its imports by 54%; significant jumps in that year were also recorded by South Korea, Switzerland, Japan, and West Germany.

Top traders in ores, minerals, and nonferrous metals

1987 RANK		1980 VALUE	1987 VALUE	1980 SHARE	1987 SHARE	1980-87 CHANGE	1987 CHANGE	1980 DEPEND	1987 DEPEND
	EXPORTERS								
1	Canada	9	8	9	9	-4	11	13	8
2	Germany (W)	7	7	7	8	-2	20	4	3
3	United States	12	7	12	8	-11	16	5	3
4	Australia	5	5	5	6	-1	13	22	21
5	USSR	5	5	5	6	-2	8	7	5
6	Brazil	2	5	2	5	7	56	10	17
7	United Kingdom	6	4	6	5	-8	9	6	3
8	France	4	4	5	5	-5	17	4	3
9	Belgium-Lux	4	3	5	4	-7	14	7	4
10	Chile	3	3	3	4	-5	31	63	56
11	Netherlands	3	3	3	3	-5	17	4	3
12	Norway	2	2	2	3	-1	27	11	11
13	Japan	2	2	3	3	-3	10	2	1
14	South Africa	2	2	2	2	-5	14	8	8
15	Italy	1	2	2	2	0	18	2	2
	Top 15	66	60	69	69				
	Top 10	56	50	58	58				
	Top 5	37	32	38	37				
	IMPORTERS								
1	Japan	14	13			-5	24	10	9
2	United States	13	12			-2	2	5	3
3	Germany (W)	12	10			-6	20	6	5
4	United Kingdom	9	6			-10	18	8	4
5	France	7	5			-6	14	5	4
6	Italy	6	5			-6	16	10	4
7	Belgium-Lux	6	4			-7	14	8	6
8	So Korea	1	3			7	39	6	7
9	Netherlands	3	3			-5	11	4	3
10	Canada	2	3			4	1	4	3
11	Taiwan	1	2			2	54	6	6
12	Spain	2	2			-4	10	7	4
13	Switzerland	3	2			-10	24	7	4
14	Sweden	2	1			-4	12	5	4
15	USSR	1	1			-2	4	9	9

Figure 4–34

Billions of dollars and percentages.
Depend(ency) = share of product in economy's merchandise exports or imports.
1980-87 change = average annual change.
Source: General Agreement on Tariffs & Trade (2).

GATT, the world trade organization, has sponsored eight rounds of negotiations aimed at reducing tariffs. Since the first round in 1947, these years-long negotiations have reduced average tariffs from 40% to 5%. The eighth (Uruguay) round began in 1986 and was scheduled to finish by the end of 1990, a deadline not met. This round, GATT's most complex and ambitious ever, extends negotiations into such new areas as intellectual property rights, investments, and services. Negotiators also hoped to make progress in eliminating agriculture subsidies, but had failed to do so by midyear 1991.

Tariff and nontariff barriers distort trade patterns and increase the cost of trading. Tariffs on imports are the "classic," visible barriers usually justified as necessary to protect new or temporarily weak domestic industries. Nontariff barriers, some of them called "hardcore," are more subtle but perhaps even more restrictive. Structural impediments (not analyzed here) are trade barriers that arise from macroeconomic policies, national traditions, and other broad cultural sources.

Tariff and nontariff barriers

Trend in tariffs on manufactures

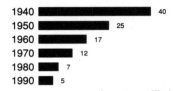

Average tariffs (percent)

Source: The Economist (1).

Figure 4–35

Hardcore nontariff barriers to imports

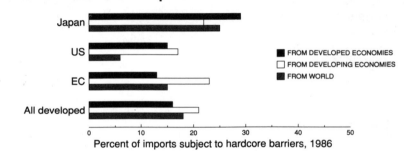

Percent of imports subject to hardcore barriers, 1986

IMPORTER	DEVELOPED		DEVELOPING		WORLD	
	1981	1986	1981	1986	1981	1986
Japan	29	29	22	22	25	25
US	9	15	14	17	11	6
EC	10	13	22	23	12	15
All developed	**13**	**16**	**9**	**21**	**15**	**18**

Figure 4–36

Percent of imports subject to hardcore nontariff measures.
Hardcore nontariff measures are those most likely to have significant restrictive effects; e.g., import prohibitions, variable levies, multifibre restrictions, and nonautomatic licensing.
Source: Twentieth Century Fund (1).

Barriers of all types are anathema to a global free-trade regime, which postulates that open competition across borders makes all producers more efficient and brings benefits to all consumers through lower prices.

Hardcore nontariff barriers affect one-fifth of all imports from developed into developing economies. Japan erects the most hardcore barriers to imports from both developed and developing economies. The European Community imposes the most (slightly more than Japan's) barriers to imports from developing economies.

The Twentieth Century Fund studied the potential effects of removing both tariff and nontariff barriers. They found that nontariff barriers have the greater effect, especially in Japan, and that a tariff-free regime would increase imports more than exports in the three main economies. Removing tariffs would expand trade the most in the European Community — an expansion that would balance new exports with new imports.

Differing casts of gainers and losers also emerged among developing regions,

Potential expansion of trade without tariff and nontariff barriers

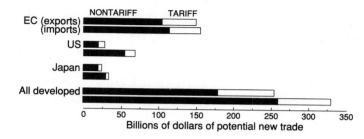

Billions of dollars of potential new trade

	EXPORTS				IMPORTS			
	NONTARIFFS	PCT	TARIFFS	PCT	NONTARIFFS	PCT	TARIFFS	PCT
Japan	20	8	5	2	30	20	4	2
US	20	8	8	3	55	13	14	3
EC	105	11	45	5	115	12	41	5
All developed	**180**	**10**	**75**	**4**	**260**	**15**	**71**	**4**

Figure 4–37

Billions of dollars, estimated expansion of trade with no barriers.
Percentage of potential trade expansion.
Source: Twentieth Century Fund (1).

with African economies coming out losers in all scenarios. Some of these gains and losses would come from increased world prices; i.e., higher prices raise import bills and cause foreign-exchange losses.

With complete liberalization, prices would go up on most agriculture products, with biggest increases in rice (43%), sugar (27%), and wheat (20%). With gradual liberalization, prices in general would rise less than one-third as much for rice, sugar, and wheat and a much smaller amount for other products. Eliminating export subsidies would leave prices unchanged, except for wheat, beef, veal, and groundnut oil.

5 Trade geography

During the 1980s, world trade increasingly flowed around three regional nodes: Asia, North America, and Western Europe. Together, these regions accounted for 80% of world exports in 1989.

In analyzing trade patterns, it is useful to keep in mind the differences between national economies, trading areas, and geographic regions.

In the main, Western Europe comprises the European Community (EC) and the European Free Trade Association (EFTA). The EC is moving steadily toward its goal of becoming an integrated single market by the end of 1992. EFTA is harmonizing its trade, legal, fiscal, and monetary policies with those of the EC. Analysts expect this trend to lead to a European Economic Area (EEA) encompassing all of Western Europe — and eventually some of the economies of Central and Eastern Europe. It is reasonable to compare EC trade with that of the United States as a whole, and to treat the national economies of the EC like states of the US. In this approach, "trade" between, say, France and Germany is like interstate commerce in the United States. It is also reasonable to compare the North American free-trade area — encompassing the US, Canada, and probably Mexico in 1993 — to Western Europe.

Asia's trade is dominated by a single national economy, Japan's, with a population about half that of either the EC or North America. No Asian free-trade area is on the horizon.

The composition of merchandise trade varied significantly among regions. Manufactures dominated the trade of the three most-dynamic regions. Latin America traded a high proportion of agricultures, as did Africa. North America was not far behind. Mining products dominated trade in the Middle East and Africa.

Trade in commercial services was more balanced within regions and less varied across regions.

Despite the tightening of regional bonds, trade **between** regions was more dynamic than trade **within** regions. If this trend holds, it should ease fears that emerging free-trade areas, most notably Western Europe and North America, will become inward-looking trade blocs at the expense of the multilateral global trading system.

Asia was clearly the most dynamic region, where 60% of the volume growth of both trade and output were contributed by the newly-industrializing economies (Hong Kong, Singapore, South Korea, Taiwan) and China. During the 1980s, the volume of China's merchandise trade increased 13%, double the average for Asia and 50% higher than China's growth in gross domestic product (GDP).

China's dynamic growth had a direct, powerful effect on the economy of Hong Kong. During the last decade, Hong Kong's re-exports to and from China grew from about one-third to four-fifths of total exports (including value added by Hong Kong manufacture).

For both Western Europe and North America, Asia was by far the fastest-growing regional trading partner. For Western European traders, on average, half of their main export and import markets lay outside the region. During the decade, Western Europe shifted from being a net importer to being a net exporter of cereals as a result of the cumulative effects of price supports in the 1970s and '80s.

Exports from the United States expanded at well above the world average in 1989, making it the world's leading merchandise exporter in that year. By mid–1991, Germany had regained its position as the world's leading exporter. The US remained the world's leading importer.

This chapter divides the world geographically — twice. First it considers the trading patterns of every economy in its geographic region. The last section looks at only the developing economies in their geographic regions.

Western Europe continued to be the world's biggest trading region in 1989, although exports grew faster in North America and Asia during that and the previous year. North America's imports continued to exceed exports by a substantial margin, while Asia had a trade surplus of a smaller amount. However, in 1989 North America's exports grew faster than those of the other two regions, while Asia's imports grew much faster. This came on top of even bigger changes in the same direction in 1988, narrowing the trade imbalances between the regions.

The developed world accounts for 70% of world trade; over half of this trade is between developed economies. The eastern trading area, including the socialist economies of eastern Europe and Asia, accounts for 10% of world trade, and half of that is with other eastern economies.

Merchandise trade by region

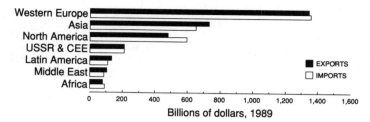

Billions of dollars, 1989

	EXPORTS			IMPORTS		
	1989 VALUE	1988 CHANGE	1989 CHANGE	1989 VALUE	1988 CHANGE	1989 CHANGE
Western Europe	1345	11.0	6.5	1355	12.5	7.5
Asia	730	19.5	8.5	650	26.5	13.5
North America	480	25.0	10.5	595	10.5	7.5
USSR & CEE	210	5.0	-2.0	210	8.0	0.5
Latin America	135	17.0	10.0	110	15.0	7.5
Middle East	105	-3.5	23.5	85	7.0	-2.0
Africa	80	0.5	-2.0	90	16.5	1.0
World	**3095**	**14.0**	**7.5**	**3095**	**14.0**	**7.5**

Figure 5–1

Billions of dollars and annual percent change.
CEE = Central and Eastern Europe: Bulgaria, Czechoslovakia, Germany (E), Hungary, Poland, Romania.
Source: General Agreement on Tariffs & Trade (4).

Distribution of world merchandise trade

DESTINATION ORIGIN	DEVELOPED SHARE	VALUE	DEVELOPING SHARE	VALUE	EASTERN SHARE	VALUE	WORLD SHARE	VALUE
Developed	55	1584	13	373	3	76	**70**	**2033**
Developing	13	389	5	144	1	39	**20**	**572**
Eastern	3	75	2	58	5	145	**10**	**277**
							100	**2882**

Table 5–1

Billions of dollars and percentages, 1988.
Eastern economies = USSR and Central Europe, plus China and centrally-planned Asian economies.
Source: General Agreement on Tariffs & Trade (2).

Origins and destinations of merchandise trade

DESTINATION ORIGIN	NO AM	LAT AM	WEST EUR	CEE	AFRICA	MID EAST	ASIA	OTHER	WORLD
Western Europe	113	24	904	39	47	38	92	11	1268
Asia	197	13	125	12	13	21	283	7	670
North America	151	47	99	5	8	12	113	4	438
USSR & CEE	3	9	50	128	4	5	18	9	226
Latin America	55	16	27	8	2	2	12	1	122
Middle East	12	6	24	4	2	6	31	1	85
Africa	10	2	39	3	5	1	6	9	74
World	**540**	**116**	**1267**	**198**	**81**	**84**	**555**	**41**	**2882**
World share	19	4	44	7	3	3	19	1	100

Table 5–2

Exports in billions of dollars, 1988.
Source: General Agreement on Tariffs & Trade (2).

Economies in Asia, Western Europe, and North America have similar patterns of trade: predominantly manufactures, a small portion of agricultures, and about half that in mining products.

The transitioning socialist economies trade less in manufactures, more in mining products, and about one-tenth of the total in agricultures.

Trade in Latin America is more balanced, with manufactures a rapidly growing share. Agricultures are more heavily traded in this region than in any other.

In the Middle East, about three-fourths of trade is in mining products — mostly oil. High as it is, this share is well below the nearly total dependence on oil at the start of the decade.

Half of Africa's trade is in mining products; the rest is in equal shares of agricultures and manufactures.

The world's trading pattern resembles North America's pattern more than that of any other region.

Composition of trade by region

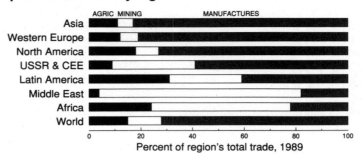

Percent of region's total trade, 1989

Product composition of main trading regions: merchandise products

	EXPORTS		IMPORTS	
	1980	1988	1980	1988
ASIA				
Agricultures	18	11	18	16
Mining products	15	6	37	16
Manufactures	65	81	44	64
WESTERN EUROPE				
Agricultures	13	12	15	14
Mining products	12	7	28	11
Manufactures	73	79	55	73
NORTH AMERICA				
Agricultures	23	18	10	7
Mining products	13	9	35	11
Manufactures	59	66	52	78
USSR AND CEE				
Agricultures	11	9	20	14
Mining products	31	28	18	20
Manufactures	51	55	59	65
LATIN AMERICA				
Agricultures	31	31	12	12
Mining products	50	28	28	16
Manufactures	18	39	58	69
MIDDLE EAST				
Agricultures	1	4	16	17
Mining products	93	78	9	5
Manufactures	5	18	73	74
AFRICA				
Agricultures	14	20	17	17
Mining products	67	50	10	8
Manufactures	7	18	72	71
WORLD				
Agricultures	15	14		
Mining products	27	12		
Manufactures	55	70		

Figure 5–2

Percent of total trade in merchandise and commercial services.
Figures for world exports are for 1989, not 1988.
No figures for commercial services from USSR and CEE.
Shares may not add up to 100 because of products not shown.
OPS (other private services and income) = telecommunications, nonmerchandise insurance, banking.
Source: General Agreement on Tariffs & Trade (4).

Trade among the three dominant regions is comparable in value. Asia and North America are each other's major trading partners, and that trade grew faster than that of any other partnership in the 1980s.

Trading partners of the world's regions

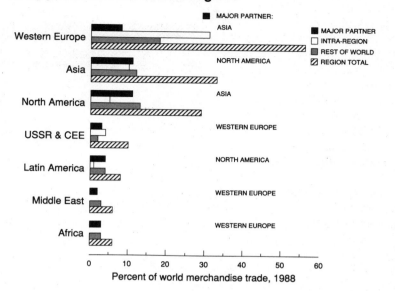

Percent of world merchandise trade, 1988

	1973	1980	1988
Western Europe			
Asia*	5	5	8
Intra-W Europe	31	27	31
Rest of world	23	25	18
W Europe total	60	56	56
Asia			
North America*	7	7	11
Intra-Asia	6	7	10
Rest of world	10	12	12
Asia total	23	25	33
North America			
Asia*	7	7	11
Intra-N America	6	4	5
Rest of world	14	15	13
N America total	27	25	29
USSR & CEE			
Western Europe*	4	4	3
Intra-USSR/CEE	5	4	4
Rest of world	3	3	2
USSR/CEE total	12	11	10

	1973	1980	1988
Latin America			
North America*	4	4	4
Intra-Latin America	1	1	1
Rest of world	5	5	4
Latin Am total	10	10	8
Middle East			
Western Europe*	3	6	2
Intra-Middle East	0	1	0
Rest of world	3	8	3
Middle East total	7	15	6
Africa			
Western Europe*	5	6	3
Intra-Africa	0	0	0
Rest of world	3	4	2
Africa total	8	10	5

Figure 5–3

Percentages of world merchandise trade.
Percentages add to more than 100 due to double counting.
Trade between regions is sum of exports.
*Region's major trading partner.
Source: General Agreement on Tariffs & Trade (2).

For developed econo-
mies, manufactures
make up about 80% of
merchandise trade and
the same share of their
exports to developing
economies. However,
imports from developing
into developed econo-
mies are about equally
divided between manu-
factures and primary
products. The same
ratios hold for trade with
the socialist eastern
economies, although at
a much lower level.

Merchandise trade
surpluses and deficits
reveal a global trading
system still far out of
balance. West Germany
and Japan have large
surpluses, while the
United States continues
deep in deficits. Such
severe disparities strain
the internal economies
of both deficit and
surplus countries and
create imbalances in
capital accounts that distort interest rates, ex-
change rates, and
trade. In the past two
years, both surpluses
and deficits have fallen,
a trend which many
analysts expect to con-
tinue.

Exports from the
United States expanded
at well above the world
average in 1989,
making it once again
the world's leading mer-
chandise exporter.

Merchandise trade of developed economies

Source: General Agreement on Tariffs & Trade (2).

Figure 5–4

Merchandise trade balances

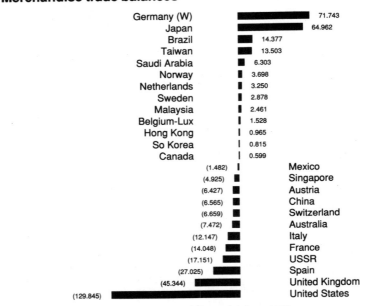

Billions of dollars, 1989

Source: International Monetary Fund (2).

Figure 5–5

Top merchandise traders

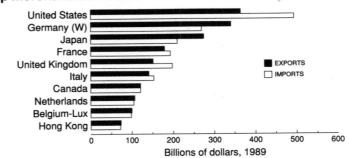

Billions of dollars, 1989

Trade Geography

In 1989, West Germany's surplus of $72 billion was 12% of its total trade (exports plus imports); Japan's slightly smaller surplus was about the same share of its total trade; Brazil's surplus was 26% of its total trade.

Among deficit economies, the huge US deficit was 15% of its total trade; the United Kingdom's large deficit was about the same share; the USSR's was 18%. Spain's was 26%.

The European Community, which exports and imports a husky 39% of world totals, had a slight deficit of only 1.4% of its total trade. Taken together, developing economies had a slight trade surplus. Oil-exporting economies had a surplus that amounted to 17% of its total trade.

In a world of perfect data, the world's total exports would exactly equal imports. The $90 billion "deficit" in this account is a measure of the substantial errors and omissions that create a fog of uncertainty around all trade figures.

Top merchandise traders

	EXPORTS			IMPORTS			TRADE BALANCE	
	RANK	VALUE	SHARE	RANK	VALUE	SHARE	VOLUME	SHARE
United States	1	364	12	1	494	16	-130	-15.14
Germany (W)	2	341	12	2	270	9	72	11.74
Japan	3	275	9	3	210	7	65	13.42
France	4	179	6	5	193	6	-14	-3.78
United Kingdom	5	152	5	4	198	7	-45	-12.95
Italy	6	141	5	6	153	5	-12	-4.13
Canada	7	121	4	7	120	4	1	0.25
Netherlands	8	107	4	8	104	3	3	1.54
Belgium-Lux	9	100	3	9	98	3	2	0.77
Hong Kong	10	73	3	10	72	2	1	0.66
Taiwan	11	66	2	16	53	2	14	11.36
So Korea	12	62	2	12	62	2	1	0.66
China	13	52	2	13	58	2	-7	-5.96
Switzerland	14	52	2	14	58	2	-7	-6.07
Sweden	15	51	2	18	48	2	3	2.90
Singapore	16	45	2	17	50	2	-5	-5.21
Spain	17	44	2	11	71	2	-27	-23.34
USSR	18	40	1	15	57	2	-17	-17.64
Australia	19	37	1	19	45	1	-7	-9.14
Brazil	20	34	1	25	20	1	14	26.41
Austria	21	32	1	20	39	1	-6	-9.01
Saudi Arabia	22	32	1	22	26	1	6	10.96
Norway	23	27	1	23	23	1	4	7.37
Malaysia	24	25	1	24	23	1	2	5.17
Mexico	25	25	1	21	26	1	-1	-2.91
Top 15		2136	73		2177	73		
Top 10		1853	64		1768	59		
Top 5		1311	45		1548	52		
Industrial economies		2125	73		2237	75	-112	-2.56
European Community		1134	39		1166	39	-32	-1.40
Developing economies		787	27		765	25	22	1.40
Non-oil developing econ		632	22		656	22	-23	-1.81
Asia developing economies		405	14		415	14	-10	-1.21
Oil exporting economies		155	5		110	4	45	17.05
Middle East		122	4		104	3	17	7.62
West Hemisphere developing		119	4		103	3	16	6.99
CMEA		92	3		100	3	-8	-4.17
Europe developing econ		65	2		66	2	-1	-1.09
World total		**2912**	**100**		**3002**	**100**	**-90**	**-1.52**

Figure 5–6

Billions of dollars, 1989.
Export (import) share = percent of total world exports (imports).
Trade balance volume = exports - imports.
Trade balance share = percent of total exports + imports.
Source: International Monetary Fund (2).

An economy's current-account balance includes merchandise trade and invisibles. While both Japan and Germany had large surpluses in 1988, both also had large deficits in trading commercial services, part of the invisibles category.

The United Kingdom had a modest surplus in invisibles and France a slight surplus. Otherwise, all of the main developed economies had deficits.

The United States and Japan had about the same pattern of trade with each other, the European Community, and the rest of the world. Exports to the US were a larger share of Japan's total exports than were US exports to Japan. In both economies, imports from the other partner were of about the same importance.

Current-account balances of main developed economies

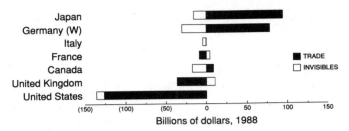

Billions of dollars, 1988

	TRADE BALANCE		INVISIBLES, NET		CURRENT ACCOUNT BALANCE	
	1987	1988	1987	1988	1987	1988
Japan	96.5	94.5	-9.5	-15.5	87.0	79.0
Germany (W)	70.0	78.5	-24.5	-30.0	45.5	48.5
Italy	0.0	-0.5	-1.0	-3.5	-1.0	-4.0
France	-9.5	-8.5	5.0	4.5	-4.5	-4.0
Canada	9.0	8.5	-16.5	-17.5	-7.5	-9.0
United Kingdom	-16.5	-36.5	12.0	10.5	-4.5	-26.0
United States	-160.5	-126.5	6.5	-9.0	-154.0	-135.5

Figure 5–7

Billions of dollars.
Invisibles includes commercial services, investment income, official services and income, and unrequited transfers.
Source: General Agreement on Tariffs & Trade (1).

Dominant trading relationships

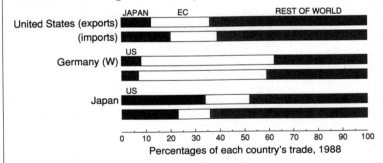

Percentages of each country's trade, 1988

Trading relationships of main developed economies

\DESTINA ORIGIN\	US		CANADA		JAPAN		EC		DEVELOPED		DEVELOPING	
	EXP	IMP	EXP	IMP	EXP	IMP	EXP	IMP	EXP	IMP	EXP	IMP
Germany	26	17	3	2	7	16	176	130	278	207	31	31
US			69	81	38	93	76	89	205	286	107	162
Japan	90	42	6	8			47	24	163	95	86	78
France	12	14	2	1	3	7	107	100	132	145	26	23
UK	19	19	4	4	3	12	73	99	117	163	24	22
Italy	11	8	1	1	2	4	73	79	105	110	17	19
Canada	83	71			7	8	9	13	102	95	8	11

Figure 5–8

Billions of dollars, 1988.
Source: General Agreement on Tariffs & Trade (2).

The importance of trade in an economy flows from the size of its domestic market, its mix of comparative advantages, and many other factors. Small, competitive economies tend to depend heavily on trade to enlarge their gross domestic product (GDP). But rigid definitions can mislead analysis. The huge economies of the United States and Japan are the developed world's most self-sufficient, yet both are big traders: in 1988 they were the world's second and third in the value of exports.

Among all GATT members, trade averaged 31% of GDP, the same percentage as among nonmembers. Among the main economies, West Germany's GDP depended most on trade, and Canada's and the United Kingdom's did so a little less. (In making comparisons, keep in mind that trade between the national economies of Europe is in many respects comparable to commerce between states in the United States.)

GATT members, with 86% of the world's GDP, had the same share of the world's trade.

Importance of merchandise trade in selected developed economies

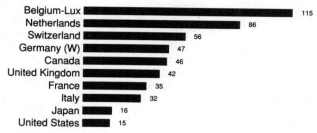

Exports + imports as percent of GDP, 1988

	1988 VALUE		EXP + IMP			EXP + IMP
	EXPORTS	IMPORTS	PCT OF GATT	POP	GDP	PCT OF GDP
Germany (W)	323,370	250,570	11.3	61.2	1118	47
United States	321,600	459,570	15.3	243.9	4473	15
Japan	264,860	187,380	8.9	122.1	2373	16
France	167,780	178,860	6.8	55.6	880	35
United Kingdom	145,170	189,340	6.6	56.9	675	42
Italy	128,530	138,590	5.2	57.4	756	32
Canada	116,840	111,460	4.5	25.7	411	46
Netherlands	103,190	99,440	4.0	14.7	213	86
Belgium-Lux	92,100	92,290	3.6	9.9	145	115
Switzerland	50,620	56,490	2.1	6.6	171	56
Sweden	49,750	45,630	1.9	8.4	159	54
Spain	40,340	60,530	2.0	38.8	289	29
Australia	33,070	36,070	1.4	16.3	195	29
Austria	31,030	36220	1.3	7.6	117	51
Denmark	27,780	25,920	1.1	5.1	101	51
Norway	22,440	23,220	0.9	4.2	83	53
Finland	21,750	21,130	0.8	4.9	90	44
South Africa	21,550	18,760	0.6	33.0	63	62
Ireland	18,720	15,570	0.7	3.5	29	101
New Zealand	8,780	7,340	0.3	3.3	35	41
Iceland	1,420	1600	0.1	0.3	5	55
Total GATT parties	2,504,500	2,585,160	100.0	3120.3	14612	
Total world trade	**2882320**	**2980000**		**4909**	**17000**	**31**
GATT share in world	87.0	86.5		63.5	86	31

Figure 5–9

Value of exports and imports in millions of dollars.
Share = percent of total merchandise trade of GATT parties.
Population in millions.
GDP = gross domestic product in billions.
Source: General Agreement on Tariffs & Trade (2).

Taken as a whole, in 1988 the rich OECD economies exported close to 3% of their GDP to developing economies. About 2.4% of their aggregate GDP was non-oil imports from developing economies, and 1.5% was imports of manufactures.

Belgium did the most trade with developing economies, leading in exports and non-oil imports. The United States imported the most manufactures.

Importance of OECD trade with developing economies

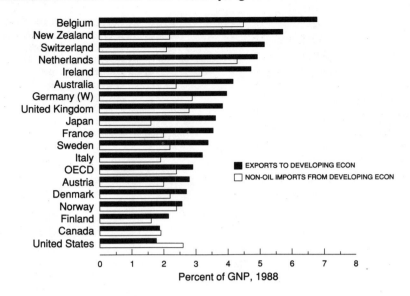

| | EXPORTS---- | IMPORTS------------------------ | |
		NON-OIL	MFRS
Belgium	6.79	4.5	1.47
New Zealand	5.73	2.2	1.48
Switzerland	5.15	2.1	1.19
Netherlands	4.93	4.3	1.99
Ireland	4.73	3.2	1.94
Australia	4.17	2.4	1.95
Germany (W)	3.97	2.9	1.78
United Kingdom	3.84	2.8	1.83
Japan	3.63	1.6	0.66
France	3.55	2.0	1.12
Sweden	3.39	2.2	1.45
Italy	3.21	1.9	0.93
OECD	2.91	2.4	1.53
Austria	2.80	2.0	1.19
Denmark	2.71	2.2	1.36
Norway	2.57	2.4	1.63
Finland	2.15	1.6	0.88
Canada	1.87	1.9	1.48
United States	1.76	2.6	2.05

Figure 5–10

Percent of GNP.
Source: Organization for Economic Cooperation and Development (1).

Western Europe's trade was mainly in manufactures, in which it had a surplus with the rest of the world in 1988. The region has a small deficit in agricultures and a larger one in mining products.

The overwhelming majority of this trade occurred within the region. During most of the 1980s, the region posted above-average increases in exports to North America and Asia — while exports to Africa, USSR and CEE, the Middle East, and Africa declined. This trend changed sharply in 1988. Exports to Asia doubled its decade growth average; exports to North America grew only a third as fast; exports to Africa and the USSR and CEE dramatically reversed their earlier trend; exports to the Middle East snapped back.

In 1988, imports from the rest of the world changed their growth trends even more. Growth of imports from Asia, North America, and Latin America shot up dramatically. In all, imports from the rest of the world grew slightly faster than exports in that year, reversing the earlier trend.

Europe

Western Europe's trade by product group

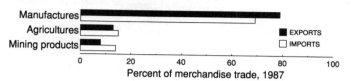

Percent of merchandise trade, 1987

	EXPORTS		IMPORTS	
	1980	1987	1980	1987
Manufactures	72	79	55	69
Agricultures	13	13	16	15
Mining products	12	8	28	14

Percentage shares, by value.
Shares do not add up to 100 due to products not specified.
Source: General Agreement on Tariffs & Trade (2).

Western Europe = the EC (Belgium, Denmark, France, Germany, Greece, Ireland, Italy, Luxembourg, the Netherlands, Portugal, Spain, United Kingdom); EFTA (Austria, Finland, Iceland, Norway, Sweden, Switzerland); and Gibraltar, Malta, Turkey, Yugoslavia.

Figure 5–11

Western Europe's trade with other regions

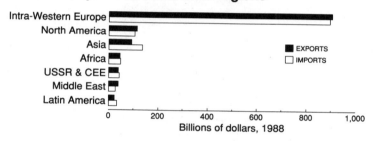

Billions of dollars, 1988

	1988 VALUE	1980-87 CHANGE	1988 CHANGE	1988 SHARE
EXPORTS				
Intra-Western Europe	904	6	13	71
North America	113	12	4	9
Asia	92	10	19	7
Africa	46	-5	10	4
USSR & CEE	39	-1	11	3
Middle East	38	-2	2	3
Latin America	24	-1	-1	2
Inter-regional	353	4	9	28
World	**1268**	**5**	**11**	**100**
IMPORTS				
Intra-Western Europe	896	6	12	69
Asia	136	9	21	10
North America	104	0	20	8
Africa	48	-5	7	4
USSR & CEE	42	0	3	3
Latin America	34	-1	19	3
Middle East	27	-14	-6	2
Inter-regional	392	-1	14	30
World	**1296**	**3**	**13**	**100**

Figure 5–12

Billions of dollars and percentages.
CEE = Central and Eastern Europe: Bulgaria, Czechoslovakia, Germany (E), Hungary, Poland, Romania.

In 1989, West Germany, Europe's strongest economy, had substantial trade surpluses with its main trading partners: France, Italy, and the United Kingdom. With the EC as a whole, Germany exported $50 billion more than it imported.

By far, the EC's biggest trading partners in that year were the EFTA group, with which it had a small surplus, and North America, with which it had a small deficit.

In 1989, the EC had an ECU 30 billion trade deficit (about $35 billion) with the rest of the world.

West Germany's main trading partners

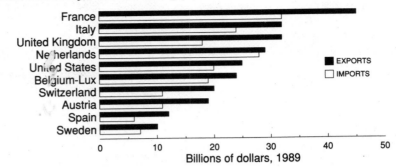

Billions of dollars, 1989

	EXPORTS VOLUME	SHARE	IMPORTS VOLUME	SHARE	TRADE BALANCE VOLUME	SHARE
France	45	13	32	12	13	2.08
Italy	32	9	24	9	8	1.27
United Kingdom	32	9	18	7	13	2.14
Netherlands	29	8	28	10	1	0.21
United States	25	7	20	8	4	0.73
Belgium-Lux	24	7	19	7	6	0.96
Switzerland	20	6	11	4	9	1.47
Austria	19	5	11	4	8	1.24
Spain	12	3	6	2	6	1.02
Sweden	10	3	7	11	3	0.49
Asia developing	16	5	18	7	-2	-0.38
EC	188	55	138	51	50	8.23
World	**341**	**100**	**270**	**100**	**72**	**11.74**

Figure 5–13

Billions of dollars, 1989.
Export (import) share = percent of total exports (imports).
Trade balance volume = exports-imports.
Trade balance share = percent of total exports + imports.
Source: International Monetary Fund (2).

European Community's main trading partners

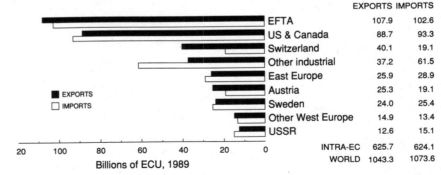

Billions of ECU, 1989

	EXPORTS	IMPORTS
EFTA	107.9	102.6
US & Canada	88.7	93.3
Switzerland	40.1	19.1
Other industrial	37.2	61.5
East Europe	25.9	28.9
Austria	25.3	19.1
Sweden	24.0	25.4
Other West Europe	14.9	13.4
USSR	12.6	15.1
INTRA-EC	625.7	624.1
WORLD	1043.3	1073.6

Figure 5–14

Trade Geography

For the EC as a whole, about 60% of its trade was between its own members. Trade with EFTA economies was another 10%, with about 30% traded outside Western Europe.

Only one class of product, power-generating machinery, was exported in greater volume outside Western Europe.

Imports of fuels came mainly from outside Western Europe. A few other products were imported primarily from outside the region: ores and minerals, power-generating machinery, office and telecommunications equipment, and apparel.

The region was most self-sufficient in iron and steel, automotive products, chemicals, "other" semi-manufactures, and "other" non-electrical machinery.

In trade with EFTA, the biggest share of exports was in apparel; the most-imported class of product was "other" semi-manufactures.

Distribution of European Community's merchandise trade

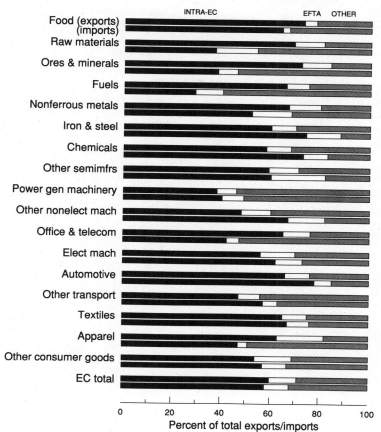

Percent of total exports/imports

	EXPORTS			IMPORTS		
	INTRA-EC	EFTA	OTHER	INTRA-EC	EFTA	OTHER
Food	73	5	23	64	3	34
Raw materials	69	12	20	37	17	47
Ores and minerals	72	12	17	38	8	55
Fuels	66	9	25	29	11	61
Nonferrous metals	67	13	21	52	16	33
Iron and steel	60	10	31	74	14	12
Chemicals	58	10	32	73	10	18
Other semi-manufactures	59	12	29	60	22	19
Power generating machinery	38	8	54	40	9	52
Other nonelectrical mach	48	12	41	67	15	19
Office and telecom equip	65	11	24	42	5	53
Electrical machinery	56	14	31	62	11	28
Automotive products	66	10	24	78	7	16
Other transport equip	47	9	45	57	6	38
Textiles	65	10	25	67	9	25
Apparel	63	19	19	47	4	50
Other consumer goods	54	15	31	57	10	34
EC total	**60**	**11**	**30**	**58**	**10**	**32**

Figure 5–15

Percentage shares of EC's total exports/imports, 1988.
Source: General Agreement on Tariffs & Trade (2).

Only 3% of Western Europe's trade was with the USSR and central and eastern Europe. Of that tiny amount, the heaviest trade was the import of fuels, mostly from the USSR. The biggest export products were "other" nonelectrical machinery and chemicals. The majority of these exports went to the CEE economies, except for iron and steel products, which went mostly to the USSR.

Fuels dominated the list of imports — most of it from the USSR. Food and chemicals were also more heavily imported products.

Western Europe's main product trade with USSR and CEE

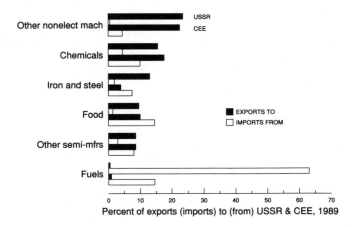

Percent of exports (imports) to (from) USSR & CEE, 1989

	EXPORTS TO		IMPORTS FROM	
	CEE	USSR	CEE	USSR
Primary products	**17.5**	**12.5**	**41.5**	**83.5**
Food	10.0	9.5	14.5	1.5
Raw materials	4.0	1.5	5.5	9.0
Nonferrous metals	1.5	0.5	4.5	7.5
Ores and minerals	1.0	0.5	2.5	2.5
Fuels	1.0	0.5	14.5	63.0
Manufactures	**81.5**	**86.5**	**57.5**	**15.0**
Other nonelect mach	22.5	23.5	4.5	0.5
Chemicals	17.5	15.5	10.0	4.5
Other semi-manfrs	8.5	8.5	8.0	3.0
Textiles	6.0	2.0	3.0	0.5
Automotive products	4.0	1.5	2.0	2.0
Iron and steel	4.0	13.0	7.5	2.0
Office mach & telecom	3.5	3.5	0.5	0.5
Electrical mach	3.5	2.5	2.5	0.5
Other transport equip	2.5	5.5	1.5	1.0
Apparel	1.5	1.0	7.5	0.0
Power machinery	1.0	0.5	1.0	0.0

Figure 5–16

Percent of Western Europe's total exports (imports), 1989.
Western Europe = EC (12) and EFTA (6).
CEE = Central and Eastern Europe: Bulgaria, Czechoslovakia, Germany (E), Hungary, Poland, Romania.
Figures exclude trade between West and East Germany.
Source: General Agreement on Tariffs & Trade (4).

The biggest share of EFTA's exports went to the EC in a trade pattern that was similar for each of the six member economies.

In the 1980s, all of the economies except Iceland substantially increased the value of their total exports.

Distribution of EFTA's merchandise exports

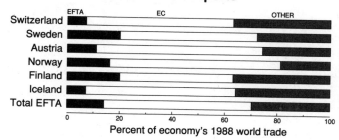

Percent of economy's 1988 world trade

	INTRA-EFTA			EC			OTHER			WORLD		
	1980 VALUE	1988 VALUE	1988 SHARE	1980 VALUE	1988 VALUE	1988 SHARE	1980 VALUE	1988 VALUE	1988 SHARE	1980 VALUE	1988 VALUE	1988 SHARE
Switzerland	3	4	7	16	28	56	11	19	37	30	51	100
Sweden	6	10	20	16	26	52	9	14	28	31	50	100
Austria	2	3	11	10	18	63	6	7	26	18	28	100
Norway	2	4	16	13	15	65	3	4	19	19	23	100
Finland	3	4	20	6	9	43	5	8	37	14	22	100
Iceland	0	0	7	0	1	57	0	0	29	1	1	100
Total	**17**	**25**	**14**	**61**	**97**	**56**	**34**	**53**	**30**	**112**	**174**	**100**

Figure 5–17

Billions of dollars and percentage shares of economy's 1988 world exports.
Source: General Agreement on Tariffs & Trade (2).

Manufactures dominated the merchandise trade of the two North American economies. The large increase of manufactures as a share of this trade is more apparent than real because it is an automatic consequence of sharply reduced trade in mining products (mainly fuels).

Exports between the United States and Canada led those to other regions, but imports from Asia exceeded intra-region growth rate.

During most the 1980s, exports to other regions grew moderately, due entirely to increased exports to Asia. In this period, exports to the USSR and CEE dropped sharply, and exports to Latin America, the Middle East, and Africa dropped a little. Exports to Western Europe were flat.

In 1988, this picture changed dramatically. Exports to the USSR and CEE economies jumped 63%; to Asia, 40%; to Western Europe and Latin America, substantially. Even exports to the Middle East and Africa turned around.

During most of the 1980s, imports from the USSR and CEE economies also grew in per-

North America

North American trade by product group

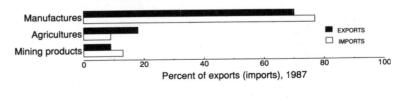

	EXPORTS		IMPORTS	
	1980	1987	1980	1987
Manufactures	61	70	53	77
Agricultures	23	18	11	9
Mining products	13	9	34	13

Figure 5–18

Percentage shares based on value.
Source: General Agreement on Tariffs & Trade (2).

North America's trade with other regions

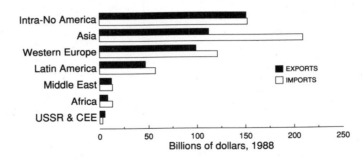

	EXPORTS				IMPORTS			
	1988 VALUE	1980-87 CHANGE	1988 CHANGE	1988 SHARE	1988 VALUE	1980-87 CHANGE	1988 CHANGE	1988 SHARE
Intra-No America	151	7	14	5	152	7	16	5
Asia	112	4	40	4	209	15	11	7
Western Europe	99	0	28	3	121	11	8	4
Latin America	47	-2	22	2	57	3	10	2
Middle East	12	-3	16	0	13	-8	6	0
Africa	8	-5	16	0	13	-13	-6	0
USSR & CEE	5	-10	63	0	4	19	0	0
Inter-regional	283	1	31	10	416	8	9	14
World	**438**	**3**	**24**	**15**	**571**	**7**	**11**	**19**

Figure 5–19

Billions of dollars.
Change = average annual percent changes in region's exports/imports to regional partners.
Share = percent of total world exports/imports.
CEE = Central and Eastern Europe: Bulgaria, Czechoslovakia, E Germany, Hungary, Poland, Romania.
Source: General Agreement on Tariffs & Trade (2).

centage (although at a low value level). Imports from Asia grew moderately, as did those from Western Europe. These trends continued into 1988, except that imports from the USSR and CEE economies abruptly halted their rate of increase. The growth rate of imports from Latin America was triple the early-decade rate. Imports from Africa continued their downward trend.

Exports from North America (excluding Mexico) were 15% of the world total, and imports 19%, in 1988. For reference, we show the relatively small amount of Mexican trade that would be included in a North America Free Trade Area.

In 1989, the European Community, Canada, and Japan continued as the main trading partners of the United States. The US's merchandise trade deficit with Japan was a very large $53 billion. (It is on a declining trend.) The US also had large deficits with Taiwan and other Asian developing economies — which, notably, provided the same share of total imports as Japan did. Trade with the EC was nearly in balance.

North America's merchandise trade

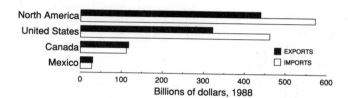

	EXPORTS				IMPORTS			
	1988 VALUE	1980-87 CHANGE	1988 CHANGE	1988 SHARE	1988 VALUE	1980-87 CHANGE	1988 CHANGE	1988 SHARE
North America	**438**	**3**	**24**	**15**	**571**	**7**	**11**	**19**
United States	322	2	27	11	460	8	9	15
Canada	117	6	19	4	112	5	21	4
Mexico	30	13	10	1	28			

Billions of dollars and percentages.
Share = percent of world total.
Source: General Agreement on Tariffs & Trade (2).

Figure 5–20

United States' main trading partners

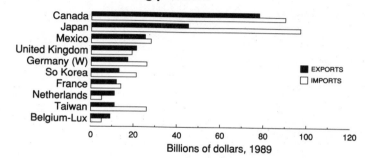

	EXPORTS		IMPORTS		TRADE BALANCE	
	VOLUME	SHARE	VOLUME	SHARE	VOLUME	SHARE
Canada	78	22	90	18	-11	-1.32
Japan	45	12	97	20	-53	-6.13
Mexico	25	7	28	6	-3	-0.31
United Kingdom	21	6	19	4	2	0.23
Germany (W)	17	5	26	5	-9	-1.03
So Korea	13	4	21	4	-7	-0.82
France	12	3	14	3	-2	-0.22
Netherlands	11	3	5	1	6	0.74
Taiwan	11	3	26	5	-14	-1.67
Belgium-Lux	9	2	5	1	4	0.45
Asia developing	57	16	101	21	-44	-5.13
EC	87	24	89	18	-2	-0.26
World	**364**	**100**	**494**	**100**	**-130**	**-15.14**

Figure 5–21

Billions of dollars, 1989.
Export (import) share = percent of total exports (imports).
Trade balance volume = exports-imports.
Trade balance share = percent of total exports + imports.
Source: International Monetary Fund (2).

Office and telecom-
munications equipment
was the most-traded
class of product for the
United States economy
— although not much
ahead of food and
chemicals, the two
main products in which
exports exceeded im-
ports. The other was
raw materials. All other
products posted deficits.

Exports of the three
leading products grew
substantially in 1988,
as did those of many
others. The biggest
gainer was nonferrous
metals, though still a
mere one percent of
total exports. The small-
est gainer was fuels,
also a small share of
total exports. Exports of
automotive products in-
creased substantially.

Automotive products
also led the list of im-
ports, with a 17% share
of the total. Imports of
office and telecom-
munications equipment
rose sharply in 1989,
as did several products
traded at lower value
levels. Imports declined
in fuels, food, and tex-
tiles.

Overall, the growth
rate of imports was
about half that of ex-
ports, which reduced
the trade deficit but left
it at a worrisome high
level.

Main traded products of the United States

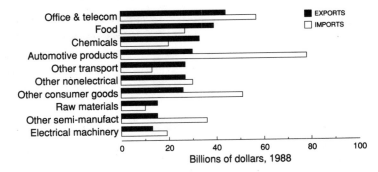

Billions of dollars, 1988

EXPORTS	VALUE	SHARE	CHANGE
Office & telecom equip	44	14	28
Food	39	12	32
Chemicals	33	10	23
Automotive products	30	10	17
Other transport equip	27	9	16
Other nonelec mach	27	9	28
Other consumer goods	26	8	26
Raw materials	15	5	25
Other semimfrs	15	5	25
Electrical machinery	13	4	33
Power generating mach	9	4	30
Fuels	8	3	6
Ores and minerals	6	2	35
Nonferrous metals	4	1	63
Textiles	4	1	24
Iron and steel	3	1	64
Clothing	2	1	36
Total main exports	**322**		**27**
Total exports	**438**	**100**	**24**

IMPORTS	VALUE	SHARE	CHANGE
Automotive products	78	17	2
Office & telecom equip	57	13	18
Other consumer goods	51	11	9
Fuels	44	10	-6
Other semimfrs	36	8	12
Other nonelec mach	30	7	15
Food	27	6	-1
Clothing	23	5	5
Chemicals	20	5	22
Electrical machinery	19	4	21
Other transport equip	13	3	13
Iron and steel	12	3	26
Nonferrous metals	11	3	29
Raw materials	10	2	10
Textiles	6	2	-4
Power generating mach	5	1	13
Ores and minerals	5	1	29
Total main imports	**460**		**9**
Total imports	**571**	**100**	**11**

Figure 5–22

Billions of dollars and percentages, 1988.
Change = annual percentage change.
Source: General Agreement on Tariffs & Trade (2).

Trade Geography

The United States had a net deficit in its trading of capital goods in 1988, posting surpluses only in "other" transport equipment and in power machinery. However, in that year exports grew significantly more than imports in every main category of capital goods except power machinery, where growth was slight.

Main traded capital goods of the United States

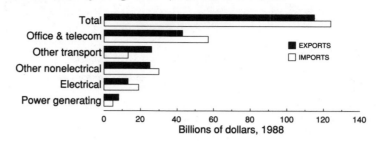

Billions of dollars, 1988

| | EXPORTS-------------------------------------- | | | | IMPORTS-------------------------------------- | | | |
	WESTERN EUROPE	ASIA	WORLD	CHANGE	WESTERN EUROPE	ASIA	WORLD	CHANGE
Office and telecom equip	16	15	43	30	4	46	57	18
Other transport equip	9	7	26	28	5	4	13	13
Other nonelectrical mach	7	6	25	28	14	11	30	15
Electrical machinery	4	3	13	33	4	10	19	21
Power generating mach	4	2	8	16	3	1	5	13
Total	**39**	**33**	**115**	**26**	**30**	**72**	**124**	**17**

Figure 5–23

Billions of dollars and percent change, 1988.
Source: General Agreement on Tariffs & Trade (2).

Manufactures accounted for four-fifths of Asia's merchandise exports in 1987. The region's economies had a large surplus in their aggregate trade in manufactures. Both exports and imports of both agricultures and mining products declined during the 1980s — much more in mining products (mostly fuels).

Japan, the world's third-largest trader, accounted for half of the region's total exports of manufactures in 1987. This trade was 97% of the economy's total merchandise exports. Manufactures also accounted for nearly all of the exports of Taiwan, Hong Kong, and South Korea, whose trade in manufactures almost exactly matched one another.

The top five Asian traders accounted for 87% of the region's total exports in manufactures.

Asia

Asia's trade by product group

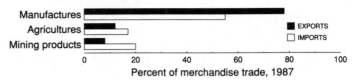

Percent of merchandise trade, 1987

	EXPORTS		IMPORTS	
	1980	1987	1980	1987
Manufactures	65	87	39	55
Agricultures	18	12	19	17
Mining products	16	8	38	20

Figure 5–24

Percentage shares, by value.
Shares do not add up to 100 due to products not specified.
Source: General Agreement on Tariffs & Trade (2).

Leading exporters of manufactures in Asia

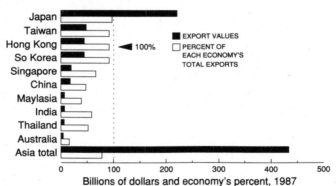

Billions of dollars and economy's percent, 1987

	1987 VALUE	ASIA'S SHARE	ECONOMY'S SHARE
Japan	221	51	97
Taiwan	48	11	92
Hong Kong	44	10	92
So Korea	44	10	92
Singapore	19	5	66
China	18	4	47
Malaysia	7	2	39
India	7	2	58
Thailand	6	2	52
Australia	4	1	16
Asia total	**434**	**100**	**78**
Top 10	418	96	
Top 5	376	87	

Figure 5–25

Billions of dollars and percentages, 1987.
Figures for Hong Kong and Singapore include substantial reexports.
Economy's share is share of merchandise exports.
Source: General Agreement on Tariffs & Trade (2).

Asian exports of agricultures accounted for 12% of total merchandise exports. This share was highest for New Zealand, whose agriculture exports were 69% of their total. These products were also a large share of Thailand's total exports.

Exports of mining products were an even smaller share — 8% — of the region's total exports. They accounted for 61% of Indonesia's total and 39% of Australia's.

Leading exporters of agricultures in Asia

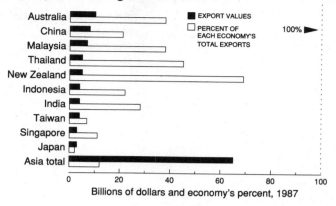

Billions of dollars and economy's percent, 1987

	1987 VALUE	ASIA'S SHARE	ECONOMY'S SHARE
Australia	10	15	38
China	8	13	21
Malaysia	7	11	38
Thailand	5	8	45
New Zealand	5	8	69
Indonesia	4	7	22
India	4	6	28
Taiwan	4	6	7
Singapore	3	5	11
Japan	3	5	2
Asia total	**65**	**100**	**12**
Top 10	53	81	
Top 5	35	54	

Figure 5–26

Billions of dollars and percentages. Figures for Singapore include substantial reexports. Economy's share = share of merchandise exports. Economy's share for India and Indonesia are for 1986, not 1987. Source: General Agreement on Tariffs & Trade (2).

Leading exporters of mining products in Asia

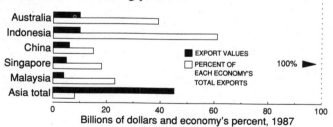

Billions of dollars and economy's percent, 1987

	1987 VALUE	ASIA'S SHARE	ECONOMY'S SHARE
Australia	10	23	39
Indonesia	10	23	61
China	6	13	15
Singapore	5	12	18
Malaysia	4	9	23
Asia total	**45**	**100**	**8**
Top 5	36	80	

Figure 5–27

Billions of dollars and percentages. Figures for Singapore include substantial reexports. Economy's share = share of merchandise exports. Economy's share for Indonesia is for 1986 rather than 1987. Source: General Agreement on Tariffs & Trade (2).

Among the developing economies of Asia, four newly-industrializing economies dominate both exports and imports, with a slight surplus of exports. Southeast Asia is the region in Asia with the largest trade.

By far, Japan's most important trading partner is the United States, which accounts for nearly 10% of total trade. (For comparison, Japan accounts for about 6% of the total trade of the US.) In 1989, 34% of Japan's exports went to the US, while 46% of imports came from there. (This compares with 12% and 20% for trade going in the other directions.) The European Community accounted for less than half as much — about 4% — of Japan's total trade.

Japan's trade with Asian developing economies was almost exactly balanced — both exports and imports accounted for about 30% of total trade.

Japan had a $65 billion trade surplus with the world, a very large 13% of Japan's total trade, in 1989.

Trade of Asian developing economies, by region

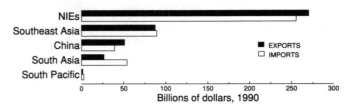

	EXPORTS			IMPORTS		
	1989	1990	1991	1989	1990	1991
NIEs	246.6	270.3	300.5	229.3	255.5	288.7
Southeast Asia	76.6	87.4	101.7	76.8	89.6	104.2
China	46.0	50.6	56.7	36.6	39.3	42.5
South Asia	24.1	26.7	29.8	51.5	54.1	57.9
South Pacific	1.6	1.5	1.6	2.0	2.4	2.5
Total	**394.9**	**436.6**	**490.3**	**396.2**	**440.8**	**495.8**

Figure 5–28

FOB basis, in billions of dollars. Figures for 1990 and 1991 are estimates and projections.
NIEs = newly industrializing economies: Hong Kong, Taiwan, So Korea, Singapore.
Southeast Asia = Malaysia, Indonesia, Thailand, Philippines, Viet Nam, Laos.
South Asia = India, Pakistan, Sri Lanka, Bangladesh, Myanmar (formerly Burma), Nepal.
South Pacific = Papua New Guinea, Fiji.
Figures for 1990 and 1991 are estimates and projections.
Source: Asia Development Bank (1).

Japan's main trading partners

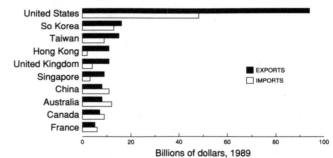

	EXPORTS		IMPORTS		TRADE BALANCE	
	VOLUME	SHARE	VOLUME	SHARE	VOLUME	SHARE
United States	94	34	48	23	46	9.44
So Korea	16	6	13	6	4	0.74
Taiwan	15	6	9	4	6	1.33
Hong Kong	11	4	2	1	9	1.91
United Kingdom	11	4	4	2	6	1.29
Singapore	9	3	3	1	6	1.29
China	8	3	11	5	-3	-0.54
Australia	8	3	12	5	-4	-0.77
Canada	7	2	9	4	-2	-0.38
France	5	2	6	3	0	-0.05
Asia developing econ	83	30	65	31	18	3.64
EC	48	17	28	13	20	4.10
World	**275**	**100**	**210**	**100**	**65**	**13.42**

Figure 5–29

Billions of dollars. Export (import) share = percent of total exports (imports).
Trade balance volume = exports – imports. Trade balance share = percent of total exports + imports.
Source: International Monetary Fund (2).

Among the developing economies of Asia, the four newly-industrializing economies and China led in both exports and imports. Forecasters expect the relative positions of these traders to remain unchanged in the current period.

Malaysia is emerging as a significant trader in manufactures; during the 1980s, this trade doubled as a share of the economy's total trade. Thailand's trade in manufactures also doubled its share of total trade in this period. Indonesia's trade increased nine-fold, though at lower values.

Top traders among Asian developing economies

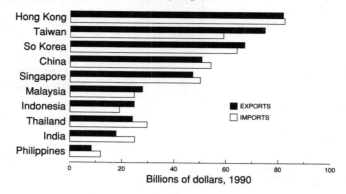

Billions of dollars, 1990

	EXPORTS			IMPORTS		
	1989	1990	1991	1989	1990	1991
Hong Kong	74.6	81.7	94.0	75.1	82.3	95.1
Taiwan	67.7	74.7	80.4	51.5	58.8	65.4
So Korea	61.1	66.9	74.6	56.7	64.0	72.5
China	46.0	50.6	56.7	51.5	54.1	57.9
Singapore	43.2	47.0	51.5	46.0	50.4	55.8
Malaysia	25.3	28.0	33.2	21.0	24.8	28.9
Indonesia	21.9	24.8	27.9	16.6	19.1	21.9
Thailand	20.3	24.2	28.3	25.2	29.8	34.6
India	15.8	17.8	19.9	22.8	24.9	27.1
Philippines	7.6	8.4	9.7	10.8	11.9	13.7
Pakistan	4.6	4.9	5.4	7.3	7.5	7.8
Viet Nam	1.5	2.0	2.6	3.1	3.8	4.8
Sri Lanka	1.5	1.6	1.8	2.0	2.1	2.2
Bangladesh	1.4	1.6	1.8	3.1	3.4	3.7
Papua New Guinea	1.2	1.1	1.1	1.5	1.8	1.8
Myanmar (Burma)	0.6	0.7	0.7	0.6	0.7	0.7
Nepal	0.2	0.2	0.2	0.7	0.8	0.8
Laos	0.1	0.1	0.1	0.2	0.3	0.3
Fiji	0.4	0.5	0.5	0.5	0.6	0.7
Total	**394.9**	**436.6**	**490.3**	**396.2**	**440.8**	**495.8**

Figure 5–30

FOB basis, in billions of dollars.
Figures for 1990 and 1991 are estimates and projections.
NIEs = newly industrializing economies.
Source: Asian Development Bank (1).

Emerging Asian exporters of manufactures

	1987 VALUE	ECONOMY'S SHARE	
		1980	1987
Malaysia	7	19	39
India	7	59	58
Thailand	6	25	52
Indonesia	3	2	18
Pakistan	3	49	72
Philippines	2	21	31

Table 5–3

Billions of dollars and percentages.
Economy's share = share of merchandise exports.
Economy's share for India and Indonesia are for 1985 and 1986 rather than 1987.
Source: General Agreement on Tariffs & Trade (2).

Asia's developing economies had a modest $2 billion trade deficit in 1990, a balance that masks wide disparities among regions and economies. The small newly-industrializing economies had a $21 billion surplus, while the populous economies of south Asia had a deficit of about $12 billion. China had a small deficit in 1990, but this is expected to become an even smaller surplus in 1991.

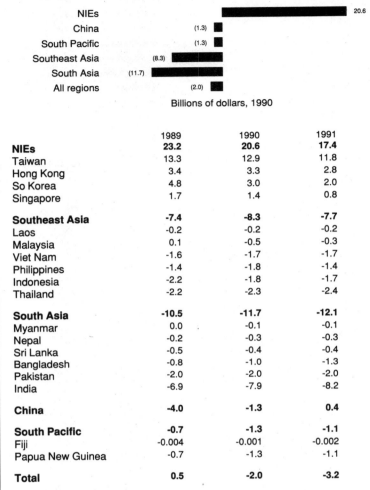

Current-account balances, Asian developing economies

Billions of dollars, 1990

	1989	1990	1991
NIEs	**23.2**	**20.6**	**17.4**
Taiwan	13.3	12.9	11.8
Hong Kong	3.4	3.3	2.8
So Korea	4.8	3.0	2.0
Singapore	1.7	1.4	0.8
Southeast Asia	**-7.4**	**-8.3**	**-7.7**
Laos	-0.2	-0.2	-0.2
Malaysia	0.1	-0.5	-0.3
Viet Nam	-1.6	-1.7	-1.7
Philippines	-1.4	-1.8	-1.4
Indonesia	-2.2	-1.8	-1.7
Thailand	-2.2	-2.3	-2.4
South Asia	**-10.5**	**-11.7**	**-12.1**
Myanmar	0.0	-0.1	-0.1
Nepal	-0.2	-0.3	-0.3
Sri Lanka	-0.5	-0.4	-0.4
Bangladesh	-0.8	-1.0	-1.3
Pakistan	-2.0	-2.0	-2.0
India	-6.9	-7.9	-8.2
China	**-4.0**	**-1.3**	**0.4**
South Pacific	**-0.7**	**-1.3**	**-1.1**
Fiji	-0.004	-0.001	-0.002
Papua New Guinea	-0.7	-1.3	-1.1
Total	**0.5**	**-2.0**	**-3.2**

Figure 5–31

FOB basis, in billions of dollars.
Figures for 1990 and 1991 are estimates and projections.
NIEs = newly industrializing economies.
Source: Asian Development Bank (1).

Trade Geography

Two-thirds of China's exports were to other Asian economies, as were over half of its imports. This distribution has held nearly constant through the 1980s.

Hong Kong received almost half of China's exports in 1989, far more than did Japan or any other trading partner. However, many of these products were reexported to the rest of the world.

It is estimated that over 30% of China's foreign exchange comes through Hong Kong.

China's main trading partners

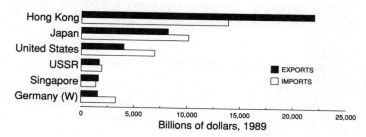

Billions of dollars, 1989

	EXPORTS		IMPORTS	
	1983	1989	1983	1989
Hong Kong	5797	22003	1710	13829
Japan	4517	8180	5495	10105
United States	1713	3988	2753	6918
USSR	319	1699	441	1945
Singapore	567	1642	114	1400
Germany (W)	859	1562	1209	3265
World	**22177**	**51626**	**21336**	**58282**

Millions of dollars.
Source: International Monetary Fund (2).

Figure 5–32

China's merchandise trade

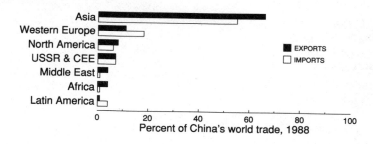

Percent of China's world trade, 1988

	EXPORTS			IMPORTS		
	1988 VALUE	1980 SHARE	1988 SHARE	1988 VALUE	1980 SHARE	1988 SHARE
North America	4	6	8	9	24	6
Western Europe	5	16	11	10	18	18
Asia	31	60	66	30	42	55
USSR & CEE	3	10	7	4	10	7
Middle East	2	4	4	1	1	1
Latin America	0	2	1	2	4	4
Africa	2	4	4	0	2	1
World	**48**	**100**	**100**	**55**	**100**	**100**

Billions of dollars and percentages.
CEE = Central and Eastern Europe: Bulgaria, Czechoslovakia, Germany (E), Hungary, Poland, Romania.

Figure 5–33

Exports of mining products (mostly fuels) bulked larger in the trade of the USSR and CEE (central and eastern Europe) economies than it does in other developed and near-developed economies. The distribution of trading by product group changed hardly at all during the 1980s, except that imports of agricultures dropped significantly.

Well over half of the group's trade was intra-regional. Western Europe was the only region with which the group had any significant trade during the 1980s. Trade with Asia grew moderately through the 1980s and twice that fast in 1988. Trade with Africa and the Middle East bounced back in 1988 after declining slightly through the decade.

USSR & CEE

USSR & CEE trade by product group

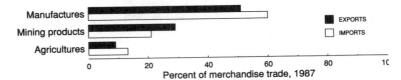

Percent of merchandise trade, 1987

	EXPORTS		IMPORTS	
	1980	1987	1980	1987
Manufactures	50	51	59	60
Mining products	31	29	17	21
Agricultures	11	9	20	13

Percentage shares, by value.
Shares do not add up to 100 due to products not specified.
Source: General Agreement on Tariffs & Trade (2).

Figure 5–34

USSR & CEE regional trade

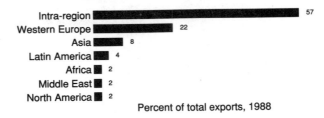

Percent of total exports, 1988

	1988 SHARE	1980-88 CHANGE	1988 CHANGE
Intra-region	57	6	4
Western Europe	22	1	8
Asia	8	8	19
Latin America	4	7	2
Africa	2	-1	9
Middle East	2	-2	9
North America	2	8	8
Inter-region	40	2	9
World	**100**	**5**	**6**

Share = percent of total exports. Percentages based on value.
Shares do no add up to 100 due to exports to unspecified destinations.
Change = average annual change.
Source: General Agreement on Tariffs & Trade (2).

Figure 5–35

Trade Geography

The group of transitioning socialist economies increased their total trade slightly during the 1980s. In 1989, exports fell 2% and imports barely increased.

The USSR accounted for a little over half of total exports and imports of the group.

Poland's were the only exports to fall during most of the 1980s, but all except East Germany's fell in 1989. In that year of political and economic upheavals, the ties that bound the socialist economies together as a bloc began to unravel. However, it was not possible to quickly rearrange patterns of highly integrated, specialized trade that had been formally set in place by the Council for Economic Assistance (CMEA) over the preceding thirty years. So, although CMEA was dissolved in 1991, the old trading patterns persisted, and the group entered a period of confusion and painful restructuring.

USSR & CEE merchandise trade

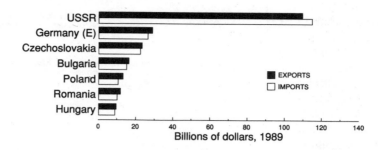

Billions of dollars, 1989

	1989 VALUE	1989 SHARE	1980-88 CHANGE	1989 CHANGE
EXPORTERS				
USSR	109.4	51.5	4.5	-1.0
Germany (E)	29.0	13.5	6.0	5.0
Czechoslovakia	23.5	11.0	6.0	-5.5
Bulgaria	16.2	7.5	6.5	-6.5
Poland	13.2	6.0	-3.5	-6.0
Romania	11.8	5.5	1.5	-9.0
Hungary	9.6	4.5	1.5	-3.5
USSR & CEE	212	100	4	-2
IMPORTERS				
USSR	114.8	55.0	6.0	7.0
Germany (E)	26.5	12.5	4.5	-1.0
Czechoslovakia	22.4	10.5	6.0	-7.5
Bulgaria	15.2	7.5	7.5	-10.0
Poland	10.6	5.0	-5.5	-12.5
Romania	10.2	5.0	-3.5	2.0
Hungary	8.8	4.0	0.0	-5.5
USSR & CEE	208	100	4	1

Billions of dollars and percent of total group trade.
Source: General Agreement on Tariffs & Trade (5).

Figure 5–36

The overall patterns of trade between the individual transitioning socialist economies and the developed world are remarkably similar. Trade with the European Community far exceeds that with either the United States or Japan. Two differences stand out: compared with the CEE economies, the USSR has large deficits with the US and a bigger trade with Japan.

Trade of USSR and CEE with developed economies

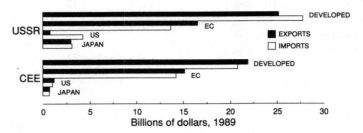

Trade of CEE with developed economies

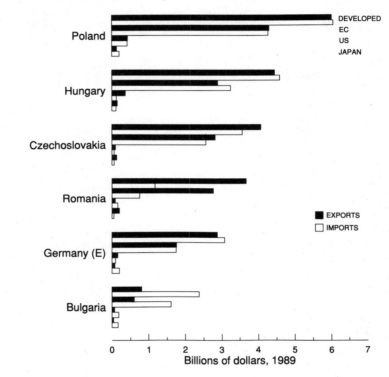

\DESTINATION ORIGIN\	DEVELOPED EXPORTS	IMPORTS	EC EXPORTS	IMPORTS	US EXPORTS	IMPORTS	JAPAN EXPORTS	IMPORTS
USSR	**25.180**	**27.770**	**16.533**	**13.642**	**0.782**	**4.271**	**3.005**	**3.082**
CEE	**21.871**	**20.808**	**15.154**	**14.212**	**1.190**	**1.021**	**0.738**	**0.673**
Poland	6.011	6.054	4.301	4.280	0.423	0.414	0.130	0.200
Hungary	4.448	4.584	2.887	3.250	0.361	0.122	0.148	0.108
Czechoslovakia	4.067	3.562	2.829	2.571	0.095	0.054	0.130	0.056
Romania	3.673	1.169	2.777	0.752	0.086	0.156	0.202	0.050
Germany (E)	2.870	3.070	1.763	1.753	0.158	0.094	0.083	0.195
Bulgaria	0.802	2.372	0.597	1.606	0.067	0.181	0.045	0.164

Figure 5–37

Billions of dollars, 1989.
CEE = Central and Eastern European economies as shown.
Figures for developed economies do not include trade between East and West Germany.
Source: General Agreement on Tariffs & Trade (4).

Trade Geography

At the decade's end, Latin America's exports were about equally divided among manufactures, agricultures, and mining products. However, the region had a large deficit in manufacturing trade and strong surpluses in agricultures and mining products. During the 1980s, the export share of mining products fell sharply and that of manufactures rose by a like percentage.

The United States and Canada took nearly half of the region's merchandise exports in 1988, a big jump from the growth of that trade during most of the 1980s. Exports to Western Europe grew by a large amount in 1988, after declining in the earlier years of the decade. Exports to Asia grew even more in 1988, after years of moderate growth. In all, the region's exports grew 17% in 1988 after declining slightly in the earlier 1980s.

Latin America

Latin America's trade by product group

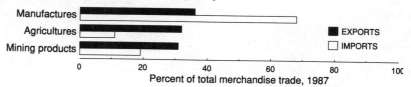

Percent of total merchandise trade, 1987

	EXPORTS		IMPORTS	
	1980	1987	1980	1987
Agricultures	32	32	12	11
Mining products	51	31	28	19
Manufactures	17	36	59	68

Percentage shares, by value.
Shares do not add up to 100 due to products not specified.
Source: General Agreement on Tariffs & Trade (2).

Figure 5–38

Latin America's trade with other regions

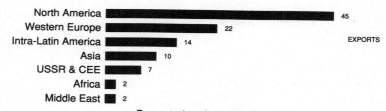

Percent of total merchandise trade, 1988

DESTINATION \	1988 SHARE	1980-87 CHANGE	1988 CHANGE
North America	45	2	12
Western Europe	22	-3	24
Intra-Latin America	14	-7	14
Asia	10	4	37
USSR & CEE	7	-1	20
Africa	2	-8	14
Middle East	2	-5	8
Inter-regional	86	1	18
World	**100**	**-1**	**17**

Shares do not add up to 100 due to exports to unspecified destinations.
CEE = Central and Eastern Europe: Bulgaria, Czechoslovakia, Germany (E), Hungary, Poland, Romania,
Source: General Agreement on Tariffs & Trade (2).

Figure 5–39

Brazil was Latin America's biggest trader, also posting the region's largest trade surplus. The four leading exporters (Brazil, Mexico, Venezuela, and Argentina) accounted for two-thirds to total exports. In 1989, Latin America had a trade surplus of $27.2 billion, which was 8% of the region's total trade.

During the 1980s, world recession, inflation, and the debt crisis caused imports to shrink as Latin Americans struggled to adjust their trade imbalances. By the decade's end, trading partners had "lost" nearly $400 billion in exports to the region, when compared with 1980 values and trends. If previous patterns apply, most of this "lost" trade would have gone to the United States.

Latin American trade in goods and services

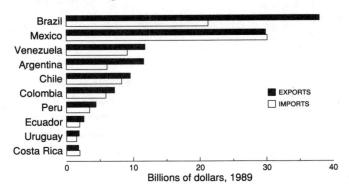

	EXPORTS	IMPORTS	BALANCE
Brazil	37.9	21.3	16.6
Mexico	29.9	30.1	-0.2
Venezuela	11.8	9.2	2.6
Argentina	11.6	6.1	5.5
Chile	9.6	8.3	1.3
Colombia	7.2	5.9	1.3
Peru	4.4	3.5	0.9
Ecuador	2.6	2.0	0.5
Uruguay	1.9	1.5	0.4
Costa Rica	1.8	2.0	-0.1
Dominican Republic	1.8	2.3	-0.5
Jamaica	1.8	1.9	-0.1
Trinidad & Tobago	1.8	1.0	0.8
Panama	1.6	1.3	0.3
Guatemala	1.4	1.8	-0.4
Paraguay	1.1	1.6	-0.5
Honduras	1.1	1.1	-0.1
El Salvador	0.8	1.2	-0.5
Bolivia	0.7	0.9	-0.2
Barbados	0.7	0.8	-0.1
Nicaragua	0.4	0.7	-0.3
Guyana	0.3	0.3	0.0
Haiti	0.2	0.5	-0.2
Latin America total	**133.0**	**105.8**	**27.2**

Figure 5–40

Billions of dollars, 1989.
Source: Inter-American Development Bank (1).

Reductions of imports into Latin America

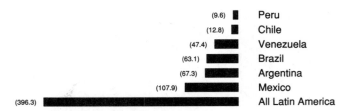

Billions of dollars, 1980-89

Figure 5–41

Source: Inter-American Development Bank (1).

Trade Geography

Mining products (fuels) were 80% of the Middle East's exports in 1987, and manufactures were 73% of imports.

Saudi Arabia was the region's biggest exporter by a wide margin. Although its exports had dropped sharply during the 1980, they grew moderately in 1988. Exports of the other oil-exporting economies fell during the decade, including 1988.

Israel's exports continued their decade-long growth, but the economy posted a substantial trade deficit in 1988.

Imports of the oil-exporting economies grew significantly in 1988 — except for Iran, Bahrain, and Syria — after posting declines through the 1980s.

Middle East

Middle East's trade by product group

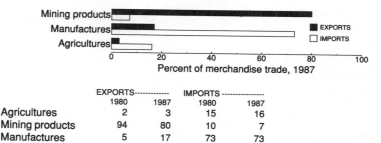

Percent of merchandise trade, 1987

	EXPORTS		IMPORTS	
	1980	1987	1980	1987
Agricultures	2	3	15	16
Mining products	94	80	10	7
Manufactures	5	17	73	73

Figure 5–42

Percentage shares, by value. Shares do not add up to 100 due to products not specified.
Source: General Agreement on Tariffs & Trade (2).

Leading traders in the Middle East

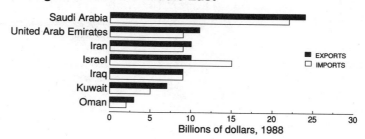

Billions of dollars, 1988

	1988 VALUE	1988 SHARE	1980-87 CHANGE	1988 CHANGE
EXPORTERS				
Saudi Arabia	24	29	-20	5
United Arab Emirates	11	13	-6	-12
Iran	10	11	-3	-24
Israel	10	12	7	14
Iraq	9	11	-11	2
Kuwait	7	9	-12	-16
Oman	3	3	-1	-18
Qatar	2	3	-9	-17
Bahrain	2	3	-6	1
Syria	1	2	-6	-1
Top 10	80	94		
IMPORTERS				
Saudi Arabia	22	26	-6	9
Israel	15	18	6	5
Iran	9	11	-4	-6
Iraq	9	10	-9	15
United Arab Emirates	9	10	-3	18
Kuwait	5	6	-3	1
Jordan	3	3	2	1
Bahrain	3	3	-4	-5
Oman	2	3	-1	21
Syria	2	3	-7	-11
Top 10	78	91		

Figure 5–43

Billions of dollars and percentages of total Middle East exports (imports).
Source: General Agreement on Tariffs & Trade (2).

Mining products of various kinds dominated the exports of African economies, which had a massive trade deficit in manufactures in 1987.

South Africa was the region's biggest trader by far, with 29% of total exports and a moderate trade surplus.

Egypt had huge trade deficit in 1988: imports were nearly four times exports. Even though exports increased by a third in that year, imports nearly doubled.

Imports to the region generally grew. The only exception was Cote D'Ivoire, whose imports fell 17% in 1988.

Africa

Africa's trade by product group

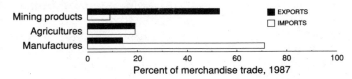

	EXPORTS -----------------		IMPORTS -----------------	
	1980	1987	1980	1987
Agricultures	13	19	17	17
Mining products	67	53	10	9
Manufactures	7	14	72	71

Figure 5—44

Percentage shares, by value. Shares do not add up to 100 due to products not specified.
Source: General Agreement on Tariffs & Trade (2).

Leading traders in Africa

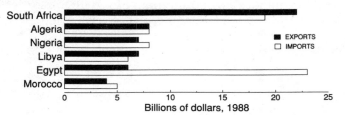

	1988 VALUE	1988 SHARE	1980-87 CHANGE	1988 CHANGE
EXPORTERS				
South Africa	22	29	-3	-9
Algeria	8	11	-3	-7
Nigeria	7	10	-15	-8
Libya	7	9	-17	0
Egypt	6	8	5	35
Morocco	4	5	2	28
Cote d'Ivoire	3	4	0	-10
Angola	3	4	2	15
Tunisia	2	3	-1	12
Zimbabwe	2	2	0	13
Top 10	62	83		
IMPORTERS				
Egypt	23	26	14	95
South Africa	19	21	-3	23
Algeria	8	9	-6	7
Libya	6	6	-5	13
Morocco	5	6	0	13
Nigeria	4	5	-19	3
Tunisia	4	4	-2	22
Cote d'Ivoire	2	2	-3	-17
Kenya	2	2	-6	13
Angola	2	2	1	23
Top 10	73	80		

Figure 5—45

Billions of dollars and percentages of total African exports (imports).
Source: General Agreement on Tariffs & Trade (2).

Trade Geography

The International Monetary Fund classifies developing economies according to the kind of export that accounted for over 50% of total exports in 1984–86. Economies that export primarily manufactures account for half of the developing world's total exports, and fuel-exporting economies another one-quarter.

The main exporters of manufactures are the four newly-industrializing economies of Asia plus China and Brazil.

The three main fuel-exporting economies are located in three continents. While a large share of petroleum reserves are located in the Persian Gulf, most of the traded oil comes from other sources. The world's biggest oil exporter, the USSR, is not considered a developing economy, as is also the case of the United Kingdom, Canada, Norway, and the United States.

The developing world

Exports of developing economies

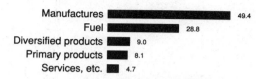

Percent of developing economies' total exports, 1985-87

Figure 5–46

Services includes private transfers.
Source: International Monetary Fund (1).

Manufactures-exporting economies

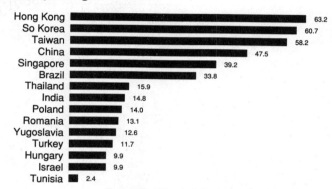

Exports in billions of dollars, 1988

Figure 5–47

Source: World Bank (1).

Fuel-exporting economies

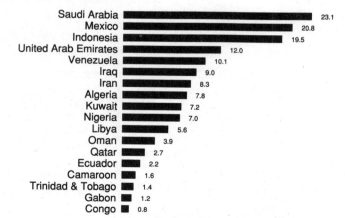

Exports in billions of dollars, 1988

Figure 5–48

Exports of fuels accounted for over 50% of total exports in 1984–86.
Source: World Bank (1).

While 37 developing economies are primarily exporters of agricultures, only Argentina and Colombia are major exporters.

Chile dominates trade in minerals. In recent years, Chile has reduced its dependence on this trade.

Agricultures-exporting economies

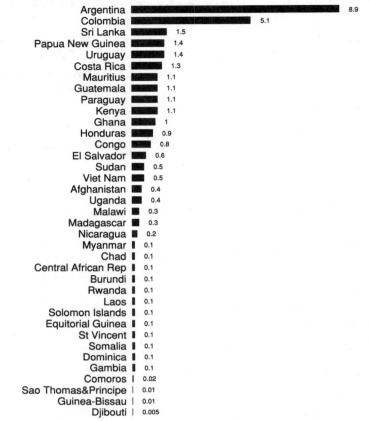

	Total exports in billions of dollars, 1988
Argentina	8.9
Colombia	5.1
Sri Lanka	1.5
Papua New Guinea	1.4
Uruguay	1.4
Costa Rica	1.3
Mauritius	1.1
Guatemala	1.1
Paraguay	1.1
Kenya	1.1
Ghana	1
Honduras	0.9
Congo	0.8
El Salvador	0.6
Sudan	0.5
Viet Nam	0.5
Afghanistan	0.4
Uganda	0.4
Malawi	0.3
Madagascar	0.3
Nicaragua	0.2
Myanmar	0.1
Chad	0.1
Central African Rep	0.1
Burundi	0.1
Rwanda	0.1
Laos	0.1
Solomon Islands	0.1
Equitorial Guinea	0.1
St Vincent	0.1
Somalia	0.1
Dominica	0.1
Gambia	0.1
Comoros	0.02
Sao Thomas&Principe	0.01
Guinea-Bissau	0.01
Djibouti	0.005

Total exports in billions of dollars, 1988

Figure 5–49

Source: World Bank (1).

Minerals-exporting economies

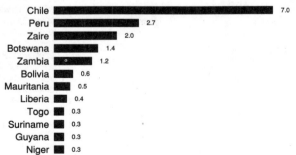

	Exports in billions of dollars, 1988
Chile	7.0
Peru	2.7
Zaire	2.0
Botswana	1.4
Zambia	1.2
Bolivia	0.6
Mauritania	0.5
Liberia	0.4
Togo	0.3
Suriname	0.3
Guyana	0.3
Niger	0.3

Exports in billions of dollars, 1988

Figure 5–50

Source: World Bank (1).

Egypt and Pakistan lead the developing economies whose primary exports are services, which in these two cases are mainly remittances from workers abroad. Tourism is the other main kind of service exported by this group.

South Africa and Malaysia lead the group of economies in which no one type of export accounts for more than half of total exports.

Services-exporting economies

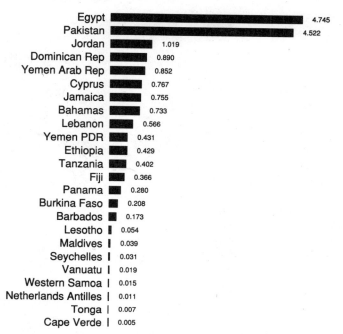

Total exports in billions of dollars, 1988

Includes private transfers.
Source: World Bank (1).

Figure 5–51

Economies with diversified exports

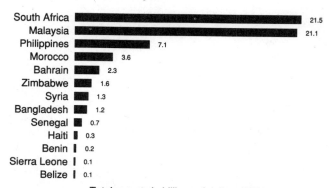

Total exports in billions of dollars, 1988

Exports of these economies were not dominated by any one IMF classification.
Source: World Bank (1).

Figure 5–52

6 Trade in services

Trade in commercial services — totaling $680 billion in 1989, up 9% from the previous year — was about 20% of world trade, the same share it held in 1970. The value of trade in commercial services was twice the value of trade in mining products and nearly twice that of agricultures.

Commercial services include transportation of freight and passengers, travel-related goods and services, and other private services and income (communications, professional and technical services, labor income abroad, and royalties and license fees). Worldwide, commercial services are about half of the current-account category of *invisibles* — which also includes investment income, the transfer of official goods, services, and income, and "unrequited" (one-way) private and official transfers of assets.

The United States is the biggest trader in commercial services; in 1989, it had a huge $24.5 billion surplus in this trade. France and Spain also recorded substantial surpluses. Japan, the biggest importer of commercial services, had a whopping deficit of $41 billion. West Germany also had a very large deficit.

Balances of trade in commercial services

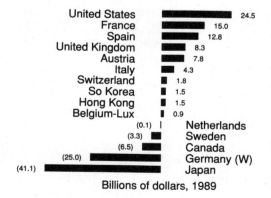

Billions of dollars, 1989

Source: General Agreement on Tariffs & Trade (4).

Figure 6–1

The "export" of invisibles consists mostly of commercial services and investment income. Since 1970 the share of the latter has risen sharply and of the former has fallen almost as much.

Trade in telecommunications, nonmerchandise insurance, banking, and other professional services grew faster than any other category of commercial services in 1989. Growth of trade in transportation and travel services slowed from the year earlier and was in both cases less than the average growth of all commercial services.

Trend in export of invisibles

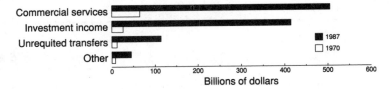

	1970 VALUE	1987 VALUE	1970 SHARE	1987 SHARE
Commercial services	64	505	58	47
Investment income	26	415	24	39
Other	8	45	7	3
Unrequited transfers	12	114	11	11
Total invisibles	**110**	**1080**	**100**	**100**

Figure 6–2

Billions of dollars and percentages of total invisibles exports.
Source: General Agreement on Tariffs & Trade (1).

Exports of commercial services

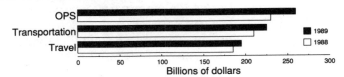

	1988 VALUE	CHANGE	SHARE	1989 VALUE	SHARE	SHARE
Transportation	210	12.5	34	225	7.0	33
Travel	185	15.5	30	195	6.5	29
OPS	230	9.5	37	260	13.0	38
All comml services	625	12	100	680	9	100

Figure 6–3

Billions of dollars.
Annual percentage change.
Share = percent of total commercial services.
OPS = Other private services and income: telecommunications, nonmerchandise insurance, banking.
Source: General Agreement on Tariffs & Trade (4).

The pattern of trade in commercial services varied little between regions. Worldwide, the share of trade in transportation services fell sharply, while that of travel and other professional services rose a little between 1980 and 1988.

The share of trade in transportation services was above average in Africa. The share of travel services was largest in Latin America, substantially above the world average. In "Other" private services, the regional share was greatest in the Middle East, largely the automatic result of declining trade in the other two categories.

Composition of trade in commercial services by region

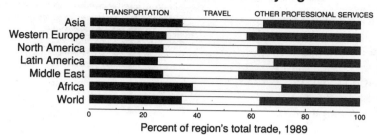

Percent of region's total trade, 1989

	EXPORTS		IMPORTS	
	1980	1988	1980	1988
ASIA				
Transportation	50	34	54	37
Travel	19	30	16	30
OPS	30	35	30	35
WESTERN EUROPE				
Transportation	35	28	37	31
Travel	25	30	26	30
OPS	40	42	36	39
NORTH AMERICA				
Transportation	37	27	43	32
Travel	32	35	37	45
OPS	31	38	20	24
LATIN AMERICA				
Transportation	32	25	45	41
Travel	41	44	33	32
OPS	27	33	22	31
MIDDLE EAST				
Transportation	39	27	51	32
Travel	35	28	29	21
OPS	26	45	20	47
AFRICA				
Transportation	47	38	48	49
Travel	26	35	15	19
OPS	27	31	36	34
WORLD				
Transportation	**44**	**34**		
Travel	**24**	**29**		
OPS	**35**	**37**		

Figure 6–4

Percent of world trade in commercial services, based on value.
Shares may no add up to 100 because of products not shown.
OPS (other private services and income) = telecommunications, nonmerchandise insurance, banking.
Source: General Agreement on Tariffs & Trade (4).

In the 1980s, the United States and Hong Kong had the biggest increases in exports of commercial services. Exports of the United Kingdom and the Netherlands grew the least during the decade.

Japan moved up from second to first place among importers of commercial services. Taiwan's imports grew twice as fast as Japan's during the 1980s; Saudi Arabia's imports fell by 10%.

Trade in commercial services increased in each of the seven regions, except for Africa on the import side. North America and Asia outpaced world growth in imports.

Leading traders in commercial services

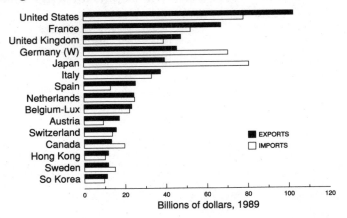

Billions of dollars, 1989

RANK		VALUE	SHARE	CHANGE	BALANCE
	EXPORTERS				
1	United States	102.5	15.7	241	24.5
2	France	67.1	10.3	81	15.0
3	United Kingdom	47.3	7.2	63	8.3
4	Germany (W)	45.4	7.0	113	-25.0
5	Japan	39.4	6.0	164	-41.1
6	Italy	37.3	5.7	87	4.3
7	Spain	25.1	3.8	146	12.3
8	Netherlands	24.4	3.7	64	-0.1
9	Belgium-Lux	23.1	3.5	85	0.9
10	Austria	17.2	2.6	105	7.8
11	Switzerland	15.5	2.4	135	1.8
12	Canada	13.1	2.0	114	-6.5
13	Hong Kong	11.6	1.8	205	1.5
14	Sweden	11.6	1.8	78	-3.3
15	So Korea	11.0	1.7	149	1.5
	World	**653**	**100**		
	Top 15	492	75		
	Top 10	429	66		
	Top 5	302	46		
	IMPORTERS				
1	Japan	80.5	12.0	195	
2	United States	78.0	11.7	187	
3	Germany (W)	70.4	10.5	67	
4	France	52.1	7.8	94	
5	United Kingdom	39.0	5.8	94	
6	Italy	33.0	4.9	152	
7	Netherlands	24.5	3.7	68	
8	Belgium-Lux	22.2	3.3	97	
9	Canada	19.6	2.9	134	
10	Sweden	14.9	2.2	133	
11	Taiwan	14.0	2.1	417	
12	Switzerland	13.7	2.0	145	
13	Spain	12.8	1.9	220	
14	Australia	12.4	1.9	125	
15	Saudi Arabia	10.5	1.6	-10	
	World	**669**	**100**		
	Top 15	498	74		
	Top 10	434	65		
	Top 5	320	48		

Figure 6–5

Billions of dollars and percentages, 1989. Share = percent of world total. Change = 1989 over 1979.
Source: General Agreement on Tariffs & Trade (4).

Trade in Services

Over decades, Western Europe had by far the largest share of world tourist receipts. North America's fell sharply in the 1970s and held steady in the 1980s. Asia's share grew moderately in the 1980s.

Among OECD economies, tourist receipts were the greatest share of gross domestic product in Austria and the lowest in Japan. The importance of tourism was also relatively slight in the United States and West Germany.

International tourism receipts by region

| | SHARES | | |
	1970	1980	1987
North America	20	12	12
Latin America	7	13	9
Western Europe	60	57	57
USSR & CEE	2	2	1
Africa	2	3	3
Middle East	2	4	4
Asia	7	9	14
World	**100**	**100**	**100**

Table 6–1

Percentages of world tourism receipts.
CEE = Central and Eastern Europe: Poland, Hungary, Czechoslovakia, Romania, E Germany, Bulgaria.
Source: General Agreement on Tariffs & Trade (1).

Importance of tourist receipts in OECD economies

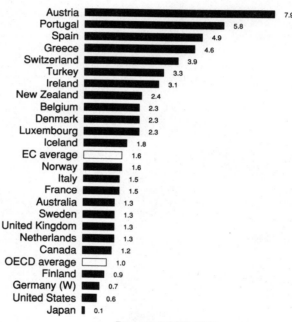

Austria	7.9
Portugal	5.8
Spain	4.9
Greece	4.6
Switzerland	3.9
Turkey	3.3
Ireland	3.1
New Zealand	2.4
Belgium	2.3
Denmark	2.3
Luxembourg	2.3
Iceland	1.8
EC average	1.6
Norway	1.6
Italy	1.5
France	1.5
Australia	1.3
Sweden	1.3
United Kingdom	1.3
Netherlands	1.3
Canada	1.2
OECD average	1.0
Finland	0.9
Germany (W)	0.7
United States	0.6
Japan	0.1

Percent of GDP, 1988

Source: Organization for Economic Cooperation and Development (1).

Among OECD countries, Spain welcomed the most tourists at its borders in 1988, and tourist receipts were well above the European Community average. France, the United States, and Yugoslavia also hosted far more than the average number of tourists. These receipts were 25% of Spain's total exports, a greater share than for any other OECD economy. Greece's receipts were almost as large a share of exports. The US hosted fewer tourists than Spain did but received more from each one. Even so, these receipts were only a small share of total US exports.

Tourists from the United States were the OECD's biggest spenders abroad, "importing" far more foreign goods and services in this way than did the average OECD or European Community economy. Tourist expenditures were the largest shares of total imports in Austria, New Zealand, and Iceland.

Tourism in OECD countries

	ARRIVALS	RECEIPTS	EXP SHARE	EXPEND	IMP SHARE
Spain	54178	16836	25.1	2457	3.3
Greece	7778	2440	21.1	734	4.6
Austria		9937	18.9	6000	11.7
Portugal	6624	2425	16.4	534	2.7
Turkey	4173	2355	13.2	358	1.9
New Zealand	865	1054	8.4	1071	10.4
Switzerland	11560	5636	8.1	5034	7.7
Australia	2249	3273	7.5	2860	5.1
Italy		12399	7.3	6053	3.4
Denmark		2423	6.0	3081	7.4
France	38288	13784	5.6	9713	4.0
United States	31557	29202	5.5	32112	5.0
Iceland	129	108	5.3	200	10.2
EC average		6423	5.0	6188	5.0
OECD average		5871	4.9	6530	5.5
Ireland	2345	997	4.5	959	4.2
Norway		1444	4.1	3406	9.1
Canada	15526	4600	4.1	6318	5.3
United Kingdom	15800	11016	3.8	14636	4.7
Sweden		2347	3.7	4573	7.1
Finland		984	3.5	1843	6.1
Belgium		3437	2.4	4427	3.3
Luxembourg		3437	2.4	4427	3.3
Netherlands		2873	2.1	6736	5.2
Germany (W)		8449	2.1	24923	7.6
Japan	2355	2894	0.8	18703	6.5
Yugoslavia	29635	2024			

Figure 6–6

Figures are for 1988.
In descending order of export share.
Tourist arrivals in thousands.
Tourist receipts (exports) in millions of dollars.
Tourist expenditures (imports) in millions of dollars.
Exp (imp) share = tourist receipts as percent of exports (imports) of goods and services.
Source: Organization for Economic Cooperation and Development (1).

Trade in Services

The United States dominates trade in patents, in 1987 collecting more than fourteen times as much in payments as did the United Kingdom and Japan. The US also paid more for use of patents than did any other OECD economy; but it still had a huge surplus of payments while most other OECD economies were posting deficits. West Germany had by far the greatest deficit.

Balance of payments for patents

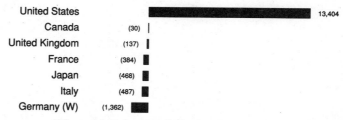

Billions of dollars at official exchange rates, 1987

	BALANCE OF PAYMENTS		
	RECEIPTS	PAYMENTS	BALANCE
United States	22281	8877	13404
Ireland	785	359	426
Sweden	149	52	97
Denmark	184	161	23
Portugal	4	33	-30
Canada	561	591	-30
Norway	28	77	-48
Australia	42	163	-121
United Kingdom	1535	1672	-137
Austria	41	194	-153
Belgium	177	389	-212
France	1348	1732	-384
Netherlands	301	688	-387
Japan	1490	1958	-468
Italy	301	788	-487
Spain	172	925	-753
Germany (W)	1081	2443	-1362

Figure 6–7

Data is for 1987.
Balance of payments: millions of dollars at official exchange rates.
Source: Organization for Economic Cooperation and Development (1).

7 Foreign Exchange

Throughout the 1980s, policymakers groped for a universal system — or nonsystem — to replace the fixed-rate exchange system abandoned in 1973. The United States and Japan entered the decade committed to a floating-rate system consistent with the growing movement toward unfettered flows of capital. Members of the European Community opened the decade with a new European Monetary System (EMS) aimed at creating a near-fixed exchange system based on a basket of key currencies moving within narrow bands.

Both beginnings were challenged by unexpected events. In mid-decade, the United States relented on its pledges of nonintervention and was leading coordinated central-bank assaults on market rates in order to bring down the high-flying dollar. At the same time, the European Community reawakened its dormant plan for full economic and monetary union by the end of the century — a plan that included irrevocably fixed exchange rates and a common currency. Some economists talked of adding the dollar and the yen to the European basket of currencies.

The unexpected event that challenged both systems was the need for a global adjustment to the large imbalances of the US economy. For developed economies, this meant exchange rates that kept up a steady flow of capital into the United States to help finance growing budget and trade deficits too large to be financed by domestic savings. The counterpart of this capital flow was an ever-growing trade surplus with the rest of the world. Because Germany trades mostly within Europe, the entire continent felt the stimulus. Japan's surplus savings flowed into the United States and its Asian neighbors. Its trade surpluses grew — mostly with the US, its main trading partner.

By 1985, the dollar was so high that it was dangerously accelerating growth of the US trade deficits and throwing the global trading system further out of balance. Some economists said — as they had been saying for five years — that the dollar would fall of its own weight sooner or later. Others, including the US treasury secretary, said that only concerted action would bring it down. Thereafter, annual meetings of the G–7 finance ministers included judgments on whether the dollar was too high or too low or just right, with the unveiled threat of coordinated intervention in the markets by central banks if the dollar strayed outside its limits (which were a tightly held secret). At times this intervention was massive: some $2 billion a day in 1988 to bring the dollar up, and about the same to bring it down again the next year.

The new interventionist regime seemed to accomplish its main purpose; external imbalances narrowed and the dollar was reasonably stable by 1991.

Meanwhile, the European Commuity moved resolutely toward monetary and economic union, setting ambitious goals for the rest of the century.

The goals of stage one, beginning in 1990, are to complete the infrastructure for an "internal financial space" and to see all EC members join the Exchange Rate Mechanism (ERM, the operational arm of EMS, the European Monetary System). The United Kingdom reluctantly joined the ERM in 1990, commiting itself to keep its currency within plus or minus 6% of its central rate versus the Deutsche mark. Italy agreed to narrow its margin to the standard 2.25% from 6%. Greece and Portugal had not joined the ERM in 1991. But outside the European Community, Norwegian officials agreed to keep the krone within 2.25% of the central rate, and Sweden committed its krona to a narrow band of 1.5%.

The main goal of stage two, set to begin in 1994, is to establish a European System of Central Banks (ESCB, popularly known as the Eurofed), which will eventually control a centralized monetary system.

In stage three, from 1997 to the end of the century, the Eurofed would take firm control of the monetary system; exchange rates would be irrevocably fixed; and the European Community — doubtless much enlarged by then — would have a single currency, the ecu, for public, business, and household transactions.

The ecu already exists as a basket of currencies, used mostly as a common denominator for official EC purposes. It is also increasingly used as a denominator for sovereign and supranational bond offerings. During the transition to a single currency, the ecu will coexist with national currencies. One test of the efficacy of the ERM is how often the ecu is revalued. Experience is encouraging. The ecu basket was revalued seven times from its inception in 1979 to 1983, only rarely over the next four years — and not at all since 1987. [Historical footnote: the name "ecu" (pronounced ay-KOO) is an acronym for European currency unit, and at the same time resurrects of the name of a coin used throughout Europe during the Renaissance.]

Exchange rates of developing economies are formally or informally tied to those of the developed economies. Besides this, the interest rates and trade policies of the developed economies critically influence current-account balances and thereby the perceived need of developing economies to adjust their exchange rates to encourage exports.

Throughout the 1980s, the yen and the mark fluctuated wildly against the dollar, with the rest of the world's currencies following suit. By 1985, the dollar was 31% higher than it was in 1981, measured against the currencies of US trading partners.

The dollar began climbing against the yen in 1978; by 1985 it was 13% higher. Similarly, the dollar rose 30% against the D-mark between 1980 and 1985.

At the now-famous Plaza accords in September 1985, finance ministers of the G–7 committed themselves to bringing down the dollar. And down it came, for whatever reasons.

By the end of 1990, the dollar had fallen 34% against US trading partners. The yen rose 39% and the mark 45% against the dollar in that period.

On the basis of purchasing-power parities, the dollar is still "undervalued." However, some analysts think that the global stocks of financial assets shifted so much during the 1980s that only a long period of undervaluation will help bring up US competitiveness to a level where the "correct" value of the dollar can be maintained.

Exchange rates of major currencies

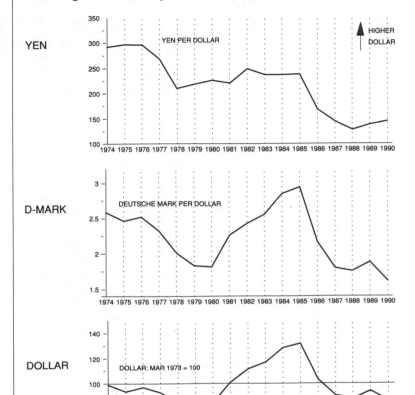

	DOLLAR	YEN	DMARK
1974	99.2	291.84	2.5868
1975	93.9	296.78	2.4614
1976	97.2	296.45	2.5185
1977	93.0	268.62	2.3236
1978	84.2	210.39	2.0097
1979	83.1	219.02	1.8343
1980	84.8	226.63	1.8175
1981	100.9	220.63	2.2632
1982	111.7	249.06	2.4281
1983	117.1	237.55	2.5539
1984	128.5	237.46	2.8455
1985	131.9	238.47	2.9420
1986	103.3	168.35	2.1705
1987	90.6	144.60	1.7981
1988	88.0	128.17	1.7570
1989	94.2	138.07	1.8808
1990	86.4	145.00	1.6166

Figure 7–1

Multilateral trade-weighted value of the dollar; March 1973 = 100.
Yen and mark are currency units per dollar.
Source: Council of Economic Advisers (1).

An "effective" exchange rate pairs a currency against a trade-weighted average of other currencies. Using this measure, the currencies of Taiwan, Singapore, Spain, South Korea, and Canada appreciated more than those of other developed economies in the period 1987–1990. Italy's lira was unchanged, along with the pound sterling, Swiss franc and Norwegian krone. Both the yen and the dollar depreciated.

Going back to 1980, the Danish krone was the biggest gainer among the currencies of developed economies, measured in real (inflation-adjusted) terms against currencies of either developing or other developed economies. The yen and mark appreciated slightly in both pairings. The dollar was lower in 1990 than it was in 1980.

Trends in effective exchange rates in selected economies

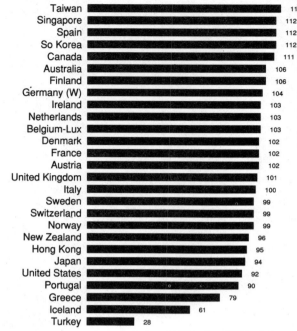

Index of 1990 rates; 1987 = 100

Source: Organization for Economic Cooperation and Development (4).

Figure 7–2

Real effective exchange rates of developed economies

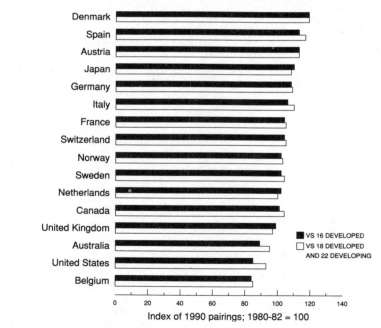

Index of 1990 pairings; 1980-82 = 100

Source: J P Morgan (1).

Purchasing power parities (PPP) are a way of defining an exchange rate — one that would allow a shopper to buy the same basket of goods for the same price in a reference currency, usually the US dollar.

Although even the architects of PPPs say that they shouldn't be used as the sole measure of a currency's value, it indicates trends and relative values.

Using PPP-derived rates, only the currencies of Turkey, Portugal, Greece, and Spain were "undervalued" in 1989. By definition, the US dollar was exactly "right" when measured against its own purchasing power, although it was significantly "undervalued" in relation to the mark and yen.

Effective exchange rates of developed economies

	AGAINST 16 DEVELOPED		AGAINST 18 DEVELOPED + 22 DEVELOPING
	NOMINAL	REAL	REAL
Denmark	105	118	119
Spain	82	113	117
Austria	112	111	113
Japan	157	106	108
Germany (W)	125	107	109
Italy	81	106	110
France	88	104	104
Switzerland	121	102	105
Norway	85	102	103
Sweden	79	103	104
Netherlands	116	99	100
Canada	101	104	104
United Kingdom	79	95	97
Australia	62	94	95
United States	87	88	93
Belgium	98	84	85

Effective exchange rates = weighted for trading partners.
Index of 1990 pairings;1980-82 average = 100.
Each currency vs weighted composite of the others.
Real = adjusted for changes in consumer prices.
Source: J P Morgan (1).

Figure 7–3

OECD exchange rates

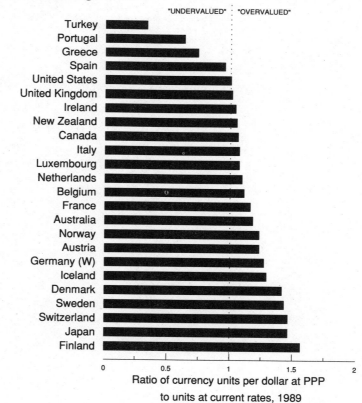

Ratio of currency units per dollar at PPP
to units at current rates, 1989

Based on PPPs, the yen appreciated 23% in the 1980s, while the mark appreciated 12%. Both currencies were still "overvalued" at the end of the decade.

Projections of "spot" (nominal) rates for 1991 have both the yen and mark appreciating significantly. Indeed, only a few currencies depreciated in terms of the dollar: those of Greece, Turkey, Taiwan, and South Korea.

Current and PPP-based exchange rates in OECD economies

	MONETARY UNIT	EXCH RATES PER US$	PER SDR	PPP FOR GDP 1989	INDEX	1980
Turkey	Lira	2120	2717	708	0.33	39
Portugal	Escudo	157.1	201.4	98.6	0.63	31.6
Greece	Drachma	162.1	207.8	120	0.74	39.2
Spain	Peseta	118.4	151.8	112	0.95	71.3
United States	Dollar	1.0	1.282	1.00	1.00	1.00
United Kingdom	Pound	0.611	0.783	0.620	1.01	0.522
Ireland	Punt	0.706	0.905	0.734	1.04	0.553
New Zealand	Dollar	1.674	2.146	1.76	1.05	1.02
Canada	Dollar	1.184	1.518	1.26	1.06	1.17
Italy	Lira	1372	1759	1466	1.07	862
Luxembourg	Franc	38.40	50.51	41.1	1.07	40.5
Netherlands	Guilder	2.121	2.719	2.32	1.09	2.76
Belgium	Franc	39.40	50.51	43.7	1.11	43.3
France	Franc	6.380	8.179	7.38	1.16	6.00
Australia	Dollar	1.265	1.622	1.49	1.18	1.07
Norway	Krone	6.903	8.85	8.48	1.23	7.43
Austria	Schilling	13.23	19.96	16.3	1.23	16.8
Germany (W)	Deutsche mark	1.880	2.41	2.39	1.27	2.72
Iceland	Krona	57.11	73.22	73.7	1.29	6.87
Denmark	Krone	7.310	9.372	10.3	1.41	8.69
Sweden	Krona	6.446	8.264	9.21	1.43	6.97
Switzerland	Franc	1.635	2.096	2.39	1.46	2.48
Japan	Yen	138	176.9	202	1.46	262
Finland	Mark	4.288	5.497	6.67	1.56	5.08

Figure 7–4

PPP = Purchasing Power Parity: the sum of money, at current exchange rates, which will buy the same basket of goods and services in pairs of countries (usually compared with the United States).
Index = ratio of currency units per dollar at PPP to units per dollar at the current exchange rate. An index greater than 1 suggests that, at PPP, the local currency at its present exchange rate is overvalued relative to the US$.
Source: Organization for Economic Cooperation and Development (1).

Spot rates in OECD economies

	1990	1991		1990	1991
United States	1.000	1.000	Netherlands	1.821	1.684
Japan	144.100	127.300	Norway	6.257	5.822
Germany (W)	1.616	1.492	Portugal	142.200	130.700
France	5.442	5.013	Spain	101.800	93.800
Italy	1198	1122	Sweden	5.914	5.566
United Kingdom	0.562	0.509	Switzerland	1.391	1.280
Canada	1.167	1.159	Turkey	2629	3405
Austria	11.370	10.500	Australia	1.278	1.275
Belgium-Lux	33.420	30.750	New Zealand	1.673	1.630
Denmark	6.184	5.709	Singapore	1.809	1.700
Finland	3.818	3.557	Taiwan	26.690	27.270
Greece	158.400	165.100	So Korea	708.200	715.500
Iceland	58.440	55.120	Hong Kong	7.789	7.796
Ireland	0.604	0.556			

Table 7–1

Spot rates, national currency per US dollar. 1991 figures are projections.
Source: Organization for Economic Cooperation and Development (4).

The volatility of the world's main currencies, measured against the US dollar, followed roughly similar patterns in the second half of the 1980s, with the Japanese yen showing slightly less volatility in 1986 and 1987. The most-volatile currency was the pound sterling in the most-volatile year, 1985.

Measuring exchange-rate changes from various milestones to November 1990 tells the same story as other data. The yen and mark have been gaining value since the early 1970s — although at smaller and smaller rates. This tends to support the view that the Plaza accords in 1985 confirmed a robust trend rather than reversed one. Changes in the dollar are near mirror images of trends in the yen and mark — except for the dollar's sharp drop from its peak in March 1985.

Volatility of main currencies vs US dollar

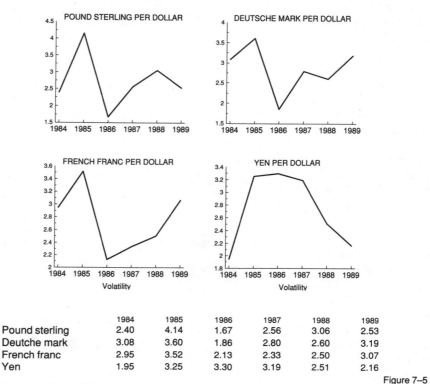

	1984	1985	1986	1987	1988	1989
Pound sterling	2.40	4.14	1.67	2.56	3.06	2.53
Deutche mark	3.08	3.60	1.86	2.80	2.60	3.19
French franc	2.95	3.52	2.13	2.33	2.50	3.07
Yen	1.95	3.25	3.30	3.19	2.51	2.16

Figure 7–5

Changes in currencies vs US dollar.
Volatility = standard deviation of monthly proportionate changes versus the US dollar in average exchange rates over the period.
Source: International Monetary Fund (5).

Exchange-rate changes in main currencies

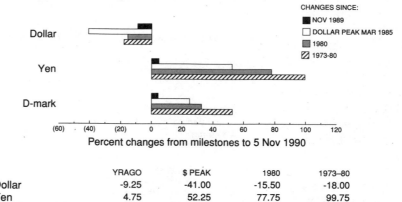

Percent changes from milestones to 5 Nov 1990

	YRAGO	$ PEAK	1980	1973–80
Dollar	-9.25	-41.00	-15.50	-18.00
Yen	4.75	52.25	77.75	99.75
Deutsche mark	4.50	25.00	32.50	52.50

Figure 7–6

Percentage changes to 5 Nov 1990 from milestones.
Yrago = Nov 1989. $ Peak = dollar peak 4–8 Mar 1985. 1980 average rate. 1973–80 average rate.
Source: Organization for Economic Cooperation and Development (4).

While the yen and mark were rising rapidly against the dollar in the second half of the decade, the yen was slowly falling against the D-mark.

In early 1990, the dollar began rising vs the yen, reaching its highest level of four years before falling back again. In Feb 1991, the dollar hit an alltime low (DM1.45) vs the German currency.

The ecu, European Currency Unit, is a basket of currencies moving within narrow bands relative to "central rates." The accompanying table translates those rates into currency units per ecu.

The SDR (Special Drawing Right) is the reserve currency of the International Monetary Fund, available to members for working out temporary trade-payments problems. The IMF has allocated 21.4 billion SDR to its members since the SDR was created in 1970. Members use about SDR12 billion annually to purchase each other's currencies as they need them to balance their trade accounts. The IMF has committed over SDR15 billion in special-purpose adjustment loans to lower- and middle-income members.

Changes in foreign exchange cross rates

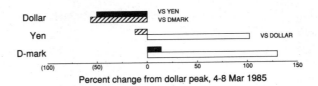

Percent change from dollar peak, 4-8 Mar 1985

	DOLLAR	YEN	DMARK
Vs yen	-50.58		13.76
Vs D-mark	-56.56	-12.1	
Vs dollar		102.35	130.2

Figure 7–7

Percent changes from dollar peak, 4-8 Mar 1985.
Source: Organization for Economic Cooperation and Development (4).

Composition of the European Currency Unit (ecu)

Belgian franc	42.4032
Danish krone	7.84195
Deutsche mark	2.05586
Spanish paseta	133.631
French franc	6.89509
Irish pound	0.767417
Italian lira	1538.24
Luxembourg franc	42.4032
Dutch guilder	2.31643
Pound sterling	0.696904
Greek drachma	205.311
Portugese escudo	178.735
US dollar*	1.31

Table 7–2

National currency rates per ecu, as of October 8, 1990.
*As of Sept 27, 1990.
Source: European Community (3).

Composition of the IMF's Special Drawing Right (SDR)

	CURRENCY AMOUNT	EXCHANGE RATE	US DOLLAR EQUIVALENT	CURRENCY UNITS PER SDR
US dollar	0.572	1.00000	0.57200	1.33456
Deutsche mark	0.453	1.74780	0.259183	2.33802
French franc	0.800	5.93500	0.134794	7.93996
Japanese yen	31.800	136.96000	0.232185	182.835
Pound sterling	0.0812	1.67980	0.13640	0.791344
SDR			1.42872	

US$ 1 = SDR 0.749310

Table7–3

Exchange rates per US dollar are for Aug 26, 1991.
US dollar equivalent of an SDR is that required to purchase an SDR at market rates.
Currency units per SDR are those required to purchase an SDR in local currencies.
Currencies per SDR are for Aug 26, 1991.
Source: International Monetary Fund (9).

Foreign Exchange

Early in the 1980s, the SDR basket attracted attention as a stable alternative to the then-high dollar and was used for awhile to denominate official and private (non-IMF) bond issues. This private use of the SDR fell off in the mid–1980s when the dollar declined. The ecu is currently preferred as a currency basket for private use.

In terms of volatility — irregularity of changes — Argentina's austral was the developing world's most erratic currency in the second half of the 1980s. Its changes, mostly downward, averaged over 12% a month. Brazil's crusado was almost as volatile in its generally downward movements.

Volatility of developing-economy currencies vs US dollar

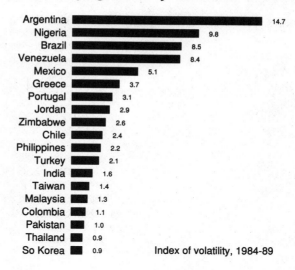

Index of volatility, 1984-89

	VOLATILITY	CHANGE
Argentina	14.70	-12.25
Nigeria	9.79	-2.97
Brazil	8.46	-11.97
Venezuela	8.35	-2.45
Mexico	5.11	-4.15
Greece	3.66	-0.26
Portugal	3.10	0.25
Jordan	2.92	-0.71
Zimbabwe	2.62	-0.63
Chile	2.36	-1.35
Philippines	2.23	-0.14
Turkey	2.12	-2.67
India	1.61	-0.49
Taiwan	1.38	0.70
Malaysia	1.27	-0.17
Colombia	1.12	-2.16
Pakistan	1.02	-0.53
Thailand	0.88	0.10
So Korea	0.88	0.34

Figure 7–8

For the years 1984–89.
The exchange rate of a country's currency changes from month to month vs the US dollar. (The changes can be large or small and still have a low volatility, if they are consistent.)
Volatility = the standard deviation of monthly changes.
Changes = mean of monthly percent changes.
Source: International Finance Corporation (2).

The currencies of most Asian developing countries depreciated during the 1980s. Exceptions were those of Myanmar and the four newly-industrializing economies: Hong Kong, Taiwan, South Korea, and Singapore.

At the other end of the scale, China's yuan lost almost half its value in the 1980s. Most of the loss was induced by an austerity program set in place to slow down too-rapid growth in the early part of the decade. The program culminated in a 21% devaluation in mid-December 1989.

The sharp drop in Indonesia's rupiah is attributed almost entirely to the collapse of oil prices and exchange rates in mid-decade.

Exchange rates rose in most Latin American economies during the 1980s. The main exception was Brazil's reinstated cruzeiro, which fell by one-quarter — most of it in early 1990 — as the new president initiated drastic measures to choke off hyperinflation.

Real effective exchange rates of Asian developing economies

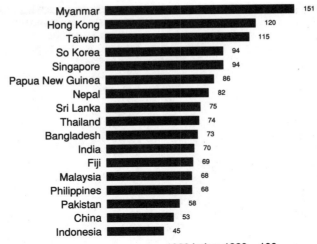

1989 index; 1980 = 100

Figure 7–9

Real effective exchange rates = nominal rates adjusted for inflation and weighted for trading partners.
Source: Asian Development Bank (1).

Real effective exchange rates in Latin America

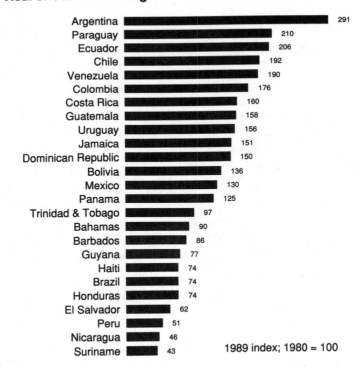

1989 index; 1980 = 100

Figure 7–10

Source: Inter-American Development Bank (1).

8 Balance of Payments

The balance-of-payments accounting system records the financial relations between each national economy and its trading partners. Imbalances in the accounts of the main trading economies generate powerful financial forces that drive global markets, as private players and both national and international policymakers react to pressures transmitted through interest and exchange rates.

The 1980s began with a surge of current-account imbalances among the main trading economies — huge, growing deficits in the United States and corresponding surpluses in Japan and Germany.

In the balance-of-payments accounting system, deficits or surpluses in an economy's current account (trade in goods and services plus investment income) must be offset by inflows or outflows of funds from the capital accounts — direct investments, purchases of stocks and bonds, and bank deposits.

The need for massive flows of capital into the United States translated into an appreciating dollar that reached its peak in March 1985. A few months later, leaders of the seven main developed economies (G–7) agreed to coordinate internal policies and, when necessary, intervene in the exchange markets. The goal was to bring down the dollar, thereby enhancing US competitiveness in world trade and helping to reduce the current-account deficit.

Later in the decade, the US current account was on its way down, as was Japan's surplus. Germany's surplus remained high through the decade, but by mid–1991, it had turned into a deficit.

By 1990, net purchases of United States bonds by foreigners declined sharply. Indeed, in that year, for the first time ever, Japanese investors were net sellers of US Treasury securities. Reductions in the US current account did not equal the reductions in Japanese investment, but tens of billions of foreign dollars flowed into the US economy via unaccounted-for routes identified only as "errors and omissions."

The German current-account surpluses impelled net outflows of portfolio investments (stocks and bonds), most of which went to fellow states of the European Community. German investors also increased their direct investments in Europe while decreasing them in the United States.

Looking ahead, economists see the 1990s as a quieter decade than its predecessor in terms of world trade. They expect current-account surpluses and deficits to continue to converge, thereby lessening the pressure on global capital flows. Some see the 1990s as a time when investors and bankers prefer to do business at home.

The United States current-account deficit dropped sharply in 1991, a one-time effect of payments received from its allies to cover the costs of the Gulf war. Even so, by 1992, the US deficit is forecast to be only about a third of what it was at its peak in 1987. Expert opinion is divided about whether it will ever reach zero — or even if it should, since it stimulates world trade.

Meantime, the US net international investment position continues to get worse. This measure of the economy's global assets and liabilities, sometimes referred to as its external debt, will reach one trillion dollars by mid-decade. This measure is roughly the accumulation of the economy's current-account deficits, so it will not even begin to go down until this account turns positive.

Current-account balances of the United States and Japan narrowed in the later years of the 1980s, after diverging widely in the early years. Germany's surplus remained high, though it was expected to fall in 1992 and through at least mid-decade as the economy coped with the financial demands of unification.

Net direct investment is a vehicle, of growing importance, for acquiring ownership or management control of foreign assets. For most of the decade, direct investment flowed into the United States, offsetting part of its massive current-account deficits. Indeed, from 1981–88, the US absorbed over half of all foreign direct investment. But in 1990, the US placed more abroad than it absorbed from abroad.

Japan's outward investments continued to grow in the latter years of the decade, even as its trade surplus declined.

Germany and the United Kingdom reversed earlier trends, as inward investments exceeded outward. France accelerated the pace of its net outward investments.

Current-account balances

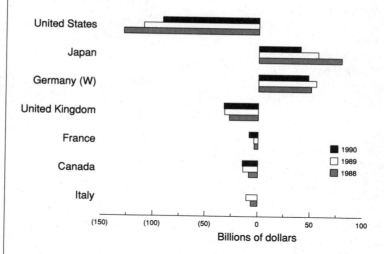

Net direct investment

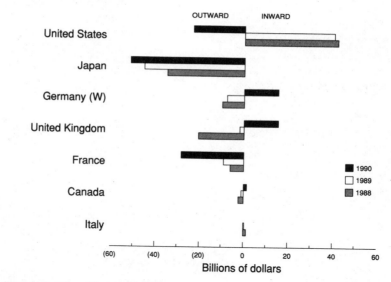

Source: International Monetary Fund (7).

The accompanying table summarizes the balance-of-payments accounts of the G–7 economies. In accounting logic, the current account must equal the algebraic sum of all the capital-account items. The "errors and omissions" item has become a substantial factor for every economy — especially the United States, where in 1990 its $71 billion outweighed all of the identified capital flows. (Errors and omissions can occur in either the trade or capital flows.)

Errors and omissions were also a large factor in Germany's balance of payments, in 1990 almost equaling its investments in foreign bonds. In the United Kingdom's accounts, errors and omissions outweighed all other capital flows.

Throughout the 1980s, the United States was the developed world's biggest taker of foreign direct investment. Inflows exceeded outflows by a wide margin, serving to partially offset very large current-account deficits.

Balance of payments of main developed economies

	CURRENT ACCOUNT BALANCE	NET DIRECT INVEST-MENT	PORTFOLIO BONDS	EQUITIES	BANK FLOWS	OTHER	CHANGES IN RESERVS	ERRORS AND OMISS
US								
1988	-129.0	42.2	41.7	-1.4	16.1	2.5	36.3	-8.3
1989	-110.0	40.5	54.9	-10.1	8.2	10.8	-16.8	22.6
1990 (3Q)	-69.0	-17.4	-1.9	-15.7	27.0	14.1	8.9	53.7
1990 (proj)	-92.0	-23.2	-2.5	-20.9	36.0	18.8	11.9	71.6
1990 (act)	-99.3							
JAPAN								
1988	79.6	-34.7	-56.6	3.8	38.4	-17.1	-16.5	3.1
1989	57.0	-45.2	-21.6	-10.9	3.7	26.1	12.8	-21.8
1990 (2Q)	20.2	-25.7	1.3	-18.0	-14.0	30.8	9.8	-4.4
1990 (proj)	40.4	-51.4	2.6	-36.0	-28.0	61.6	19.6	-8.8
1990 (act)	35.7							
GERMANY (W)								
1988	50.5	-9.9	-36.4	-7.3	-2.8	-14.9	18.4	2.4
1989	55.4	-7.7	-12.1	7.6	-25.0	-32.1	10.6	3.0
1990 (3Q)	36.0	11.6	-15.8	-1.7	-2.2	-15.9	-2.4	14.0
1990 (proj)	48.0	15.5	-21.1	-2.3	-2.9	-21.2	-3.2	18.7
1990 (act)	44.5							
UK								
1988	-27.3	-20.5	3.0	3.6	18.5	6.9	1.9	14.0
1989	-32.1	-1.8	-15.5	-24.3	20.4	11.4	16.2	25.7
1990 (3Q)	-24.4	11.8	-6.3	8.7	-14.5	0.1	6.6	17.8
1990 (proj)	-32.5	15.7	-8.4	11.6	-19.3	0.1	8.8	23.7
1990 (act)	-22.8							
FRANCE								
1988	-3.5	-6.0	6.8	0.9	3.8	-3.1	0.1	0.9
1989	-3.8	-9.1	16.8	5.6	5.2	-15.2	2.5	-1.9
1990 (2Q)	-4.3	-14.1	8.6	3.2	33.3	-16.7	-6.0	-4.3
1990 (proj)	-8.6	-28.2	17.2	6.4	66.6	-33.4	-12.0	-8.6
1990 (act)	-7.5							
CANADA								
1988	-8.2	-2.3	12.9	-2.8	3.2	8.2	-7.6	-3.4
1989	-14.1	-1.0	13.1	2.6	-0.7	4.9	-0.3	-4.6
1990 (3Q)	-10.7	1.1	7.2	-0.4	5.3	2.1	-0.7	-3.8
1990 (proj)	-14.3	1.5	9.6	-0.5	7.1	2.8	-0.9	-5.1
1990 (act)	-13.7							
ITALY								
1988	-6.2	1.3	0.4		8.0	4.0	-7.5	
1989	-10.6	0.5	3.3		11.1	11.5	-11.1	-4.6
1990 (act)	-15.7							

Figure 8–1

Billions of dollars. For changes in reserves: (–) = decrease.
Source: International Monetary Fund (7).

Main flows of direct investment

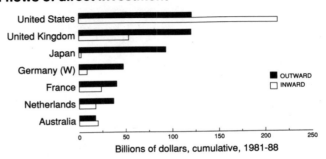

Billions of dollars, cumulative, 1981-88

The flow of direct investment by OECD economies follows the course of the post-World War II global economy.

In the 1960s, when the United States as the world's pre-eminent exporter generated current-account surpluses, it accounted for 66% of all outward investment. By the end of the 1980s, the US share was down to 22%. Over that period, inward investment grew from 15% to 54% of the OECD total.

The United Kingdom's share of the outward investment doubled over the two decades, while its share of inward investments was doubling in the 1970s and then falling back to the earlier level.

Japan's share of outward investments grew from 2% of the OECD total in the 1960s to 17% in the 1980s, most of it in the last decade. Meanwhile, its economy absorbed less than 1% of total investment in the 1980s.

Mexico and Argentina hosted about three-fifths of Latin America's total inward investment in 1989.

Direct investment, OECD economies

OUTWARD	1961-70	% SHARE	1971-80	% SHARE	1981-88	% SHARE
United States	46.822	66.3	134.354	44.4	121.230	21.6
United Kingdom	7.398	10.5	55.112	18.2	120.520	21.4
Japan	1.438	2.0	18.052	6.0	93.672	16.7
Germany (W)	4.091	5.8	23.130	7.7	47.745	8.5
France	2.641	3.7	13.940	4.6	40.556	7.2
Netherlands	2.692	3.8	27.829	9.2	36.926	6.6
Canada	1.483	2.1	11.335	3.7	29.437	5.2
Italy	1.667	2.4	3.597	1.2	18.805	2.4
Australia	0.493	0.7	2.510	0.8	17.592	3.1
Sweden	1.074	1.5	4.597	1.5	11.400	2.0
Switzerland					8.877	1.6
Norway	0.060	0.1	1.079	0.4	5.379	1.0
Belgium-Lux	0.323	0.5	3.213	1.1	5.131	0.9
Finland	0.146	0.2	0.605	0.2	5.024	0.9
Spain	0.090	0.1	1.274	0.4	2.654	0.5
Austria	0.055	0.1	0.578	0.2	1.591	0.3
Denmark	0.103	0.1	1.063	0.4	0.476	0.1
Portugal			0.038		0.070	
Total	**70.576**	**100**	**302.306**	**100**	**561.635**	**100**
INWARD						
United States	6.282	14.9	56.276	30.0	213.690	53.8
United Kingdom	4.310	10.2	40.503	21.6	53.940	13.6
France	2.804	6.7	16.908	9.0	24.127	6.1
Australia	5.402	12.8	11.295	6.0	20.329	5.1
Netherlands	2.294	5.5	10.822	5.8	17.771	4.5
Spain	1.201	2.9	7.060	3.8	16.870	4.3
Italy	3.634	8.6	5.698	3.0	16.148	2.3
Germany (W)	6.270	15.0	13.957	7.4	8.716	2.2
Belgium-Lux	1.358	3.2	9.215	4.9	8.299	2.1
Switzerland					4.595	1.1
Canada	5.489	13.1	5.534	2.9	3.665	0.9
Greece					3.481	0.9
Japan	0.624	1.5	1.424	0.8	2.582	0.7
Austria	0.360	0.9	1.455	0.8	2.061	0.5
Norway	0.372	0.9	3.074	1.6	2.045	0.5
Sweden	0.889	2.1	0.897	0.5	1.955	0.5
Portugal			0.535	0.3	1.475	0.4
Ireland			1.659	0.9	0.919	0.2
Finland	0.081	0.2	0.376	0.2	0.754	0.2
Denmark	0.698	1.7	1.561	0.8	0.308	0.1
Total	**42.060**	**100**	**187.873**	**100**	**396.891**	**100**

Figure 8–2

Billions of dollars. Includes reinvested earnings.
For Belgium-Lux: 1965–70. For Portugal: 1975–80. For Switzerland: 1983–86.
Source: Organization for Economic Cooperation and Development (6).

Main hosts for foreign direct investment in Latin America

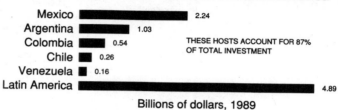

THESE HOSTS ACCOUNT FOR 87% OF TOTAL INVESTMENT

	Billions of dollars, 1989
Mexico	2.24
Argentina	1.03
Colombia	0.54
Chile	0.26
Venezuela	0.16
Latin America	4.89

Figure 8–3

Figures for Barbados, Costa Rica, Jamaica, and Uruguay are for 1988. Figure for Suriname is for 1987.
Source: Inter-American Development Bank (1).

In 1990, the United States purchased slightly more foreign bonds than it sold to foreigners, reversing a strong trend of the two previous years.

Japan's experience was the mirror image of that of the United States: in 1988 and 1989, Japanese investors bought far more foreign bonds (mostly in the United States and Pacific-Rim economies) than they sold in domestic and foreign markets.

Germans continued to be net investors in foreign bonds as the 1990s got underway.

US investors were net purchasers of foreign equities by an ever-growing margin. In Japan, too, investors bought more foreign securities than Japanese firms sold to all buyers. These net purchases abroad strongly reversed the actions of investors in 1988.

Investors in the United Kingdom swung sharply from being net buyers of foreign equities in 1989 to net investing abroad in 1990.

The flow of capital through banks continued to decline through the 1980s.

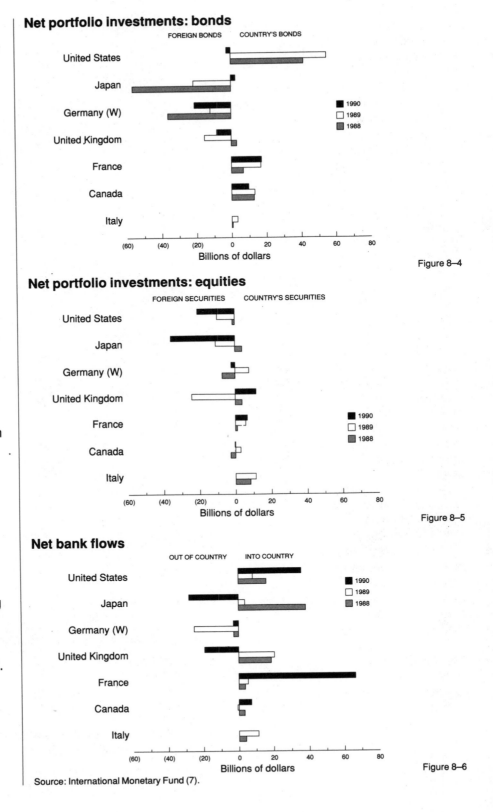

Net portfolio investments: bonds

Figure 8–4

Net portfolio investments: equities

Figure 8–5

Net bank flows

Figure 8–6

Source: International Monetary Fund (7).

Over the three years shown, the patternless buying and selling of reserves was a response to G–7 commitments to intervene in the exchange markets to meet goals for the value of their currencies.

Mergers and acquisitions (M&A) of European firms jumped ahead of those in other regions in 1990, reflecting managers' impulses to position their businesses for the European single market. These moves more than doubled in total value, compared with the previous year. In 1986, Europe was the destination for only about a tenth as much M&A activity as was North America (mainly the United States).

M&A activity in North America dropped 20% in 1990, compared with the previous year. In 1986, it had accounted for about three-fourths of such deals.

Japanese firms have been conspicuous non-players throughout the period.

Changes in reserves

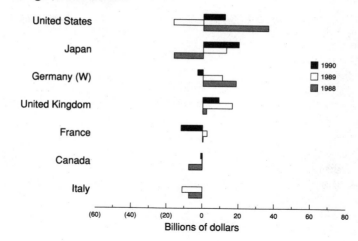

Figure 8–7

Cross-border mergers and acquisitions

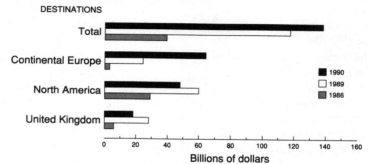

DESTINATIONS	1986 VALUE	1989 VALUE	1989 SHARE	1989 CHANGE	FIRST HALF 1990 VALUE	FIRST HALF 1990 SHARE	1990 (PROJ) VALUE	1990 (PROJ) CHANGE
Cont. Europe	3.2	24.2	21	656	32.0	46	64.0	164
North America	29.0	59.7	51	106	23.9	35	47.8	-20
United Kingdom	5.9	28.1	24	376	9.1	13	18.2	-35
Rest of world	1.1	5.4	5	391	4.0	6	8.0	48
Japan		0.1	0.1					
Total	**39.2**	**117.5**	**100**	**200**	**69.1**	**100**	**138.2**	**18**

Billions of dollars and percentages.
Source: International Monetary Fund (7).

Figure 8–8

The United States current-account deficits are offset by inflows from all of the capital accounts. The modest exception to this pattern was the purchase of official reserves in 1988 and, even more so, in 1989.

Net inward direct investments stayed strong through the 1980s.

Net portfolio sales to foreigners exceeded purchases by increasing amounts. (A reversal in bond sales in 1990 is not shown.)

Foreign bank deposits continued to decline in importance as capital inflows through the decade.

Errors and omissions grew in 1989 and (not shown) even more in 1990 as unaccounted-for inflows of trade receipts or capital.

United States balance of payments

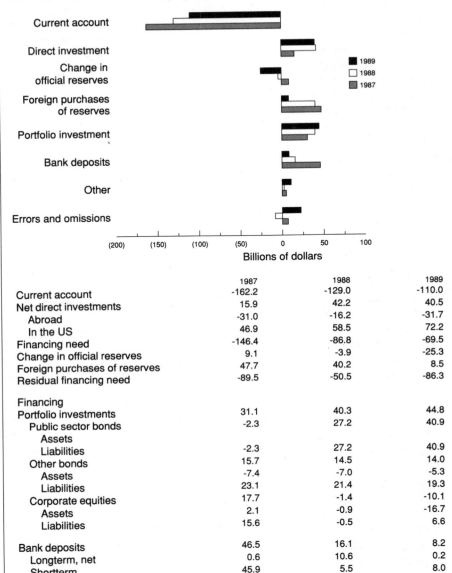

	1987	1988	1989
Current account	-162.2	-129.0	-110.0
Net direct investments	15.9	42.2	40.5
Abroad	-31.0	-16.2	-31.7
In the US	46.9	58.5	72.2
Financing need	-146.4	-86.8	-69.5
Change in official reserves	9.1	-3.9	-25.3
Foreign purchases of reserves	47.7	40.2	8.5
Residual financing need	-89.5	-50.5	-86.3
Financing			
Portfolio investments	31.1	40.3	44.8
Public sector bonds	-2.3	27.2	40.9
Assets			
Liabilities	-2.3	27.2	40.9
Other bonds	15.7	14.5	14.0
Assets	-7.4	-7.0	-5.3
Liabilities	23.1	21.4	19.3
Corporate equities	17.7	-1.4	-10.1
Assets	2.1	-0.9	-16.7
Liabilities	15.6	-0.5	6.6
Bank deposits	46.5	16.1	8.2
Longterm, net	0.6	10.6	0.2
Shortterm	45.9	5.5	8.0
Assets	-40.9	-57.3	-41.6
Liabilities	86.7	62.8	49.6
Other	5.3	2.5	10.8
Errors and omissions	6.7	-8.3	22.6

Figure 8–9

Billions of dollars. Note: The sign of a number indicates direction of money flow: + = into the country.
Everything below the current-account line is in the capital account, which must balance with the current account.
Deficits in the current account are balanced by direct investments, changes in official reserves, portfolio investments, and foreign deposits in domestic banks.
Portfolio investments exclude bonds held by foreign monetary authorities.
Source: International Monetary Fund (7).

The United States net investment position — sometimes referred to as its external debt — began to decline in 1982, when the current account went negative. A strong net positive position was totally eroded by mid–1985. Thereafter, the net position continued to decline and will as long as the current account is in deficit — even though that deficit is getting smaller.

The US government used to calculate the net investment position using historical valuation of US and foreign assets. In 1991 it changed its methods to present the information in alternative ways: measuring current costs (a kind of perpetual inventory) and estimating market values. Of three possibilities, the net position is worst using the historic method — in 1989, $664 billion. Using the current-cost method illustrated in the graph, the net position was $423 billion in 1990. Using the market-value method, the net position was $361 billion in 1990.

The choice of which method to use depends on the purposes for which the information is to be used.

The United States as the world's biggest "debtor"

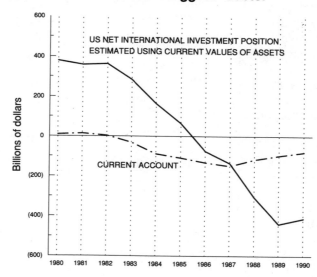

	CURR ACCT	NET INT'L INVESTMENT POSITION		
		CURR COST	MKT VALUE	HISTORIC
1980	8.4	379.623		
1981	14.1	359.441		
1982	2.5	363.993	258.473	136.703
1983	-31.5	284.970	224.124	89.004
1984	-88.2	163.972	111.034	-2.162
1985	-108.8	64.306	64.502	-117.214
1986	-131.4	-74.122	14.588	-273.686
1987	-149.7	-134.960	-42.237	-378.066
1988	-115.7	-305.976	-150.562	-531.084
1989	-96.6	-439.656	-267.711	-663.747
1990	-79.3	-412.163	-360.598	

Figure 8–10

Billions of dollars.
Note: Current-cost, market-value, and historic-value figures are alternative ways of estimating the US net international investment position. In 1991, the US Commerce Department discontinued using the historic-value method on the grounds that it does not accurately represent the current value of US assets abroad.
Source: US Department of Commerce (1).

Japan's current-account surpluses are offset primarily by direct foreign investments abroad, portfolio investments, and the purchase of reserves. In recent years, portfolio investments are playing a smaller role.

For some years, Japan has been a net taker of bank funds, mainly interbank deposits, but this inflow was virtually extinguished in 1989.

Errors and omissions are a growing factor, turning sharply toward net capital outflows in 1989.

Japan balance of payments

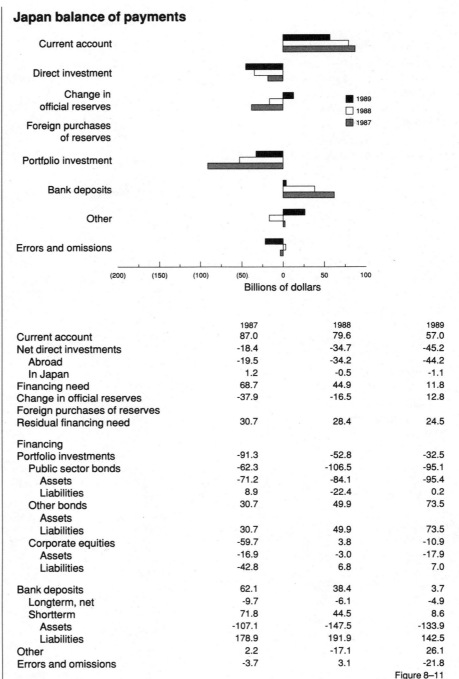

	1987	1988	1989
Current account	87.0	79.6	57.0
Net direct investments	-18.4	-34.7	-45.2
Abroad	-19.5	-34.2	-44.2
In Japan	1.2	-0.5	-1.1
Financing need	68.7	44.9	11.8
Change in official reserves	-37.9	-16.5	12.8
Foreign purchases of reserves			
Residual financing need	30.7	28.4	24.5
Financing			
Portfolio investments	-91.3	-52.8	-32.5
Public sector bonds	-62.3	-106.5	-95.1
Assets	-71.2	-84.1	-95.4
Liabilities	8.9	-22.4	0.2
Other bonds	30.7	49.9	73.5
Assets			
Liabilities	30.7	49.9	73.5
Corporate equities	-59.7	3.8	-10.9
Assets	-16.9	-3.0	-17.9
Liabilities	-42.8	6.8	7.0
Bank deposits	62.1	38.4	3.7
Longterm, net	-9.7	-6.1	-4.9
Shortterm	71.8	44.5	8.6
Assets	-107.1	-147.5	-133.9
Liabilities	178.9	191.9	142.5
Other	2.2	-17.1	26.1
Errors and omissions	-3.7	3.1	-21.8

Figure 8–11

Billions of dollars.
Note: The sign of a number indicates direction of money flow: + = into the country.
Everything below the current-account line is in the capital account, which must balance with the current account.
Deficits in the current account are balanced by direct investments, changes in official reserves, portfolio investments, and foreign deposits in domestic banks.
Portfolio investments exclude bonds held by foreign monetary authorities.
Source: International Monetary Fund (7).

Germany's current-account surpluses were offset primarily by bank deposits abroad and by "other" outward flows of capital.

Portfolio investment was strongly outward in 1988 but was not a big factor in other years.

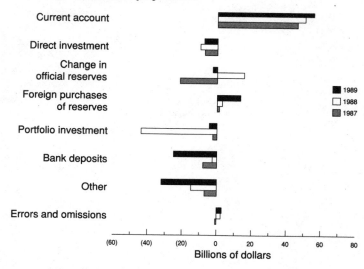

Germany balance of payments

Billions of dollars

	1987	1988	1989
Current account	46.1	50.5	55.4
Net direct investments	-7.3	-9.9	-7.7
Abroad	-9.2	-11.2	-13.6
In Germany	1.9	1.4	5.9
Financing need	38.8	40.6	47.8
Change in official reserves	-21.5	15.4	-2.8
Foreign purchases of reserves	1.2	3.0	13.4
Residual financing need	18.5	59.0	58.4
Financing			
Portfolio investments	-2.5	-43.8	-4.4
Public sector bonds	11.7	2.6	8.9
Assets			
Liabilities	11.7	2.6	8.9
Other bonds	-12.9	-39.0	-21.0
Assets	-13.6	-31.2	-21.5
Liabilities	0.7	-7.8	0.6
Corporate equities	-1.3	-7.3	7.6
Assets	-0.1	-10.3	-5.0
Liabilities	-1.2	3.0	12.6
Bank deposits	-8.0	-2.8	-25.0
Longterm, net	-1.3	6.9	6.3
Shortterm	-6.7	-9.6	-31.3
Assets	-8.8	-15.8	-43.2
Liabilities	2.1	6.2	12.0
Other	-7.1	-14.9	-32.1
Errors and omissions	-0.8	2.4	3.0

Figure 8–12

Billions of dollars.
Note: The sign of a number indicates direction of money flow: + = into the country.
Everything below the current-account line is in the capital account, which must balance with the current account.
Deficits in the current account are balanced by direct investments, changes in official reserves, portfolio investments, and foreign deposits in domestic banks.
Portfolio investments exclude bonds held by foreign monetary authorities.
Source: International Monetary Fund (7).

The United Kingdom off-
set its current-account
deficits mainly through
the receipt of bank
deposits by foreigners.
Recordkeeping errors
and omissions, along
with "other" capital in-
flows, also offset the
trade deficits.

In 1989, $40 billion
in portfolio investments
abroad added to the
payments deficit, sharp-
ly accelerating the
trend of the previous
two years.

United Kingdom balance of payments

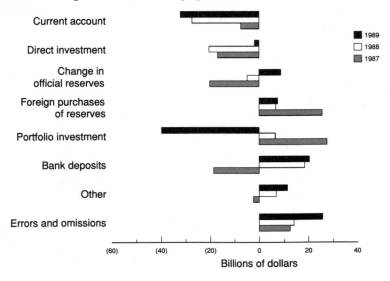

	1987	1988	1989
Current account	-7.4	-27.3	-32.1
Net direct investments	-17.0	-20.5	-1.8
Abroad	-31.1	-37.0	-32.0
In the UK	14.1	16.5	30.2
Financing need	-24.4	-47.8	-33.9
Change in official reserves	-20.2	-4.9	8.8
Foreign purchases of reserves	25.5	6.8	7.4
Residual financing need	-19.0	-45.9	-17.7
FINANCING			
Portfolio investments	27.6	6.5	-39.9
Public sector bonds	3.9	1.5	-2.7
Assets			
Liabilities	3.9	1.5	-2.7
Other bonds	11.8	1.5	-12.8
Assets	4.2	-12.2	-27.6
Liabilities	7.6	13.7	14.8
Corporate equities	11.9	3.6	-24.3
Assets	2.5	-5.6	-30.9
Liabilities	9.4	9.1	6.5
Bank deposits	-18.6	18.5	20.4
Longterm, net	1.8	1.0	1.0
Shortterm	-20.4	17.5	19.5
Assets	-86.8	-35.9	-50.9
Liabilities	66.4	53.4	70.4
Other	-2.4	6.9	11.4
Errors and omissions	12.5	14.0	25.7

Figure 8–13

Billions of dollars.
Note: The sign of a number indicates direction of money flow: + = into the country.
Everything below the current-account line is in the capital account, which must balance with the current
account.
Deficits in the current account are balanced by direct investments, changes in official reserves, portfolio
investments, and foreign deposits in domestic banks.
Portfolio investments exclude bonds held by foreign monetary authorities.
Source: International Monetary Fund (7).

9 Capital Markets

The global economy is most fully realized in financial markets, which every year get closer to the ideal of untrammeled flows of capital across transparent borders to markets governed only by supply and demand. Global capital markets are large: $250 trillion flow through the international bank-payments system yearly — more than ten times the value of all the goods and services produced in the world and fifty times the value of the global trade in goods and services.

Through almost all of the 1980s, capital flows were governed by growing current-account imbalances among the three main economies. In the later years of the decade, investment binges in the United States, Europe, and Japan — much of them fueled by borrowed money — inflated the value of assets and led eventually to recessions, first in the English-speaking economies: the United States, the United Kingdom, Canada, and Australia. The 1990s opened with a global mood of contraction, caution, and fears of a credit crunch — a newly unified Germany being the notable exception to all of these trends.

Meanwhile, regulators were rewriting the ground rules for international capital transactions. The trend to liberalize the flow of capital across national borders picked up speed and spread from the United States to the European Community and finally to Japan, whose policymakers were more reluctant to change apparently successful formulas for interest-rate control and managed capital flows. Augmenting the liberalization (deregulation) of capital flows and interest rates, a stream of financial innovations in private markets served to increase capital flows.

A necessary — though seemingly contradictory — counterpart of liberalization was a tightening of the regulations governing the growth of assets, particularly in banks. In 1988, the Basle Committee on Banking Supervision put out, and banking authorities of the main economies approved, a sweeping set of regulations that tightened capital standards and started a rush by international banks to increase the ratio of (primarily) equity capital to assets (mostly, loans). With the supply of equity capital shrinking at the same time, this led banks to dispose of some of the assets they had and/or to become increasingly stingy about acquiring new assets (mostly, loans). Many feared that this contraction would bring on a global credit crunch: banks unwilling to finance even sound projects by creditworthy borrowers.

Economists and policymakers worried that a credit crunch could only prolong and worsen the recession, which began in 1990.

Germany and Japan seemed immune from recession, for different reasons — although some analysts felt it was just a matter of time until those economies, too, turned down. In Germany, reunification triggered a burst of public and private investment in the eastern states. At the same time, massive unemployment led to massive outlays for social safety-nets. These outlays, some economists think, served as a Keynesian-style stimulus to the German economy. In Japan, the tightly linked capital markets were jolted by a drop in the stock market, which lost almost 30% of its value between December 29, 1989 and early April, 1990. This led to a repatriation of capital: foreign direct investments fell off, as did purchases of US Treasury bonds.

Interest rates and bond prices were the media transmitting these captial shifts. In the early 1980s, interest rates stayed high to assure the flow of capital into the United States to offset the growing trade deficits. But as the current-account disparities narrowed, the situation changed abruptly. By spring 1990, for the first time since the early 1970s, longterm nominal interest rates in the United States were at the same level as Germany's. Longterm rates in Japan started going up in 1989. By the end of 1990, amid evidence of weakness in the economy, US longterm rates were below the average of the main economies. This trend reversed in late 1990, as rates declined in most countries — although not in Germany until 1991. Japanese rates were expected to go down. Bond prices followed, inversely, the ups and downs of interest rates, serving as a banner proclaiming private investors' longterm expectations for inflation.

Capital markets in the developing economies were dominated by the debt crisis which suddenly emerged in 1982. For several years, many analysts feared that massive defaults could severely damage the whole global financial system. But in the later years of the decade, the debt problem came under control, and capital markets in the developing world were mostly perceived as insignificant. In 1990 and 1991, Mexico and Venezuela took the first steps of reentering the private bond markets.

Transitioning economies, too, were insignificant players in capital markets, although for awhile some analysts thought that new capital demands in eastern Germany, the USSR, and central and eastern Europe might contribute to a global capital crunch.

The outstanding value of domestic bonds matched almost exactly those of domestic equities in 1990 in the $25 trillion of outstanding securities of all kinds. The value of international bonds (those held by nonresidents, plus bonds issued by governments and international organizations) was well over twice the value of equities held by nonresidents. The $1.6 trillion in total outstandings of futures and options equaled those of international bonds.

At $3.35 trillion, net international bank credit was almost triple the value of new international bond financing and ten times the value of Euronote placements.

The markets for short- and medium-term Euronotes (especially the latter), jumped sharply in 1990, as bank credits tightened generally and some banks lost credit standing. The market for Euro commercial paper (shortterm loans not placed through banks) also more than doubled.

The share of dollar-denominated Euronotes declined somewhat in 1990, while more issues were denominated in ecus, Italian lire, yen, and sterling.

Structure of global financial markets

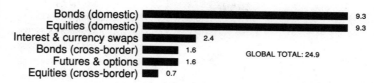

Outstandings in trillions of dollars, mid-1990

Figure 9–1

Domestic = assets held by residents, and bonds issued by all governments in the Euromarkets and by international organizations in all markets.
Cross-border = assets held by nonresidents, and bonds issued by all governments in the Euromarkets and by international organizations in all markets.
Source: J P Morgan (1).

Net new lending in international markets

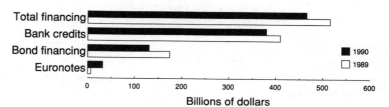

	1989	1990	STOCKS DEC90
Net international bank credit	410.0	380.0	3350.0
Net new Euronote placements	6.9	32.0	111.2
Net international bond financing	174.3	131.0	1472.5
Total net international financing*	**515.0**	**465.0**	**4375.0**

Figure 9–2

Billions of dollars.
International bank credits = cross-border claims in all currencies plus local claims in foreign currency.
*Adjusted for double counting.
Source: Bank for International Settlements (1).

The Euronote market

	1989	1990	% CHANGE 1990	STOCKS DEC90	SHARE
New facilities announced	**72.5**	**72.8**	**0**		
Euro-commercial paper	49.3	44.4	-10		
Other shortterm Euronotes	10.3	3.0	-71		
Medium-term notes	12.9	25.4	97		
Net new issues	**6.9**	**32.0**	**364**	**111.2**	**100**
Euro-commercial paper	5.3	11.8	123	70.3	63
Other shortterm Euronotes	-2.4	8.0	-433	19.1	17
Medium-term notes	4.0	12.3	208	21.9	20
Currency of new issues					
US dollars		17.0		84.0	76
Australian dollar		2.3		9.4	8
Ecu		4.9		8.4	8
Other		7.8		9.4	8

Table 9–1

Billions of dollars.
Source: Bank for International Settlements (1).

The United States market for commercial paper continued to grow robustly, reaching nearly one-fifth of total bank credit in 1990. Only Norway's market, at 13%, was comparable.

Longterm interest rates of United States bonds fell below those of every other G–7 economy in 1990 for the first time in nearly twenty years. Japanese rates dropped below those of the US and the G–7 average in early 1991.

Shortterm rates, more easily controllable by central-bank policy-makers, followed a similar pattern. Here, US rates had been forced below those of Japan and the G–7 average by early 1991, responding to the continuing recession.

Commercial paper markets

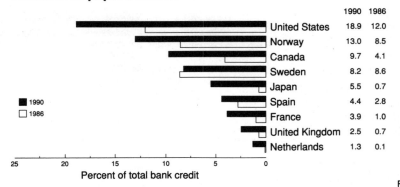

	1990	1986
United States	18.9	12.0
Norway	13.0	8.5
Canada	9.7	4.1
Sweden	8.2	8.6
Japan	5.5	0.7
Spain	4.4	2.8
France	3.9	1.0
United Kingdom	2.5	0.7
Netherlands	1.3	0.1

■ 1990
□ 1986

Percent of total bank credit

Figure 9–3

Amounts outstanding as percentages of bank credit to nonfinancial companies.
Japan's earlier figure is for 1987.
Spain's figures exclude substantial private placements.
Source: Bank for International Settlements (3).

Interest rates in main economies

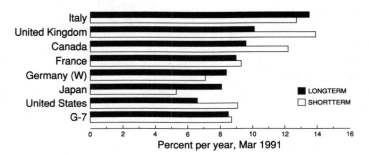

Percent per year, Mar 1991

■ LONGTERM
□ SHORTTERM

	1989	1990	MAR 1991
LONGTERM			
Italy	13.3	13.6	13.5
United Kingdom	10.2	11.7	10.1
Canada	9.9	10.8	9.6
France	8.8	10.0	9.0
Germany (W)	7.0	8.7	8.4
United States	8.5	8.6	8.1
Japan	5.1	7.0	6.6
G–7	8.1	9.0	8.5
SHORTTERM			
Italy	12.7	12.2	13.3
United Kingdom	13.9	14.8	12.4
Canada	12.2	13.0	9.9
France	9.3	10.3	9.6
Germany (W)	7.1	8.4	9.0
Japan	5.3	7.6	7.9
United States	9.1	8.1	6.5
G–7	8.7	9.1	8.4

Figure 9–4

Percent per year.
Longterm rates for ten-year instruments.
Shortterm rates for three-month instruments.
Source: Internatonal Monetary Fund (10).

Japan held the greatest total reserves (excluding gold) in 1990, as it had throughout the decade. Taiwan's small economy generated nearly SDR54 billion in 1990, more than those of the United States by a small margin. Germany's reserves, which had ranked highest in 1983, had fallen to fourth by 1990.

Japan also had the greatest reserves of foreign exchange, followed by Germany, Italy, and the United States.

At the end of 1990, the United States held by far the greatest amount of Special Drawing Rights (SDR), the reserve currency created by the International Monetary Fund.

Total international reserves of selected economies

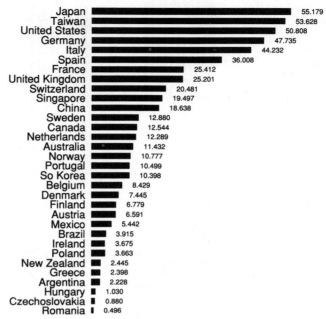

Billions of SDR, Dec 1990 or nearest month

	FOREIGN EXCHANGE 1990	TOTAL RESERVES		SDR HOLDINGS 1990
		1983	1990	
Japan	48.843	23.498	55.179	2.138
Taiwan		11.327	53.628	
United States	36.704	21.612	50.808	7.724
Germany	44.266	40.760	47.735	1.321
Italy	42.298	19.203	44.232	.729
Spain	34.722	7.070	36.008	.489
France	23.535	18.961	25.412	.902
United Kingdom	23.144	10.831	25.201	.878
Switzerland	20.480	14.360	20.481	.001
Singapore	19.346	8.849	19.497	.081
China	17.938	14.315	18.638	.395
Sweden	12.444	3.853	12.880	.204
Canada	11.108	3.310	12.544	1.073
Netherlands	11.266	9.715	12.289	.504
Australia	10.969	8.560	11.432	.218
Norway	10.054	6.332	10.777	.316
Portugal	10.355	.368	10.499	.040
So Korea	10.163	2.241	10.398	
Belgium	7.716	4.502	8.429	.398
Denmark	7.073	3.458	7.445	.152
Finland	6.475	1.182	6.779	.153

(MORE)

Developed economies held nearly 90% of all of the IMF's outstanding SDRs in 1990.

The accumulation of reserves by developing economies followed an erratic pattern of extreme ups and downs through the 1980s, reflecting the vicissitudes of managing current-account balances in an era of declining values for commodity exports.

International reserve positions, cont'd

	FOREIGN EXCHANGE 1990	TOTAL RESERVES 1983	1990	SDR HOLDINGS 1990
Austria	6.153	4.313	6.591	.196
Mexico	5.060	3.737	5.442	.293
Brazil	3.913	4.160	3.915	.008
Ireland	3.413	2.521	3.675	.158
Poland	3.663	.731	3.663	.001
New Zealand	2.400	.743	2.445	.0004
Greece	2.323	.860	2.398	.0002
Argentina	2.184	1.120	2.228	.209
Hungary	1.027	1.176	1.030	.001
Czechoslovakia	.527	.767	.880	
Romania	.420	.502	.496	.0001
All countries	**577.823**	**361.546**	**621.110**	**20.354**
Developed	372.757	206.184	409.371	17.615
Developing	205.066	155.362	211.740	2.739

Figure 9–5

Billions of SDR.
In descending order of total reserves, 1990.
Foreign exchange = monetary authorities' claims on nonresidents, certain claims on central banks, and some other types of claims.
Holdings in International Monetary Fund at yearend, 1990.
Total reserves: minus gold.
Source: International Monetary Fund (9).

Year-by-year accumulation of reserves in developing economies

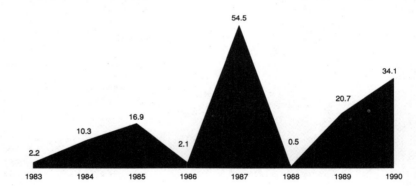

Billions of dollars.
Source: International Monetary Fund (7).

Figure 9–6

The official reserves of developing economies were substantially higher at the end of the decade than they were in 1983. Most of the growth was in the prospering Asian economies. The only group to lose reserves were the economies of the Middle East.

The ratio of reserves to imports also grew during the 1980s, most strongly in developing economies in Europe, which doubled the share of imports covered by official reserves.

Official reserves of developing economies

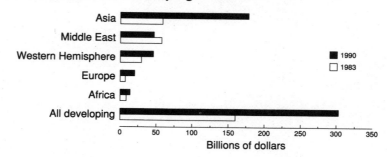

Reserves/import ratios of developing economies

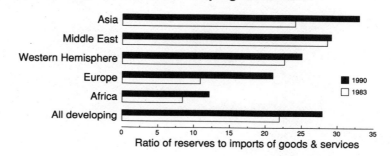

	RESERVES		IMPORT RATIO	
	1983	1990	1983	1990
Asia	58.6	178.1	24.1	33.0
Middle East	57.1	46.4	28.6	29.1
Western Hemisphere	29.3	45.2	22.6	25.0
Europe	6.9	19.5	10.9	21.0
Africa	7.9	13.8	8.4	12.1
All developing	**159.7**	**303.0**	**21.9**	**27.9**

Figure 9–7

Billions of dollars and percentages.
Ratio of reserves to imports of goods and services.
Source: International Monetary Fund (10).

10 Bond Markets

Innovation was the motif of all international financial markets in the 1980s, affecting every sector: bonds, banking, foreign exchange, interest rates, and even the conduct of monetary policy. The thrust to innovation originated in specific problems of the economic environment in the 1980s — changing regulations, expanding technology, volatile markets, growing competition. But it's most likely that the effects will outlast the causes. Not only the specific innovations of the 1980s, but the culture of innovation itself, will surely be the legacy of this period.

"Securitizaton" is a main thread in the web of innovations. In it, a creditworthy corporate borrower goes directly to the credit markets for funds rather than to a bank to syndicate a loan or line of credit. In the early 1980s, syndications fell fourfold while international bonds and notes grew in about the same proportion. In some cases, banks get involved by helping to arrange the credit for lesser-known corporate borrowers, or by enhancing the credit with their own endorsements.

Both the cause and effect of innovation is the globalization of financial markets. Deregulation and the dismantling of capital controls provided the opportunity, and technology provided the means for globalization, which is now linking international and national financial markets ever more tightly.

The payoff of innovation is greater efficiency in arranging and maintaining credits by providing a greater range of instruments and tailoring them to borrowers' requirements.

One of the main innovations of the 1980s is the Note Issuance Facility (NIF), an arrangement that enables a borrower to issue a stream of notes, known as Euronotes, over a medium-term period, bypassing bank syndication. NIFs evolved into a Euro-commercial paper (ECP) market. Between 1985 and 1990, the ECP market grew to $70 billion in outstandings.

Commercial paper markets have existed in the United States and Canada since before 1960, primarily for very short-term, unsecured notes. In 1990, outstandings in the US market were $558 billion. That amounted to nearly one-fifth of total US bank credits to nonfinancial companies and 70% of the world commercial paper market. Japan has the second-largest market, with outstandings of $117 billion. Other developed economies have also inaugurated commercial paper markets — Australia in the mid-1970s and others in the 1980s.

Currency or interest-rate swaps, forms of "derivative" instruments, were created in 1982. With these instruments, borrowers exchange streams of payments over time. Their purpose may be to lower costs or raise yields in their portfolios, to hedge risks, earn fees, or to speculate.

Currency and interest-rate options aren't new, but trading them is. Use of this type of instrument surged in the early 1980s; but its use is limited by its complexity.

Forward-rate agreements allow two parties to hedge their interest-rate exposures without touching the principal of an instrument.

The innovations of the 1980s take their place along with older ones: floating-rate notes, asset-backed notes, and financial futures. Skeptics of this plethora of innovations say that their main purpose is to accommodate portfolio risks to the unprecedented fluctuations in foreign exchange during the early 1980s. Net flows were much smaller than gross flows, raising the thought that if exchange rates were under control, so much innovation might not be necessary.

The international bond market fell in 1990, although the net volume of funds raised was higher by 10% ($121 billion) than in the previous year.

The developing world continued to be an insignificant player in bond markets. Although individual countries' sovereign debt to banks had, in most cases, fallen below investment grade in rating, several countries continued to service their bonds. In 1990, large amounts of Mexico's and Venezuela's bank debt were converted to bonds — called Brady bonds after the US Treasury Secretary who initiated a debt-relief program that includes enhancing developing-country bonds by backing them with bonds of the US Treasury and government agencies.

By mid–1991, Mexico had issued $45 billion and Venezuela $21 billion in Brady bonds, thereby securitizing most of their bank debts. In the new, more-optimistic financial climate, corporate issuers are expected to play an increasingly important role in the bond markets of the seriously reforming major countries: Mexico, Venezuela, Brazil, and Argentina.

Most of the $13 trillion global bond market — 60% — was in public domestic issues, mostly by central governments. Another 29% of the total market was in the domestic private sector, most of it issued by business firms and banks. The international sector — i.e., bonds from international issuers or bonds sold primarily in international markets — continued to account for a little over 10% of the total market.

The linkages between domestic and international markets are becoming ever stronger.

The United States dollar continued to be, by a wide margin, the preferred denomination of issues in the global market.

Structure of global bond market

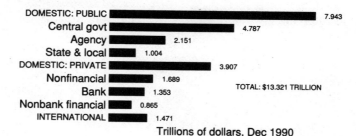

Trillions of dollars, Dec 1990

	AMOUNT	% SHARE
DOMESTIC: PUBLIC SECTOR	7.943	60
Central govt	4.787	36
Agency	2.151	16
State & local	1.004	8
DOMESTIC: PRIVATE SECTOR	3.907	29
Nonfinancial	1.689	13
Bank	1.353	10
Nonbank financial	0.865	6
INTERNATIONAL SECTOR	1.471	11
Total	**13.321**	**100**

Trillions of dollars and percentages.
Nominal values outstanding at end-1990.
Source: Bank for International Settlements (1).

Figure 10–1

Main currencies of the global bond market

Nominal outstandings in trillions of $ equivalents, Dec 1990

Source: Bank for International Settlements (1).

Figure 10–2

Issuers in developed economies accounted for 83% of the value of all bonds in the main international markets. International organizations issued most of the rest.

Issuers in developing economies accounted for only 2% of the value of bonds in all international markets.

Fixed-rate instruments continued to be the preferred type of bond in international markets, accounting for 70% of the total in 1990.

Floating-rate issues gained market share in 1990, largely due to uncertainties generated by recession fears and, in the fall, by the Gulf crisis.

Equity-related issues dropped sharply in 1990, as Japanese warrents (bonds with an option to convert to equities) lost favor following the stock market crash.

International bond issues and placements

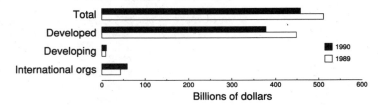

	1985	1989	1990 VALUE	CHANGE	SHARE
FOREIGN BONDS					
Developed economies	19.736	31.755	36.316	14	77
Developing economies	1.815	1.843	1.373	-26	3
International orgs	9.350	8.172	8.539	4	18
Other	0.327	1.142	0.680	-40	1
Total	**31.229**	**42.932**	**46.907**	**9**	**100**
EUROBONDS					
Developed economies	118.194	192.653	152.606	-21	84
Developing economies	6.681	2.871	3.834	34	2
International orgs	8.543	13.451	20.541	53	11
Other	3.124	3.878	4.889	26	3
Total	**136.543**	**212.853**	**181.870**	**-15**	**100**
INTERNATIONAL BONDS					
Developed economies	137.931	224.428	188.922	-16	83
Developing economies	8.497	4.714	5.206	10	2
International orgs	17.893	21.623	29.080	34	13
Other	3.450	5.020	5.569	11	2
Total		**255.785**	**228.777**	**-11**	**100**
TOTALS, ALL BONDS					
Developed economies	275.861	448.836	377.844	-16	83
Developing economies	16.993	9.428	10.413	10	2
International orgs	35.786	43.246	58.160	34	13
Other	6.901	10.040	11.138	11	2
Grand total	**335.541**	**511.550**	**457.555**	**-11**	**100**

Figure 10–3

Billions of dollars and percentages.
Excludes special issues by development institutions directly placed with governments or central banks.
Excludes bonds issued in the context of commercial bank restructuring and financing agreements.
Source: International Monetary Fund (7).

International bond instruments

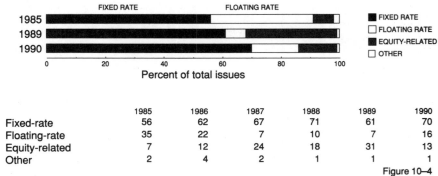

	1985	1986	1987	1988	1989	1990
Fixed-rate	56	62	67	71	61	70
Floating-rate	35	22	7	10	7	16
Equity-related	7	12	24	18	31	13
Other	2	4	2	1	1	1

Figure 10–4

Percent of total issues.
Source: International Monetary Fund (7).

Yen displaced dollars as the preferred denomination of fixed-rate issues in 1990; yen issues increased 61%, while dollar issues declined 38%.

In floating-rate instruments, the dollar overtook the Deutsche mark and sterling in their shares of issues.

Equity-related issues of all denominations fell in value by 69% in 1990, with dollar denominations taking an even greater loss: 74%.

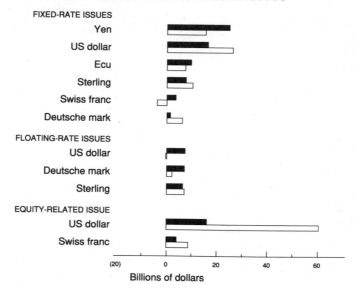

Currencies of new international bond issues

	1989	1990	% CHANGE 1990	STOCKS DEC90	SHARE
STRAIGHT FIXED-RATE ISSUES					
US dollar	26.1	16.1	-38	322.7	32
Yen	15.3	24.7	61	159.4	16
Swiss franc	-3.9	3.5	-190	119.8	12
Deutsche mark	6.2	1.3		110.7	11
Ecu	7.4	9.6	30	68.7	7
Sterling	10.2	7.6	-25	62.8	6
Other	27.7	17.8	-36	164.0	16
Total	**89.0**	80.7	**-9**	**1008.1**	**100**
FLOATING-RATE ISSUES					
US dollar	-0.5	7.3	-1560	115.6	56
Sterling	7.0	6.4	-9	42.7	21
Deutsche mark	2.2	7.0	218	20.8	10
Other	1.8	6.4	256	26.6	13
Total	**10.5**	27.1	**158**	205.7	**100**
EQUITY-RELATED ISSUES					
US dollar	60.4	16.0	-74	169.2	65
Swiss franc	8.8	4.0	-55	54.3	21
Other	5.5	3.1	-44	35.2	14
Total	**74.8**	23.2	**-69**	**258.7**	**100**

Figure 10–5

Billions of dollars and percentages.
Source: Bank for International Settlements (1).

Japan continued to lead international institutions and all countries as the source of new international bonds in 1990. The total value of completed new bond issues fell by 25% in 1990.

Japan's outstandings of international bonds in 1990 was more than those of the United States and the United Kingdom combined.

Asian countries continued to lead other developing countries as issuers of international bonds, although their volume declined by half between 1985 and 1990.

Developing countries in Europe tripled the value of their new issues in the second half of the 1980s. But the value of African issues was 37 times as great in 1985 as it was in 1990.

Issuers of new international bonds

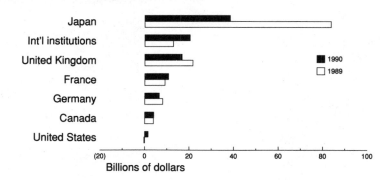

Billions of dollars

	1989	1990	% CHANGE 1990	STOCKS DEC90	SHARE
Japan	83.8	38.5	-54	317.7	22
United States	-0.3	1.5	-600	170.3	12
United Kingdom	21.6	16.8	-22	127.8	9
Canada	4.1	4.2	2	107.9	7
France	9.2	10.8	17	90.8	6
Germany	8.3	6.7	-19	64.5	4
Australia	4.4	0.1	-98	46.3	3
Other BIS-reporters	27.5	28.3	3	288.8	20
Other countries	2.7	3.7	37	70.8	5
International institutions	12.9	20.5	59	187.7	13
Total	**174.3**	**131.0**	**-25**	**1472.5**	**100**

Figure 10–6

Billions of dollars and percentages.
Source: Bank for International Settlements (1).

International bond issues by developing-country borrowers

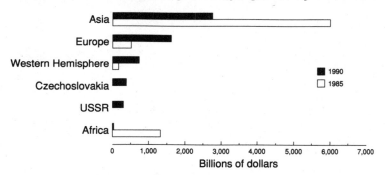

Billions of dollars

The net volume of new completed bond issues in the international market fell 25% in 1990.

The biggest drop came in equity-related issues — in the preceding few years a favorite of Japanese investors, who received warrants (options) to convert their bonds to securities in the high-flying stock market.

New floating-rate issues more than doubled in 1990, at least partly due to uncertainties in the financial environment.

New issues of straight fixed-rate bonds fell a little in 1990 but still made up two-thirds of the total stock of bonds outstanding.

International bond issues by developing-country borrowers

	1985	SHARE 1985	1989	SHARE 1989	1990	SHARE 1990
Asia	6005.4	74	2217.9	49	2757.4	54
Europe	509.6	6	2138.4	47	1607.4	31
Western Hemisphere	168.8	2			730.9	14
Czechoslovakia			74.0	2	376.6	7
USSR			891.5	20	297.6	6
Africa	1322.5	16	159.0	4	35.5	1
Middle East	82.0	1				
All developing*	**8113.3**	**100**	**4515.3**	**100**	**5131.2**	**100**

Figure 10–7

Millions of dollars and percentages of all developing countries; i.e., excluding Czechoslovakia and USSR. Percentages for Czechoslovakia and USSR are shown for comparison.
Foreign bonds and Eurobonds.
Excludes bonds issued in the context of commercial bank restructuring and financing agreements.
* Excludes offshore banking centers.
Source: International Monetary Fund (7).

The international bond market

	1989	1990	% CHANGE 1990	STOCKS DEC90	SHARE
New issues announced	261.8	241.7	-8		
Straight fixed-rate issues	149.5	166.5	11		
Floating-rate notes	27.1	42.1	55		
Equity-related issues	85.2	33.2	-61		
Net new completed issues	174.3	131.0	-25	1472.5	100
Straight fixed-rate issues	89.0	80.7	-9	1008.1	68
Floating-rate issues	10.5	27.1	158	205.7	14
Equity-related issues	74.8	23.2	-69	258.7	18

Table 10–1

Billions of dollars and percentages.
Equity-related = convertible bonds and bonds with equity warrants.
Source: Bank for International Settlements (1).

Currencies of international bonds

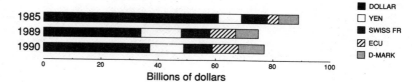

International interest rates

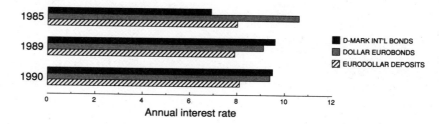

Over 80% of all bonds continued to be issued by developed countries. The small share issued by developing countries declined in the later years of the decade.

The dollar lost ground as the main denominator of bond issues, its share falling by half since 1985. Ecu-denominated bonds, mostly by European Community public agencies and international institutions, rose in the latter part of the decade to become a major factor in bond financing.

Interest rates continued to rise for D-mark international bonds, righting the 1985 yield curve as longterm rates topped Eurodollar deposits in 1990.

Trends in international bond markets

	1985	1989	1990
GROSS INTERNATIONAL BONDS			
Amortization	36	90	111
Net issues	132	166	118
Purchased by banks	55	68	
Nonbanks	77	98	
Developed economies	63	81	
Developing economies	4	2	
Total	**168**	**256**	**229**
TOTAL BONDS ISSUED			
Developed economies	137	224	189
Percent of total	82	88	83
Developing economies	10	5	5
Percent of total	6	2	2
Other*	21	27	35
Percent of total	12	10	15
BY CURRENCY OF DENOMINATION			
US dollar	61	50	34
Percent of total	36	20	15
Japanese yen	8	9	14
Percent of total	5	4	6
Swiss franc	9	7	10
Percent of total	5	3	4
Ecu	4	5	9
Percent of total	2	2	4
Deutsche mark	7	6	8
Percent of total	4	2	3
Other	11	23	25
Percent of total	7	9	11
INTEREST RATES			
D-mark international bonds	6.9	7.9	9.6
Dollar Eurobonds	10.6	10.6	8.7
Eurodollar deposits	8.0	8	8.4

Figure 10–8

Billions of dollars and annual percentages.
* Includes international organizations.
Ecu = European currency unit.
Eurodollar deposits: 3-month deposits, end of period.
Bond rates for bonds with remaining maturity of 7-15 years, at end of period.
Source: International Monetary Fund (7).

Total returns of Australia's government bonds led other government issues in early 1991. Returns on Japanese bonds continued to be lowest of the major economies.

Yields on Italy's longterm government bonds led those of all other main economies as the new decade opened. Yields of most of these bonds declined in 1990 and early 1991, Australia's most of all.

Yields on Japan's longterm government bonds increased notably in the same period, although these yields continued to be below those of government bonds of all other main economies.

Total returns on government bonds

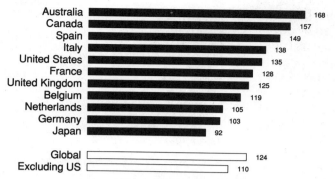

Index of March 1991 returns; Dec 1987 = 100

	DEC 1989	DEC 1990	MARCH 1991
Australia	136.50	158.68	167.58
Canada	138.06	148.03	156.95
Spain	117.52	154.03	148.73
Italy	114.27	147.29	138.07
United States	121.70	132.22	134.77
France	111.33	136.22	127.89
United Kingdom	98.66	129.55	124.89
Belgium	102.74	128.85	119.31
Netherlands	97.90	114.76	104.79
Germany	98.56	113.14	103.33
Japan	87.70	94.01	92.41
Global	**112.14**	**125.34**	**124.28**
Excluding US	99.25	114.78	109.86

Index of total return for traded bonds.
Index: Dec 31, 1987 = 100
Source: J P Morgan (1).

Figure 10–9

Yields on longterm government bonds

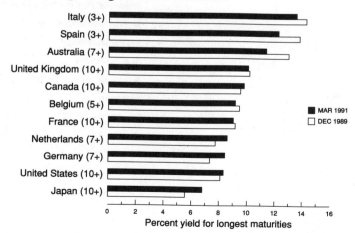

Percent yield for longest maturities

The market for fixed-rate bonds grew slightly (4%) in 1990, but bonds issued by developed economies contracted slightly (2%). In the second half of the decade, the global market grew at an average annual rate of 14%, as did the markets in developed economies.

Dollar-denominated issues continued their decade-long decline. Ecu-denominated issues continued to rise strongly, moving past the Swiss franc to become the number three currency for fixed-rate bonds — this despite the fact that use of the Swiss franc also increased sharply in 1990 to a value well over its 1985 level.

Yields on longterm government bonds

	DEC 1989	DEC 1990	MAR 1991
Italy (3+)	14.25	14.04	13.52
Spain (3+)	13.77	14.11	12.25
Australia (7+)	12.97	12.04	11.37
United Kingdom (10+)	10.17	10.79	10.07
Canada (10+)	9.51	10.33	9.75
Belgium (5+)	9.44	9.73	9.14
France (10+)	9.14	9.80	8.99
Netherlands (7+)	7.71	8.96	8.58
Germany (7+)	7.33	8.85	8.39
United States (10+)	8.08	8.31	8.31
Japan (10+)	5.54	6.52	6.80

Figure 10–10

For traded bonds included in the J P Morgan Government Bond Index.
For longest maturities (yrs).
Source: J P Morgan (1).

Market for fixed-rate bonds

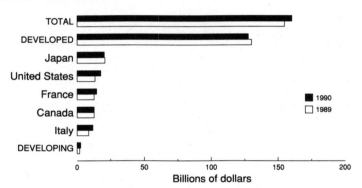

Currencies of fixed-rate bonds

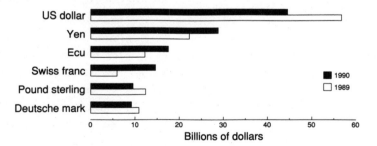

In 1990, the value of fixed-rate bonds issued by most of the developed economies declined — Norway's tiny share by 78% and New Zealand's by almost as much. However, the value of issues by Italy and the United States each increased by about one-third.

The total market for floating-rate issues grew smartly in 1990, in the context of uncertainties about interest rates and inflation. The United Kingdom continued as the biggest borrower in this market, though by 1990 its volume had still not recovered its 1985 position.

Market for fixed-rate bonds

BORROWERS	1985	1989	1990 VALUE	1990 CHANGE	1990 SHARE
Developed countries	77.3	130.0	127.6	-2	80
Japan	11.4	20.7	20.2	-2	13
United States	26.2	13.3	17.6	32	11
France	4.8	12.6	14.4	14	9
Canada	7.5	12.5	12.3	-2	8
Italy	0.8	8.4	11.5	37	7
United Kingdom	2.5	12.3	9.0	-27	6
Germany	1.6	7.2	7.4	3	5
Finland	0.9	5.0	5.9	18	4
Sweden	3.9	6.0	5.1	-15	3
Denmark	2.2	4.3	4.2	-2	3
Austria	2.0	4.7	3.3	-30	2
Belgium	0.7	2.3	2.9	26	2
Australia	5.1	5.9	2.8	-53	2
Netherlands	1.2	2.8	2.0	-29	1
Norway	1.4	2.7	0.6	-78	0
New Zealand	1.3	1.7	0.5	-71	0
Developing countries	2.3	1.7	2.4	41	1
Other	15.2	23.0	23.0	0	14
Total	**94.8**	154.6	**160.2**	**4**	**100**
CURRENCY DISTRIBUTION					
US dollar	45.1	56.8	44.5		28
Yen	11.3	22.2	28.8		18
Ecu	6.0	12.3	17.6		11
Swiss franc	10.5	5.9	14.7		9
Pound sterling	3.1	12.4	9.5		6
Deutsche mark	6.7	10.9	9.2		6
Canadian dollar	2.2	11.3	6.2		4
Australian dollar	3.1	6.3	4.8		3
Nertherlands guilder	1.6	1.8	1.3		1
Other	5.2	14.7	23.6		15
Total	**94.8**	**154.6**	**160.2**		100

Figure 10–11

Billions of dollars and percentages.
Source: International Monetary Fund (7).

Market for floating-rate issues

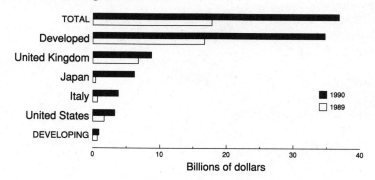

Billions of dollars

The dollar continued as the preferred currency for floating-rate issues, taking a wide lead over issues in pound sterling. Deutsche mark issues also increased sharply, approaching the pound's share of total issues, as it had in 1985.

The ecu lept from nowhere to hold a significant position in the market, though a position well below the pound and D-mark.

The market for equity-related bonds contracted sharply in 1990, due almost entirely to the rejection of these instruments by Japanese investors accostomed to moving from bonds to equities when the stock market was flying high. The market crash spoiled the appeal of that option. More ominous is the prospect that the Yen 20 trillion of these bonds outstanding could become a drag on interest rates when they mature in 1993 and 1994.

The tiny market for UK issues more than doubled in 1990, while the even tinier market for US issues shrank by about one-quarter of its year-earlier value.

Currencies of floating-rate issues

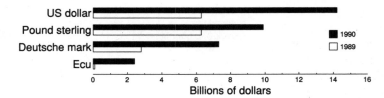

Market for floating-rate issues

	1985	1989	1990 VALUE	% CHANGE	% SHARE
BORROWERS					
Developed countries	48.5	16.7	34.7	108	94
United Kingdom	12.2	6.8	8.7	28	24
Japan	2.3	0.4	6.2	1450	17
Italy	4.4	0.7	3.8	443	10
United States	10.5	1.7	3.3	94	9
France	6.5		1.7		5
Sweden	2.2		1.0		3
Belgium	1.8	0.6	0.8	33	2
Canada	2.1	0.6	0.6	0	2
Denmark	0.6	0.5	0.2	-60	1
Developing countries	6.2	0.7	0.9	29	2
Other	4.0	0.4	1.2	200	3
Total	**58.7**	**17.8**	**36.8**	**107**	**100**
CURRENCY DISTRIBUTION					
US dollar	50.5	6.3	14.2	125	39
Pound sterling	3.4	6.3	9.9	57	27
Deutsche mark	3.2	2.8	7.3	161	20
Ecu	1.0	0.1	2.4	2300	7
Other	0.6	2.3	3.0	30	**8**
Total	**58.7**	**17.8**	**36.8**	**107**	**100**

Figure 10–12

Billions of dollars and percentages.
Source: International Monetary Fund (7).

Market for equity-related bonds

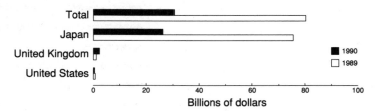

The dollar continued to dominate the market for interest-rate swaps, although by a gradually decreasing margin. Swaps of yen, sterling, and D-marks held their small positions in this market.

The dollar also led the market for currency swaps, but it shared that market with transactions in yen. Sterling and D-marks continued to get only minor plays.

The total market for both kinds of swaps continued to grow, although the value of interest-rate swaps is three times that of deals in currencies.

Market for equity-related bonds

	1985	1989	1990 VALUE	% CHANGE	% SHARE
BORROWERS					
Japan	5.9	75.7	26.3	-65	86
United Kingdom	0.7	1.0	2.3	130	8
United States	3.2	0.7	0.5	-29	2
Germany	1.0	0.6	0.5	-17	2
Switzerland	0.1		0.1		0.3
Other OECD countries	0.4	0.3	0.1	-67	0.3
Other borrowers		2.0	0.8	-60	3
Total	**11.3**	**80.3**	**30.6**	**-62**	**100**
CURRENCY DISTRIBUTION					
US dollar	5.3	63.5	18.1	-71	59
Swiss franc	3.9	12.3	8.1	-34	26
Deutsche mark	1.3	2.7	1.8	-33	6
Other	0.8	1.8	2.6	44	8
Total	**11.3**	**80.3**	**30.6**	**-62**	**100**

Figure 10–13

Billions of dollars and percentages.
Source: International Monetary Fund (7).

Swap transactions

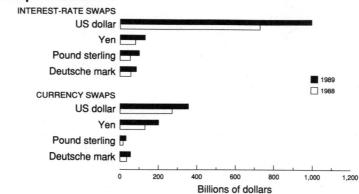

Billions of dollars

	1987 VALUE	SHARE %	1988 VALUE	SHARE %	CHANGE %	1989 VALUE	SHARE %	CHANGE %
INTEREST RATE SWAPS								
US dollar	541.517	79	728.166	72	34	993.746	66	36
Yen	40.498	6	78.488	8	94	128.022	9	63
Pound sterling	29.706	4	52.265	5	76	100.417	7	92
Deutsche mark	31.640	5	56.466	6	78	84.620	6	50
Other	39.528	6	94.820	9	140	195.795	13	106
Total	**682.888**	**100**	**1010.203**	**100**	**48**	**1502.600**	**100**	**49**
CURRENCY SWAPS								
US dollar	162.606	89	269.477	84	66	354.166	79	31
Yen	59.746	33	131.034	41	119	201.145	45	54
Pound sterling	10.505	6	17.704	6	69	33.466	7	89
Deutsche mark	21.377	12	33.979	11	59	53.839	12	58
Other	113.328	62	187.062	59	65	256.045	57	37
Total*	**183.781**	**200**	**319.628**	**200**	**74**	**449.331**	**200**	**41**

Figure 10–14

Billions of dollars and percentages.
* Each currency swap involves two currencies.
To avoid double counting, the total is half the sum of individual currency amounts.
Percentages in each currency add up to 200% of the adjusted total.
Source: International Monetary Fund (7).

11 Stock Markets

Equity shares vie with bonds for positions in investors' port-folios — with bonds, historically, getting the bigger play by about four to one. Yet by 1989, after a decade of unparalleled portfolio investment, global holdings of equities had caught up with those of bonds — at $11 trillion. During the 1980s, international equity transactions grew more than seven-fold to $1.3 trillion. This was a doubling to a 13.5% share of global trading (transactions for both resident and nonresident clients). The volume of international equity transactions (adjusting for rises in share prices) grew almost six-fold in the decade. Some 95% of the value of all the equity shares in the world are traded on stock markets in the developed economies. In 1990, the total value of all these shares declined 18%.

A major cause of surging foreign portfolio investment in both equities and bonds was the suddenly large presence in the international markets of big nonbank financial institutions: pension funds, insurance firms, and investment trusts. The United States lagged behind Europe and Japan in this diversification into foreign investments. Analysts expect diversification to continue into the 1990s, with US institutional investors also placing more money abroad.

International equity investment was set back a little for a couple of years after the worldwide stock-market crash in 1987 but then rebounded and grew at an even faster rate. Before that

Growth of world stock markets

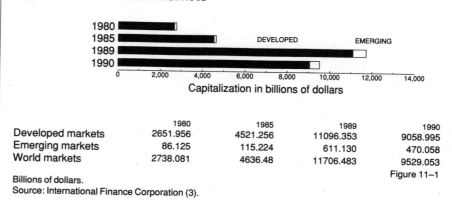

	1980	1985	1989	1990
Developed markets	2651.956	4521.256	11096.353	9058.995
Emerging markets	86.125	115.224	611.130	470.058
World markets	2738.081	4636.48	11706.483	9529.053

Billions of dollars.
Source: International Finance Corporation (3).

Figure 11–1

crash, the United States market had attracted the biggest proportion of equity investments, closely followed by the United Kingdom. Investments in the European Community had grown, but not much. Investments in Japan had declined.

Following the crash, investment in the United States dropped off; in Japan it turned up; and it took off in the European Community, which in 1989 received half of total international inflows.

A hybrid instrument, the equity warrant (a bond with an option to convert it into an equity share), had a spectacular rise in popularity among Japanese investors, shooting up from $4 billion in 1985 to $62 billion in 1989. This bubble burst with the Japanese stock market in 1990, when warrants dropped to $17 billion.

The strong inflows of portfolio capital into the United States "covered" much of that country's huge and growing current-account deficits. This, some say, eased the pressure to make fundamental corrections in the domestic economy — most importantly, increasing savings. Some analysts think that the world's financial markets are fairly uniformly liberalized now and that investors will continue to diversify their portfolios away from the US. Both of these developments would put pressures on the US economy.

While equity markets in developing economies weren't a big share of global trading, several of these markets emerged to prominence during the decade. There are strong reasons to expect that these emerging markets will grow in size and importance during the 1990s. Some developing countries, most notably Venezuela and Mexico, have reformed their economies and now stand on the threshhold of reentering the global financial markets. More shares are coming into play as a result of debt-for-equity swaps. In transitioning economies of Eastern Europe, most notably Hungary, the work of privatizing state-owned enterprises will create a potentially bottomless market for equity investments.

Venezuela, the world's worst performer in 1989, was its best in 1990 — up 572%; Greece's market was up 90%; Mexico's 25%. Specific local conditions — in Venezuela, the sharp rise in oil prices at the onset of the Gulf war — accounted for some of the market growth. Beyond that, reforming economies were nurturing world-class companies in Chile, South Korea, Mexico, Portugal, and Thailand, among others.

Among the more-advanced economies of Asia, liberalizing rules were opening up equity markets in South Korea and Taiwan. Country funds grew apace, appearing for the first time in Latin America and Eastern Europe. By 1990 there were close to 140 country funds with $12 billion in net assets.

International (cross-border) trading of equity shares now makes up about 13% of the value of all shares traded on the world's stock markets.

Trading at the end of the decade was five times what it was at the beginning, measured by volume (adjusting for price increases).

The United Kingdom continues to be the biggest investor in equities and Germany the smallest.

Equity investments in continental Europe doubled in the later years of the decade.

Investments in Japanese markets recovered somewhat in the later years, after being heavily negative (more selling than buying) in 1986.

Trading in equity markets

INT'L EQUITY MARKETS	1986	1987	1988	1989
Trading value	800.8	1344.4	1212.6	1528.3
% of world total	11	12	11	13
Change (%)	108	68	-10	26
Volume (1979 = 100)	403	591	440	483
Change (%)	46	47	-26	10
World total (value)	**7024.6**	**11551.6**	**10598.9**	**11716.9**

Billions of dollars and year-to-year changes.
Source: International Monetary Fund (7).

Table 11–1

Net international equity flows

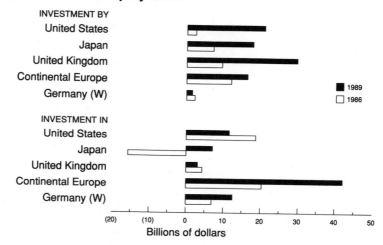

	1986	1989	FIRST Q 1989	FIRST Q 1990
INVESTMENT BY				
United States	2.4	20.9		
Japan	7.1	17.9	-0.1	4.0
United Kingdom	9.5	29.8	5.7	0.8
Continental Europe	12.0	16.4		
Germany (W)	2.3	1.6	0.8	-0.3
Rest of world	0.8	7.4		
INVESTMENT IN				
United States	18.7	11.5		
Japan	-15.8	7.0	9.0	-11.7
United Kingdom	4.3	3.1	-2.0	0.1
Continental Europe	20.3	42.1		
Germany (W)	6.9	12.4	1.3	4.3
Rest of world	4.1	28.6		
Total	**31.7**	**92.3**		

Figure 11–2

Billions of dollars.
Purchases minus sales of equity associated with international portfolio investment.
Japanese investments include Euro-warrants.
UK investments includes only pension funds, insurance companies, and open- and closed-ended mutual funds.
German investments exclude investment certificates.
Source: International Monetary Fund (7).

Stock markets in the United States and Japan each list about one-third of the $9.5 trillion worth of equity shares traded in the world.

South Korea's is the largest of the stock markets emerging in the dynamic Asian economies.

India's market is the largest in the developing world.

Capitalization of world stock markets

	Billions of dollars
United States	3,072.303
Japan	2,917.679
United Kingdom	867.599
Germany (W)	379.399
France	341.695
Canada	241.920
Switzerland	165.913
Italy	148.766
Netherlands	148.521
So Africa	137.540
Spain	111.404
So Korea	110.594
Australia	106.915
Taiwan	100.710
Sweden	92.102
Hong Kong	83.397
Belgium	65.449
Malaysia	48.611
Denmark	39.063
India (Bombay)	38.567
Singapore	34.308
Mexico	32.725
Austria	26.320
Norway	26.130
Thailand	23.896
Finland	22.721
Turkey	19.065
Brazil (Sao Paulo)	16.354
Greece	15.228
Chile	13.645
Israel	10.560
Luxembourg	10.456
Portugal	9.201
New Zealand	8.835
Venezuela	8.361
Indonesia	8.081
Philippines	5.927
Argentina	3.268
Pakistan	2.985
Zimbabwe	2.395
Jordan	2.001
Colombia	1.416
Nigeria	1.372

SHARE OF TOTAL

32%	UNITED STATES
31%	JAPAN
9%	UNITED KINGDOM
4%	GERMANY (W)
4%	FRANCE
80%	TOP FOUR

TOTAL CAPITALIZATION
$9.5 TRILLION

Billions of dollars, yearend 1990

Figure 11–3

Billions of dollars, yearend 1990.
Market capitalization = share price times total number of shares outstanding.
Note: "Emerging" stock markets are markets in 20 developing countries, within which the International Finance Corporation (IFC) monitors more than 800 stocks. For indexes of performance, IFC selects stocks based on trading activity, market size, and sectoral diversity.
Source: International Finance Corporation (3).

In 1990, the eight top-performing stock markets in the world were emerging new markets. Venezuela's led all others, with a 572% year-to-year increase in the value of its index.

Markets in the United Kingdom and Austria were the only established ones to show an increase in the value of their indexes in 1990.

On average, stocks throughout the world lost 19% in 1990. Performance of markets in the United States was well above the world average. Japan's market was one of the worst-performing; Brazil's was the worst.

Price performance of world stock markets

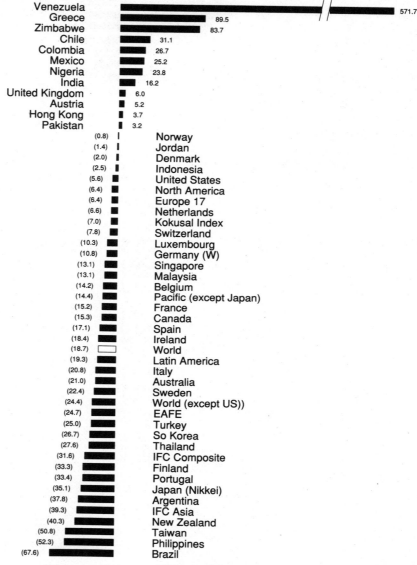

Price percent change, 1990 over 1989

Source: International Finance Corporation (3).

Figure 11–4

The two stock markets with the highest capitalization, those of the United States and Japan, had the first- and third-largest number of listed stocks. India's market was second.

Among the established markets, those of Finland and Austria had among the fewest listed stocks.

Number of companies listed in world stock markets

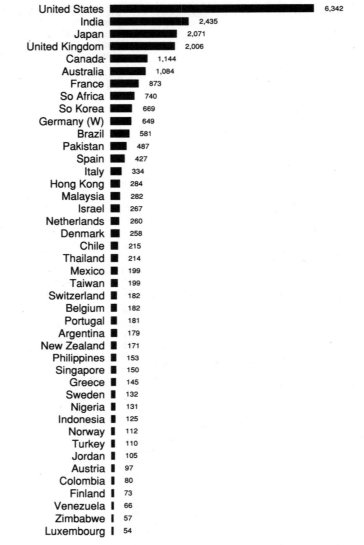

United States	6,342
India	2,435
Japan	2,071
United Kingdom	2,006
Canada	1,144
Australia	1,084
France	873
So Africa	740
So Korea	669
Germany (W)	649
Brazil	581
Pakistan	487
Spain	427
Italy	334
Hong Kong	284
Malaysia	282
Israel	267
Netherlands	260
Denmark	258
Chile	215
Thailand	214
Mexico	199
Taiwan	199
Switzerland	182
Belgium	182
Portugal	181
Argentina	179
New Zealand	171
Philippines	153
Singapore	150
Greece	145
Sweden	132
Nigeria	131
Indonesia	125
Norway	112
Turkey	110
Jordan	105
Austria	97
Colombia	80
Finland	73
Venezuela	66
Zimbabwe	57
Luxembourg	54

Number of listed domestic companies, yearend 1990

Figure 11–5

Source: International Finance Corporation (3).

Stock Markets

The International Finance Corporation, an arm of the World Bank, has constructed a composite index of 838 stocks among emerging markets, which represent the total list of 29,000. (For comparison, the 23 developed markets list a little under 18,000 stocks.)

In the 1980s, the capitalization (total value of all shares) of East Asian markets of the IFC index increased three-fold; Latin American markets lost about the same proportion of their capitalization.

In 1990, the average price/earnings ratio of Taiwan's stocks were the highest in world markets at almost three times the world average — which was 15.3.

The average p/e in Japan was 31, twice the world average in 1990 and down dramatically from the year earlier.

In 1990, the average p/e in the United States was 14.1, exactly what it was a year earlier.

Regional weights of emerging stock markets

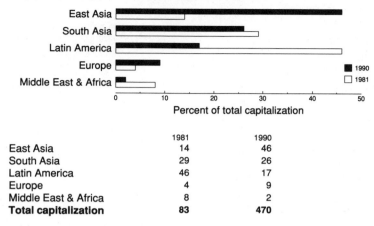

	1981	1990
East Asia	14	46
South Asia	29	26
Latin America	46	17
Europe	4	9
Middle East & Africa	8	2
Total capitalization	**83**	**470**

Percent of total capitalization. Capitalization in billions of dollars.
Source: International Finance Corporation (3).

Figure 11–6

Price/earnings ratios

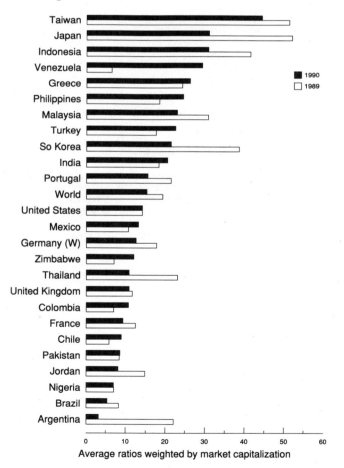

Over $115 billion worth of shares in manufacturing firms are traded in emerging stock markets, more than those of any other industry.

The only industry group that comes close to matching that total value are firms in finance, insurance, and real estate — capitalized at $108 billion.

Price/earnings ratios

	END 1990	RELATIVE TO WORLD 1990	END 1989
Taiwan	44.41	2.90	51.17
Japan	31.00	2.03	51.90
Indonesia	30.84	2.02	41.50
Venezuela	29.31	1.92	6.44
Greece	26.23	1.71	24.30
Philippines	24.51	1.60	18.50
Malaysia	23.01	1.50	30.75
Turkey	22.50	1.47	17.64
So Korea	21.48	1.40	38.57
India	20.59	1.35	18.34
Portugal	15.47	1.01	21.42
World	**15.30**	**1.00**	**19.30**
United States	14.10	0.92	14.10
Mexico	13.20	0.86	10.66
Germany (W)	12.60	0.82	17.80
Zimbabwe	12.01	0.78	7.00
Thailand	10.90	0.71	23.07
United Kingdom	10.90	0.71	11.70
Colombia	10.66	0.70	6.96
France	9.30	0.61	12.50
Chile	8.86	0.58	5.82
Pakistan	8.53	0.56	8.44
Jordan	8.15	0.53	14.93
Nigeria	7.01	0.46	6.99
Brazil	5.34	0.35	8.30
Argentina	3.11	0.20	22.14

Figure 11–7

Average ratios weighted by market capitalization.
Source: International Finance Corporation (3).

Industries traded on emerging stock markets

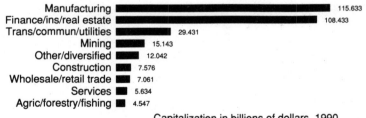

	Capitalization
Manufacturing	115.633
Finance/ins/real estate	108.433
Trans/commun/utilities	29.431
Mining	15.143
Other/diversified	12.042
Construction	7.576
Wholesale/retail trade	7.061
Services	5.634
Agric/forestry/fishing	4.547

Capitalization in billions of dollars, 1990

Stock Markets

The average value of firms listed on developed markets was $510,000 in 1990.

The average value manufacturing firms listed on emerging markets was about $250,000 at the end of 1990. The average value of firms in the financial, insurance, and real estate group was about $630,000.

Industries traded on emerging stock markets

	STOCKS	CAPITALIZATION
MANUFACTURING		
Cement	41	18.151
Electrical & electronic	35	12.639
Transportation	30	9.515
Food, etc.	61	9.104
Chemicals, etc.	44	8.877
Petroleum refining	25	8.065
Primary metal	18	7.472
Paper, etc.	32	7.383
Rubber & misc plastics	21	7.237
Fabricated metal	36	6.325
Apparel	26	6.307
Textiles	32	4.343
Total	**465**	**115.633**
FINANCE/INSURANCE/REAL ESTATE		
Banking	88	74.724
Credit agencies	30	12.185
Insurance	9	8.809
Security & commodity brokers	18	8.265
Total	**171**	**108.433**
TRANSPORTATION/COMMUNICATION/UTILITIES		
Electric, gas, sanitary	15	17.296
Communication	11	7.094
Total	**37**	**29.431**
MINING		
Metals	27	11.190
Oil and gas extraction	14	3.054
Total	**44**	**15.143**
OTHER/DIVERSIFIED		
Total	**31**	**12.042**
CONSTRUCTION		
Total	**23**	**7.576**
WHOLESALE/RETAIL TRADE		
Total	**24**	**7.061**
SERVICES		
Hotels	15	3.743
Total	**19**	**5.634**
AGRICULTURE/FORESTRY/FISHING		
Total	**22**	**4.547**

Figure 11–8

Coverage for 1991.
Number of stocks traded.
Capitalization in billions of dollars.
Source: International Finance Corporation (3).

12 Banking

For all financial institutions, the 1990s began in the turbulent wake of a decade in which three powerful trends transformed their industry. The trends were liberalization, globalization, and innovation.

Liberalization freed financial operations from constraints of regulations and eroded many cartel-like arrangements, which together had curbed capital flows and distorted market disciplines. Some observers say that liberalization is now nearly complete in the main developed economies. It started in the United States in the 1970s with a gradual casting off of controls on interest rates and capital flows, and it will most likely conclude sometime in the early 1990s when the US removes then-60-year-old regulations limiting banks' lines of business and their geographic reach. Some economies — Austria, France, Japan, and Switzerland — still retain some of the old controls, but the trend is irresistible.

Globalization followed naturally from liberalization. With capital free to go where it was wanted most, national governments lost control over longterm interest rates and much of their ability to influence shortterm rates.

Innovation in information technology and in the design of financial instruments made it increasingly easy for operators to react to moment-by-moment changes and challenges in the financial environment.

All of these trends begat a fourth: heightened competition among banks and between banks and nonbank providers of financial services. Large corporations, once the mainstay of banking services, found that they could reduce costs by going directly to investors. Japanese banks reached out globally for low-margin interbank deposits, trade financing, and corporate lending. By 1990 they were the world's largest, and the top United States bank ranked 23rd in assets.

These trends delivered on their central promise: efficiency and lower costs. And the freer, more flexible, globalized system proved to be remarkably resiliant. It bounced back from the recession of the early 1980s. It survived a debt crisis in the developing world which at its outset threatened to swamp the whole global financial system. It brushed off a worldwide stockmarket crash in

1987 and a local one in Japan in 1990. And most impressively, it confounded predictions that imbalances in current accounts — the string of huge trade deficits in the United States and surpluses in Japan and Germany — would soon lead to severe global dislocations. That didn't happen. Instead, the financial system accommodated itself to the imbalances until they started to go away at the end of the decade.

However, these successes didn't come cost-free. Rapid deregulation led to runaway inflation in asset prices, most notably for real-estate in the United States and for equity shares in Japan. Asset inflation of the mid–1980s led to asset deflation in the early 1990s. Since assets are the collateral that backs up bank loans, the rapid fall in asset prices led quickly to the need to set aside greater provisions against possible loan losses. Inevitably, the scarcity of sound assets led to fewer business loans.

Important to the global economy was a series of new rules covering the capital requirements of international banks. The new rules generally increased the amount of equity capital that banks must have in relation to their assets. The intended effect was to make banks sounder — that is, better able to withstand external shocks — and to make them more responsible to shareholders. The rules were promulgated in 1988 by the Basle Committee, an international group of bank regulators, and adopted the next year by the main dozen or so economies. Well before the committee's end–1992 deadline, the overwhelming majority of international banks had met either the interim standards or the final ones. While some observers say that the stricter capital requirements worsened the recession and could lead to a capital crunch, most seemed to feel that enhanced soundness was more important for these times.

In this environment, international bank lending moved sharply down as the new decade began; new lending by Japanese and United States banks in 1990 was only one-fourth of what it was a year earlier.

Japanese banks continued to hold the biggest share, by far, of total international assets, although their share fell to 35.5% in 1990 from 38% in 1988. Part of this fall was a cutback in claims on its United States affiliates. Loans to European clients increased, especially in France and Belgium.

Japan's share of the $6 trillion of international bank assets fell slightly in 1990, but was still three times the United States' share. Assets of West Germany and France approached those of the US.

Counting local claims in foreign currencies and adjusting for double counting of deposits, total net international credits were $3.35 trillion.

New bank lending dropped sharply in 1990, while lending by nonbanks grew a little.

Lending by banks in the developed economies to those outside it fell by $17 billion in 1990.

Banks' international assets

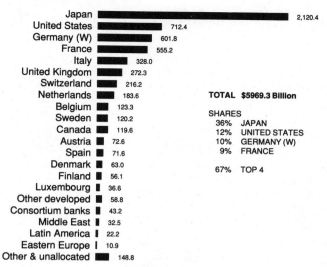

Japan	2,120.4
United States	712.4
Germany (W)	601.8
France	555.2
Italy	328.0
United Kingdom	272.3
Switzerland	216.2
Netherlands	183.6
Belgium	123.3
Sweden	120.2
Canada	119.6
Austria	72.6
Spain	71.6
Denmark	63.0
Finland	56.1
Luxembourg	36.6
Other developed	58.8
Consortium banks	43.2
Middle East	32.5
Latin America	22.2
Eastern Europe	10.9
Other & unallocated	148.8

TOTAL $5969.3 Billion

SHARES
36%   JAPAN
12%   UNITED STATES
10%   GERMANY (W)
9%   FRANCE

67%   TOP 4

Billions of dollars, Dec 1990

Figure 12–1

International lending by main banks

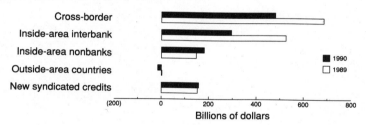

Cross-border
Inside-area interbank
Inside-area nonbanks
Outside-area countries
New syndicated credits

■ 1990
□ 1989

(200)   0   200   400   600   800

Billions of dollars

	1989	1990	STOCKS DEC90
Cross-border claims	684.9	480.0	5907.2
Inside-area interbank	525.0	294.9	3997.5
Inside-area nonbanks	146.6	179.7	1029.2
Outside-area countries	1.7	-17.0	718.6
Unallocated	15.0	22.4	161.9
Local foreign currency claims	122.2	109.0	1309.4
Claims on nonbanks	82.9	61.3	655.2
Net int'l bank credit	410.0	380.0	3350.0
New syndicated credits	151.7	156.9	

Figure 12–2

Billions of dollars.
For banks reporting to the BIS.
Excludes non-spontaneous credits and renegotiated loans where only spreads are changed.
Source: Bank for International Settlements (1).

Japanese banks accounted for 40% of total outstanding international loans among developed economies, although their lending in 1990 dropped by 64%.

Lending within European economies grew 15% in 1990, surpassing Japanese loans for the year, although not their share of all outstanding loans.

Loans by United States banks to other developed economies contracted 70% in 1990, and the US share of outstanding loans fell below that of European economies.

The dollar continued to be the currency most used in international lending, although its use declined in 1990.

Yen-denominated loans also declined in 1990, although not nearly as much as loans denominated in Swiss francs. The use of French francs more than doubled.

World interbank market among main developed economies

	1989	1990	% CHANGE 1990	STOCKS DEC90	SHARE
Cross-border claims	525.0	294.9	-44	3997.5	100
Between Japan & others	244.1	87.6	-64	1583.6	40
Between Euro countries	122.5	141.2	15	1130.0	28
Between US & others*	115.5	34.8	-70	781.3	20
Others	43.0	31.2	-27	502.6	12
Local claims**	39.3	47.7		654.2	

Table 12–1

Billions of dollars.
* Except Japan.
** Local interbank claims in foreign currency.
Source: Bank for International Settlements (1).

Currencies of international bank assets

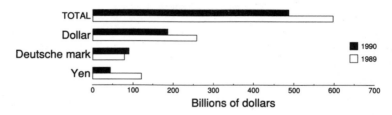

	1989	1990	% CHANGE 1990	STOCKS DEC90	SHARE
Dollars	257.8	185.8	-28	2939.2	50
Other	338.5	301.2	-11	2912.0	50
Deutsche mark	79.5	89.9	13	850.6	15
Yen	121.5	43.5	-64	678.4	12
Swiss francs	-12.5	5.9	-147	284.3	5
Sterling	28.2	37.2	32	250.3	4
Ecu	24.6	23.8	-3	194.6	3
French francs	17.4	38.1	119	164.9	3
Dutch guilders	10.3	10.7	4	80.6	1
Italian lire	18.9	26.2	39	73.8	1
Other	50.6	25.9	-49	334.5	6
Total	**596.3**	**487.0**	**-18**	**5851.2**	**100**

Figure 12–3

Billions of dollars and percentages.
Source: Bank for International Settlements (1).

Total international longterm bank credits within developed economies declined a little in 1990. The seven main economies hold over half of all longterm credits.

Longterm credits to developing economies were virtually unchanged in 1990, but they had declined over 40% since 1985. Credits to Africa were 60% higher than the year earlier, and credits to Asian developing economies grew 28%. The relatively small amount of credits to borrowers in the Middle East dropped precipitously.

In the second half of the 1980s, credits became the dominant form of international bank lending, growing to almost ten times the amount of lending through bonds.

International longterm bank credits

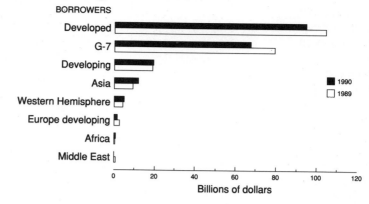

	1985 VALUE	1989 VALUE	1990 VALUE	% SHARE	% CHANGE
BORROWERS IN					
Developed countries	80.1	104.6	94.8	74	-9
G-7	52.1	79.2	67.3	53	-15
Other	28.0	25.4	27.5	22	8
Developing countries	35.4	18.9	19.2	15	2
Africa	0.8	0.5	0.8	1	60
Asia	10.5	9.3	11.9	9	28
Europe	2.0	2.8	1.7	1	-39
Middle East	0.4	0.7	0.1	0.1	-86
Western Hemisphere	20.4	4.3	4.8	4	12
Offshore banking centers	1.4	2.7	3.3	3	22
Other countries	1.9	1.6	3.0	2	88
Int'l orgs and unallocated	4.1	3.5	7.3	6	109
Total	**122.7**	**131.4**	**127.6**	**100**	**-3**

Figure 12–4

Billions of dollars and percentages.
External credit commitments and other international longterm bank facilities.
Source: International Monetary Fund (7).

International bank lending

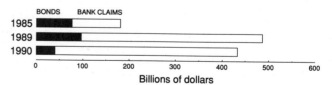

Billions of dollars

In the first three quarters of 1990, bank credits through loans to developed economies were about 90% of total lending, including bonds.

Of bond issues, 83% were to developed economies.

Mexico, the USSR, and China hold the largest shares of bank loans to developing economies.

International bank lending

	1985	1989	FIRST 3Q 1989	FIRST 3Q 1990
THROUGH BANKS AND BOND MARKETS				
Bonds	77	97	78	30
Changes in bank claims	105	390	270	295
Growth (%)	8	17	12	12
Total	**182**	**487**	**348**	**325**
TO DEVELOPED ECONOMIES				
Bonds	63	81	68	25
Changes in bank claims	58	231	168	237
Growth (%)	5	10	7	9
Total	**121**	**312**	**236**	**262**
TO DEVELOPING ECONOMIES				
Bonds	4	2	1	1
Changes in bank claims	13	-12	-13	-18
Growth (%)	3	-2	-2	-3
Total	**17**	**10**	**-12**	**-17**
GROSS BOND ISSUES				
Developed economies	138	224	172	143
Developed (%)	82	88	87	83
Developing economies	8	5	3	4
Developing (%)	6	2	2	3
Total	**168**	**256**	**197**	**172**

Figure 12–5

Billions of dollars and percentages.
BIS figures, net of bond redemptions and repurchases and net of redepositing to banks.
Excluding changes attributed to exchange-rate movements.
Developing countries excludes 7 offshore centers.
Source: International Monetary Fund (7).

Bank lending to developing countries

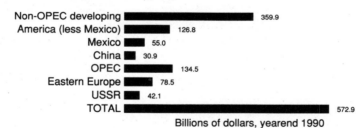

Non-OPEC developing	359.9
America (less Mexico)	126.8
Mexico	55.0
China	30.9
OPEC	134.5
Eastern Europe	78.5
USSR	42.1
TOTAL	572.9

Billions of dollars, yearend 1990

Figure 12–6

Billions of dollars, yearend 1990.
Borrowings from banks reporting to the BIS.
Source: Bank for International Settlements (1).

In the welter of inter-bank transactions, changes in claims (mostly loans) almost match changes in liabilities (deposits), leaving a relatively small net change. In the first three quarters of 1990, the $531 billion in total transactions netted out to a $21 billion increase in claims.

Banks in the United States were net lenders, while banks in Japan continued to be, though slightly, net takers of funds.

All developing economies received a net $29 billion from the rest of the world in the first three quarters of 1990.

Changes in bank and nonbank claims

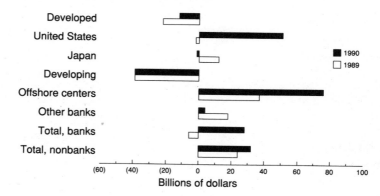

Changes in interbank claims and liabilities

	1985	1989	FIRST 3Q 1989	FIRST 3Q 1990
Total change in bank claims	**217**	**637**	**458**	**276**
Developed economies	183	436	323	256
United States	33	59	33	11
Japan	40	136	94	31
Developing economies	8		-2	-4
Offshore centers	19	171	109	36
Other transactors	7	30	27	-13
Total change in bank liabilities	**213**	**643**	**448**	**255**
Developed economies	168	458	340	266
United States	8	60	38	-27
Japan	40	125	108	32
Developing economies	1	38	17	25
Offshore centers	37	135	76	-20
Other transactors	8	12	15	-16
Changes in total net claims	**4**	**-6**	**10**	**21**
Developed economies	16	-22	-17	-9
United States	25	-2	-5	38
Japan	-1	12	-14	-1
Developing economies	6	-39	-19	-29
Offshore centers	-18	37	33	57
Other transactors	-1	18	13	3
Total change in nonbank claims	59	183	123	157
Total change in nonbank liabilities	89	158	117	132
Change in total net nonbank claims	**-30**	**24**	**5**	**24**

Figure 12–7

Billions of dollars.
Source: International Monetary Fund (7).

Bank lending to developing economies in the Western Hemisphere fell by $22 billion in the first three quarters of 1990, due largely to debt-reduction agreements by Mexico and Venezuela.

Lending to Asian developing economies grew 11% in that period, continuing solid growth through the decade.

Brazil is the largest developing-economy debtor to western banks. Mexico's debt dropped $15 billion in 1990 after its debt-reduction agreement with bank creditors.

The USSR's debt is third-highest. Poland is more heavily indebted than the accompanying graph indicates; most of its debt is owed to official creditors. The same is true of most African debtors.

Changes in bank claims on developing economies

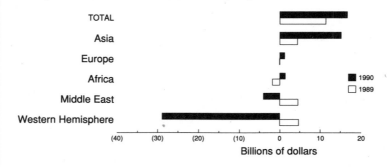

Billions of dollars

0

Total change in claims on	1985	1989	FIRST 3Q 1989	FIRST 3Q 1990
	3.6	**11.3**	**6.4**	**12.6**
Asia	6.7	4.3	3.7	11.3
Europe	1.3	-0.1	-0.3	0.9
Africa	0.9	-1.9	-0.3	0.1
Middle East	-1.9	4.4	0.4	-3.1
Western Hemisphere	-3.3	4.6	2.8	-21.7

Figure 12–8

Billions of dollars. Excluding effects of exchange-rate changes. Excluding offshore centers.
Source: International Monetary Fund (7).

Selected developing-country debt to western banks

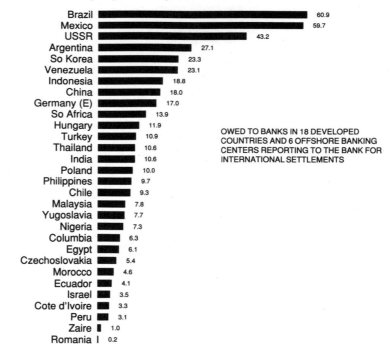

OWED TO BANKS IN 18 DEVELOPED COUNTRIES AND 6 OFFSHORE BANKING CENTERS REPORTING TO THE BANK FOR INTERNATIONAL SETTLEMENTS

Billions of dollars, yearend 1989
Includes undisbursed credit commitments

The total bank debt of developing countries did not grow at all in the last half of the 1980s.

It also remained flat in Africa during that period.

It declined appreciably in the Western Hemisphere and slightly in the Middle East.

It grew appreciably in Asia and in the USSR, and it grew moderately in developing Europe.

Selected developing-country debt to western banks

	1985	1988	1989
WESTERN HEMISPHERE			
Brazil	66.7	63.9	60.9
Mexico	71.7	62.8	59.7
Argentina	29.4	32.4	27.1
Venezuela	27.1	25.0	23.1
Chile	14.3	11.0	9.3
Colombia	6.4	6.6	6.3
Ecuador	5.0	4.5	4.1
Peru	4.7	3.7	3.1
Other	13.1	13.7	15.1
Total	**238.4**	**223.6**	**208.7**
ASIA			
So Korea	28.7	21.5	23.3
Indonesia	14.1	17.9	18.8
China	6.6	16.7	18.0
India	4.9	9.3	10.6
Thailand	6.9	8.3	10.6
Philippines	12.9	11.6	9.7
Malaysia	10.1	8.4	7.8
Other	9.7	20.0	17.0
Total	**93.9**	**113.5**	**115.8**
AFRICA			
So Africa	17.0	14.6	13.9
Nigeria	9.2	9.0	7.3
Morocco	4.5	4.6	4.6
Cote d'Ivoire	2.9	3.3	3.3
Zaire	0.8	1.1	1.0
Other	28.8	34.4	34.3
Total	**63.2**	**67.0**	**64.4**
EUROPE			
Hungary	8.6	11.7	11.9
Turkey	6.5	10.7	10.9
Poland	9.9	10.3	10.0
Yugoslavia	10.3	8.8	7.7
Romania	3.0	0.7	0.2
Other	1.2	2.5	3.3
Total	**39.5**	**44.7**	**44.0**
MIDDLE EAST			
Egypt	6.7	6.1	6.1
Israel	5.6	4.3	3.5
Other	3.7	4.8	4.5
Total	**16.0**	**15.2**	**14.1**
All developing	**478.1**	**492.5**	**478.9**
OTHER			
USSR	22.0	36.1	43.2
Germany (E)	10.3	16.0	17.0
Czechoslovakia	2.7	4.5	5.4
Other	5.2	9.7	10.7
Total	**40.2**	**66.3**	**76.3**

Figure 12–9

Billions of dollars at yearend. Includes undisbursed credit commitments.
External assets (claims) of banks in 18 developed countries and 6 offshore banking centers reporting to the Bank for International Settlements (BIS).
Source: International Monetary Fund (7).

Asian borrowers accounted for more than half of all longterm bank credit commitments to developing economies in 1990.

Of notable significance for the future, "spontaneous" (market-based) lending to developing economies in the Western Hemisphere continued to increase in 1990, as it had the year before. For Mexico, Venezuela, and Chile, this could mean the beginning of the end of their debt crises.

Interbank interest rates in the Eurocurrency markets were lowest for the United States and Japan.

Longterm bank credit commitments to developing countries

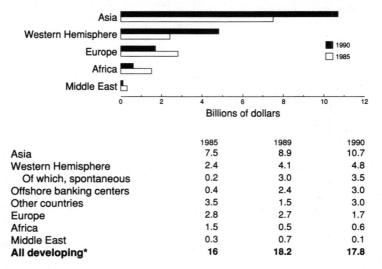

	1985	1989	1990
Asia	7.5	8.9	10.7
Western Hemisphere	2.4	4.1	4.8
Of which, spontaneous	0.2	3.0	3.5
Offshore banking centers	0.4	2.4	3.0
Other countries	3.5	1.5	3.0
Europe	2.8	2.7	1.7
Africa	1.5	0.5	0.6
Middle East	0.3	0.7	0.1
All developing*	**16**	**18.2**	**17.8**

Figure 12–10

Billions of dollars.
* Excludes offshore banking centers. Offshore banking centers = The Bahamas, Bahrain, Cayman Islands, Hong Kong, Netherlands Antilles, Panama, and Singapore.
Spontaneous lending indicates reentry into voluntary credit markets; includes two large "semi-spontaneous" loans to Columbia.
Other countries = mostly Eastern European, but not Poland and Hungary.
Source: International Monetary Fund (7).

Eurocurrency deposit rates

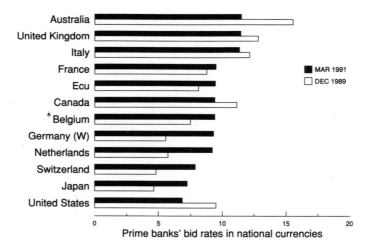

Eastern European borrowers continued to get the best rates in the longterm market in 1990, rates slightly better than those offered in the developed countries. The spread rose slightly from the previous year. Over a five-year period, rates fell by one-half a percentage point.

The average spread for all bank loans fell a little in 1990 and by one-tenth of a percentage point over the previous five years. Spreads for loans to OECD borrowers also fell in 1990, but they rose over the five-year period.

For all developing-country borrowers, spreads were considerably lower in 1990 than they had been five years earlier.

The average rate for Eurodollar interbank loans dropped by almost a full percentage point in 1990 and by about one-third of that over the last five years.

The United States prime rate also fell by nearly a full percentage point in 1990. But it was a little higher in that year than it had been five years earlier.

Eurocurrency deposit rates

	DEC 1989	DEC 1990	MAR 1991
Australia	15.56	16.22	11.48
United Kingdom	12.81	14.56	11.44
Italy	12.13	13.00	11.31
France	8.75	11.06	9.50
European currency unit	8.13	11.19	9.44
Canada	11.13	11.63	9.38
Belgium	7.50	10.19	9.38
Germany (W)	5.56	8.38	9.31
Netherlands	5.75	8.56	9.19
Switzerland	4.81	8.50	7.88
Japan	4.63	6.75	7.25
United States	9.50	8.13	6.88

Figure 12–11

Prime banks' bid rates, at or near end of month.
For 12-month maturities.
Source: J P Morgan (1).

Interest-rate spreads for longterm bank loans

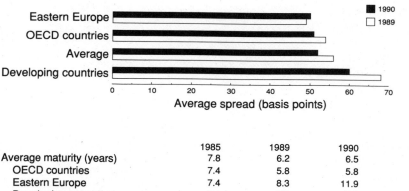

Average spread (basis points)

	1985	1989	1990
Average maturity (years)	7.8	6.2	6.5
OECD countries	7.4	5.8	5.8
Eastern Europe	7.4	8.3	11.9
Developing countries	8.4	7.3	8.6
Average spread (basis points)	62	56	52
OECD countries	47	54	51
Eastern Europe	55	49	50
Developing countries	92	68	60
Other rates (percent)			
6-month Eurodollar*	8.64	9.27	8.35
US prime	9.93	10.92	10.01

Figure 12–12

* Average interbank rate.
Source: International Monetary Fund (7).

In the later years of the 1980s, international bank supervisors initiated a system of risk-based capital requirements for banks in the main economies. The new standards, which were adopted, call for capital-to-asset ratios of 8% by the end of 1992.

By 1989, the largest banks in Switzerland, the United States, and the United Kingdom had met the new requirements. Subsequently, most banks in developed economies had met either the final or interim capital requirements.

Since 1985, shortly after the onset of the developing world's debt crisis, United States banks have substantially improved their exposures to these debts. Claims fell by one-half as a percent of total assets, and the ratio of capital to claims more than doubled.

Capital/asset ratios of banks

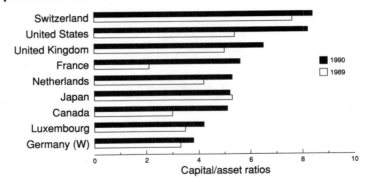

	1980	1989
Switzerland	7.6	8.4
5 largest	7.6	8.7
United States*	5.4	8.2
9 money-center	4.5	9.3
Next 15	5.5	7.9
United Kingdom	5.0	6.5
4 largest	6.9	8.0
France	2.1	5.6
Netherlands	4.2	5.3
Japan	5.3	5.2
Canada	3.0	5.1
Luxembourg	3.5	4.2
Germany (W)	3.3	3.8

Figure 12–13

* 155 banking organizations.
Note: Methods of accounting for bank assets and capital vary greatly from country to country. Changes over time within a single country are more accurate than cross-country comparisons.
Source: International Monetary Fund (7).

Capital coverage of United States banks' claims on borrowers in developing countries

	1985	1989	FIRST 3Q 1990
Claims	129	79	68
Total assets	1529	1770	1802
Capital	105	145	147
RATIOS (%)			
Capital to total assets	7	8	8
Claims to total assets	8	5	4
Capital to claims	82	184	217

Table 12–2

Billions of dollars and percent.
Claims are exposures; i.e., adjusted for guarantees and other risk transfers.
Source: International Monetary Fund (7).

Japan's commercial banks are by far the world's biggest in terms of assets. But because of their low margins, they are below the median in profitability.

Banks in Germany are the most profitable among the main economies.

CHIPS, the interbank payments system, handles 90% of the world's international settlements. In 1990, more than $222 trillion flowed through this system — about ten times the output of all the world's economies. The average amount of the 149 million transactions in that year was $6 million.

Commercial bank profitability in the 1980s

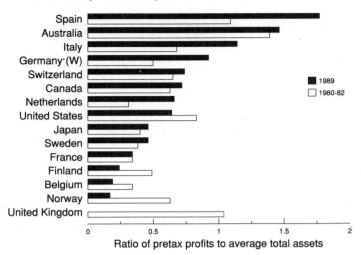

Ratio of pretax profits to average total assets

	1980-82	1983-85	1986-87	1988-89	1989
Spain	1.09	0.91	1.10	1.72	1.77
Australia	1.39	1.33	1.23	1.50	1.46
Italy	0.68	0.78	1.01	1.02	1.14
Germany (W)	0.50	0.92	0.80	0.90	0.92
Switzerland	0.65	0.69	0.71	0.69	0.74
Canada	0.63	0.76	0.86	1.03	0.72
Netherlands	0.31	0.61	0.73	0.63	0.66
United States	0.83	0.78	0.44	0.93	0.64
Japan	0.40	0.46	0.56	0.55	0.46
Sweden	0.38	0.39	0.82	0.52	0.46
France	0.34	0.21	0.31	0.35	0.34
Finland	0.49	0.48	0.54	0.51	0.24
Belgium	0.34	0.35	0.41	0.27	0.19
Norway	0.63	0.85	0.22	-0.08	0.17
United Kingdom	1.04	0.92	0.68	0.74	-0.03

Figure 12–14

Ratio of pretax profit to average total assets of commercial banks.
Source: Bank for International Settlements (3).

World automated interbank payments

	YEARLY VOLUME ($Billions)	DAILY VOLUME ($Billions)	YEARLY XACTIONS (Millions)	DAILY XACTIONS (Millions)	$ PER PAYMENT ($Millions)
1980	37121	148	13244	53	2.803
1989	190212	758	36520	145	5.208
1990	222108	885	37324	149	5.951

Table 12–3

For Clearing House Interbank Payments System (CHIPS).
Note: CHIPS handles over 90% of the world's interbank payments.
Source: Clearing House Interbank Payments Systems (1).

13 External Debt

For developing countries in the 1980s, the governing force of their economic lives was the debt crisis. It arrived like a clap of thunder on the international financial scene in the summer of 1982 when Mexican officials came to Washington to announce that they weren't able to service their debts to commercial banks. Over a weekend, the world's most powerful financial leaders put together a rescue package in the belief — which they would hold for three stressful years — that the basic problem was liquidity: a temporary shortage of international cash to service their trade deficits.

Over the next few months, other heavily indebted developing countries would follow Mexico's lead to the brink of default. Banks immediately stopped making new loans, except to refinance arrears in interest payments. The International Monetary Fund stepped in with loans to cover the "temporary" balance-of-payments difficulties.

In the fall of 1985, the US treasury secretary acknowledged that the crisis was more serious than at first admitted. He outlined a plan whereby commercial banks would resume lending, supported by loans from the IMF and the World Bank. The two international banks continued their lending. But commerical banks still held back, not satisfied that the investment climate in the debtor economies justified adding new debts to the old ones.

Growth of total external debt in all developing countries

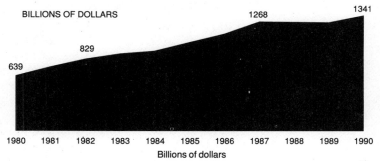

BILLIONS OF DOLLARS

639   829   1268   1341

1980 1981 1982 1983 1984 1985 1986 1987 1988 1989 1990

Billions of dollars

Figure 13–1

In the spring of 1987, the biggest US commercial banks initiated their own plan for extricating themselves from the problem. Each bank would find its own way out by selecting from a long "menu of options" for getting the loans off their books: selling them at a discount, swapping debt for equity or for "exit bonds," and other financial inventions.

However, the banks' strategems did nothing to relieve the plight of the debtors. By now, it was generally agreed that the problem was not liquidity, a temporary shortage of cash, but solvency, a basic inability to handle financial needs. During most of the 1980s, the flow of money seemed to be going the wrong way: from less-developed to more-developed economies. That is, the heavily indebted middle-income countries were sending tens of billions of dollars to the developed economies in loan payments and getting much less back in new loans and investments, thereby impairing their ability to get back on a sustainable growth path. Also, the stern conditions under which they got IMF loans were hurting their own poorest people.

Building on concepts first advanced by European leaders, in 1989 a new US treasury secretary announced a new plan for handling the continuing crisis, based on debt relief. Banks were encouraged to reduce either the principal or interest of their loans. US treasury bonds were used as collateral. The IMF and World Bank loaned money for debt reductions and conversions.

By the end of 1990, the new plan seemed to be working. Mexico and Venezuela had used it to reduce their debts by billions. Those reductions, coupled with reforms in their economic systems, brought the two countries to the threshhold of "spontaneous" borrowing in the capital markets via loans and bond issues.

Such bright success stories were rare among the 76 countries that have had to refinance their loans. The total debt grew 6% in 1990 to $1.341 trillion. (Half of this increase was attributed to depreciation of the US dollar.) Forecasters expect total debt to grow by 3.25% a year in 1991 and '92. They also look for a significant decline in debt as a percent of gross national product. They predict that official creditors will step up their lending rates to $32–$38 billion in 1992, compared with $6 billion in 1990. Observers expect banks to continue to ease their way out of the debt scene, making loans on a very selective basis and then mostly to finance trade and specific projects. General-purpose "sovereign" loans, secured only by faith in the perpetuity of the debtor government, are out of the picture, at least in the near future.

At the Paris Club, where official creditors meet to reschedule debts, member countries continue to press for wholesale debt forgiveness — 100% of it in one proposal and two-thirds in another. They have agreed to reduce Poland's huge debt by half, in two stages. (Unlike most middle-income debtors, Poland owes most of its debt to official creditors.) Most debt forgiveness will be offered to the undeveloped countries of Asia and Sub-Saharan Africa.

Debtor countries in Latin America and the Caribbean owe more than a third of all external debt, more than twice as much as countries in East Asia and the Pacific.

The biggest class of debtors were severely indebted middle-income countries, with half of the total debt. Low-income debtors owe only about a tenth of the total.

Increasingly, country debt is migrating from private to official holders, as commercial banks work their way out of involvement and official sources step in to provide relief and to "enhance" existing debt. By 1990, a little more than half of all longterm debt was owed to official creditors; in 1980 about one-third was.

External debt by region and group

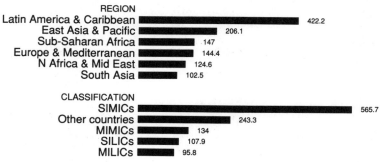

Billions of dollars, 1989

	1988	1989	CHANGE
REGION			
Latin America & Caribbean	427.5	422.2	-0.7
East Asia & Pacific	206.1	206.1	3.1
Sub-Saharan Africa	141.5	147.0	4.6
Europe & Mediterranean	143.7	144.4	1.8
North Africa & Mid East	122.0	124.6	2.5
South Asia	95.5	102.5	8.8
CLASSIFICATION			
Severely-indebted middle income (SIMIC)	567.8	565.7	0.4
Other countries	237.1	243.3	4.5
Moderately-indebted middle income (MIMIC)	132.3	134.0	1.8
Severely-indebted low income (SILIC)	105.9	107.9	3.2
Moderately-indebted low income (MILIC)	93.4	95.8	5.7
All developing countries	**1136.5**	**1146.7**	**2.1**

Figure 13–2

Billions of dollars of total debt.
Change = 1989 percent, adjusted for currency changes.
Source: World Bank (5).

Longterm private and official debt

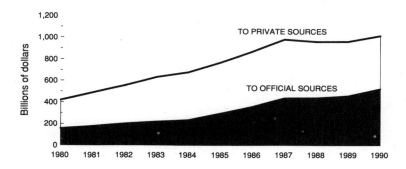

The external debt of all developing countries doubled during the 1980s.

Longterm debt, the most worrisome component of the total, grew much faster than shortterm debt, most of which finances trade and is usually serviced faithfully.

The debt of countries with servicing problems was 272% of their exports in 1989. (Analysts say that a ratio of 200% is the threshhold of severe debt problems.) For low-income debtors, the ratio was 493%. The average for all developing countries approached the danger level.

External debt of developing economies

	DRS ECONOMIES						OTHER	ALL
	TOTAL	LONGTOTAL	LONGOFF	LONGPRIV	SHORT	IMF		
1980	562	421	157	264	129	12	77	639
1981	656	487	177	310	151	18	83	739
1982	743	552	197	354	167	24	86	829
1983	807	633	219	414	140	34	86	893
1984	843	675	233	442	133	36	81	924
1985	937	768	294	473	129	40	89	1026
1986	1028	867	357	511	118	43	99	1127
1987	1152	980	433	547	128	43	116	1268
1988	1137	960	437	523	142	35	128	1265
1989	1147	959	454	505	156	32	114	1261
1990	1221	1015	521	494	169	36	120	1341

Figure 13–3

Billions of dollars.
DRS = 107 countries reporting to the World Bank Debtor Reporting System.
Longtotal = total longterm debt.
Longoff = total longterm debt to official sources.
Longpriv = total longterm debt to private sources.
Short = shortterm debt.
IMF = use of IMF credit.
Other = total debt of non-DRS countries.
All = total external debt of all developing countries.
Source: World Bank (5).

Debt indicators by groups and regions

	SHARE	DEBT/ EXPORTS	DEBT SERVICE
Without debt-service problems	18	86	14
With debt-service problems	82	272	29
SIMICs	49	294	29
SILICs	9	493	23
Moderately indebted	24	194	31
BY REGION			
Latin America & Caribbean	37	284	31
East Asia and Pacific	18	90	16
Sub-Saharan Africa	13	371	22
Europe & Mediterranean	11	131	19
Middle East & No Africa	11	250	31
South Asia	9	273	25
All developing countries	**100**	**187**	**22**

Table 13–1

Percentages and ratios, 1989.
Debt indicators are based on total external debt and associated payments of debt service.
Source: World Bank (5).

Commercial banks hold more than one-third of the total longterm debt, almost all of which is guaranteed by some kind of public agency.

Multilateral creditors like the International Monetary Fund and World Bank more than doubled their lending during the 1980s.

Concessional — below market rate — lending tripled over the decade.

Official creditors hold 67% of the debt of severely-indebted low income countries; the comparable figure for severely-indebted middle income countries is 35%.

Structure of longterm debt of developing economies

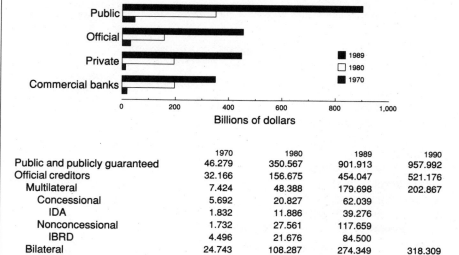

Billions of dollars

	1970	1980	1989	1990
Public and publicly guaranteed	46.279	350.567	901.913	957.992
Official creditors	32.166	156.675	454.047	521.176
Multilateral	7.424	48.388	179.698	202.867
Concessional	5.692	20.827	62.039	
IDA	1.832	11.886	39.276	
Nonconcessional	1.732	27.561	117.659	
IBRD	4.496	21.676	84.500	
Bilateral	24.743	108.287	274.349	318.309
Concessional	21.213	73.896	143.613	
Private creditors	14.112	193.892	447.866	436.817
Bonds	1.893	13.055	48.821	
Commercial banks	3.797	127.612	293.950	
Other private	8.422	53.225	105.096	
Private nonguaranteed	15.645	70.101	56.911	57.144
Commercial banks	19.442	197.713	350.861	
Total longterm debt	**61.923**	**420.668**	**958.824**	**1015.136**

Figure 13–4

Billions of dollars.
1990 figures are projections.
Bilateral = loans by individual governments.
Source: World Bank (5).

External debt of country groups

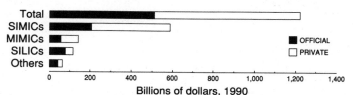

Billions of dollars, 1990

	DEBT 1990	OFFICIAL %	OFFICIAL	PRIVATE
SIMICs	588	35	206	382
MIMICs	141	40	56	85
SILICs	116	67	78	38
Others	66	66	44	22
Total	**911**		**384**	**527**

Figure 13–5

Billions of dollars and percent, 1990. Projections.
SILICs - 26 severely indebted lower income countries.
SIMICs = 20 severely indebted middle income countries.
MIMICs = 13 moderately indebted middle income countries.
Official = percent of total debt from official sources.
Source: World Bank (5).

Some patterns of country indebtedness changed notably during the 1980s.

In 1985–87, exchange-rate adjustments accounted for most of the growth in the stock of debt; in later years, the effects were still considerable but much less.

Net flows of debt continued to decline, due to the halt in lending by commerical banks and the conversion of debt to equity.

In 1990, bank claims on Latin American economies fell appreciably. For all developing economies, the rise in Asian debt accounted wholly for the rise in the debt of the developing economies.

Trade-related credits remained about the same in 1990 as they were the year earlier.

Changes in developing-country debt

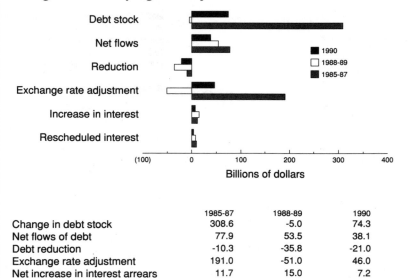

	1985-87	1988-89	1990
Change in debt stock	308.6	-5.0	74.3
Net flows of debt	77.9	53.5	38.1
Debt reduction	-10.3	-35.8	-21.0
Exchange rate adjustment	191.0	-51.0	46.0
Net increase in interest arrears	11.7	15.0	7.2
Rescheduled interest	9.6	7.8	4.0
Residual	28.7	5.5	0.0

Figure 13–6

Billions of dollars. Figures for 1990 are projected. For 107 main debtors.
Source: World Bank (5).

Bank and nonbank claims on developing countries

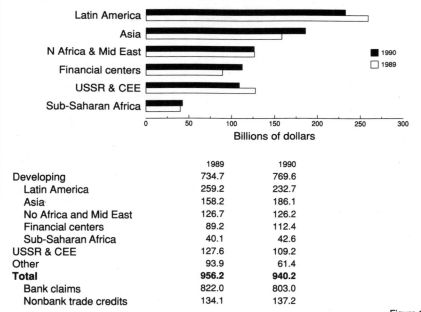

	1989	1990
Developing	734.7	769.6
Latin America	259.2	232.7
Asia	158.2	186.1
No Africa and Mid East	126.7	126.2
Financial centers	89.2	112.4
Sub-Saharan Africa	40.1	42.6
USSR & CEE	127.6	109.2
Other	93.9	61.4
Total	**956.2**	**940.2**
Bank claims	822.0	803.0
Nonbank trade credits	134.1	137.2

Figure 13–7

Billions of dollars. 1990 = as of June 30. As reported to the Bank for International Settlements (BIS).
CEE = Central and Eastern Europe: Bulgaria, Czechoslovakia, Germany (E), Hungary, Poland, Romania, Yugoslavia.
Source: Bank for International Settlements (2).

Brazil is the developing world's biggest debtor to commercial banks at the end of the decade, followed closely by Mexico. The USSR is a solid third.

Bank debts of South Korea and China are not considered to be problems.

In the 1980s, net resource flows to developing economies (including direct investment) fell by 14%, while transfers from official sources rose by 44%.

Foreign direct investment more than doubled.

Bottomline net transfers fell by 75% over the decade; they had been negative since 1984.

Country debts to commercial banks

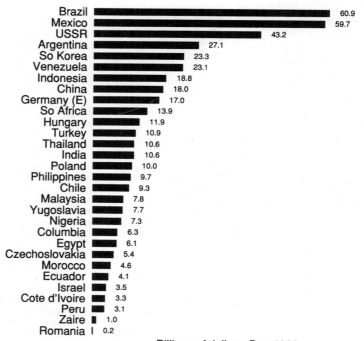

Billions of dollars, Dec 1989

Figure 13–8

Billions of dollars at yearend.
External assets (claims) of banks in 18 developed countries and 6 offshore banking centers reporting to the Bank for International Settlements (BIS).
Includes undisbursed credit commitments.
Source: International Monetary Fund (7).

Net resource flows and transfers to developing economies

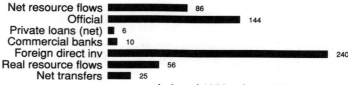

Index of 1990 values; 1980 = 100.

Among severely in-debted middle income countries, which hold the biggest share of total debt, three Latin American countries were by far the biggest debtors.

Net resource flows to developing economies

	1980	1990	INDEX
Net resource flows	82.8	71.0	86
Official development finance	32.6	46.9	144
Private loans (net)	41.1	2.3	6
Commercial banks	30.8	3.0	10
Foreign direct investment	9.1	21.8	240
Real net resource flows*	109.3	61.4	56
Net transfers	37.0	9.3	25

Figure 13–9

Billions of dollars, longterm borrowings.
Index of 1990 values; 1980 = 100.
*Deflated by OECD deflator.
Commercial bank loans are for 1989, not 1990.
Source: World Bank (5).

Notes for comment:
Aggregate net transfers were negative in 1984 (-0.9), 1985 (-7.4), 1986 (-10.0), 1987 (-16.8), 1988 (-9.5), 1989 (1.0).
Total transfers, 1981-90: $47.3 billion, about same as 1981 ($45.7 billion).
Net resource flows = New loans less amortizations plus official grants plus foreign direct investment.
Net transfers = Net resource flows less interest payments less FDI profits.

Total debt of severely-indebted middle income countries

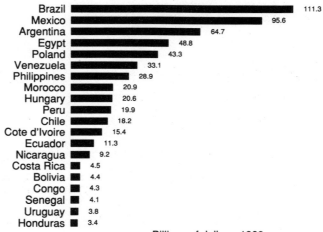

Billions of dollars, 1989

For severely-indebted middle income countries, interest payments accounted for 16.5% of export earnings. For low-income countries, the interest burden was less because of concessional lending.

Over $100 billion flowed from severely-indebted middle income countries to developed economies during the 1980s. (Historically, resources flow from richer to poorer economies.) The net outflow impaired the debtors' ability to revive their economies.

Debt and debt service in severely-indebted countries

	TOTAL DEBT	PRIVATE PERCENT	DEBT SERVICE TOTAL	INTEREST	DEBT/ GNP	INTEREST/ EXPORTS
Brazil	111.3	73.0	11.6	5.7	24.1	15.5
Mexico	95.6	79.1	14.4	9.3	51.2	25.5
Argentina	64.7	81.4	4.4	2.1	119.7	17.7
Egypt	48.8	17.7	3.0	1.5	159.0	11.0
Poland	43.3	31.5	1.5	0.9	68.3	5.3
Venezuela	33.1	96.8	3.9	3.2	79.9	20.3
Philippines	28.9	47.0	3.4	2.2	65.7	17.1
Morocco	20.9	23.4	2.0	1.2	95.9	18.4
Hungary	20.6	88.3	3.4	1.5	72.9	11.1
Peru	19.9	53.3	0.3	0.2	70.8	3.6
Chile	18.2	67.1	2.7	1.6	78.3	16.8
Cote d'Ivoire	15.4	58.9	1.4	0.5	182.2	15.6
Ecuador	11.3	61.4	1.0	0.5	112.9	17.1
Nicaragua	9.2	17.7	0.0	0.0	623.6	7.7
Costa Rica	4.5	47.4	0.4	0.2	91.2	10.5
Bolivia	4.4	18.3	0.3	0.1	103.1	14.3
Congo	4.3	41.6	0.3	0.1	214.9	11.9
Senegal	4.1	6.1	0.4	0.2	93.2	14.6
Uruguay	3.8	76.8	0.6	0.3	46.5	15.3
Honduras	3.4	18.6	0.1	0.1	72.5	6.2
SIMICs	565.7	61.8	55.1	31.4	54.9	16.5
Nigeria	32.8	52.4	1.8	1.3	119.3	15.6
SILICs	107.9	26.9	5.0	2.5	99.5	11.8

Billions of dollars and percentages or ratios, 1989.
Debt/GNP and Interest/exports for Hungary are for 1988.
Interest/exports for Nicaragua is for 1988. Nigeria is officially classified a SILIC.
Source: World Bank (5).

Figure 13–10

Net transfers to severely-indebted middle income developing economies

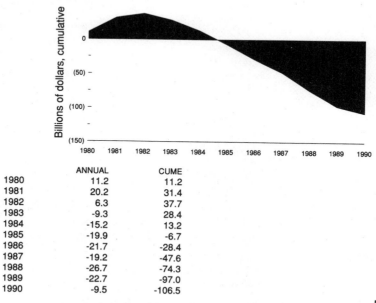

	ANNUAL	CUME
1980	11.2	11.2
1981	20.2	31.4
1982	6.3	37.7
1983	-9.3	28.4
1984	-15.2	13.2
1985	-19.9	-6.7
1986	-21.7	-28.4
1987	-19.2	-47.6
1988	-26.7	-74.3
1989	-22.7	-97.0
1990	-9.5	-106.5

Billions of dollars. Transfers on longterm private and official loans.
1990 is a projection. Cume = cumulating transfers, 1980–90.
Source: World Bank (5).

Figure 13–11

The main difference between low- and middle-income debtors is their per-capita outputs — a ratio of well over five to one. For middle-income debtors, manufactures accounted for about five times the share of exports.

Latin American countries, the biggest debtor group, owe some $250 billion, 60% of their total debt, to commercial banks.

At the decade's end, multilateral and bilateral official creditors accounted for equal shares of the region's debt.

Structural differences between SILICs and SIMICs

	SILICs	SIMICs
Annual population growth (1988)	3.2	2
Per-capita GNP in dollars, 1988	288	1632
Gross domestic investment/GDP (1987-88)	14	22
Exports/GDP (1987-88)	18	16
Manufacturing share of exports (1987-88)	8	43
Infant mortality (deaths/1000 live births, 1987)	109.8	55
Primary school enrollment (percent of age group, 1986)	67.3	103
Official development assistance (% of GDP, 1987)	8.2	0.6
Longterm official debt, percent of total debt	67	35

Table 13–2

Source: World Bank (5).

Composition of Latin America's external debt

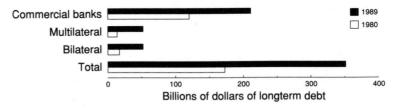

Billions of dollars of longterm debt

■ 1989
□ 1980

	1980	1989
COMMERCIAL BANKS		
Long term	120	211
Long term pct	50	50
Short term	68	39
Short term pct	28	9
Interest arrears	0	16
Total comml banks	188	250
Comml banks pct	78	59
Arrears pct	0	4
MULTILATERAL		
Long term	14	52
Long term pct	6	12
IMF	1	17
IMF pct	1	4
BILATERAL		
Long term	17	52
Long term pct	7	12
OTHERS		
Long term	22	36
Long term pct	9	9
TOTAL		
Total long term	173	351
Long term pct	71	83
Total short term	70	56
Short term pct	29	13
Total debts	**243**	**424**
Total pct	100	100

Figure 13–12

Billions of dollars and percent of total indebtedness.
Debts to commercial banks include those guaranteed by the public sector.
Source: Inter-American Development Bank (1).

Among transitioning economies, the USSR's hard-currency debt totaled $54 billion. The size of this debt is not worrisome in itself, given the size of the Soviet economy and its excellent debt-servicing record. The country's debt-service ratios are not excessive. However, all the trends are running in the wrong direction, and most analysts expect the USSR — or its successor confederation — to have mounting problems in the 1990s.

Debt burdens in Poland and Bulgaria have crossed the "problem" threshhold; Hungary's debt is also considered excessive. Debt relief being offered to Poland will help. Poland's courageous attempt to make the transition from socialist to market economy through "shock therapy" is keeping exchange rates stable, but the economy as a whole was depressed in the early years of the decade.

Hard-currency debt of USSR and Central & Eastern Europe

Billions of dollars, 1989

	EXTERNAL DEBT	OFFICIAL PERCENT	DEBT/ EXPORTS	DEBT SERVICE/ EXPORTS
USSR	54.0	na	125	21.0
Poland	43.3	55	263	9.4
Hungary	20.6	12	159	29.0
Yugoslavia	19.7	38	84	16.0
Bulgaria	9.2	17	230	na
Czechoslovakia	7.9	3	104	19.0
Romania	0.5	na	na	na
Central & Eastern Europe	101.2	35	156	

Figure 13–13

Billions of dollars and percentages, 1989.
Official percent: of longterm debt owed to official creditors.
Source: World Bank (5).

Per-capita debt in Sub-Saharan Africa

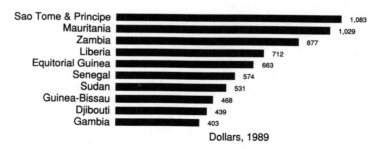

Dollars, 1989

Per-capita debt in Sub-Saharan Africa is high for every country; for the most heavily in-debted, it is four times the average of countries receiving loans from the World Bank's concessional lending agency.

Debt indicators for developing countries in Sub-Saharan Africa

	TOTAL PERCAP	TOTAL DEBT	OFFICIAL PERCENT	IMF CREDITS	DEBT SERVICE
IDA ONLY					
Sao Tome & Principe*	1083	131	84	1	100
Mauritania*	1029	2010	90	69	33
Zambia*	877	6874	64	900	38
Liberia	712	1761	68	299	26
Equitorial Guinea	663	228	92	9	54
Senegal*	574	4139	88	316	41
Sudan	531	12965	60	884	97
Guinea-Bissau*	468	449	89	5	63
Djibouti	439	180	73	0	7
Gambia*	403	342	89	38	12
Guinea*	392	2176	89	61	35
Comoros	383	176	92	0	23
Cape Verde	352	130	95	0	31
Somalia*	351	2137	90	150	85
Togo*	338	1186	82	75	18
Madagascar*	323	3607	89	165	118
Mozambique*	310	4766	70	56	246
Mali*	263	2157	97	55	35
Sierra Leone	261	1056	50	105	28
Zaire*	257	8843	84	628	36
Benin*	256	1177	66	10	20
Kenya*	244	5690	66	415	34
Central African Republic*	240	707	92	35	18
Ghana*	213	3078	93	737	23
Niger*	211	1578	70	85	42
Tanzania*	192	4918	89	129	69
Lesotho	188	324	90	10	4
Malawi*	169	1394	92	101	23
Burundi*	164	867	96	40	43
Uganda*	108	1808	88	225	57
Rwanda	95	652	92	1	20
Burkina Faso	86	756	86	1	11
Chad*	69	380	82	24	4
Ethiopia	62	3013	85	30	46
Total IDA	**258**	**81655**	**78**	**5659**	**43**
OTHER SUB-SAHARAN AFRICA					
Gabon	2661	2940	37	135	11
Seychelles	2485	169	61	0	10
Congo	1955	4316	46	12	77
Cote d'Ivoire	1316	15412	34	370	58
Mauritius	783	832	67	63	7
Botswana	422	513	90	0	4
Cameroon	395	4560	50	113	37
Swaziland	378	288	97	0	4
Zimbabwe	323	3087	40	29	29
Nigeria	289	32832	36	0	57
Total other	**427**	**65360**	**47**	**722**	**41**
SPA countries	236	49431	81	3542	43

Figure 13–14

IDA = International Development Agency, concessional unit of the World Bank.
Debt per capita in dollars, 1989.
Total debt in millions of dollars, 1989.
Official percent of total debt owed to official creditors.
Use of IMF credit in millions of dollars, 1989.
Longterm debt service = 1990 scheduled/1989 exports (%).
*Countries participating in SPA = Special Program of Assistance providing extraordinary concessional assistance to adjusting low-income African countries.
Source: World Bank (5).

External Debt

Developing-country debts to United States banks are owed mostly to nine large money-center banks. The share for Latin American debtors is even higher. Asia is the second-biggest regional debtor to US banks; most of those claims are on borrowers in dynamic economies which have no problems servicing their debts.

Mexico is the largest single debtor to United States banks, with $13 billion (6%) of the $212 billion outstanding. Brazil is not far behind with $11 billion (5%).

All developing-country loans to United States banks are 139% of total capital and 12% of total assets. Both figures are much more favorable than they were in mid-decade at the height of the debt crisis.

Main debtors of largest US banks

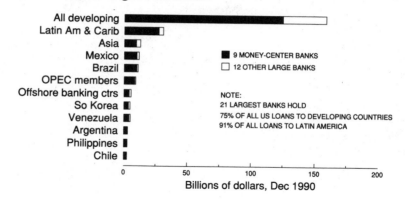

Billions of dollars, Dec 1990

	ALL BANKS	% OF ALL DEBT	9 MONEY CENTER	12 OTHER BANKS	21 LARGE BANKS	MONEY CENTER %	21 BANKS %
LOANS							
Latin Am & Caribn	33.549	15.81	26.947	3.695	30.642	80	91
Asia	15.088	7.11	9.475	2.921	12.396	63	82
Mexico	12.990	6.12	9.875	1.644	11.519	76	89
Brazil	11.270	5.31	9.925	0.856	10.781	88	96
OPEC members	9.894	4.66	8.462	0.717	9.179	86	93
Offshore bank ctrs	6.629	3.12	4.049	1.324	5.373	61	81
So Korea	6.016	2.83	3.514	1.113	4.627	58	77
Venezuela	5.797	2.73	4.142	0.717	4.859	71	84
Argentina	3.271	1.54	2.588	0.550	3.138	79	96
Philippines	2.848	1.34	2.452	0.349	2.801	86	98
Chile	2.813	1.33	2.215	0.351	2.566	79	91
Hong Kong	2.302	1.08	1.383	0.514	1.897	60	82
Singapore	1.991	0.94	1.265	0.466	1.731	64	87
USSR, CEE	1.818	0.86	1.378	0.312	1.690	76	93
Colombia	1.740	0.82	1.341	0.164	1.505	77	86
Taiwan	1.721	0.81	0.927	0.562	1.489	54	87
Thailand	1.420	0.67	0.648	0.422	1.070	46	75
Africa	1.244	0.59	1.037	0.144	1.181	83	95
Int'l & regional orgs	1.118	0.53	0.779	0.150	0.929	70	83
Yugoslavia	1.112	0.52	0.860	0.200	1.060	77	95
India	1.090	0.51	0.764	0.177	0.941	70	86
Indonesia	1.007	0.47	0.658	0.174	0.832	65	83
Total all developing	**212.260**	**100**	**124.782**	**34.100**	**158.882**	**59**	**75**
CAPITAL							
All loans	**153**		**59**	**28**	**87**		
Loans/capital (%)	139		210	122	183		
ASSETS							
All loans	**1764**		**623**	**327**	**950**		
Loans/assets (%)	12		20	10	17		

Figure 13–15

Billions of dollars, Dec 1990. Includes both guaranteed and nonguaranteed borrowings.
9 money center banks: Bank of America, Citibank, Chase Manhattan, Manufacturers Hanover, Morgan Guaranty, Chemical, Continental Illinois, Bankers Trust, First National Bank of Chicago.
12 other large banks: Security Pacific, Wells Fargo, Marine Midland, Mellon, First Interstate, First National Bank of Boston, National Bank of Detroit, Texas Commerce, Bank of New York, NCNB, Texas National, Republic Bank of New York, First City National Bank of Houston.
Source: Federal Reserve Board (1).

A main part of the strategy of United States banks for protecting themselves from the effects of default was to increase reserves against possible loan losses.

On average, by mid-1990 the largest US banks had set aside 46% of total developing-country loan values as provisions against default. Two banks had made even greater provisioning, and three others were above the average.

(Note: Since then, several of the banks shown have merged with one another or with other large banks.)

Provisioning of reserves by United States banks was below the lowest of European banks, but above that of Japanese banks. The highest provisioning of Japanese banks was also well below that of US and European banks.

Reserves of largest US commercial banks against developing-world loan losses

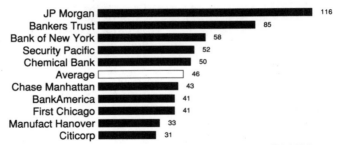

Percent of longterm loans, Q2 1990

	EXPOSURE	RESERVES	RESERVES PERCENT
Citicorp	7800	2415	31.0
Manufactures Hanover	4500	1481	32.9
BankAmerica	4050	1739	42.9
Chase Manhattan	4000	1730	43.3
Chemical Bank	2370	1187	50.1
Bankers Trust	2271	1930	85.0
J.P.Morgan	1500	1736	115.7
Bank of New York	544	313	57.5
First Chicago	450	183	40.7
Security Pacific	250	130	52.0
Total/average	**27735**	**12844**	**46.3**

Figure 13–16

Millions of dollars, June 1990.
Exposures and loan-loss reserves vs developing-country loans.
Source: World Bank (5).

Reserve positions of non-US banks

	1989	1990
United Kingdom	50-70	52-84
France	53-57	56-61
Germany (W)	38-77	50-78
Japan	15-20	25-30
United States		31-116

Table 13–3

Percent of developing-country loans covered by reserves.
UK banks: Natwest, Lloyds, Barclays, Midland.
French banks: Banque Nationale de Paris, Credit Lyonnais, Societe General.
German banks: Deutsche Bank, Dresdner Bank, Commerzbank.
Japanese banks: Dai-Ichi Kangyo, Sumitomo, Fuji, Mitsubishi, Sanwa, Bank of Tokyo.
Source: World Bank (5).

Arrearages in debt obligations (effectively, nonpayment of interest) is a big problem for banks, since regulators can require banks to set aside reserves out of profits against non-performing loans.

By the end of the decade, arrears in all debtor groups had risen for both private and official creditors.

Among low-income debtors, arrears were greater to official than to private creditors. Among middle-income debtors, arrears are greater to private creditors, a sore point among bankers.

In a pathbreaking "Brady" debt reduction package, Mexico's debt was effectively reduced by $7 billion. Added to this was an equivalent debt reduction of $8 billion gained from reductions in interest rates. Thus for Mexico the total net reduction of debt was $15 billion.

Other countries also got reductions in their debt or debt burdens in the 1989–90 packages.

Arrears in debt obligations

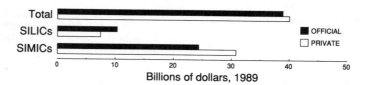

Billions of dollars, 1989

	1985 INTEREST	1985 TOTAL	1987 INTEREST	1987 TOTAL	1989 INTEREST	1989 TOTAL
Total						
Official	4.3	13.2	11.1	30.1	17.8	38.9
Private	3.5	14.1	9.0	24.6	17.2	40.0
SILICs						
Official	1.3	3.9	3.0	8.1	4.0	10.3
Private	0.5	2.1	1.3	3.8	1.7	7.4
SIMICs						
Official	2.8	9.8	7.7	20.8	12.4	24.4
Private	2.9	11.2	7.5	19.4	15.1	30.8

Figure 13–17

Billions of dollars of arrears.
Source: World Bank (5).

Debt reduction

Billions of dollars of effective total reduction

	COSTA RICA	MEXICO	NIGER	PHILIP-PINES	URU-GUAY	VENE-ZUELA
Public sector debt before	1.7	66.2	0.1	12.8	1.6	20.2
Eligible bank debt before	1.6	48.5	0.1	7.0	1.6	19.8
Bank debt extinguished	0.8	7.1	0.1	1.3	0.6	2.0
Interest (equiv reduction)	0.2	7.9			0.1	2.6
Effective total reduction	1.0	15.0	0.1	1.3	0.8	4.6
Debt incurred for enhancements	0.2	5.7		0.3	0.2	1.2
Use of own reserves	0.04	1.4	0.02	0.4	0.25	1.4
Net effective reduction	0.8	7.9	0.1	0.6	0.3	2.0
New money		1.1		0.7	0.1	1.2

Figure 13–18

Billions of dollars.
Debt-reduction packages negotiated between 1989–91.
"Before" = before debt-reducing operations.
Interest factor = the debt-reduction equivalent of reduced interest rates.
This factor applies to $22.5 billion of Mexico's debt, $10.5 billion of Venezuela's, and lesser face values of other countries' debts.
Niger's "own reserves" were to be obtainedthrough IDA grants and bilateral donors.
Uruguay's "own reserves" to be replenished through new borrowings.
Source: International Monetary Fund (7).

One way of reducing debt is to convert some it to equity shares in public or private enterprises. A total of nearly $34 billion in debt has been extinguished in this way.

Brazil is Latin America's most-active debt swapper, with $11 billion. Chile has reduced a greater proportion of debt in this way and is regarded as the pacesetter of the method.

The clearest advantage of debt swapping is that it eliminates the never-ending burden of interest payments. Opinion divides on whether or not it stimulates privatization of firms that would otherwise have remained publicly owned. In all, debt swapping is considered constructive. For various reasons, however, its role in debt management will probably be limited over the long run.

Debt-for-equity swaps

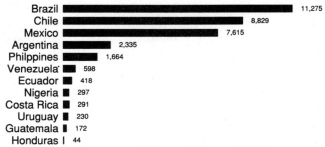

Millions of dollars, 1985-89

	1985	1986	1987	1988	1989	TOTAL 1985-89
Brazil	530	206	300	5515	4724	11275
Chile	332	981	1950	2782	2784	8829
Mexico		363	1786	2919	2547	7615
Argentina	467			1354	514	2335
Philppines		11	353	826	474	1664
Venezuela				51	547	598
Ecuador			127	259	32	418
Nigeria				40	257	297
Costa Rica			145	100	46	291
Uruguay			36	144	50	230
Guatemala				152	20	172
Honduras				10	34	44
Jamaica				9	24	33
Total	**1329**	**1561**	**4697**	**14161**	**12053**	**33801**

Figure 13–19

Millions of dollars.
Debt-for-equity swaps (conversions) are various forms of debt reduction under which a debtor country government agrees to permit creditor banks to sell their claims for local currency at a discount, provided that the proceeds are used to make equity investments in resident enterprises.
Source: World Bank (5).

External Debt

14 Development Aid

The global economy reaches all geographic regions and, in ways large and small, is the product of the economic actions of every person, business, and government. Yet perhaps the most striking feature of the global economy is its concentration: 15% of the world's people produce 68% of its output . . . and, it follows, get 68% of its income. This egregious disparity suggests to all parties the need to redistribute the wealth. Since each party approaches this distribution from its own perspective, the result is a hodge-podge of often-inconsistent motives, goals, and means.

For the developed economies, which control the redistribution, a broad range of involvements with the rest of the world provide the motivation. First, a relatively small but important segment of the developed world's trade is with transitioning, developing, and undeveloped economies. The traditional goal of having a secure source of raw materials and basic commodities is still important. The poorer economies are also a substantial — and potentially huge — market for industrial goods, services, and investments. Besides trade, developed economies have ideological reasons for parting with some of their wealth: religious affinities, geopolitical strategies, and internal politics. There are also prudential reasons: the fear of mass migration from benighted regions and awareness that poverty can lead to deforestation, desertification, pollution, and other hazards to the common global environment. Finally, and not necessarily least, is the humanitarian motive: consciences touched by the knowledge that more than one billion human beings live in poverty.

For potential aid recipients, the most striking fact is the gross disparity — and, most say, unfairness — of the system as it is. For decades, their advocates have called for some kind of "new internatonal economic order" with more-equitable dynamics.

The United Nations and its multilateral economic agencies are currently focusing on a less-confrontational version of a new order — one with human development as its central goal. UN analysts are looking beyond broad indicators such as growth of gross domestic product to find the real-life impact of programs in two main areas: reducing poverty and increasing private entrepreneural incentives.

The UN's agencies have come up with an analytical approach to development aid which they hope will lead donor countries to rethink and restructure their aid programs so as to emphasize human development. Their hierachical approach starts with setting appropriate goals for public expenditures: roads, telecommunications, defense, and other infrastructures. The analysis tracks how much of this spending goes to meet real human needs — education, health, welfare, water, sanitation, housing. With this analysis, UN policymakers hope to avoid misplaced or unintended outcomes — such as overspending on military weapons, aid that benefits middle and upper classes more than the general population, funds wasted on showcase projects such as world-class airports and grand public buildings, and technical aid that funds foreign expertise rather than developing indigenous capabilities. Overall, the UN estimates, about 40% of external aid goes to middle- and upper-income developing countries.

Using the UN's method of analysis, the present aid programs are too small and too poorly focused to make much of a difference in human development. The overall quantitative target for international aid is a modest seven-tenths of one percent (0.7%) of the gross national products of the main developed economies. The average actual contribution is less than half of that. Thus, on average, the wealthiest countries donate one-third of one percent (0.32%) of their GNP to aid programs. But only about one-tenth of that (0.026%) actually goes to the priority areas for human development, as defined by the United Nations.

Most aid (about 85%) comes from the Development Assistance Committee (DAC), consisting of 18 of the 24 members of the OECD. The aid is composed of bilateral aid (74%) flowing from donor government to recipient government and multilateral aid (26%) flowing through the international development agencies — primarily the World Bank group, the International Monetary Fund, and regional development banks.

In 1989, Japan became the biggest aid donor, at about the DAC's average level. The United States was the second-biggest donor in dollar amount but lowest in percent of GNP. On average, donations increased about two percent. Finland's contribution increased 17% and Italy's 14%.

The aggregate of long-term official development finance — aid from governments and international agencies — to all developing countries resumed a declining trend in 1989.

Net transfers, which include interest and principal payments on loans, were negative in 1989, as they had been in the two previous years. A negative net transfer means that more money flows out of the country (in payments of principal and interest on loans, plus profits repatriated from foreign investments) than flows into the country (in new loans and grants).

The International Monetary Fund was a net taker of funds from developing countries.

Net transfers of funds to severely-indebted middle income countries turned sharply negative in 1983 and remained negative throughout the decade.

Longterm aid to all developing countries

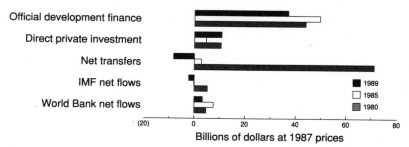

Note: Scale differs from chart below.

Longterm aid to severely-indebted middle income countries

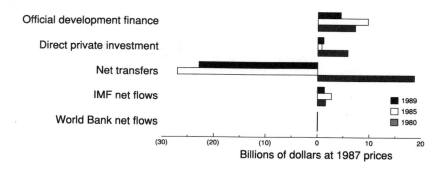

	ALL COUNTRIES			SEVERELY-INDEBTED MIDDLE INCOME COUNTRIES		
	1980	1985	1989	1980	1985	1989
Official development finance	44.0	49.7	37.0	7.2	9.7	4.4
Official development assistance	30.4	36.3	30.9	2.6	4.4	2.8
Official grants	17.5	23.1	18.2	0.6	1.9	1.5
Official concessional loans	12.9	13.3	12.7	2.1	2.5	1.3
Official nonconcessional loans	13.6	13.3	6.1	4.6	5.3	1.6
Private flows	69.6	30.4	11.6	36.9	7.6	-1.5
Private loans	56.0	21.7	-2.3	31.2	6.9	-2.8
Direct private investment	10.5	4.6	10.6	5.8	0.8	1.2
Private grants	3.0	4.1	3.4	0	0.0	0.1
Aggregate net flows	113.6	80.1	48.6	44.1	17.3	2.9
Aggregate net transfers	71.1	2.8	-8.2	18.7	-27.0	-22.9
IMF net flows	5.1	-0.2	-2.2	0.7	2.3	-0.4
World Bank net flows	4.7	7.6	3.2	1.6	2.7	1.4
IDA net flows	2.0	3.9	3.2	0.1	0.1	0.1

Figure 14–1

Billions of dollars at 1987 prices and exchange rates.
1989 figures are projections.
Net flows and transfers include payments to principal and interest.
Source: World Bank (4).

Longterm official
development finance
and net transfers of
funds remained positive
for low-income Asian
countries. Direct invest-
ments and flows from
the IMF and World
Bank were small.

Longterm flows to
low-income African
countries showed the
same pattern.

Longterm aid to low-income Asian countries

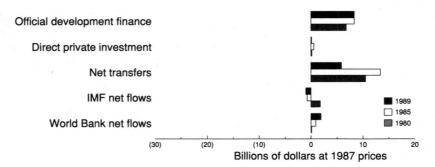

Billions of dollars at 1987 prices

Longterm aid to low-income African countries

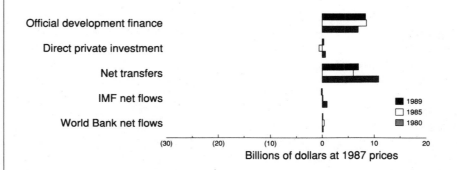

Billions of dollars at 1987 prices

	ASIAN COUNTRIES			AFRICAN COUNTRIES		
	1980	1985	1989	1980	1985	1989
Official development finance	6.8	8.3	8.3	6.9	8.5	8.3
Official development assistance	6.3	7.1	6.4	6.0	8.4	8.0
Official grants	3.3	2.5	2.6	3.4	5.3	4.7
Official concessional loans	3.1	4.6	3.8	2.6	3.1	3.3
Official nonconcessional loans	0.5	1.2	2.0	1.0	0.1	0.4
Private flows	5.2	8.6	4.3	5.7	0.6	1.2
Private loans	3.3	5.5	3.3	3.6	-1.4	0.0
Direct private investment	0.2	0.5	0.1	0.6	-0.6	0.3
Private grants	1.7	2.6	0.9	1.5	2.6	0.9
Aggregate net flows	12.0	17.0	12.6	12.7	9.2	9.4
Aggregate net transfers	10.5	13.4	5.8	10.8	6.0	7.0
IMF net flows	1.8	-0.8	-1.0	0.9	0.1	-0.2
World Bank net flows	0.1	0.9	1.9	0.2	0.4	0.1
IDA net flows	1.2	2.5	1.5	0.5	1.2	1.5

Figure 14–2

Billions of dollars at 1987 prices and exchange rates.
1989 figures are projections.
Net flows and transfers include payments to principal and interest.
Source: World Bank (4).

In 1989, Japan passed the United States as the biggest donor of official development assistance to developing countries.

The Nordic countries and the Netherlands donated the greatest share of their gross national products to development aid in the final years of the decade.

Contributions of Japan and the United Kingdom were at the average level.

France's contribution was slightly above the level of aid targeted by international agencies.

As a percent of GNP, the contributions of the United States continued to be lowest in the OECD.

Official development assistance by OECD countries

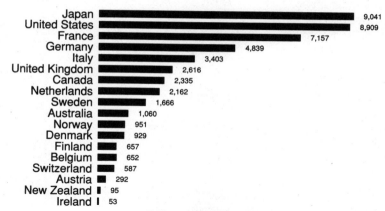

Billions of dollars, 1988-89 average

Aid as share of GDP

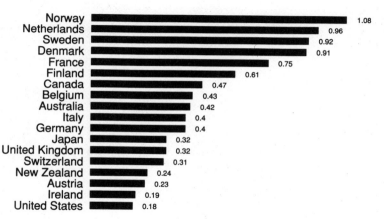

Percent of GDP, 1989

The United Nations is trying to get donors to restructure their aid budgets to emphasize human development.

Using their analysis, bilateral (government to government) aid for both health and education were very small percentages of total aid — and the levels declined in 1989.

Official development assistance by OECD countries

	VALUE	GDP%	% SHARE	MULTILAT ODA%
Japan	9041	0.32	19.1	27.1
United States	8909	0.18	18.8	23.7
France	7157	0.75	15.1	18.0
Germany	4839	0.40	10.2	34.3
Italy	3403	0.40	7.2	32.5
United Kingdom	2616	0.32	5.5	44.7
Canada	2335	0.47	4.9	32.2
Netherlands	2162	0.96	4.6	29.2
Sweden	1666	0.92	3.5	30.7
Australia	1060	0.42	2.2	37.4
Norway	951	1.08	2.0	40.8
Denmark	929	0.91	2.0	46.2
Finland	657	0.61	1.4	38.0
Belgium	652	0.43	1.4	40.9
Switzerland	587	0.31	1.2	26.1
Austria	292	0.23	0.6	37.8
New Zealand	95	0.24	0.2	11.1
Ireland	53	0.19	0.1	61.0
Total DAC	**47405**	**0.35**	**100**	**28.9**

Figure 14–3

Millions of dollars and percentages, 1988-89 average.
Multilateral aid as a percent of ODA.
DAC (Development Assistance Committee) = OECD members shown.
Other OECD members also contributed: Greece $38 million, Iceland $2 million, + Luxembourg $18 million, Portugal $83 million, Spain $241 million.
Source: Organization for Economic Cooperation and Development (5).

Allocation of international aid

	BILATERAL		MULTILATERAL
	1979	1989	1988
Social and administrative infrastructure	30.8	25.7	19.9
Health and population	8.0	6.7	7.8
Education	16.5	10.7	4.3
Agriculture	17.9	11.3	23.2
Other (incl military)	51.3	63.0	56.9

Table 14–1

Percent of total aid.
Bilateral aid is that from OECD countries, which account for 85% of total bilateral aid.
Source: United Nations (4).

Development Aid

The United Nations' analysis looks at the percent of total aid that goes to support basic social needs. Switzerland allocated by far the greatest percentage to this area; allocations of Italy, France, Australia, Canada, and Finland were less than a third of Switzerland's.

The proposed United States budget for international aid programs in fiscal year 1992 called for a total of $7 billion in economic aid.

About half of the total US budget for international affairs goes to economic assistance and 21% to military assistance in the proposed budget.

Aid allocated to basic social needs

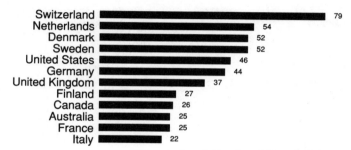

Percent of social-sector aid to priority areas

Figure 14–4

Percent of social-sector aid allocated to basic education, family planning, and rural water supply. Figures cover about 75% of total bilateral official development assistance.
Source: United Nations (4).

United States 1992 budget requests for international aid programs

Economic aid	6.560
Development assistance	2.788
Economic support funds	3.228
Special assistance initiative	0.560
Selected aid recipients	
Latin America & Caribbean	1.296
Israel	1.200
Africa	0.958
Egypt	0.815
Eastern Europe	0.400
Nicaragua	0.179
El Salvador	0.178
Military assistance	4.703
International affairs (%)	
Economic assistance	51.7
Administrative	25.2
Military assistance	20.6
Export-import/IMF	2.5
Total	**100**

Table 14–2

Billions of dollars and percentages. Note: Figures may appear inconsistent due to their presentation in several accounting categories.
Source: United States Agency for International Development (1).

Combined, all of the international financial institutions committed $38 billion to developing countries in 1990.

Throughout the 1980s, the International Bank for Reconstruction and Development (IBRD), the main agency of the World Bank, led all other multilateral institutions in lending for development. In 1990, the IBRD loaned $15 billion at market rates and made a profit of over $1 billion.

The International Development Association (IDA), the concessional arm of the World Bank, makes loans to low-income countries at below-market rates. In 1990 these loans totaled more than $6.3 billion.

Commitments of multilateral financial institutions

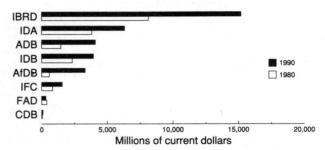

Millions of current dollars

Note: See accompanying table for full names of institutions.

Commitments of development-finance groups

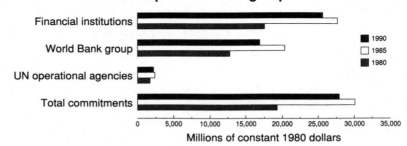

Millions of constant 1980 dollars

	1980	1985 CURR	1985 DEFL*	1990 CURR	1990 DEFL*
Financial Institutions	**17583**	**23809**	**27685**	**34814**	**25598**
World Bank Group	12780	17527	20380	23043	16943
Int'l Bank for Reconstruction & Development (IBRD)	8148	12952	15061	15176	11159
Int'l Development Association (IDA)	3817	3541	4117	6300	4632
Int'l Finance Corporation (IFC)	815	1034	1202	1567	1152
Asian Development Bank (ADB)	1452	1845	2145	4099	3014
Inter-American Development Bank IDB)	2341	3102	3607	3938	2896
African Development Bank (AfDB)	571	1154	1342	3300	2426
Int'l Fund for Agricultural Dev (FAD)	394	131	152	323	237
Caribbean Development Bank (CDB)	45	50	58	101	74
United Nations Operational Agencies	**1735**	**2032**	**2363**	**3012**	**2215**
World Food Programme	671	872	1014	1145	842
UN Development Programme	639	567	659	1111	817
UN Children's Fund	279	452	526	545	401
UN Population Fund	146	141	164	211	155
Total commitments					
Current dollars	19318	25841		37882	
1980 purchasing-power equivalent*	19318	30048		27854	

Figure 14–5

Millions of dollars.
*Deflated by the UN index of manufactured export prices; 1980 = 100.
Source: United Nations (3).

15 Prices and Wages

Prices play the starring role in free-market theory. Responding to changes in demand, they direct the flow of resources to the producers and consumers who want them most. When prices don't respond faithfully to the supply and demand of real goods and services, price signals are distorted by inflation or deflation, confounding the decisions that people and businesses make in the marketplaces. Internationally, inflation and deflation are transmitted through exchange rates, sometimes visiting unwanted and undeserved distortions upon more-stable economies.

So the control of inflation — price stability — is a primary concern in every free-market economy and in the global economy. Inflation is one of the indicators that financial ministers of the group of seven main economies (G–7) monitor and try to control.

Inflation played the leading role in the global economy in the 1970s and '80s. In the developed economies, led by the United States, inflation soared to alarming heights due to the oil-price shocks and the cost of waging the Viet Nam war. When milder remedies failed, the US federal reserve board invoked the ultimate remedy: recession. It worked. The US economy led the world into its deepest recession since World War II; prices came down.

Middle-income developing economies that had built their growth on the assumption of perpetual inflation got an additional, unwanted byproduct of disinflation: external debts that would plague them through the decade.

As the recovery proceeded, inflation began to creep up. But in 1986, oil prices dropped suddenly, and so did inflation. The global economy shrugged off the stock market crash in 1987. But it responded with surprising giddiness to the possibility of higher oil prices as the crisis in the Persian Gulf heated up in late 1990. The Gulf war quickly won, oil prices came quickly down again.

The economies of the United States, Canada, and the United Kingdom slipped into a recession that was already showing its face when the Gulf crisis stunned the confidence of both consumers and business people. The dollar rose sharply though briefly, pushing down import prices. The Japanese economy was still in shock after its own stock market crash in the first months of 1990. All of these developments should have been a recipe for lower inflation. But instead, in the first months of 1991, prices

Inflation in developed economies

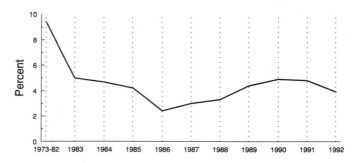

	1973-82	1983	1984	1985	1986	1987	1988	1989	1990	1991	1992
All developed	9.4	5.0	4.7	4.2	2.4	3.0	3.3	4.4	4.9	4.8	3.9
United States	8.7	3.2	4.4	3.5	2.0	3.6	4.1	4.8	5.3	4.9	4.0
Japan	8.6	1.8	2.3	2.0	0.6	0.1	0.7	2.3	3.1	4.0	3.2
Germany (W)	5.2	3.3	2.4	2.2	-0.1	0.2	1.3	2.8	2.7	3.5	3.2
All developing	24.8	32.9	38.3	38.8	30.2	41.0	70.2	105.0	117.7	40.9	18.0

Figure 15–1

1973–82 = compound annual rates of change. Excludes China. Figures for 1991 and 1992 are forecasts. Source: International Monetary Fund (10).

went up 5% in the developed economies — 6% in three of the G–7 economies and 4% in Japan.

Wages, the price of labor, are also headed up in the 1990s, forecasters say, to higher levels than any year of the 1980s.

What it all added up to for some observers was a worrisome underlying inflationary pressure throughout the developed world.

The developing economies were moving in the opposite direction, as many of them resolutely pushed ahead with economic reforms. After adjusting to the Gulf-war spike in oil prices, the average inflation in all developing economies is forecast to fall to its lowest level in more than two decades. Forecasters expect this trend to hold even for economies in the Western Hemisphere, where they say inflation will fall from a record 768% in 1990 to 36% in 1992.

However, for many developing economies, falling prices aren't all good news. For all but the most dynamic economies, production of primary agriculture and mining products is still the most important economic activity, contributing more than 30% of gross domestic product. Not counting fuel exporters, some 90 developing economies depend on commodities for more than half their export earnings. Worse, in many cases they depend on one or two commodity products. Lower prices and earnings from commodities usually reverberate throughout already fragile economies. Unfortunately for these economies, forecasters expect the price index of all commodities, excluding energy, to be about 42% lower in 2000 than it was in 1980.

Comparative prices measure differences in purchasing power without regard for exchange rates.

Prices are relatively higher in all developed economies than they are in the United States. Highest relative prices occur in the Nordic countries and in Germany, where in 1990, prices were 48% higher than they were in the US.

Inflation in all of the transitioning economies continued to rise sharply in the final years of the decade. Poland and Yugoslavia were in the grip of hyperinflation.

Prices

Comparative price levels in OECD economies

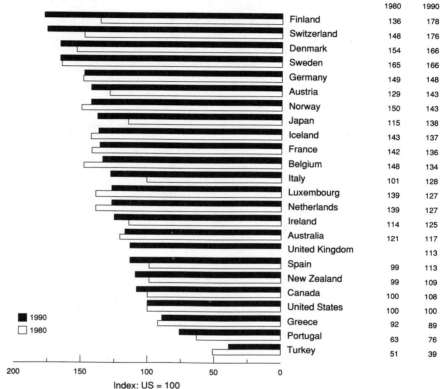

	1980	1990
Finland	136	178
Switzerland	148	176
Denmark	154	166
Sweden	165	166
Germany	149	148
Austria	129	143
Norway	150	143
Japan	115	138
Iceland	143	137
France	142	136
Belgium	148	134
Italy	101	128
Luxembourg	139	127
Netherlands	139	127
Ireland	114	125
Australia	121	117
United Kingdom		113
Spain	99	113
New Zealand	99	109
Canada	100	108
United States	100	100
Greece	92	89
Portugal	63	76
Turkey	51	39

■ 1990
□ 1980

Index: US = 100

Figure 15–2

Comparative price levels show the number of US dollars required in each country to buy the same representative basket of final goods and services costing $100 in the United States.
Source: Organization for Economic Cooperation and Development (5).

Inflation in transitioning economies

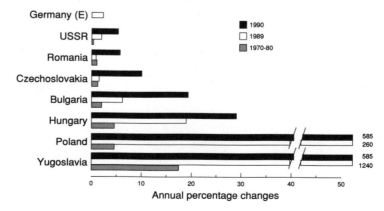

■ 1990
□ 1989
▨ 1970-80

Annual percentage changes

Poland 585 / 260
Yugoslavia 585 / 1240

Terms of trade, the difference between the average prices of exports and imports, changed little in the developed economies in the 1980s, and forecasters expect even less change in the first years of the '90s.

Terms of trade also changed slightly in developing economies, except for shifts in 1990 and 1991 as economies responded to sharp changes in the price of oil immediately before and after the Gulf war. Still, the 22% negative terms of trade forecast for oil exporters in 1991 was less than half what it was in 1986.

Increases in the prices of traded manufactures were expected to continue their downward trend into the early 1990s.

Inflation in transitioning economies

	1970-80	1980-85	1985-88	1989	1990
Germany (E)	0.0	0.0	0.8	2.3	-4.0
USSR	0.3	1.0	2.0	1.9	5.3
Romania	1.0	5.0	0.8	0.9	5.7
Czechoslovakia	1.2	2.0	0.2	1.5	10.0
Bulgaria	2.0	1.0	2.6	6.2	19.3
Hungary	4.6	6.7	9.8	19.0	29.0
Poland	4.6	32.5	33.0	260.0	585.0
Yugoslavia	17.5	47.5	131.0	1240.0	585.0

Figure 15–3

Annual percentage changes.
1990 figures are preliminary.
Source: Bank for International Settlements (3).

Trends of prices in world trade

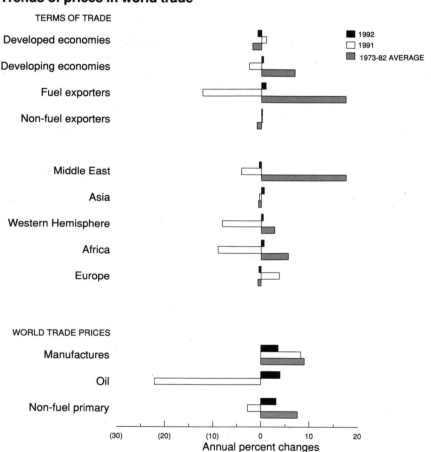

TERMS OF TRADE

Developed economies

Developing economies

Fuel exporters

Non-fuel exporters

Middle East

Asia

Western Hemisphere

Africa

Europe

WORLD TRADE PRICES

Manufactures

Oil

Non-fuel primary

■ 1992
☐ 1991
▨ 1973-82 AVERAGE

(30) (20) (10) 0 10 20
Annual percent changes

Steep jumps in oil prices in 1972 and again in 1978–80 triggered high inflation in oil-consuming economies. The net effect was a slight rise in the real price over the decade.

Oil prices doubled between August 3 and October 12, 1990 during the period of uncertainties following the Iraqi invasion of Kuwait. By February 8 they had returned to their pre-crisis level.

Trends of prices in world trade

	AVERAGE 1973-82	1990	1991	1992
TERMS OF TRADE*				
Developed economies	-1.9	0.5	1.0	-0.8
Developing economies	6.9	0.2	-2.5	0.4
Fuel exporters	17.5	11.0	-12.2	0.9
Non-fuel exporters	-1.0	-2.9	0.2	0.2
Middle East	17.6	8.6	-4.1	-0.5
Asia	-0.6	-1.0	-0.4	0.6
Western Hemisphere	2.8	-1.5	-8.1	0.4
Africa	5.6	-1.8	-9.0	0.6
Europe	-0.7	-2.1	3.8	-0.5
WORLD TRADE PRICES				
Manufactures	9.0	9.6	8.3	3.6
Oil		28.3	-22.1	4.0
Non-fuel primary	7.6	-7.9	-2.7	3.2

Figure 15–4

Compound annual rates of change, 1973-82. Excludes China. Annual percent changes.
* A positive number means that the economy receives, in the aggregate, higher prices for its exports than it pays for its imports, relative to a base period.
Figures for 1991 and 1992 are projections.
Source: International Monetary Fund (10).

Trend in average oil prices

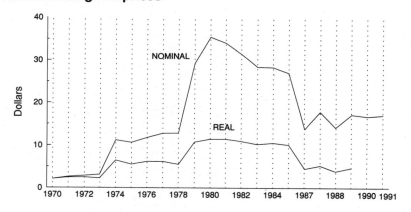

	NOMINAL	REAL			NOMINAL	REAL
1970	2.10	2.10		1981	34.10	11.51
1971	2.60	2.46		1982	31.40	10.99
1972	2.80	2.42		1983	28.40	10.27
1973	3.10	2.22		1984	28.30	10.53
1974	11.20	6.43		1985	26.98	10.12
1975	10.60	5.47		1987	13.82	4.49
1976	11.80	6.11		1987	17.79	5.18
1977	12.80	6.14		1988	14.15	3.86
1978	12.90	5.47		1989	17.18	4.69
1979	29.20	10.74		1990	16.74	
1980	35.50	11.50		1991*	17.00	

Figure 15–5

Real price in 1970 dollars, deflated by Manufacturers Export Index.
Average of three crude spot prices, reflecting relatively equal consumption of light, medium, and heavy crudes worldwide (Dubai, UK, Alaskan North Slope).
*Weekly average spot price on June 28, 1991.
Source: International Monetary Fund (10).

Prices of most commodities fell during the 1980s, least in coffee and most in sugar.

Among metals, the price of tin fell steeply in the 1980s, after a modest average rise in the preceding two decades.

Price trends for selected commodities

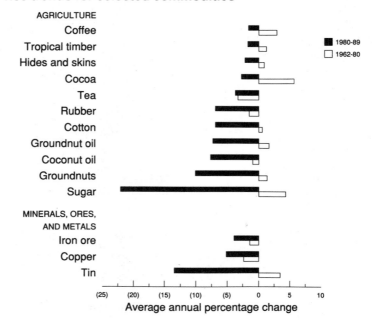

	1962-80	1980-89
AGRICULTURE		
Coffee	2.9	-1.6
Tropical timber	1.3	-1.7
Hides and skins	0.9	-2.2
Cocoa	5.7	-2.7
Tea	-3.3	-3.7
Rubber	-1.5	-6.9
Cotton	0.6	-6.9
Groundnut oil	1.7	-7.3
Coconut oil	-0.9	-7.7
Groundnuts	1.4	-10.1
Sugar	4.3	-22.1
MINERALS, ORES, AND METALS		
Iron ore	-1.4	-3.9
Copper	-2.4	-5.1
Tin	3.5	-13.4

Figure 15–6

Average annual percentage rate of change.
Constant 1980 dollars.
Prices for 1989 are for first seven months.
Source: Organization for Economic Cooperation and Development (7).

Prices and Wages

Except for timber, prices in most commodity groups are forecast to fall in the 1990s.

Forecasters expect that by 2000, the price of metals and minerals will have fallen nearly 80% from their 1970 level.

During the 1980s, terms of trade rose strongly in Japan and less in other OECD economies. Norway's terms of trade fell sharply during the decade.

Price projections for selected commodity groups

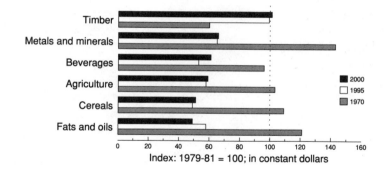

Index: 1979-81 = 100; in constant dollars

	1970	1980	1985	1995	2000
All commodities	**111**	**105**	**81**	**62**	**63**
Agriculture	103	104	81	58	59
Food	103	104	83	56	58
Beverages	96	99	95	53	61
Cereals	109	101	74	49	51
Fats and oils	121	96	76	58	49
Non-food	101	106	75	65	63
Timber	60	110	80	99	101
Metals and minerals	143	105	80	65	66

Figure 15–7

Index: 1979-81 = 100.
In constant US dollars.
Projections by the World Bank.
Source: Organization for Economic Cooperation and Development (7).

Changes in terms of trade in OECD economies

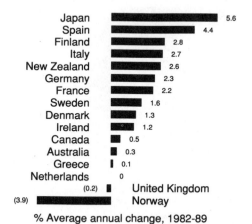

% Average annual change, 1982-89

Figure 15–8

Prices fell sharply throughout the developed economies in the 1980s, both in terms of GNP deflators and consumer indexes.

Inflation in developed economies

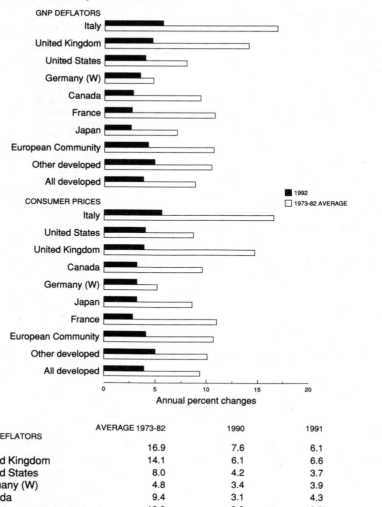

GNP DEFLATORS	AVERAGE 1973-82	1990	1991	1992
Italy	16.9	7.6	6.1	5.7
United Kingdom	14.1	6.1	6.6	4.7
United States	8.0	4.2	3.7	4.0
Germany (W)	4.8	3.4	3.9	3.5
Canada	9.4	3.1	4.3	2.8
France	10.8	3.0	3.3	2.7
Japan	7.1	1.9	2.6	2.6
European Community	10.7	5.1	5.1	4.3
Other developed	10.5	6.0	5.6	4.9
All developed	8.9	4.1	4.1	3.8
CONSUMER PRICES				
Italy	16.6	6.5	6.2	5.6
United States	8.7	5.3	4.9	4.0
United Kingdom	14.7	9.5	6.0	3.9
Canada	9.6	4.8	5.6	3.2
Germany (W)	5.2	2.7	3.5	3.2
Japan	8.6	3.1	4.0	3.2
France	11.0	3.4	3.2	2.8
European Community	10.7	5.3	4.7	4.1
Other developed	10.1	6.2	5.7	5.0
All developed	9.4	4.9	4.8	3.9

Figure 15–9

Annual changes, in percent. For 1973-82: compound annual rates of change. In descending order of 1990 rates of change. Figures for 1991 and 1992 are projections.
Source: International Monetary Fund (10).

Prices and Wages

Inflation in OECD economies was moderate in the second half of the decade, except for Turkey, Iceland, Greece, and Portugal. Consumer price rises averaged less than 2% per year during that period in Japan and Germany.

In Poland in 1990, prices rose 585% and wages fell 27%, as the economy suffered through its self-imposed "shock therapy" transition to market dynamics.

In 1991, the situation in the former Soviet Union was deteriorating so fast that forecasts are worthless — except to say that the economy is probably on the verge of hyperinflation.

Consumer price changes in OECD economies

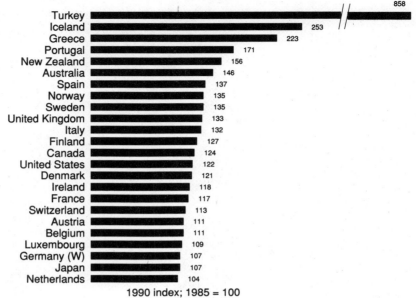

1990 index; 1985 = 100

Figure 15–10

Inflation and real wages in transitioning economies

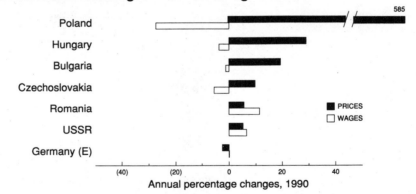

Annual percentage changes, 1990

	PRICES			WAGES		
	1980	1985	1990	1980	1985	1990
Poland	9.1	14.4	584.7	3.9	3.8	-27.3
Hungary	9.1	7	28.9	-2.8	2.6	-3.8
Bulgaria	14	1.7	19.3	-3.2	1.4	-1.2
Czechoslovakia	3.4	1.3	9.9	-1.1	0.3	-5.6
Romania	3	0.4	5.7	3.1	1.5	11.6
USSR	0.7	0.8	5.3	2.7	2.2	6.6
Germany (E)	0.4	-0.2	-2.5	1.1	3.7	0.2

Figure 15–11

Annual percentage changes. Prices calculated in various ways.
For USSR 1980 and 1985, approved "list price" changes only.
Wages in the socialist sector, excluding cooperative farmers; deflated by consumer price index.
Prices and wages for East Germany are for 1986, not 1985.
Wages for Bulgaria and East Germany are for 1989, not 1990.
Source: United Nations (3).

Among developing economies, inflation during the 1980s and into the '90s was highest in Western Hemisphere countries. By the end of 1990, prices were 15 times higher than they averaged through the 1970s. They were declining in 1991 and were expected to drop still more in 1992, to below their 1973 level.

In Asian developing economies, inflation averaged an estmated 7.5% in 1991, although it was many times that rate in Myanmar and Viet Nam.

Consumer-price changes in developing economies

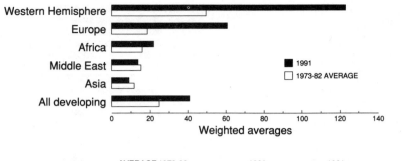

	AVERAGE 1973-82	1990	1991	1992
Western Hemisphere	49.6	768.0	122.9	35.9
Europe	18.7	166.4	60.8	22.8
Africa	16.0	15.6	21.9	9.9
Middle East	15.2	13.3	13.7	13.9
Asia	11.7	7.9	9.1	9.2
All developing	24.8	117.7	40.9	18.0

Figure 15–12

Weighted averages.
Compound annual rates of change for 1973-82. Excludes China.
Figures for 1991 and 1992 are projections.
Source: International Monetary Fund (10).

Inflation in Asian developing economies

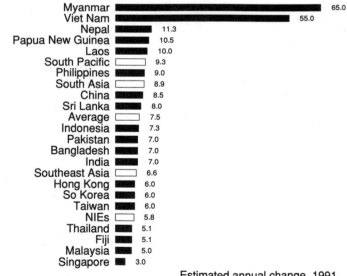

Estimated annual change, 1991

In Latin American economies, hyperinflation prevailed in 1989 in Nicaragua, Peru, Argentina, and Brazil.

Through the 1980s, inflation in Argentina had averaged 142%.

Chile's average 174% inflation in the 1980s fell to a manageable 17% in 1989.

Mexico's inflation at the end of the 1980s was much higher than its average during the 1970s, but still far lower than that of the other main economies in the region.

Inflation in Asian developing economies

	1971-80	1989	1990	1991
NIEs	12.6	5.8	5.7	5.8
Hong Kong	8.5	10.0	7.0	6.0
So Korea	16.4	5.6	6.5	6.0
Taiwan	11.1	4.7	4.5	6.0
Singapore	6.7	2.8	3.5	3.0
Southeast Asia	13.6	6.6	7.7	6.6
Viet Nam		40.0	60.0	55.0
Laos		60.0	20.0	10.0
Philippines	13.9	10.6	12.0	9.0
Indonesia	17.6	6.4	7.8	7.3
Thailand	9.8	5.8	6.5	5.1
Malaysia	6.0	4.0	4.5	5.0
South Asia	9.5	11.8	10.0	8.9
Myanmar	11.9	70.0	70.0	65.0
Nepal	8.4	10.1	13.5	11.3
Sri Lanka	8.9	11.6	10.0	8.0
Pakistan	12.0	10.4	8.5	7.0
India	8.3	10.0	8.0	7.0
Bangladesh	20.7	8.0	7.5	7.0
China	1.4	18.0	9.0	8.5
South Pacific	9.7	6.1	8.3	9.3
Papua New Guinea	9.5	6.0	9.0	10.5
Fiji	10.2	6.5	5.8	5.1
Average	8.1	11.1	8.1	7.5

Figure 15–13

Percent change per year. Figures for 1990 and 1991 are estimates and projections. NIEs = newly industrializing economies.
Source: Asian Development Bank (1).

Inflation trends in Latin America

	1961-70	1971-80	1989
Nicaragua	2	20	4770
Peru	10	32	3399
Argentina	21	142	3079
Brazil	46	37	1284
Uruguay	48	63	87
Venezuela	1	9	84
Guyana	2	10	80
Ecuador	4	13	76
Dominican Republic	2	11	45
Paraguay	3	13	29
Colombia	11	21	26
Mexico	3	17	20
El Salvador	1	11	18
Chile	27	174	17
Costa Rica	3	11	17
Bolivia	6	20	16
Suriname	4	10	15
Jamaica	4	19	14
Haiti	3	11	12
Guatemala	1	10	11
Trinidad & Tobago	3	13	11
Honduras	2	8	10
Barbados	3	15	6
Bahamas	6	8	5
Panama	1	7	-0.1

Table 15–1

Annual average changes in monthly consumer price indexes.
Source: Inter-American Development Bank (1).

Germany's average wage for production workers ($21.77 per hour) was highest among the main economies in 1990. The average wage in the European economy was $16.93.

The United States wage rate, at $14.83, was 13th among the developed economies.

Japan's average compensation of $12.85 was the lowest among the major economies.

Wages

Hourly compensation of production workers

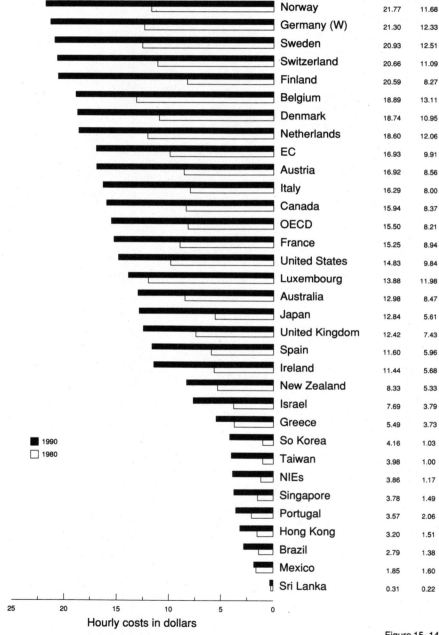

	1990	1980
Norway	21.77	11.68
Germany (W)	21.30	12.33
Sweden	20.93	12.51
Switzerland	20.66	11.09
Finland	20.59	8.27
Belgium	18.89	13.11
Denmark	18.74	10.95
Netherlands	18.60	12.06
EC	16.93	9.91
Austria	16.92	8.56
Italy	16.29	8.00
Canada	15.94	8.37
OECD	15.50	8.21
France	15.25	8.94
United States	14.83	9.84
Luxembourg	13.88	11.98
Australia	12.98	8.47
Japan	12.84	5.61
United Kingdom	12.42	7.43
Spain	11.60	5.96
Ireland	11.44	5.68
New Zealand	8.33	5.33
Israel	7.69	3.79
Greece	5.49	3.73
So Korea	4.16	1.03
Taiwan	3.98	1.00
NIEs	3.86	1.17
Singapore	3.78	1.49
Portugal	3.57	2.06
Hong Kong	3.20	1.51
Brazil	2.79	1.38
Mexico	1.85	1.60
Sri Lanka	0.31	0.22

■ 1990
□ 1980

25   20   15   10   5   0
Hourly costs in dollars

Figure 15–14

Prices and Wages

In 1975, hourly wages in manufacturing jobs in Germany were equal to those in the United States. By 1990, they were 44% higher.

In 1975, Japan's hourly wage was 48% of that in the United States. By 1990, it was 87% of the US level.

Over the same period, the average wage in the European Community grew from 80% of the US level to 114% of it.

Trends in hourly compensation

	1975	1980	1989	1990
Switzerland	96	113	117	239
Norway	107	119	131	147
Germany (W)	100	125	123	144
Sweden	113	127	123	141
Finland	72	84	116	139
Belgium	101	133	107	127
Denmark	99	111	106	126
Netherlands	103	123	108	125
EC	80	101	97	114
Austria	68	87	95	114
Italy	73	81	93	110
Canada	91	85	104	107
OECD	75	83	97	105
France	71	91	88	103
United States	100	100	100	100
25 economies			82	88
Australia	87	86	86	88
Japan	48	˙57	88	87
United Kingdom	52	76	73	84
Spain	41	61	64	78
Ireland	47	60	66	77
New Zealand	50	54	55	56
So Korea	6	10	25	28
Taiwan	6	10	25	27
NIEs	8	12	23	26
Singapore	13	15	22	25
Portugal	25	21	20	24
Hong Kong	12	15	20	22
Brazil	14	14	12	19
Mexico			11	12
Israel	35	39	54	
Luxembourg	100	122		
Greece	27	38	38	
Sri Lanka	4	2		

Table 15–2

Hourly compensation costs for production workers in manufacturing.
Index: US = 100.
Source: Bureau of Labor Statistics (1).

Real minimum wages declined in most of the Latin American economies during the 1980s, rising only in Paraguay, Costa Rica, and Colombia.

The average decline was 25% over the decade.

In 1989, minimum wages in Brazil and Argentina were two-thirds, and in Mexico less than half, of what they were in 1980.

In the transitioning economies, wage levels grew rampantly at the end of the 1980s as the former socialist satellites disengaged from the USSR. In every case, except possibly Romania and the USSR, the increases were wiped out by much greater levels of inflation.

Real minimum wages in Latin America

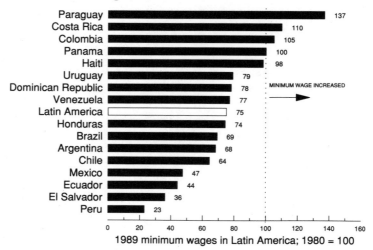

1989 minimum wages in Latin America; 1980 = 100

Figure 15–15

Index, 1980 = 100.
Source: Inter-American Development Bank (1).

Wages in transitioning economies

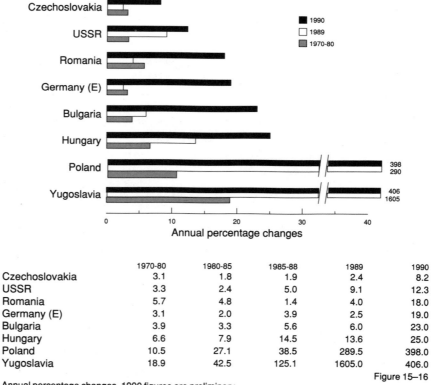

Annual percentage changes

	1970-80	1980-85	1985-88	1989	1990
Czechoslovakia	3.1	1.8	1.9	2.4	8.2
USSR	3.3	2.4	5.0	9.1	12.3
Romania	5.7	4.8	1.4	4.0	18.0
Germany (E)	3.1	2.0	3.9	2.5	19.0
Bulgaria	3.9	3.3	5.6	6.0	23.0
Hungary	6.6	7.9	14.5	13.6	25.0
Poland	10.5	27.1	38.5	289.5	398.0
Yugoslavia	18.9	42.5	125.1	1605.0	406.0

Figure 15–16

Annual percentage changes. 1990 figures are preliminary.
Source: Bank for International Settlements (3).

16 Saving & Investment

Savings are the raw material of investments. Except for savings kept under mattresses, the two quantities should be identical. From a broad perspective, they always are. People, businesses, and governments around the world save about $4 trillion every year. That's the theoretical limit on how much money is available for investment anywhere in the world.

Regardless of the demand for investment in any year, the total can't exceed the stock of savings made in that year. If investment demand grows faster than savings, the result will surely be higher interest rates. At the end of the 1980s, some dramatic changes in the global scene combined with longer term trends to raise the question: Is there going to be a global shortage of capital in the 1990s?

On the demand (investment) side, observers thought they saw some formidable new needs for investment: restructuring the former socialist economies of central and eastern Europe (including the reunification of Germany); rebuilding Kuwait after the Gulf war; in the United States, handling the savings-and-loan bailout and rebuilding the physical infrastructure; meeting the new, expanded needs of developing countries with reformed economies.

Calmer second thoughts led analysts to discount many of the investment demands, at least in the short term. Restructuring the former socialist economies would be a task of decades, maybe even generations, and so would not strain the immediate supply of savings. (The task would probably be more quickly done in eastern Germany, but that high-saving economy could probably handle it.) Rebuilding Kuwait would not absorb as much investment funds as worriers had expected. The US was already working its way out of the S&L debacle, and rebuilding the infrastructure would be spread out over many years. Developing economies would probably not come around quickly enough to be a short-term problem.

Besides this discounting of new demands on savings, some old demands also seemed likely to abate. The developed economies were in recession and investments should go down. A capital investment binge in the mid–1980s had run its natural course, and the developed economies where it occurred would need some time to absorb the new capacities.

While it's natural to think of savings and investments in each individual national economy, the globalization of financial markets in the 1980s should have made investors increasingly indifferent to where the savings come from. However, empirical evidence suggests that, despite globalization, investors seem to prefer to invest at home when they can. Of course, if domestic savings aren't sufficient, then investors must use foreign savings. This situation defines a current-account deficit. For various reasons, current-account deficits were narrowing, apparently confirming a diminished demand for savings.

Some analysts say that, while a capital shortage may not be imminent, it could happen in the medium term. This view argued for doing something to increase savings. So did statistical evidence broadly suggesting that national economies do better when they save more.

In this context, national savings (the combination of saving by households, businesses, and governments) declined throughout the 1980s in all developed economies. Over the last three decades, Germany's savings dropped the most, Canada's the least. Throughout this period, savings in the United States were the lowest of any developed economy, except the UK in the 1970s.

Demographics was a primary reason for the decline in household savings. The population of low-saving elderly folk grew in all major economies except Germany and France. Aging was especially notable in Japan and the United States. Moreover, the financial position of the elderly improved in most economies, so they felt they could save even less. During the 1980s, stock market booms and escalation of real estate prices gave household savers unexpected capital gains that made them feel they didn't have to set aside so much for retirement. The corporate scene in the 1980s, especially in the US, was characterized by what to many seemed a compulsion to go into debt to finance restructurings in such forms as takeovers and leveraged buyouts.

But all analysts agree that the main force driving down the national savings rate is the persistent "dissaving" of governments. At the end of the decade, leaders of the developed economies agreed that reducing budget deficits was a primary goal, especially in the United States. Whether or not that goal will be met will probably determine whether or not there is a capital shortage in the 1990s.

Gross national saving — the sum of saving by governments, households, and businesses — declined moderately in the main developed economies in the 1980s. The average change was less than those of most individual economies.

At 21.5%, the average national saving rate in the G–7 economies was a full ten percentage points below Japan's rate. Japan had the greatest national savings in all of the last three decades.

There is no apparent pattern in the composition of national saving among the G–7.

Only the governments of Japan and Germany were net savers. The governments of Italy, the United States, and Canada were big dissavers in the 1980s.

Gross national saving in main developed economies

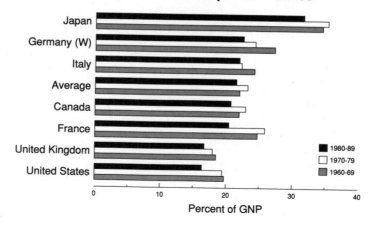

Percent of GNP

	1960-69	1970-79	1980-89
Japan	34.5	35.3	31.6
Germany (W)	27.3	24.3	22.5
Italy	24.2	22.3	21.9
Average	22.0	23.2	21.5
Canada	21.9	22.9	20.7
France	24.7	25.8	20.4
United Kingdom	18.4	17.9	16.6
United States	19.7	19.4	16.3

Percent of GNP.
Source: Bank for International Settlements (2).

Figure 16–1

Composition of national saving

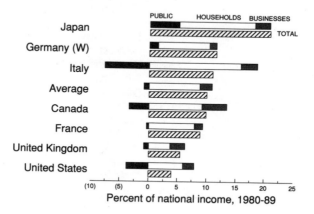

Percent of national income, 1980-89

Italian households saved more than their counterparts in the 1980s, and Canadian businesses saved most in that period.

Looking at the 24 OECD economies, those of Luxembourg, Switzerland, and Portugal saved more than Japan's did in 1989. Turkey ranks ahead of Germany.

France and Canada rank well below the median. The United States ranked lowest, with a national savings rate less than one-seventh of Switzerland's.

Net national saving in main developed economies

	US	JAPAN	(W) GERMANY	FRANCE	UK	ITALY	CANADA	AVERAGE
1960-79								
Public	0.8	6.6	6.3	4.6	2.7	1.4	2.6	2.3
Private	10.0	18.6	13.5	12.1	8.2	16.2	8.7	11.2
Households	6.2	11.9	7.6	9.4	4.3	14.1	4.0	7.2
Businesses	3.8	6.6	6.0	2.7	3.9	2.0	4.8	4.0
Total	**10.8**	**25.2**	**19.9**	**16.6**	**10.9**	**17.6**	**11.3**	**13.5**
1970-79								
Public	-1.2	5.0	3.7	2.7	1.4	-4.6	1.4	0.8
Private	10.3	20.6	11.5	14.4	6.8	19.0	11.7	12.7
Households	7.6	16.5	9.7	11.9	4.3	18.9	6.0	10.0
Businesses	2.6	4.1	1.7	2.5	2.5	0.1	5.6	2.7
Total	**9.1**	**25.6**	**15.2**	**17.0**	**8.3**	**14.4**	**13.1**	**13.5**
1980-89								
Public	-3.8	5.1	1.5	-0.4	-0.8	-7.7	-3.4	-0.9
Private	7.8	15.7	10.1	9.3	6.3	18.7	13.3	10.9
Households	6.0	13.1	8.9	7.9	3.7	15.9	9.2	8.8
Businesses	1.9	2.6	1.2	1.4	2.6	2.8	4.2	2.1
Total	**4.0**	**20.9**	**11.6**	**8.9**	**5.5**	**11.0**	**9.9**	**10.0**

Figure 16–2

Percent of national income.
Public = general government: central + local. Private = total private.
Total = net national saving.
Source: Bank for International Settlements (3).

Net national saving in OECD economies

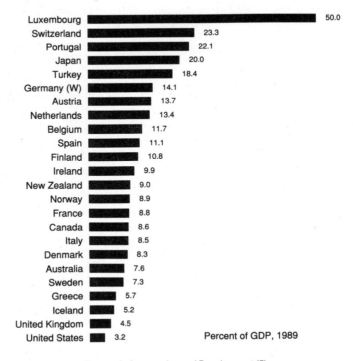

Luxembourg	50.0
Switzerland	23.3
Portugal	22.1
Japan	20.0
Turkey	18.4
Germany (W)	14.1
Austria	13.7
Netherlands	13.4
Belgium	11.7
Spain	11.1
Finland	10.8
Ireland	9.9
New Zealand	9.0
Norway	8.9
France	8.8
Canada	8.6
Italy	8.5
Denmark	8.3
Australia	7.6
Sweden	7.3
Greece	5.7
Iceland	5.2
United Kingdom	4.5
United States	3.2

Percent of GDP, 1989

Figure 16–3

Source: Organization for Economic Cooperation and Development (5).

Saving & Investment

Japan led and the United States trailed other OECD economies in total capital formation, measured as a percent of GDP in 1989.

Australia's investment in machinery and equipment topped Japan's in 1989. Canada's investment was lowest, followed by the United States, Spain, and Belgium.

In the developing economies, total investment is about the same percentage of GDP that it is in developed economies. Both public and private investment declined as shares of GDP during the 1980s.

The public sector's share of investments (42%) was exactly the same at the end of the decade as it was at the beginning of it. Public investments' share peaked in 1983 at 49%.

Capital formation in OECD economies

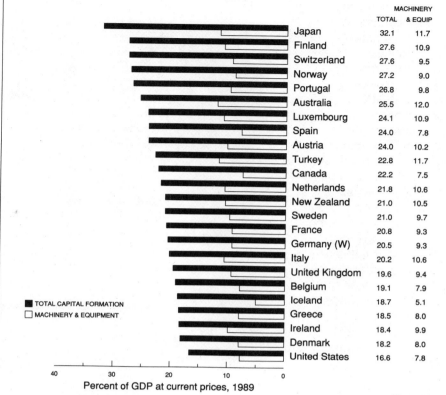

| | MACHINERY |
	TOTAL	& EQUIP
Japan	32.1	11.7
Finland	27.6	10.9
Switzerland	27.6	9.5
Norway	27.2	9.0
Portugal	26.8	9.8
Australia	25.5	12.0
Luxembourg	24.1	10.9
Spain	24.0	7.8
Austria	24.0	10.2
Turkey	22.8	11.7
Canada	22.2	7.5
Netherlands	21.8	10.6
New Zealand	21.0	10.5
Sweden	21.0	9.7
France	20.8	9.3
Germany (W)	20.5	9.3
Italy	20.2	10.6
United Kingdom	19.6	9.4
Belgium	19.1	7.9
Iceland	18.7	5.1
Greece	18.5	8.0
Ireland	18.4	9.9
Denmark	18.2	8.0
United States	16.6	7.8

■ TOTAL CAPITAL FORMATION
☐ MACHINERY & EQUIPMENT

Percent of GDP at current prices, 1989

Source: Organization for Economic Cooperation and Development (5).

Figure 16—4

Public and private investment in developing economies

	1980	1981	1982	1983	1984	1985	1986	1987
PCT OF GDP								
Public	10	11	10	9	8	8	9	8
Private	14	13	12	11	10	10	11	12
Total	**23**	**23**	**22**	**21**	**19**	**19**	**20**	**20**
PCT OF GDI								
Public	42	46	48	49	46	47	44	42
Private	58	54	52	51	54	53	56	58

Table 16—1

GDI = gross domestic investment.
Numbers may not add to 100 due to rounding.
Data from 30 representative developing economies.
Source: International Finance Corporation (1).

Among Asian developing economies, the seven "dynamic" ones — newly-industrializing plus Indonesia, Malaysia, and Thailand — saved the greatest shares of GDP in 1991 projections.

China's national savings rate ranked just below those of Singapore and Indonesia in 1991 projections.

Singapore also led other Asian developing economies in gross domestic investment in 1991 projections. South Korea's investment rate ranked second, barely ahead of China's.

Saving and investment in Asian developing economies

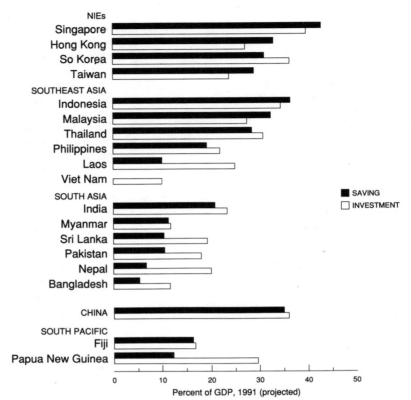

Percent of GDP, 1991 (projected)

	GROSS DOMESTIC SAVING			GROSS DOMESTIC INVESTMENT		
	1989	1990	1991	1989	1990	1991
NIEs						
Singapore	41.6	42.4	42.8	38.3	38.6	39.7
Hong Kong	33.5	33.3	33.0	27.1	26.2	27.2
So Korea	34.5	32.2	31.1	34.6	35.7	36.3
Taiwan	31.2	30.0	28.9	23.4	23.5	23.8
SOUTHEAST ASIA						
Indonesia	33.7	35.7	36.4	31.1	33.2	34.4
Malaysia	33.5	31.4	32.4	27.9	27.0	27.5
Thailand	28.1	28.2	28.5	29.4	30.4	30.8
Philippines	17.4	18.7	19.2	18.8	18.5	21.9
Laos	10.0	10.0	10.0	30.0	25.0	25.0
Viet Nam				5.0	10.0	10.0
SOUTH ASIA						
India	20.2	20.5	20.8	23.1	23.2	23.3
Myanmar	11.4	11.0	11.3	11.2	11.5	11.7
Sri Lanka	9.2	9.9	10.4	21.0	20.6	19.3
Pakistan	9.4	9.0	10.5	17.5	17.0	18.0
Nepal	7.6	6.7	6.7	20.0	19.5	20.0
Bangladesh	2.7	5.7	5.3	11.6	11.4	11.6
CHINA	36.5	34.5	35.0	37.0	35.5	36.0 (MORE)

Nicaragua led Latin American economies in its rate of gross domestic investment in 1989.

Brazil's investment rate was the highest among the big economies of the region, followed by Mexico and, distantly, Argentina.

Saving and Investment in Asian developing economies, cont'd

	GROSS DOMESTIC SAVING			GROSS DOMESTIC INVESTMENT		
	1989	1990	1991	1989	1990	1991
SOUTH PACIFIC						
Fiji	14.8	15.6	16.3	15.5	16.1	16.7
Papua New Guinea	9.4	7.3	12.3	21.7	24.1	29.6

Figure 16–5

Percent of GDP.
Figures for 1990 are estimates and projections.
NIEs = newly industrializing economies.
Source: Asian Development Bank (1).

Investment in Latin America

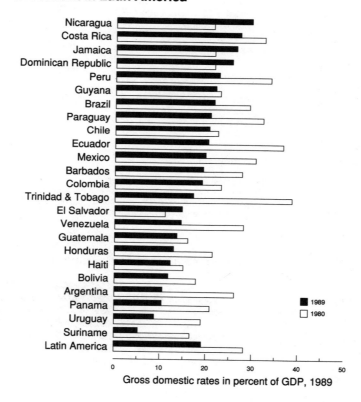

Gross domestic rates in percent of GDP, 1989

1989
1980

Brazil's rate of domestic saving topped that of the region's big economies, surpassing Mexico's and Argentina's.

Resource transfer — the difference between domestic investment and saving — measures the net amount of savings flowing into the home economy from abroad (positive number) or sent abroad (negative).

By this measure, in 1989, Mexico had an almost exact balance between domestic investment and saving. In both Brazil and Argentina, foreign savings were flowing out of the domestic economies.

In the transitioning economies, household savings is an exceptionally large share of GDP, compared with both developed and developing economies. Much of this is a worrisome "overhang" of enforced savings which, in the socialist regimes, could not be spent because of shortages and a longstanding bias against the production of consumer goods.

Saving and investment in Latin America

	SAVING		INVESTMENT		RESOURCE TRANSFER	
	1980	1989	1980	1989	1980	1989
Nicaragua	-1.9	18.1	21.4	29.6	23.3	11.5
Costa Rica	22.7	24.8	32.5	27.2	9.8	2.4
Jamaica	25.6	23.6	21.6	26.3	-4.0	2.6
Dominican Republic	4.9	16.5	21.6	25.4	16.7	9.0
Peru	30.0	25.8	33.9	22.6	3.9	-3.2
Guyana	3.9	17.0	22.9	21.9	19.0	4.9
Brazil	27.0	26.5	29.3	21.6	2.3	-4.9
Paraguay	25.9	13.3	32.3	20.8	6.4	7.5
Chile	17.7	24.5	22.4	20.5	4.7	-4.0
Ecuador	26.3	24.3	36.7	20.3	10.4	-4.0
Mexico	20.7	19.6	30.6	19.7	9.9	0.1
Barbados	16.8	13.5	27.7	19.2	10.9	5.7
Colombia	20.2	22.0	23.2	19.0	3.1	-3.0
Trinidad & Tobago	31.3	33.0	38.6	17.2	7.3	-15.8
El Salvador	6.7	6.2	11.0	14.7	4.4	8.5
Venezuela	16.5	18.9	28.1	14.5	11.6	-4.4
Guatemala	10.3	8.6	16.0	13.6	5.7	5.0
Honduras	12.3	11.6	21.3	12.9	9.0	1.3
Haiti	0.1	1.4	15.0	12.2	14.8	10.7
Bolivia	13.6	8.4	17.8	11.7	4.2	3.3
Argentina	19.1	16.8	26.1	10.4	6.9	-6.4
Panama	17.6	16.6	20.8	10.3	3.2	-6.3
Uruguay	14.6	12.7	18.9	8.7	4.3	-4.0
Suriname	27.5	15.5	16.5	5.2	-11.0	-10.3
Latin America	**22.3**	**22.2**	**28.2**	**19.0**	**5.9**	**-3.2**

Figure 16–6

Gross domestic rates in percent of GDP.
Real resource transfer = difference between domestic investment and savings rates.
A negative figure indicates resources flowing out of the economy.
Source: Inter-American Development Bank (1).

Household savings in transitioning economies

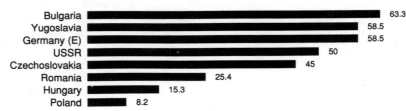

Bulgaria 63.3
Yugoslavia 58.5
Germany (E) 58.5
USSR 50
Czechoslovakia 45
Romania 25.4
Hungary 15.3
Poland 8.2

Percent of GDP in current prices, 1989

Figure 16–7

Yearend savings deposits as percent of GDP in current prices.
Hungary figure excludes convertible-currency deposits after 1987.
Source: Bank for International Settlements (3).

"Investment efficiency" can be measured by showing how much investment it takes to produce a gain in GDP (the smaller the number, the better). By this measure, efficiencies vary hugely in the transitioning economies, from the former east Germany to Yugoslavia.

East Germany's investment efficiency compares favorably with the average in Asian developing economies. Investment efficiency in Bulgaria and Romania are at about the level of all developing economies.

For years, joint ventures have been touted as an ideal way of attracting western investment in transitioning economies. Hungary has been at it longest, and by early 1991 had the most registered ventures.

Readers should note that only a fraction of the registered joint ventures have become going concerns. In the former USSR, only about one out of eight registered joint ventures were actually operating in mid–1991.

Investment efficiency in transitioning economies

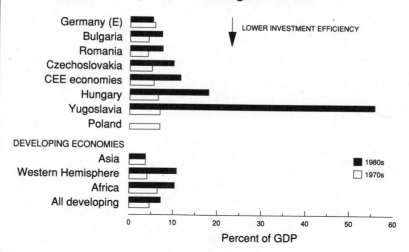

	INVESTMENT		OUTPUT CHANGE		ICOR	
	1970s	1980s	1970S	1980S	1970s	1980s
Germany (E)	27.8	20.8	4.9	4.0	5.7	5.2
Bulgaria	29.7	26.5	7.1	3.7	4.2	7.3
Romania	39.4	32.8	9.7	4.5	4.1	7.4
Czechoslovakia	24.7	21.1	5.0	2.1	5.0	10.0
CEE economies	33.8	26.8	6.1	2.3	5.5	11.6
Hungary	35.5	28.1	5.4	1.6	6.5	18.0
Yugoslavia	42.1	39.3	6.1	0.7	6.9	55.7
Poland	45.8	27.7	6.6	-0.1	6.9	
DEVELOPING						
Asia	22.7	26.0	6.1	6.9	3.7	3.7
Western Hemisphere	23.8	20.6	5.8	1.9	4.1	10.8
Africa	27.3	22.3	4.2	2.2	6.5	10.3
All developing	27.3	24.5	5.8	3.4	4.7	7.2

Figure 16–8

Percent of GDP.
Annual averages of % changes in real output.
ICOR = incremental capital-output ratio: percent of output to annual average percent growth of real output.
Shown in descending order of investment efficiency for the 1980s.
Source: Institute of International Finance (1).

Joint ventures in transitioning economies

Number of joint ventures, early 1991

Source: Deutsche Bank (1).

Figure 16–9

17 Fiscal Management

In the global economy, fiscal operations (spending and taxing) have been one of the main ways of adjusting a national economy to the pressures of unbalanced trade and fluctuating exchange rates. (When fiscal measures are unavailable or unavailing, policymakers use monetary measures.) Structural deficits are the parts of fiscal deficits that seem to be relatively permanent and not tied to the ups and downs of business cycles. When structural deficits are high, they deprive policymakers of much of the power of fiscal adjustment, either to global pressures or to the pressures of domestic inflation and unemployment.

In the second half of the 1980s, the main developed economies struggled to gain control over their fiscal deficits, which had peaked in 1985–86. They were having some successes; by 1989, deficits were down to 1% of gross domestic product, the lowest rate since the early 1970s. Several economies had achieved balances or surpluses, among them Japan, Germany, and the United Kingdom. The deficit in the United States had declined from 3.5% of GDP in 1986 to 1.75% in 1989. Public debt of the main economies had stabilized at a little less than 58% of GDP.

But as the 1990s opened, new problems pushed the deficits up again. Germany had to finance reunification. Japan had to recover from a stock market crash. The United States had to bail out failed savings and loan institutions.

Several of the main economies were in recession in 1990, but without counter-cyclical fiscal tools to restart growth. Interest payments were snowballing (interest on last year's interest) and crowding out discretionary spending. Lower inflation had reduced government revenues. In the United States, interest payments had grown to 7% of general goverment expenses (federal and state) and 15% of federal expenses.

People in the developed economies worried about their competitiveness in the global arena and what governments should do about it (i.e., "industrial" or "strategic-industry" policies). In the 1970s, subsidies had been direct — usually with the goal of trying to help declining industries get back on their feet. In the 1980s, the most popular strategem was a broad policy of assistance to research and development in general. Specific subsidies

Government outlays in main developed economies

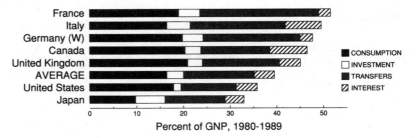

Percent of GNP, 1980-1989

CONSUMPTION · INVESTMENT · TRANSFERS · INTEREST

	FRANCE	ITALY	GERMANY	CANADA	UK	AVERAGE	US	JAPAN
1960-69								
Total	**38.0**	**32.5**	**36.7**	**30.8**	**35.4**	**30.5**	**29.0**	**18.4**
Consumption	13.1	13.9	15.0	15.5	16.8	16.0	17.6	7.9
Investment (net)	4.8	3.9	5.8	4.3	4.5	3.7	2.9	4.8
Transfers	18.9	13.2	15.2	8.0	10.1	9.0	6.6	5.3
Interest (net)	1.2	1.4	0.7	3.1	3.9	1.8	1.9	0.5
1970-79								
Total	**42.1**	**40.8**	**45.0**	**38.6**	**42.5**	**35.2**	**32.2**	**25.2**
Consumption	16.0	15.3	18.6	19.3	19.4	16.4	17.7	9.0
Investment (net)	4.9	4.3	6.0	3.7	5.6	3.9	2.0	6.2
Transfers	20.1	17.4	19.1	11.4	13.5	12.7	10.1	8.7
Interest (net)	1.1	3.7	1.2	4.2	4.0	2.2	2.4	1.3
1980-89								
Total	**51.4**	**49.5**	**47.7**	**46.5**	**45.1**	**39.6**	**35.8**	**33.0**
Consumption	19.0	16.4	19.8	20.4	20.9	16.4	17.9	9.7
Investment (net)	4.5	5.1	4.4	3.3	3.2	3.6	1.6	6.3
Transfers	25.5	20.4	20.8	14.8	16.5	15.1	11.8	12.9
Interest (net)	2.5	7.6	2.7	8.0	4.5	4.4	4.5	4.1

Figure 17–1

Percent of GNP.
Source: Bank for International Settlements (3).

took the form of grants, tax concessions, equity participations by government, "soft" loans, and loan guarantees.

Economists and some leaders saw two main problems in this: first, there was no clear evidence that the benefits of industrial subsidies outweigh their many open and hidden costs. Second, many feared that aggressive use of subsidies as a competitive strategy would lead to retaliation and costly subsidy wars.

Another fiscal-management issue that engaged policymakers was the "peace dividend," greatly reduced military spending due to the ending of the Cold War. By mid–1991, it had become an inevitability — and was being spent and respent by competing beneficiaries. When it comes, it will probably be most welcomed by people in developing countries, where military spending is a serious drag on economic development.

Fiscal deficits of the developed economies increased sharply in 1990, after declining steadily since 1986.

Japan's had a substantial fiscal surplus in 1989 — 7.5% of GDP and well above the smaller surpluses of Germany and the United Kingdom. France's accounts were nearly in balance. In the United States, the combined accounts of the federal, state, local governments remained in deficit, at 3.3% of GDP.

Government spending

Fiscal balances of main developed economies

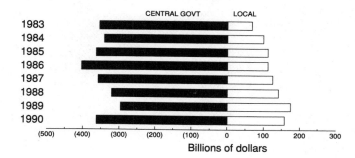

	CENTRAL	LOCAL	GENERAL
1983	-355	67	-288
1984	-341	99	-242
1985	-364	112	-252
1986	-404	112	-292
1987	-358	125	-233
1988	-321	141	-180
1989	-296	175	-121
1990	-362	158	-204

Billions of dollars.
Source: International Monetary Fund (1).

Figure 17–2

General government balances in OECD economies

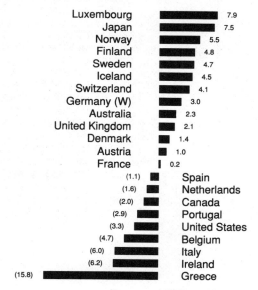

Percent of GDP, 1989

Almost one-third of Sweden's workforce is employed by governments at all levels. This is five times the government employment in Japan. The United States is a little below the median in its governments' share of the workforce, at over 14%.

The median level of government employment in OECD economies is about 17%.

Government balances and employment in OECD economies

	REVENUE	SPENDING	BALANCE	EMPLOYMENT
Luxembourg	52.9	45.0	7.9	11.3
Japan	34.3	26.8	7.5	6.3
Norway	55.1	49.7	5.5	25.7
Finland	39.9	35.1	4.8	21.9
Sweden	61.9	57.2	4.7	31.7
Iceland	36.6	32.1	4.5	17.4
Switzerland	34.1	29.9	4.1	11.2
Germany (W)	44.6	41.6	3.0	15.5
Australia	34.2	31.9	2.3	16.7
United Kingdom	39.7	37.6	2.1	20.3
Denmark	57.4	56.0	1.4	29.8
Austria	47.0	45.9	1.0	20.6
France	46.5	46.2	0.2	22.8
Spain	35.0	36.1	-1.1	13.9
Netherlands	50.1	51.7	-1.6	15.1
Canada	39.6	41.6	-2.0	19.4
Portugal	37.6	40.4	-2.9	12.8
United States	31.6	34.9	-3.3	14.4
Belgium	44.1	48.7	-4.7	20.4
Italy	41.1	47.1	-6.0	15.6
Ireland	43.7	49.9	-6.2	15.0
Greece	31.8	47.7	-15.8	18.1

Figure 17–3

Percent of GDP and of total employment. Figures are for 1989 or nearest year for which available. Includes central and local governments.
Source: Organization for Economic Cooperation and Development (5).

Government employment in OECD economies

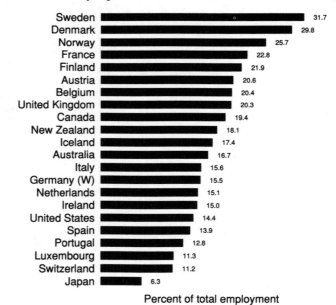

Percent of total employment

Figure 17–4

Government final consumption — mostly wages of its employees — naturally followed the pattern of employment in government.

The five Nordic countries are the five top spenders on education among the OECD economies, all at over 5% of GDP. The United States was the median spender on education. The United Kingdom, Germany, and Japan ranked near the bottom.

Government final consumption expenditures in OECD economies

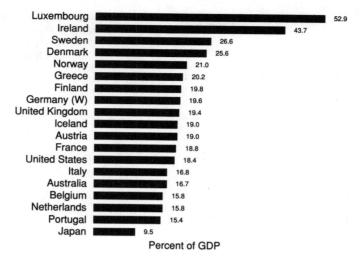

Country	Percent of GDP
Luxembourg	52.9
Ireland	43.7
Sweden	26.6
Denmark	25.6
Norway	21.0
Greece	20.2
Finland	19.8
Germany (W)	19.6
United Kingdom	19.4
Iceland	19.0
Austria	19.0
France	18.8
United States	18.4
Italy	16.8
Australia	16.7
Belgium	15.8
Netherlands	15.8
Portugal	15.4
Japan	9.5

Percent of GDP

Figures are for 1989 or nearest year for which available.
Source: Organization for Economic Cooperation and Development (5).

Education expenditures in OECD economies

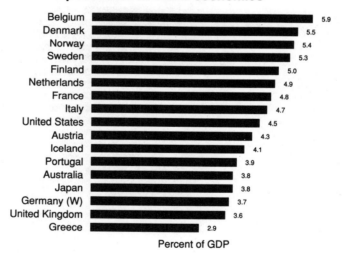

Country	Percent of GDP
Belgium	5.9
Denmark	5.5
Norway	5.4
Sweden	5.3
Finland	5.0
Netherlands	4.9
France	4.8
Italy	4.7
United States	4.5
Austria	4.3
Iceland	4.1
Portugal	3.9
Australia	3.8
Japan	3.8
Germany (W)	3.7
United Kingdom	3.6
Greece	2.9

Percent of GDP

Figures are for 1989 or nearest year for which available.
Source: Organization for Economic Cooperation and Development (5).

Among the OECD economies, Denmark spends most on social security and welfare — 6.2% of GDP — followed by Sweden at 4.7%.

Among the G–7, Germany spends most on social security and welfare, well ahead of France. The United Kingdom, Japan, and the United States spend the lowest share of its GDP in these categories — about one-sixth of Denmark's share.

The United States spends more on defense than does any other OECD economy, at over 6% of GDP. Japan spends the least, at about 1%.

Germany and Sweden are at the median level.

The United Kingdom and France spend above the median.

Social security and welfare expenditures in OECD economies

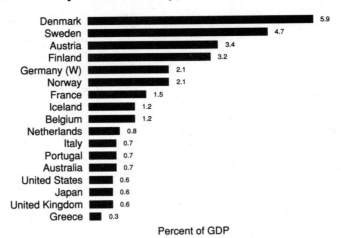

Percent of GDP

Figures are for 1989 or nearest year for which available.
Source: Organization for Economic Cooperation and Development (5).

Defense expenditures in OECD economies

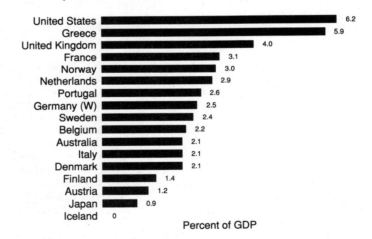

Percent of GDP

Figures are for 1989 or nearest year for which available.
Source: Organization for Economic Cooperation and Development (5).

Real spending on defense in the United States (adjusted for inflation) climbed steadily during the 1980s, growing by 50% until it reached a peak of $311 billion in 1987.

The fiscal deficit of the USSR grew rapidly after 1985, reaching a high point of 11% of GDP in 1988. However, the poor quality of current statistics, coupled with high inflation and generally chaotic economic conditions, rob current figures of any reliability.

Government final consumption expenditures in OECD economies

	TOTAL	EDUCATION	SOC SECURITY	DEFENSE
Luxembourg	52.9			
Ireland	43.7			
Sweden	26.6	5.3	4.7	2.4
Denmark	25.6	5.5	5.9	2.1
Norway	21.0	5.4	2.1	3.0
Greece	20.2	2.9	0.3	5.9
Finland	19.8	5.0	3.2	1.4
Germany (W)	19.6	3.7	2.1	2.5
United Kingdom	19.4	3.6	0.6	4.0
Iceland	19.0	4.1	1.2	0.0
Austria	19.0	4.3	3.4	1.2
France	18.8	4.8	1.5	3.1
United States	18.4	4.5		6.2
Italy	16.8	4.7	0.7	2.1
Australia	16.7	3.8	0.7	2.1
Belgium	15.8	5.9	1.2	2.2
Netherlands	15.8	4.9	0.8	2.9
Portugal	15.4	3.9	0.7	2.6
Japan	9.5	3.8	0.6	0.9

Figure 17–5

Percent of GDP. Figures are for 1989 or nearest year for which available.
Source: Organization for Economic Cooperation and Development (5).

Real defense spending in the United States

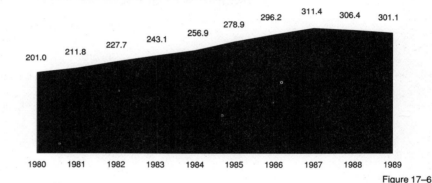

Figure 17–6

Billions of 1989 dollars.
Source: Deutsche Bank (2).

USSR's fiscal deficits

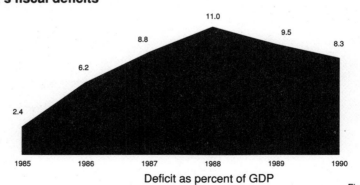

Deficit as percent of GDP

Figure 17–7

Source: International Monetary Fund (6).

Five of the six "dynamic" Asian economies had surpluses in their central government accounts in 1989. Indonesia's deficit of over 7% of GDP was below the median of developing economies in Asia.

In Latin America, Chile had a substantial surplus (5.5% of GDP) in 1989.

Among the main economies of the region, Argentina had a slight surplus; Mexico had a substantial deficit; Brazil's balance was not available.

Central government balances in Asia

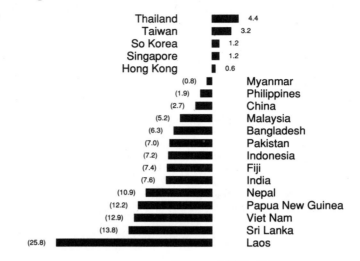

Percent of GDP, 1989

Source: Asian Development Bank (1).

Figure 17–8

Central government balances in Latin America

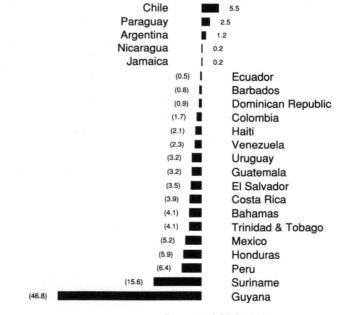

Percent of GDP, 1989

Source: Inter-American Development Bank (1).

Figure 17–9

The former socialist economies of central and eastern Europe spent relatively small shares of their GDPs on their military establishments. East Germany spent the most at 5%.

Countries in the Middle East spend more on their military establishments than do those of any other region. Biggest spenders late in the decade were Iraq and Saudi Arabia, both at around one-quarter of GDP. Iran's military spending was the lowest of the region's main countries — even so, it was a substantial 3% of GDP.

South Asia countries were relatively low spenders on their military establishments. Still, South Korea and Thailand, at about the median for the region, spent well over 4% of GDP. Among the main economies, the Philppines spent the least on its military.

Military spending in selected developing economies

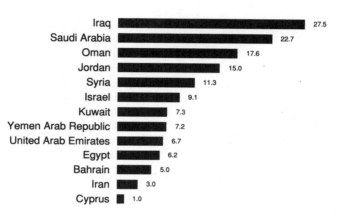

Figure 17–10a

Percent of GDP. 1988 in most cases; 1987 in others, except: 1985 for Iran and Iraq.
Source: Stockholm International Peace Research Institute (1).

In Africa, spending on military establishments was relatively low, except in Angola and Ethopia, both embroiled in civil wars at the close of the decade.

Before the end of its civil war, Nicaragua spent the most on its military establishment, as a share of GDP, in Latin America. Guyana, Cuba, and Chile spent substantial shares of their GDP on military matters. But expenditures were relatively low among most countries in the region — Mexico's only half of one percent of GDP.

Military spending in selected developing economies, cont'd

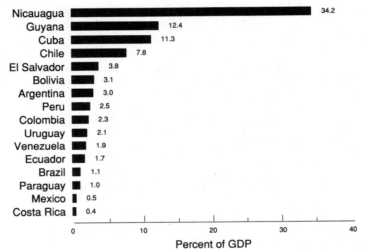

OCEANA

Australia 2.4
New Zealand 2.1

AFRICA

Angola 21.5
Ethiopia 10.0
Zimbabwe 5.8
So Africa 3.9
Algeria 1.5
Nigeria 0.9

LATIN AMERICA

Nicauagua 34.2
Guyana 12.4
Cuba 11.3
Chile 7.8
El Salvador 3.8
Bolivia 3.1
Argentina 3.0
Peru 2.5
Colombia 2.3
Uruguay 2.1
Venezuela 1.9
Ecuador 1.7
Brazil 1.1
Paraguay 1.0
Mexico 0.5
Costa Rica 0.4

Percent of GDP

Figure 17–10b

Percent of GDP. 1988 in most cases; 1987 in others, except: 1985 for Iran and Iraq.
Source: Stockholm International Peace Research Institute (1).

Fiscal Management

Total tax receipts as a share of GDP are highest in Sweden, at 55%. France collects the highest share among the main developed economies. The United States collects the lowest share (30%) and Japan the next-lowest (31%) among the main economies.

The top personal income tax rates are highest in Italy and Japan among the main OECD economies. Rates in the United States are not only the lowest among the main economies, but have the narrowest range between highest and lowest rates.

Among the main economies, the United Kingdom has the highest minimum rate (25%), followed closely by Germany (22%). Among the main economies, Japan's minimum rate is lowest (10%), slightly below Italy's (12%).

Taxes

Total tax receipts in OECD economies

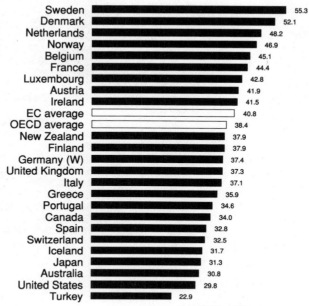

Percent of GDP, 1988

Source: Organization for Economic Cooperation and Development (5).

Personal income taxes in OECD economies

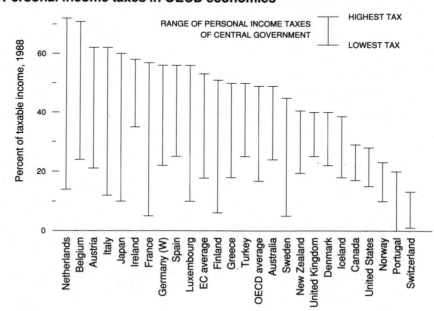

Disposable income — the percent of gross income a family "takes home" after taxes and social security contributions — is highest in Japan and France among the main developed economies. In both of these countries, a family with two children takes home about 90% of its gross income. Take-home pay in Canada is also above the European Community's average.

Take-home pay is lowest in the high-taxing Nordic countries, except for Norway, which ranked above the EC average.

Disposable income in OECD economies

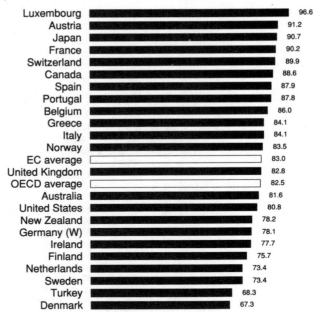

Percent of gross income for married persons with two children

	TOTAL TAX RECEIPTS	CENTRAL GOVT PERSONAL INCOME TAXES		DISPOSABLE INCOME AFTER TAXES	
		HIGHEST	LOWEST	SINGLE	MARRIED
Sweden	55.3	45.0	5.0	62.8	73.4
Denmark	52.1	40.0	22.0	53.4	67.3
Netherlands	48.2	72.0	14.0	62.8	73.4
Norway	46.9	23.0	10.0	66.6	83.5
Belgium	45.1	70.8	24.0	64.5	86.0
France	44.4	56.8	5.0	76.0	90.2
Luxembourg	42.8	56.0	10.0	73.8	96.6
Austria	41.9	62.0	21.0	73.3	91.2
Ireland	41.5	58.0	35.0	65.3	77.7
EC average	40.8	53.1	17.7	71.0	83.0
OECD average	38.4	49.0	16.7	71.9	82.5
New Zealand	37.9	40.5	19.5	76.3	78.2
Finland	37.9	51.0	6.0	64.5	75.7
Germany (W)	37.4	56.0	22.0	64.4	78.1
United Kingdom	37.3	40.0	25.0	72.1	82.8
Italy	37.1	62.0	12.0	72.6	84.1
Greece	35.9	50.0	18.0	81.6	84.1
Portugal	34.6	20.0	0.0	83.0	87.8
Canada	34.0	29.0	17.0	76.2	88.6
Spain	32.8	56.0	25.0	82.7	87.9
Switzerland	32.5	13.2	1.1	79.1	89.9
Iceland	31.7	38.5	18.0		
Japan	31.3	60.0	10.0	84.9	90.7
Australia	30.8	49.0	24.0	74.8	81.6
United States	29.8	28.0	15.0	74.0	80.8
Turkey	22.9	50.0	25.0	68.3	68.3

Figure 17–11

Total receipts as percent of GDP. Figures are for 1988.
Personal income tax rates. Incorporates tax relief, social security contributions, and local income taxes.
Disposable income of average production worker for single person and married with two children.
Source: Organization for Economic Cooperation and Development (5).

Fiscal Management

Tax structures in the developed economies show marked differences, one from another. In the accompanying graphs, countries are shown in descending order of personal income tax shares of total tax receipts, from Denmark to Portugal.

Among the main economies, personal income tax receipts in Canada and the United States are above the OECD average. Germany's receipts are a little below that, but above the European Community's average. Rates in the United Kingdom are a little below the EC average. Japan's are lowest among the main economies.

As a percent of total tax revenues, personal income taxes range from half in Denmark and New Zealand to one-eighth in France.

Tax structure in OECD economies

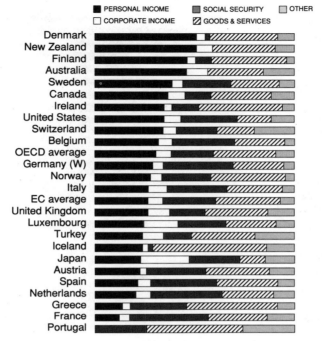

Percent of total tax receipts, 1988

Source: Organization for Economic Cooperation and Development (5).

Personal income tax share of total taxes in OECD economies

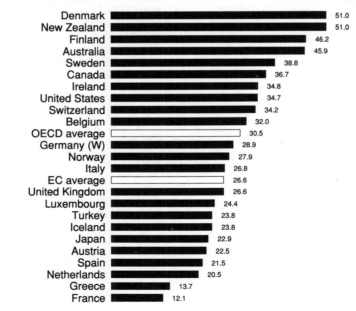

Percent of total tax receipts, 1988

Source: Organization for Economic Cooperation and Development (5).

Among the developed economies, corporate income taxes are the highest share of total tax receipts in Japan. The share in France is about one-fourth of that in Japan. The Nordic countries rely far less on corporate income taxes than does the average OECD country.

Among the main developed economies, France collects the greatest share (40%) of total tax receipts from social-security contributions; the United Kingdom collects the smallest share in this way.

Employees make contributions to their social security in all countries except Sweden, Finland, and Iceland. Employers make the biggest contributions in France, Spain, Sweden, and Belgium.

Among the main economies, employee contributions are above the OECD average in all G–7 countries except Canada.

Corporate income-tax share of total taxes in OECD economies

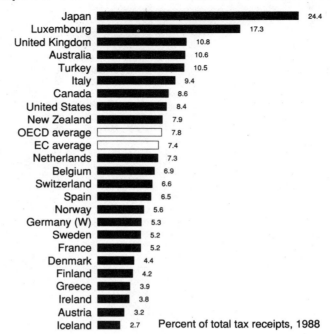

Percent of total tax receipts, 1988

Contributions to social security taxes in OECD economies

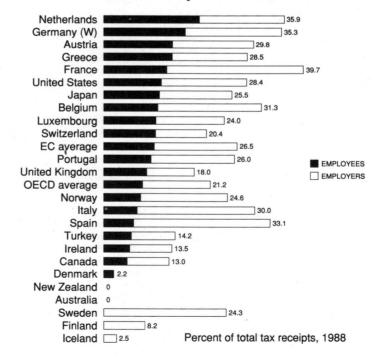

Percent of total tax receipts, 1988

Taxes on goods and services (value-added taxes) range from 57% of total tax receipts in Iceland to less than 13% in Japan and 17% in the United States.

All of the G–7 economies rely less on this tax than does the average OECD economy.

Taxes on goods and services as a share of total taxes in OECD

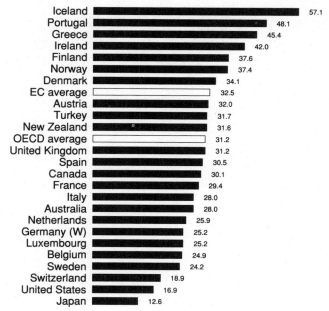

	Iceland	57.1
	Portugal	48.1
	Greece	45.4
	Ireland	42.0
	Finland	37.6
	Norway	37.4
	Denmark	34.1
	EC average	32.5
	Austria	32.0
	Turkey	31.7
	New Zealand	31.6
	OECD average	31.2
	United Kingdom	31.2
	Spain	30.5
	Canada	30.1
	France	29.4
	Italy	28.0
	Australia	28.0
	Netherlands	25.9
	Germany (W)	25.2
	Luxembourg	25.2
	Belgium	24.9
	Sweden	24.2
	Switzerland	18.9
	United States	16.9
	Japan	12.6

Percent of total tax receipts, 1988

| | INCOME TAX | | SOCIAL SECURITY | | | GOODS & | |
	PERSONAL	CORP	EMPLEE	EMPLER	TOTAL	SERVICES	OTHER
Denmark	51.0	4.4	2.0	0.2	2.2	34.1	8.3
New Zealand	51.0	7.9	0.0	0.0	0	31.6	9.5
Finland	46.2	4.2	0.0	8.2	8.2	37.6	3.8
Australia	45.9	10.6	0.0	0.0	0	28.0	15.5
Sweden	38.8	5.2	0.0	24.3	24.3	24.2	7.6
Canada	36.7	8.6	4.6	8.4	13.0	30.1	11.5
Ireland	34.8	3.8	5.1	8.4	13.5	42.0	5.9
United States	34.7	8.4	11.4	17.0	28.4	16.9	11.6
Switzerland	34.2	6.6	10.3	10.1	20.4	18.9	20.0
Belgium	32.0	6.9	10.7	20.6	31.3	24.9	5.0
OECD average	30.5	7.8	7.7	13.5	21.2	31.2	11.0
Germany (W)	28.9	5.3	16.2	19.1	35.3	25.2	5.3
Norway	27.9	5.6	7.3	17.3	24.6	37.4	4.5
Italy	26.8	9.4	6.6	23.4	30.0	28.0	5.8
EC average	26.6	7.4	10.0	16.5	26.5	32.5	10.0
United Kingdom	26.6	10.8	8.5	9.5	18.0	31.2	13.3
Luxembourg	24.4	17.3	10.4	13.6	24.0	25.2	9.1
Turkey	23.8	10.5	5.5	8.7	14.2	31.7	19.8
Iceland	23.8	2.7	0.0	2.5	2.5	57.1	13.9
Japan	22.9	24.4	11.1	14.4	25.5	12.6	14.7
Austria	22.5	3.2	13.7	16.1	29.8	32.0	12.5
Spain	21.5	6.5	5.9	27.2	33.1	30.5	8.4
Netherlands	20.5	7.3	19.0	16.9	35.9	25.9	10.3
Greece	13.7	3.9	13.6	14.9	28.5	45.4	8.6
France	12.1	5.2	12.5	27.2	39.7	29.4	13.6
Portugal		9.4	16.6	26.0	48.1	26.0	

Figure 17–12

Percent of total tax receipts, 1988.
Source: Organization for Economic Cooperation and Development (5).

18 Energy

While nearly everybody knows that oil is a vital ingredient of the modern world, it wasn't until the oil "shocks" of 1973 and 1979–80 that the supply and demand for oil became pillars of economic analysis. Indeed, the rudeness of the supply-side shocks of the 1970s seemed to many to prove the higher importance of supply over demand. This grew into expansive predictions that the global economy could and probably would be held hostage to a few countries lucky enough to be endowed with vital natural resources, like oil.

But in the 1980s, most of the producer cartels crumbled. Commodity prices fell, with no visible hope of recovery. Commodity-producing economies now scramble to diversify their outputs. But oil has held its special importance in the global economy, as the Gulf war demonstrated. And it is the demand for oil that governs the fate of alternative sources of energy.

Oil consumption continued to rise after the 1973–74 shock, reaching a maximum of 64.5 million barrels per day (mbd) in 1979. In the first half of the 1980s, as conservation measures took hold, consumption fell to 59 mbd. Prices declined in step with reduced demand, dropping precipitously in 1986.

At lower prices, demand recovered, though at a slower rate than before. By 1990, world consumption had reached a record high 65 mbd. But underneath the aggregate figure lay a changed pattern of consumption. Demand in the developed economies had come to a halt immediately in 1973; by 1990, it was 10% below its 1979 peak. Demand was flat in the socialist economies of central and eastern Europe. But the developing world's appetite for oil grew steadily as most of them urbanized their societies and industrialized their economies. By 1990, developing economies were using over one quarter of the world's supply of oil, more than twice as big a share as they used in 1970.

During the 1980s, the developed economies were driving down the "intensity" of their oil consumption — the amount of oil it takes to produce a unit of economic output. They substituted coal and natural gas for oil. More importantly, they reduced their requirements one-sixth by designing and installing more energy-efficient equipment and technologies. Overall, even though total consumption continues to rise, lower energy intensity in developed economies is holding the rise down to moderate levels.

Oil production is the other side of the coin. Here, too, the aggregates hide important differences. Producers outside the Oil Producing and Exporting Countries (OPEC) cartel provided most of the increased production of 1980–85, becoming an important new factor in the oil-supply equation. The shock of the 1970s had led to the rapid buildup of new reserves discovered in the 1970s — in Alaska, Mexico, and the North Sea. Non-OPEC production fell after 1986 (except in Norway), as lower prices discouraged exploration and drilling. Output of the USSR, the world's biggest producer, had risen briskly in the 1970s and continued to rise slowly in the 1980s. But unsettled political conditions, a falloff in investment, and lack of equipment, spare parts, and maintenance all worked together to cause significant reductions in 1989 and 1990. Production from the mature fields in the "lower forty-eight" United States also declined in the later 1980s.

Losses from USSR and US fields were made up by non-OPEC suppliers: Angola, Brazil, China, Colombia, India, Malaysia, Oman, Syria, and Yemen. OPEC made up for lost production in Kuwait and Iran after the invasion in 1990. Most of that new production came from Saudi Arabia.

Inventories of governments and the oil industry hold about a month-and-a-half of reserve supply. Some observers suggest that the government reserves be released from time to time as needed to stabilize prices. That was done when the allies began the war to liberate Kuwait in January 1991. But the usual policy is to hold the reserves for emergency use.

Analysts don't see any oil or other energy shocks on the horizon. World demand will continue to grow in the 1992–96 period, but at the modest rate of 1.5% a year. Both OPEC and non-OPEC sources of supply can easily rise to meet demand. If the USSR gets financial and technical help, its production could rise significantly in the second half of the decade. Output of the second-biggest producer, the United States, is expected to fall gradually through the 1990s.

Recently, energy economics is being linked with environment economics. The 25% decline in energy intensity that has occurred since 1973 translated into 19% less carbon emitted into the atmosphere in 1988. On the other side of the ledger, massive increases in traffic outweigh improvements in fuel efficiency and raise the level of air pollution. Energy-intensive industries account for over 75% of total CO_2 emissions and are also major sources of other air pollutants, including sulphur dioxide and nitrous oxide. The oil-dependent transport industry, which accounted for much of the growth in the demand for oil since 1973, is also a major source of CO_2.

A recent OECD study indicates that the industries that consume the most energy and emit the most CO_2 can reduce both by 10%–50%, using only proved, available technologies.

The United States is by far the biggest consumer of energy in the OECD economies, using 75% more than all 12 members of the European Community. The US uses 50% of OECD's energy to produce 36% of its output.

In the United States, the pattern of energy use is about evenly divided among industry, transport, and other sectors. In most other OECD economies, the transport sector's share is lower.

Total energy consumption in OECD economies

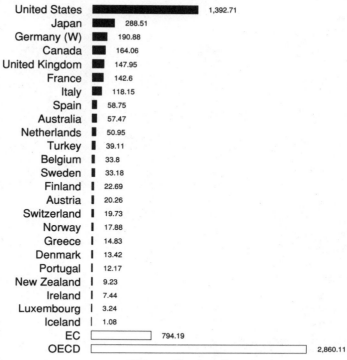

	Millions of tons of oil equivalent
United States	1,392.71
Japan	288.51
Germany (W)	190.88
Canada	164.06
United Kingdom	147.95
France	142.6
Italy	118.15
Spain	58.75
Australia	57.47
Netherlands	50.95
Turkey	39.11
Belgium	33.8
Sweden	33.18
Finland	22.69
Austria	20.26
Switzerland	19.73
Norway	17.88
Greece	14.83
Denmark	13.42
Portugal	12.17
New Zealand	9.23
Ireland	7.44
Luxembourg	3.24
Iceland	1.08
EC	794.19
OECD	2,860.11

Millions of tons of oil equivalent

Energy consumption by sector

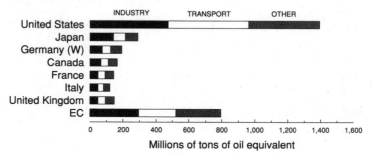

INDUSTRY   TRANSPORT   OTHER

United States
Japan
Germany (W)
Canada
France
Italy
United Kingdom
EC

0   200   400   600   800   1,000   1,200   1,400   1,600

Millions of tons of oil equivalent

On average, energy consumption in OECD economies fell by 2.4% in the 1980s. But consumption rose in the main economies, excepting Germany and France.

Turkey and Portugal had the biggest consumption increases over the decade; Denmark had the biggest decrease.

Among the main economies, industry took the biggest share of energy in Japan and the smallest in the United Kingdom. In this group, the transport sector took the biggest share in the United States and the smallest in Japan.

Consumption of energy in OECD economies

	TOTAL		INDUSTRY			TRANSPORT			OTHER		
	MTOE	CHGE	MTOE	SHARE	CHGE	MTOE	SHARE	CHGE	MTOE	SHARE	CHGE
US	1392.71	5.6	473.92	34	-5.7	488.94	35	16.9	429.85	31	8.0
Japan	288.51	15.9	142.02	49	4.2	70.48	24	30.1	76.01	26	29.7
Germ (W)	190.88	-4.0	72.79	38	-8.4	50.24	26	21.2	67.85	36	-12.9
Canada	164.06	5.9	66.24	40	5.4	42.35	26	-1.8	55.48	34	13.3
UK	147.95	8.0	46.39	31	-4.1	45.33	31	33.5	56.23	38	2.8
France	142.60	-1.5	48.88	34	-17.1	41.44	29	22.6	52.29	37	0.5
Italy	118.15	11.2	46.49	39	0.2	33.63	28	32.2	38.03	32	10.5
Spain	58.75	15.9	24.89	42	0.8	21.85	37	34.5	12.02	20	23.3
Australia	57.47	20.9	23.75	41	16.9	22.25	39	25.7	11.48	20	20.7
Netherlnds	50.95	-2.1	21.42	42	-2.5	10.34	20	17.8	19.18	38	-9.9
Turkey	39.11	44.2	13.30	34	70.9	8.79	22	57.6	17.01	43	23.6
Belgium	33.80	-2.5	14.71	44	-5.9	7.78	23	31.2	11.32	33	-13.7
Sweden	33.18	-3.8	13.78	42	-2.1	7.89	24	29.1	11.51	35	-19.5
Finland	22.69	17.3	11.26	50	18.3	4.26	19	41.6	7.17	32	5.2
Austria	20.26	2.5	7.24	36	-3.2	5.41	27	17.8	7.61	38	-1.1
Switzerlnd	19.73	11.9	3.92	20	-15.1	5.96	30	33.3	9.85	50	15.2
Norway	17.88	8.3	8.24	46	0.2	4.02	22	26.6	5.62	31	10.0
Greece	14.83	27.3	4.72	32	6.5	5.51	37	36.6	4.6	31	44.4
Denmark	13.42	-11.4	3.17	24	-10.6	4.36	32	20.3	5.89	44	-26.1
Portugal	12.17	43.5	6.07	50	50.1	3.60	30	37.6	2.50	21	37.4
N Zealand	9.23	35.3	3.80	41	60.7	3.50	38	40.4	1.93	21	-1.7
Ireland	7.44	12.8	2.57	35	8.8	1.95	26	9.9	2.92	39	18.7
Luxembrg	3.24	-2.3	1.77	55	-19.3	0.87	27	70.5	0.59	18	-2.1
Iceland	1.08	30.8	0.39	36	7.1	0.54	50	75.7	0.15	14	-1.9
EC	794.19	3.2	293.87	37	-5.8	226.90	29	27.4	273.41	34	-2.1
OECD	**2860.11**	**-2.4**	**1061.73**	**37**	**-2.4**	**891.28**	**31**	**20.3**	**907.09**	**32**	**6.4**

Figure 18–1

MTOE = millions of tons of oil equivalent.
Change = percent change since 1980.
Share = Percent of total consumpton by each sector.
Source: Organization for Economic Cooperation and Development (5).

Of the main economies, Japan used energy the most efficiently in producing its national output in the 1980s. Italy, France, Germany, and the United Kingdom were all above OECD average efficiency. The United States was a little below, and the European Community further below, the OECD average.

All of the main economies except France's increased their energy efficiency more than the OECD average in the 1980s. The European Community as a whole was less efficient at the end of the decade.

Energy intensity in OECD countries

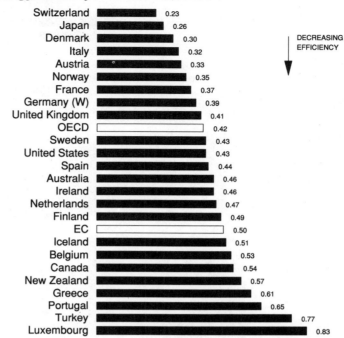

Energy units divided by GDP, 1989

Figure 18–2

Changes in energy intensity

Percent change in energy supply, 1980-89

Figure 18–3

The USSR produces more than half of the energy used in transitioning economies, an amount that grew 21% in the 1980s.

China, using 25% of the total for these economies, increased its share by 49% during the decade.

Oil prices dropped steeply among the main users. Israel's oil bill dropped by two-thirds. The cost of imported oil fell the least in the United States, but even so by one-third.

Energy consumption in transitioning economies

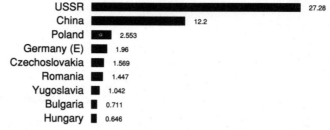

Millions of barrels per day of oil equivalent, 1988

	1980	1988	% CHANGE	% SHARE
USSR	22.470	27.280	21	55
China	8.162	12.200	49	25
Poland	2.488	2.553	3	5
Germany (E)	1.856	1.960	6	4
Czechoslovakia	1.466	1.569	7	3
Romania	1.364	1.447	6	3
Yugoslavia	0.890	1.042	17	2
Bulgaria	0.656	0.711	8	1
Hungary	0.602	0.646	7	1
Total	**39.954**	**49.408**	**24**	**100**

Figure 18–4

Millions of barrels per day oil equivalent.
Figures exclude minor fuels such as peat, shale, and fuelwood.
Source: Central Intelligence Agency (1).

Drop in oil prices to major importers

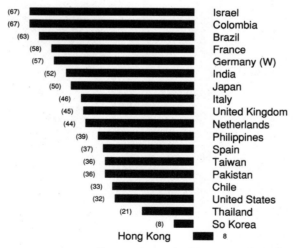

Percent change in oil import bills, 1980-89

Energy

Saudi Arabia has by far the biggest proved reserves of crude oil, 40% of the total of the Persian Gulf producers.

The USSR, the world's biggest oil producer holds a smaller portion of total reserves than do any of the Gulf producers.

Mexico and Venezuela have greater reserves than does the United States, the world's second-biggest producer.

Oil costs of major importers

	1980	1989	% CHANGE
Israel	2.1	0.7	-67
Colombia	0.6	0.2	-67
Brazil	10.3	3.8	-63
France	30.7	13.0	-58
Germany (W)	35.1	15.2	-57
India	6.1	2.9	-52
Japan	58.9	29.2	-50
Italy	24.6	13.2	-46
United Kingdom	14.0	7.7	-45
Netherlands	17.0	9.5	-44
Philippines	2.3	1.4	-39
Spain	11.9	7.5	-37
Taiwan	4.2	2.7	-36
Pakistan	1.4	0.9	-36
Chile	0.9	0.6	-33
United States	76.9	52.4	-32
Thailand	2.8	2.2	-21
So Korea	6.2	5.7	-8
Hong Kong	1.2	1.3	8

Figure 18–5

Billions of dollars.
Total cost of imported crude oil and petroleum products.
For Taiwan, crude petroleum only.
Source: Central Intelligence Agency (1).

Proved reserves of crude oil

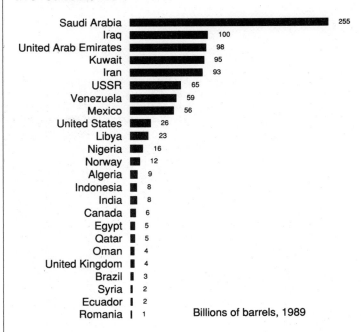

Billions of barrels, 1989

The USSR holds by far the biggest share of reserves of natural gas.

The United States and the USSR together have most of the world's coal reserves.

Proved reserves of natural gas

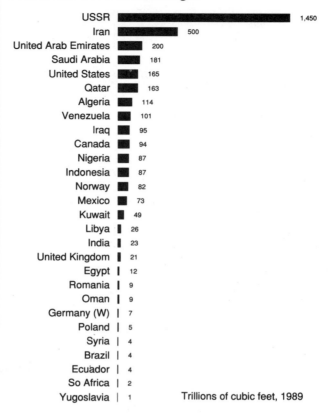

USSR	1,450
Iran	500
United Arab Emirates	200
Saudi Arabia	181
United States	165
Qatar	163
Algeria	114
Venezuela	101
Iraq	95
Canada	94
Nigeria	87
Indonesia	87
Norway	82
Mexico	73
Kuwait	49
Libya	26
India	23
United Kingdom	21
Egypt	12
Romania	9
Oman	9
Germany (W)	7
Poland	5
Syria	4
Brazil	4
Ecuador	4
So Africa	2
Yugoslavia	1

Trillions of cubic feet, 1989

Proved reserves of coal

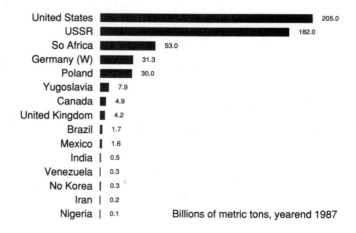

United States	205.0
USSR	182.0
So Africa	53.0
Germany (W)	31.3
Poland	30.0
Yugoslavia	7.9
Canada	4.9
United Kingdom	4.2
Brazil	1.7
Mexico	1.6
India	0.5
Venezuela	0.3
No Korea	0.3
Iran	0.2
Nigeria	0.1

Billions of metric tons, yearend 1987

Only the USSR and the United States have major proved reserves of the three primary sources of energy: crude oil, natural gas, and coal.

Of the main developed economies, only the United States, the United Kingdom, and Germany have any reserves of energy raw materials.

Proved reserves of energy sources

	CRUDE OIL	NATURAL GAS	COAL
Saudi Arabia	255	181	
Iraq	100	95	
United Arab Emirates	98	200	
Kuwait	95	49	
Iran	93	500	0.175
USSR	65	1450	182.000
Venezuela	59	101	0.340
Mexico	56	73	1.600
United States	26	165	205.000
Libya	23	26	
Nigeria	16	87	0.120
Norway	12	82	
Algeria	9	114	
Indonesia	8	87	
India	8	23	0.475
Canada	6	94	4.900
Egypt	5	12	
Qatar	5	163	
Oman	4	9	
United Kingdom	4	21	4.200
Brazil	3	4	1.660
Syria	2	4	
Ecuador	2	4	
Romania	1	9	
Germany (W)		7	31.300
Poland		5	30.000
So Africa		2	53.000
No Korea			0.272
Yugoslavia		1	7.900

Figure 18–6

The portion of total resources that has been assessed as being exploitable under local economic conditions and available technology.
Figures for crude oil and natural gas are for 1989.
Coal is for yearend 1987, in terms of coal equivalent (7000 kilocalories per kilogram), and include anthracite, bituminous and subbituminous coal, and brown coal/lignite.
Crude oil in billions of barrels.
Natural gas in trillions of cubic feet.
Coal in billions of metric tons.
Source: Central Intelligence Agency (1).

19 Human Capital

Aglobal economy — in which goods, services, people, and money move freely across national borders — raises basic questions about the appropriate role of national governments. Inexorably, the old notions of sovereignty are eroding. The former Soviet Union, which tried so hard for so long to insulate its own and its satellites' economies from the markets of the developed world, is now turning itself inside out in order to fit into that world. Developing — "third world" — countries that once proclaimed a New International Economic Order are now restructuring their own orders to align their economies with world markets. Even the hard-line Chinese government claims to be moving toward integration with the world system. The handful of holdouts — notably North Korea and Cuba — are hardly enviable models.

The developed market economies have their own adjusting to do, if they want to prosper in the global arenas. The seven main economies (the G–7) are coordinating the fiscal and monetary actions of their "sovereign" economies to deal with global imbalances. Many observers feel that the main economic mission of national governments today is to develop the human capital of their societies so they will be competitive in the global order.

This chapter deals with the ways in which natonal governments develop and maintain their human capital.

From one viewpoint, productivity is the index of how effectively physical and social resources have been organized to enable individual workers to produce more at lower cost.

In analyzing how a society employs its workers, policymakers must ask: Is the economy creating enough new jobs for its increasing population? Are all human resources — including women and minorities — being employed? Are workers being adequately supported by research and development?

Demographics define an economy's basic human potentials. Bigger populations obviously produce more output — but not necessarily more output per capita. Infant mortality and life expectancy are rough guides to a society's success in meeting the first need: life itself. Dependency ratios — the number of working-age people who support those too young and too old to work —

point to potentials for growth . . . and future demands for welfare services.

Education has always been the preferred tool for developing human capital. So we ask: How accessible is it? How do societies value education, compared with other needs? In the latter area, we look at some embarrassing data on how the number of teachers compares with the number of military people; and how spending on education and health compares with spending on military establishments.

Analysts at the United Nations are concerned that the traditional measure of development, the growth of national income, does not explicitly measure what's happening to real human beings. They are therefore attempting to collect a very broad range of data, worldwide, showing how well human needs are being met. They have created a Human Development Index (HDI), a rough "humanity score" for individual societies. Obviously, the HDI isn't perfect, and UN people are still improving it. But the index does serve to refocus attention on people.

The Human Development Index is the composite of three factors that stand for the quality of human life: longevity, knowledge, and income.

Longevity is expressed simply as life expectancy at birth, a figure that presumably reflects many aspects of lifelong health care. Knowledge is represented by a weighted combination of adult literacy and years of schooling. Income is represented by gross domestic product, weighted to include the assumption of diminishing returns — i.e., the quality of human life doesn't rise indefinitely as national income does.

This chapter ends with the HDI rankings for 160 societies. As one expects, wealthier societies get higher indexes. But the news is that the correlation between wealth and human development is not at all consistent. This inconsistency is interesting; it suggests that some societies provide more human-development services than their incomes justify in comparison with other societies. Turned around, some societies should be able to provide more human services with the amount of wealth they have — again, by comparison with world norms.

Productivity — output per employed person — is highest in the United States, as it has been since World War II. However, other economies have gained on the US since 1970.

Japanese workers now produce 77% of what US workers do; in 1970, the ratio was 47%.

The productivity of German workers went from 62% to 79% of that of US workers.

Labor forces

Productivity in selected economies

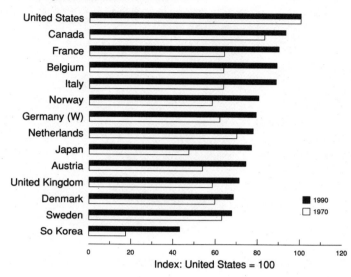

Index: United States = 100

	1960	1970	1980	1989	1990
United States	100	100	100	100	100
Canada	79.0	83.0	91.6	94.6	93.0
France	47.7	63.9	80.3	88.7	89.7
Belgium	50.7	63.5	81.8	86.9	88.7
Italy	42.1	63.6	82.5	88.4	88.4
Norway	50.5	58.2	73.9	78.9	80.4
Germany (W)	49.5	61.9	75.6	78.0	79.1
Netherlands	57.5	70.0	81.3	77.3	77.7
Japan	24.1	47.3	64.1	74.6	76.9
Austria	39.2	53.8	68.3	72.2	74.4
United Kingdom	54.7	58.6	66.9	71.5	71.2
Denmark	53.1	59.6	66.0	67.4	68.6
Sweden	52.4	63.0	67.1	68.4	67.7
So Korea	13.0	17.5	26.5	41.1	43.3

Figure 19–1

Gross domestic product per employed person.
Based on purchasing-power-parity exchange rates.
Source: Bureau of Labor Statistics (1).

The labor forces of Canada and the United States grew faster in the 1980s than did any other OECD labor force.

Japan's growth was at the OECD median, with an 11% increase in the labor force between 1980–89.

Four out of five women between the ages of 16–64 were employed in Sweden in 1989 — the highest rate of female participation in the OECD labor force.

Female participation in Japan's labor force was at the OECD median of 60%.

At 44%, women's participation in the Italian labor force was the lowest among the G–7 economies.

Growth of OECD labor force

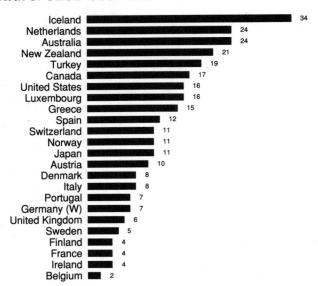

Percent change in total labor force, 1980-89

Participation of women in the OECD labor force

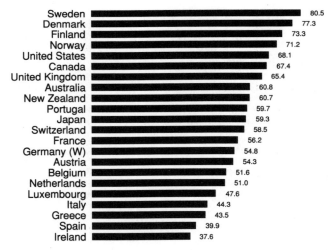

Female workers as percent of total female labor force, 1989

Worldwide, the percent- age of all Asian and Oceanic women in those labor forces is slightly higher than the percent of working women in the devel- oped economies.

The smallest percent of women are employed in the Arab states.

Women in the world labor force

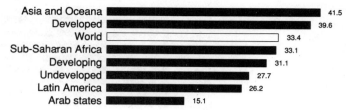

Percent of total population

Labor force in OECD economies

	TOTAL		FEMALE PARTICIPATION		
	1989	% CHANGE	1989	1980	% CHANGE
United States	125.557	16	68.1	59.7	8
Japan	62.700	11	59.3	54.9	4
Germany (W)	29.779	7	54.8	51.4	3
United Kingdom	28.508	6	65.4	58.3	7
France	24.320	4	56.2	54.4	2
Italy	24.258	8	44.3	39.6	5
Turkey	19.180	19			
Spain	15.160	12	39.9	32.2	8
Canada	13.582	17	67.4	57.2	10
Australia	8.303	24	60.8	52.7	8
Netherlands	6.713	24	51.0	35.5	16
Portugal	4.677	7	59.7	57.0	3
Sweden	4.527	5	80.5	74.1	6
Belgium	4.144	2	51.6	47.0	5
Greece	3.967	15	43.5	33.0	11
Switzerland	3.535	11	58.5	54.1	4
Austria	3.450	10	54.3	48.7	6
Denmark	2.879	8	77.3	69.9	7
Finland	2.583	4	73.3	70.1	3
Norway	2.155	11	71.2	62.3	9
New Zealand	1.573	21	60.7	44.6	16
Ireland	1.292	4	37.6	36.3	1
Luxembourg	0.184	16	47.6	39.9	8
Iceland	0.142	34			

Figure 19–2

Millions of workers.
% Change since 1980.
Female participation rate = female labor force of all ages divided by female population age 15-64.
Source: Organization for Economic Cooperation and Development (5).

Employing a high percentage of an economy's labor force in services seems to be a characteristic of more-developed economies. But differences are noteworthy.

In the United States, over 70% of all workers work in services, while in Germany and Japan, fewer than 60% do.

In mirror-image similarity, a greater percentage of German and Japanese workers are employed in industry than are in the United States.

In all of the main developed economies, only a small percent of workers are employed in agriculture. Of the main economies, Italy's labor force has the biggest share of farmers (9%), but Japan's share is a fairly close second (under 8%).

Structure of civilian employment in OECD economies

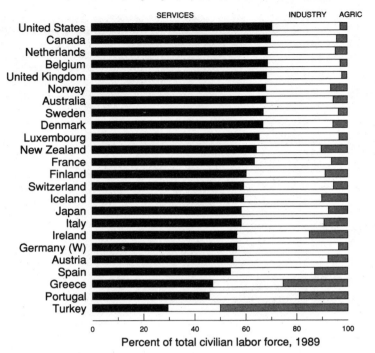

Percent of total civilian labor force, 1989

	AGRICULTURE	INDUSTRY	SERVICES
United States	2.9	26.7	70.5
Canada	4.3	25.7	70.1
Netherlands	4.7	26.5	68.8
Belgium	2.8	28.5	68.7
United Kingdom	2.1	29.4	68.4
Norway	6.6	25.3	68.1
Australia	5.5	26.5	68.0
Sweden	3.6	29.4	67.0
Denmark	5.7	27.4	66.9
Luxembourg	3.4	31.2	65.4
New Zealand	10.3	25.4	64.3
France	6.4	30.1	63.5
Finland	8.9	30.9	60.2
Switzerland	5.6	35.1	59.3
Iceland	10.2	30.6	59.2
Japan	7.6	34.3	58.2
Italy	9.3	32.4	58.2
Ireland	15.1	28.4	56.5
Germany (W)	3.7	39.8	56.5
Austria	8.0	37.0	55.1
Spain	13.0	32.9	54.0
Greece	25.3	27.5	47.1
Portugal	19.0	35.3	45.7
Turkey	50.1	20.5	29.5

Figure 19–3

Percent of total civilian labor force.
Source: Organization for Economic Cooperation and Development (5).

Human Capital

The United States spends more per capita on research and development than does any other OECD economy. Among the main economies, all but Italy are above the OECD median.

Research and development spending by industry is presumed to add to an economy's competitiveness in global product markets. Much of the spending financed by government goes for military programs and strategic industries.

In the median OECD economy, about half is financed by industry and half by government.

In the United States, slightly more than half of all research and development is financed by government.

Spending on research and development

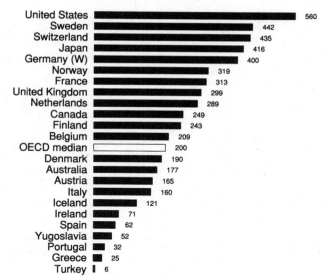

Per-capita spending, 1988

Industry financing of research and development

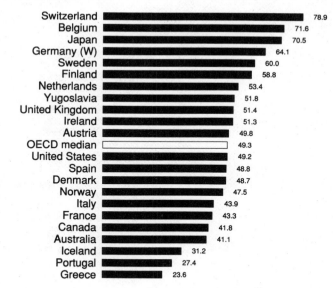

Percent of gross domestic spending financed by industry, 1988

Japan spends more of its GDP on research and development (2.91%) than any other economy. The United States (2.86%) and Germany (2.83%) are close behind. Among the main economies, Italy spends the lowest share of its GDP on research and development.

The number of researchers in an economy's labor force indicates the depth of its potential competitiveness in world markets.

Japan leads the main economies in the number of researchers, followed not very closely by the United States and Germany. The United Kingdom and Canada are at the OECD median; Italy is far below it.

Gross domestic spending on research and development

	SPENDING			% FINANCED BY	
	TOTAL	PER CAPITA	GDP %	GOVT	INDUSTRY
United States	137.816	560	2.86	48.8	49.2
Sweden	3.756	442	2.84	36.9	60.0
Switzerland	2.858	435	2.88	21.1	78.9
Japan	50.987	416	2.91	19.9	70.5
Germany (W)	24.578	400	2.83	33.9	64.1
Norway	1.350	319	1.91	48.3	47.5
France	17.512	313	2.29	49.9	43.3
United Kingdom	17.042	299	2.20	36.5	51.4
Netherlands	4.259	289	2.26	42.7	53.4
Canada	6.456	249	1.35	44.0	41.8
Finland	1.201	243	1.76	38.9	58.8
Belgium	2.060	209	1.61	26.7	71.6
OECD median		200	1.50	47.0	49.3
Denmark	0.972	190	1.43	45.9	48.7
Australia	2.931	177	1.24	54.6	41.1
Austria	1.255	165	1.32	47.5	49.8
Italy	9.164	160	1.23	51.8	43.9
Iceland	0.030	121	0.77	66.3	31.2
Ireland	0.251	71	0.87	38.4	51.3
Spain	2.433	62	0.67	48.5	48.8
Yugoslavia	1.215	52	0.98	47.0	51.8
Portugal	0.328	32	0.50	66.1	27.4
Greece	0.252	25	0.37	67.9	23.6
Turkey	0.299	6	0.13		

Figure 19–4

Figures are for 1988.
Total and per-capita expenditures converted using purchasing power parities.
Source: Organization for Economic Cooperation and Development (5).

Researchers in the labor force

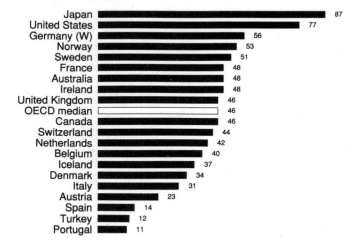

Per 10,000 in labor force

Figure 19–5

Researchers or holders of university degrees engaged in research and development.
Source: Organization for Economic Cooperation and Development (5).

Japan's inventors contribute almost 90% of the patents used in their country's domestic applications. That is a far greater percentage than any other country's (it's about 50% in the United States) and a far greater absolute number of domestic patents (about four times the US number).

Germany, the United Kingdom, and France follow not very closely in the number of domestic patent applications and in the percentage made by local inventors.

Switzerland has the greatest number of patent applications as a percent of its population, an indication of the intensity of technology in its economy. Technology intensity in Japan is second, followed by that in Sweden and Germany.

Domestic patent applications

Millions of applications

Patent applications in OECD countries

	TOTAL	DOMESTIC	FROM ABROAD	APPLIC ABROAD	TOTAL RATE
Japan	345.239	308.644	36.595	101.192	334
United States	146.904	75.215	71.689	200.842	112
Germany (W)	84.806	30.869	53.937	128.026	261
United Kingdom	79.916	19.819	60.097	54.926	133
France	66.095	12.426	53.669	53.150	118
Australia	22.096	6.342	15.754	14.069	123
Switzerland	36.940	2.844	34.096	28.633	486
Canada	31.641	2.784	28.857	9.286	46
Netherlands	40.115	2.567	37.548	20.389	156
Sweden	37.410	2.544	34.866	21.637	296
Finland	9.986	2.477	7.509	6.729	176
Spain	26.251	1.838	24.413	2.722	12
Austria	31.872	1.498	30.374	7.774	133
Yugoslavia	2.406	1.448	0.958	0.292	7
Denmark	11.080	1.197	9.883	7.639	172
Norway	9.435	0.906	8.529	2.978	92
Belgium	33.867	0.847	33.020	6.003	69
New Zealand	4.425	0.801	3.624	0.716	46
Ireland	3.901	0.726	3.175	0.939	47
Greece	13.764	0.372	13.392	0.210	16
Turkey	0.900	0.153	0.747	0.007	0
Luxembourg	23.014	0.092	22.922	0.812	
Portugal	2.464	0.054	2.410	0.105	2
Iceland	0.126	0.016	0.110	0.007	15
Italy	52.939			25.271	

Figure 19–6

Millions of applications, 1988.
Total rate = applications, domestic and from abroad, per 100,000 of total population.
Source: Organization for Economic Cooperation and Development (5).

Almost 60% of the world's people live in Asia.

Population is growing fastest in Africa, where it will double in just 24 years. It will take 33 years for the population of the less-developed countries to double their populations. The whole world's population will double in 39 years.

Slow-growing (in Germany, declining) populations in Europe will take 266 years to double at present rates.

One of every five human beings is Chinese.

The USSR as it existed in mid–1991 was the world's third-largest nation. If the Russian republic were an independent nation (population: 147 million), it would rank sixth, just behind Brazil.

Demographics

World population

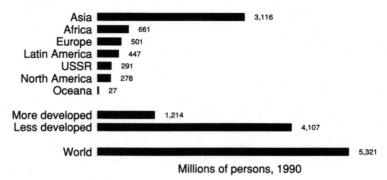

Millions of persons, 1990

Doubling time of world populations

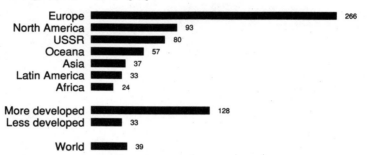

Years for population to double at current rates

Most-populous countries

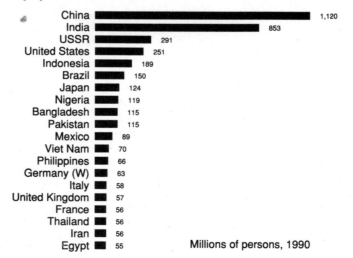

Millions of persons, 1990

Regionally, the rate of infant mortality (death in the first year of life) is lowest in North America and highest in Africa.

The infant mortality rate in less-developed countries is five times that of the more-developed.

Worldwide, the infant mortality rate is 73 per 1000 live births.

Most-populous countries

	POPULATION			DOUBLING TIME	INFANT MORTALITY
	1990	2000	2020		
China	1120	1280	1496	49	37
India	853	1043	1375	33	95
USSR	291	312	355	80	29
United States	251	268	294	92	9.7
Indonesia	189	224	287	38	89
Brazil	150	180	234	36	63
Japan	124	128	124	175	4.8
Nigeria	119	161	273	24	121
Bangladesh	115	147	201	28	120
Pakistan	115	149	251	23	110
Mexico	89	107	142	29	50
Viet Nam	70	88	120	28	50
Philippines	66	83	118	27	48
Germany (W)	63	66	62	INF	7.5
Italy	58	59	56	1155	9.5
United Kingdom	57	59	61	301	9.5
France	56	58	59	157	7.5
Thailand	56	64	78	45	39
Iran	56	76	130	20	91
Egypt	55	69	102	24	90
World	**5321**	**6292**	**8228**	**39**	**73**
Top 20, percent	74	73	71		

Figure 19–7

Population in millions.
Source: Population Reference Bureau (1).

World infant mortality rates

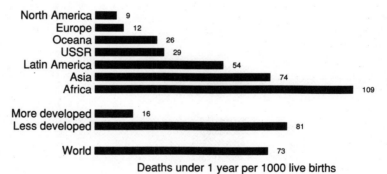

Deaths under 1 year per 1000 live births

Infant mortality is lower in Japan than in any other country. Among the developed economies, the rates are lowest in New Zealand, Ireland, the United States, and the United Kingdom.

Life expectancy at birth is highest in Japan (79 years) and close to that in several other developed economies.

Five of the ten countries with the highest infant mortality are African; four are Asian; one is Latin American.

In this group, life expectancy ranges from 41 to 56 years.

Lowest infant mortality rates

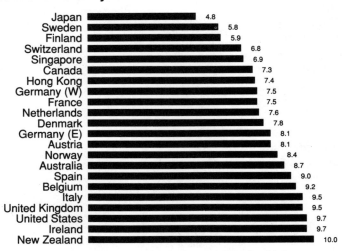

Deaths under 1 year per 1000 live births

Range of infant mortality

	POPULATION			DOUBLING	INFANT	LIFE
	1990	2000	2020	TIME	MORTALITY	EXPECT
LOWEST INFANT MORTALITY						
Japan	124	128	124	175	4.8	79
Sweden	9	9	9	311	5.8	77
Finland	5	5	5	239	5.9	75
Switzerland	7	7	7	231	6.8	77
Singapore	3	3	3	47	6.9	73
Canada	27	29	33	96	7.3	77
Hong Kong	6	6	7	82	7.4	77
Germany (W)	63	66	62		7.5	76
France	56	58	59	157	7.5	77
Netherlands	15	15	15	165	7.6	77
Denmark	5	5	5		7.8	75
Germany (E)	16	16	15	6930	8.1	73
Austria	8	8	8	1155	8.1	75
Norway	4	4	4	231	8.4	76
Australia	17	19	23	90	8.7	76
Spain	39	41	41	247	9.0	77
Belgium	10	10	9	462	9.2	74
Italy	58	59	56	1155	9.5	75
United Kingdom	57	59	61	301	9.5	75
United States	251	268	294	92	9.7	75
Ireland	4	4	3	108	9.7	74
New Zealand	3	4	4	82	10.0	74
Greece	10	10	10	408	11.0	77
Cuba	11	12	13	60	11.9	75
Czechoslovakia	16	16	17	289	11.9	71
HIGHEST INFANT MORTALITY						
Sudan		34	55	24	108	50
Pakistan		149	251	23	110	56
Bolivia		9	13	27	110	53
Nepal		24	38	28	112	52
Bangladesh		147	201	28	120	54
Madagascar		17	30	22	120	54
Nigeria		161	273	24	121	48

(MORE)

Regionally, life expectancy at birth is highest in North America and lowest in Africa. Worldwide, life expectancy is 64 years.

Thirty years from now, the regional distribution of population will have changed very little, except that Africa's share of the total will have grown substantially.

Europe and North America have the oldest populations; Africa has the youngest.

Range of infant mortality, cont'd

	POPULATION			DOUBLING TIME	INFANT MORTALITY	LIFE EXPECT
	1990	2000	2020			
Mozambique		20	32	26	141	47
Ethiopia		71	126	34	154	41
Afghanistan		25	43	27	182	41
World	**5321**	**6292**	**8228**	**39**	**73**	**64**

Figure 19–8

Population in millions.
Source: Population Reference Bureau (1).

Life expectancy

North America	75
Europe	74
Oceana	72
USSR	69
Latin America	67
Asia	63
Africa	52
More developed	74
Less developed	61
World	64

Life expectancy at birth with current mortality

Demographics by region and development status

	POPULATION						2X TIME	INFANT MORT	LIFE EXPECT
	1990	SHARE	2000	SHARE	2020	SHARE			
Asia	3116	59	3718	59	4805	58	37	74	63
Africa	661	12	884	14	1481	18	24	109	52
Europe	501	9	515	8	516	6	266	12	74
Latin America	447	8	535	9	705	9	33	54	67
USSR	291	5	312	5	355	4	80	29	69
North America	278	5	298	5	328	4	93	9	75
Oceana	27	1	31	0	38	0.5	57	26	72
More developed	1214	23	1274	20	1350	16	128	16	74
Less developed	4107	77	5018	80	6878	84	33	81	61
World	**5321**	**100**	**6292**	**100**	**8228**	**100**	**39**	**73**	**64**

Figure 19–9

Population in millions.
2X time = doubling time: years to double population at constant 1991 rate.
Infant mortality = deaths under 1 year per 1000 live births.
Life expectancy at birth, assuming current mortality levels.
Source: Population Reference Bureau (1).

Dependency on labor forces in geographic regions

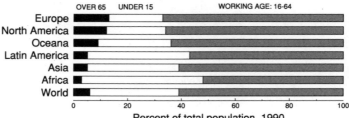

OVER 65   UNDER 15   WORKING AGE: 16-64

Europe
North America
Oceana
Latin America
Asia
Africa
World

0   20   40   60   80   100

Percent of total population, 1990

The productivity of any economy is influenced by the percent of its population in the active labor force — persons 15–64 years old. The more active workers there are in the population, the more productive the economy should be. So a lower dependency should tend to increase productivity. However, a dearth of active workers can stimulate the introduction of new technology and thereby tend to increase productivity.

Sweden has the highest dependency ratio among highly developed economies and Canada the lowest.

The dependency ratios of Japan and Germany are about the same, although Germany has has a somewhat older population.

Dependency on labor forces in developed economies

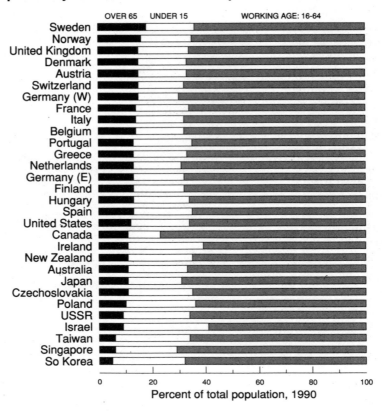

Percent of total population, 1990

	UNDER 15	OVER 65	TOTAL DEPENDENTS	WORKING AGE	DEPENDENCY RATIO
Sweden	18	18	36	64	56
Norway	19	16	35	65	54
United Kingdom	19	15	34	66	52
Denmark	18	15	33	67	49
Austria	18	15	33	67	49
Switzerland	17	15	32	68	47
Germany (W)	15	15	30	70	43
France	20	14	34	66	52
Italy	18	14	32	68	47
Belgium	18	14	32	68	47
Portugal	22	13	35	65	54
Greece	20	13	33	67	49
Netherlands	18	13	31	69	45
Germany (E)	19	13	32	68	47
Finland	19	13	32	68	47
Hungary	21	13	34	66	52
Spain	22	13	35	65	54
United States	22	12	34	66	52
Canada	12	11	23	77	30
Ireland	28	11	39	61	64
New Zealand	24	11	35	65	54
Australia	22	11	33	67	49
Japan	20	11	31	69	45
Czechoslovakia	24	11	35	65	54

(MORE)

Less-developed countries have fewer elderly and more young people than developed countries do. Because of the high proportion of people under 15, their dependency ratios are higher.

In China, the percent of young people is exceptionally small, considering its development status.

Populations in four major Middle East countries are notably young, considering their development status.

Dependency on labor forces in developed economies, cont'd

	UNDER 15	OVER 65	TOTAL DEPENDENTS	WORKING AGE	DEPENDENCY RATIO
Poland	26	10	36	64	56
USSR	25	9	34	66	52
Israel	32	9	41	59	69
China	27	6	33	67	49
Taiwan	28	6	34	66	52
Singapore	23	6	29	71	41
So Korea	27	5	32	68	47

Figure 19–10

Percent of total population, except dependency ratio.
Dependency ratio = percent of dependent population (under 15 and over 15 years) to the working-age population (between 15-64 years).
Source: Population Reference Bureau (1).

Dependency on labor forces in selected developing and undeveloped economies

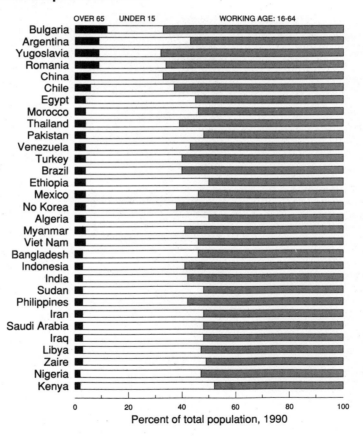

Percent of total population, 1990

The working-age population must support an equal number of dependents in several less-developed countries: Kenya, Algeria, Ethiopia, and Zaire.

The dependency ratio of China is the same as that of Bulgaria, and the lowest among less-developed countries.

Dependency ratios in selected developing and undeveloped economies

	UNDER 15	OVER 65	TOTAL DEPENDENTS	WORKING AGE	DEPENDENCY RATIO
Bulgaria	21	12	33	67	49
Argentina	34	9	43	57	75
Yugoslavia	23	9	32	68	47
Romania	25	9	34	66	52
China	27	6	33	67	49
Chile	31	6	37	63	59
Egypt	41	4	45	55	82
Morocco	42	4	46	54	85
Thailand	35	4	39	61	64
Pakistan	44	4	48	52	92
Venezuela	39	4	43	57	75
Turkey	36	4	40	60	67
Brazil	36	4	40	60	67
Ethiopia	46	4	50	50	100
Mexico	42	4	46	54	85
No Korea	34	4	38	62	61
Algeria	46	4	50	50	100
Myanmar	37	4	41	59	69
Viet Nam	42	4	46	54	85
Bangladesh	43	3	46	54	85
Indonesia	38	3	41	59	69
India	39	3	42	58	72
Sudan	45	3	48	52	92
Philippines	39	3	42	58	72
Iran	45	3	48	52	92
Saudi Arabia	45	3	48	52	92
Iraq	45	3	48	52	92
Libya	44	3	47	53	89
Zaire	46	3	49	51	96
Nigeria	45	2	47	53	89
Kenya	50	2	52	48	108

Figure 19–11

Percent of total population, except dependency ratio.
Dependency ratio = percent of dependent population (under 15 and over 15 years) to the working-age population (between 15-64 years).
Source: Population Reference Bureau (1).

Human Capital

On average, children throughout the world get 5.4 years of schooling. In undeveloped countries, where more than half of all humanity live, children go to school for only 1.4 years.

Giving very young children a "head start" on their education is a far from universal practice in developed countries — although in the United Kingdom, France, and three others, all five-year-olds are in school. In Japan, less than two out of three are in school at that age.

The United States has the highest portion of its young adults in school. The lowest portion is in the United Kingdom, where only one in twenty are still in school at age 21.

Human development

Education

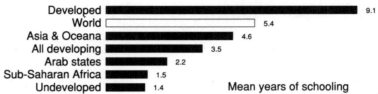

Mean years of schooling

Figure 19–12

Preschool enrollment of five-year-olds

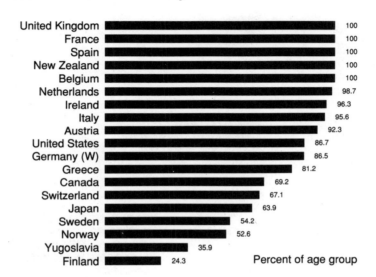

Percent of age group

Post-high school enrollment of 21-year-olds

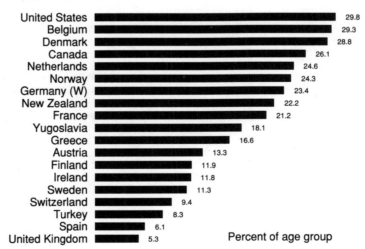

Percent of age group

In France and Belgium, nearly all children are in school from age three on through their secondary schooling. More than nine out of ten of these young people are still in school at age 17 in Belgium.

In Finland, Japan, and the United States, nine out of ten 17-year-olds are in school — although in Finland and Japan, the portion of very young children in school is relatively low.

Among less-developed countries, adult literacy is highest in Latin America. In the undeveloped world, a little more than one out of three adults are literate.

Arab governments spend $1.66 on their military establishments for every $1.00 they spend on education and health. Throughout the developing world, the amount is $1.09.

Latin American governments spend $0.29 on their military establishments for every $1.00 they spend on education and health — a lower ratio than the average developed-country government.

Enrollments in OECD preschool and post-high school classes

	3-YR-OLDS	4-YR-OLDS	5-YR-OLDS	AGE 17	AGE 21
United Kingdom	25.9	69.2	100	52.1	5.3
France	96.3	100	100	79.3	21.2
Spain	17.8	90.6	100	55.9	6.1
New Zealand	42.6	72.8	100	49.3	22.2
Belgium	94.1	98.1	100	92.7	29.3
Netherlands	0	97.9	98.7	79.2	24.6
Ireland	0.7	52.1	96.3	66.4	11.8
Italy	84.7	86.8	95.6		
Austria	28.5	63.4	92.3		13.3
United States	28.9	49.0	86.7	89.0	29.8
Germany (W)	32.3	71.6	86.5	81.7	23.4
Greece	9.1	43.2	81.2	55.2	16.6
Canada	0	41.4	69.2	75.7	26.1
Switzerland	5.4	18.7	67.1	84.6	9.4
Japan	15.6	54.6	63.9	89.3	
Sweden	38.5	42.4	54.2	83.1	11.3
Norway	31.6	44.1	52.6	75.2	24.3
Yugoslavia	18.5	22.8	35.9	66.3	18.1
Finland	16.0	19.6	24.3	90.6	11.9
Turkey				34.1	8.3
Australia				74.2	
Denmark				76.9	28.8
Luxembourg				83.4	

Figure 19–13

Percent of age group.
Enrollment rates, 1986 and 1987.
Source: Organization for Economic Cooperation and Development (8).

Adult literacy

Percent of total adult population

Military spending vs spending on education plus health

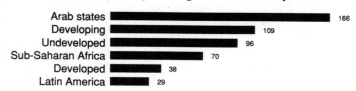

Ratio of monies spent in percent

In Arab states, 12 out of every 100 persons are in the armed forces. Worldwide, the portion is 5 out of every 100.

Latin American countries have a third as great a portion of their people in the armed forces as the developed countries do.

In Arab states, there are 9 men in the armed forces for every 5 teachers. Worldwide, there are 4 teachers for every 3 men in the armed forces.

Worldwide: life expectancy at birth increased ten years between 1960 and 1990; female children get two-thirds as much schooling as males do; a little over half as many women work as do men.

In the developed world, 139.3 persons out of every 1000 are scientists or technicians. In the developing world, 9.5 are. Worldwide, 43.9 are.

Armed forces and the population

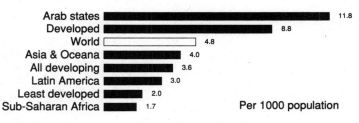

Per 1000 population

Armed forces and teaching forces

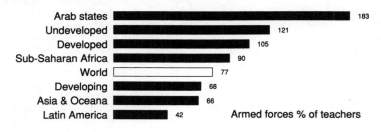

Armed forces % of teachers

Human development indicators by region

	SUB-SAHARAN AFRICA	ARAB STATES	ASIA & OCEANA	LATIN AMERICA	DEV'ED	DEV'ING	UN-DEV'ED	WORLD
LIFE EXPECTANCY								
1960	40.0	46.7	47.0	56.0	69.0	46.2	38.6	53.4
1990	51.8	62.1	68.1	67.4	74.5	62.8	50.7	63.5
ADULT LITERACY RATE (%)								
Total	45.0	53.0	72.0	82.0		60.0	36.0	
Male	56.0	66.0	82.0	84.0		70.0	47.0	
Female	34.0	39.0	61.0	80.0		49.0	24.0	
MEAN YEARS OF SCHOOLING								
Total	1.5	2.2	4.6	4.4	9.1	3.5	1.4	5.4
Male	2.0	3.0	5.7	4.6	9.4	4.4	2.1	6.1
Female	1.0	1.4	3.5	4.1	8.8	2.5	0.8	4.6
Female % of male	44.0	42.0	61.0	89.0	94.0	53.0	40.0	66.0
LABOR FORCE								
Percent of total pop	38.8	30.7	54.5	39.7	48.5	43.9	38.8	44.9
Women % of labor force	33.0	15.1	41.5	26.2	39.6	31.1	27.7	33.4
Female % of male	62.0	25.0	71.0	36.0	66.0	52.0	46.0	57.0
SCI/TECH PER 1000 POP			39.5		139.3	9.5		43.9
MILITARY								
$ Military as % of $ educ + $ health	70.0	166.0		29.0	38.0	109.0	96.0	
Armed forces /1000 pop	1.7	11.8	4.0	3.0	8.8	3.6	2.0	4.8
Armed forces /teachers (%)	90.0	183.0	66.0	42.0	105.0	68.0	121.0	77.0

Figure 19–14

Figures are for 1988–89 unless otherwise stated.
Undeveloped = per-capita GDP less than $500 annually.
Source: United Nations (4).

The United Nations human development index makes it possible to compare societies in how well they attend to the basic needs of their people. Japan ranks a solid first by this measure.

Throughout the developed world, differences in human development aren't nearly as large as differences in per-capita income.

South Africa and Brazil are two major societies with medium levels of development.

Leaders in human development

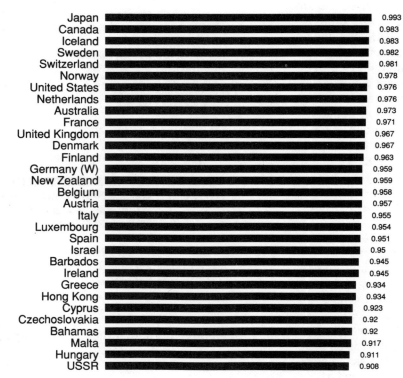

Japan	0.993
Canada	0.983
Iceland	0.983
Sweden	0.982
Switzerland	0.981
Norway	0.978
United States	0.976
Netherlands	0.976
Australia	0.973
France	0.971
United Kingdom	0.967
Denmark	0.967
Finland	0.963
Germany (W)	0.959
New Zealand	0.959
Belgium	0.958
Austria	0.957
Italy	0.955
Luxembourg	0.954
Spain	0.951
Israel	0.95
Barbados	0.945
Ireland	0.945
Greece	0.934
Hong Kong	0.934
Cyprus	0.923
Czechoslovakia	0.92
Bahamas	0.92
Malta	0.917
Hungary	0.911
USSR	0.908

United Nation's human development index

Medium levels of human development

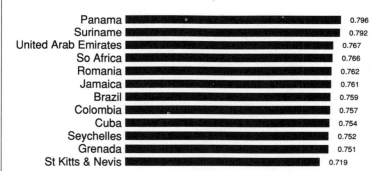

Panama	0.796
Suriname	0.792
United Arab Emirates	0.767
So Africa	0.766
Romania	0.762
Jamaica	0.761
Brazil	0.759
Colombia	0.757
Cuba	0.754
Seychelles	0.752
Grenada	0.751
St Kitts & Nevis	0.719

United Nation's human development index

Most of the societies at the lowest levels of human development are in Sub-Saharan Africa.

Nepal and Afghanistan are Asian societies in this group.

Lowest levels of development

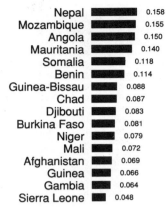

Country	Index
Nepal	0.158
Mozambique	0.155
Angola	0.150
Mauritania	0.140
Somalia	0.118
Benin	0.114
Guinea-Bissau	0.088
Chad	0.087
Djibouti	0.083
Burkina Faso	0.081
Niger	0.079
Mali	0.072
Afghanistan	0.069
Guinea	0.066
Gambia	0.064
Sierra Leone	0.048

United Nation's human development index

Human development indexes

	HUMAN DEVEL INDEX	LIFE EXPECT INDEX	EDUC INDEX			HUMAN DEVEL INDEX	LIFE EXPECT INDEX	EDUC INDEX
HIGH				41 Poland		0.863	71.8	67.8
1 Japan	0.993	78.6	69.5	42 Brunei		0.861	73.5	53.5
2 Canada	0.983	77.0	69.8	43 Argentina		0.854	71.0	65.2
3 Iceland	0.983	77.8	68.5	44 Venezuela		0.848	70.0	58.9
4 Sweden	0.982	77.4	69.1	45 Mexico		0.838	69.7	57.8
5 Switzerland	0.981	77.4	68.8	46 Antig/Barbuda		0.832	72.0	64.9
6 Norway	0.978	77.1	69.2	47 Mauritius		0.831	69.6	56.6
7 US	0.976	75.9	70.1	48 Kuwait		0.827	73.4	48.6
8 Netherlands	0.976	77.2	68.6	49 Albania		0.821	72.2	58.3
9 Australia	0.973	76.5	69.1	50 Qatar		0.812	69.2	52.0
10 France	0.971	76.4	69.1	51 Bahrain		0.810	71.0	49.3
11 UK	0.967	75.7	69.6	52 Malaysia		0.802	70.1	50.7
12 Denmark	0.967	75.8	69.2	53 Dominica		0.800	76.0	64.2
13 Finland	0.963	75.5	69.1					
14 Germany (W)	0.959	75.2	68.9	**MEDIUM**				
15 New Zealand	0.959	75.2	69.0	54 Panama		0.796	72.4	59.6
16 Belgium	0.958	75.2	68.6	55 Suriname		0.792	69.5	63.1
17 Austria	0.957	74.8	69.2	56 United Arab Em		0.767	70.5	41.0
18 Italy	0.955	76.0	66.8	57 So Africa		0.766	61.7	57.9
19 Luxembourg	0.954	74.9	68.6	58 Romania		0.762	70.8	66.2
20 Spain	0.951	77.0	65.3	59 Jamaica		0.761	73.1	67.0
21 Israel	0.950	75.9	66.3	60 Brazil		0.759	65.6	53.4
22 Barbados	0.945	75.1	68.1	61 Colombia		0.757	68.8	58.2
23 Ireland	0.945	74.6	68.6	62 Cuba		0.754	75.4	63.5
24 Greece	0.934	76.1	64.2	63 Seychelles		0.752	70.0	60.2
25 Hong Kong	0.934	77.3	60.7	64 Grenada		0.751	71.5	65.6
26 Cyprus	0.923	76.2	61.6	65 St Kitts & Nevis		0.719	67.5	62.0
27 Czechoslovakia	0.920	71.8	68.6	66 Thailand		0.713	66.1	61.6
28 Bahamas	0.920	71.5	68.1	67 Belize		0.700	69.5	62.2
29 Malta	0.917	73.4	65.3	68 St Lucia		0.699	70.5	56.0
30 Hungary	0.911	70.9	68.9	69 Saudi Arabia		0.697	64.5	39.5
31 USSR	0.908	70.6	68.5	70 Turkey		0.694	65.1	51.6
32 Uruguay	0.905	72.2	65.5	71 Fiji		0.689	64.8	55.0
33 Bulgaria	0.899	72.6	64.3	72 Syria		0.681	66.1	40.4
34 Yugoslavia	0.893	72.6	63.3	73 Paraguay		0.667	67.1	60.4
35 So Korea	0.884	70.1	65.3	74 No Korea		0.665	70.4	62.0
36 Portugal	0.879	74.0	57.9	75 Sri Lanka		0.665	70.9	59.6
37 Singapore	0.879	74.0	56.5	76 Libya		0.665	61.8	38.6
38 Chile	0.878	71.8	63.5	77 Ecuador		0.655	66.0	57.1
39 Trinidad/Tobago	0.876	71.6	65.4	78 Peru		0.644	63.0	56.6
40 Costa Rica	0.876	74.9	63.1	79 St Vincent		0.636	70.0	56.2
								(MORE)

Human development indexes, cont'd

		HUMAN DEVEL INDEX	LIFE EXPECT INDEX	EDUC INDEX			HUMAN DEVEL INDEX	LIFE EXPECT INDEX	EDUC INDEX
80	Dominican Rep	0.622	66.7	55.0	120	Pakistan	0.311	57.7	21.2
81	Samoa	0.618	66.5	61.7	121	Ghana	0.311	55.0	36.3
82	China	0.614	70.1	47.1	122	Cote d'Ivoire	0.311	53.4	33.0
83	Jordan	0.614	66.9	51.1	123	India	0.308	59.1	30.1
84	Philippines	0.613	64.2	60.7	124	Zaire	0.299	53.0	44.4
85	Nicaragua	0.612	64.8	53.2	125	Haiti	0.296	55.7	32.4
86	Oman	0.604	65.9	20.2	126	Comoros	0.274	55.0	32.3
87	Mongolia	0.596	62.5	62.7	127	Tanzania	0.266	54.0	35.3
88	Lebanon	0.592	66.1	52.7	128	Laos	0.253	49.7	34.2
89	Guyana	0.589	64.2	65.3	129	Nigeria	0.242	51.5	28.8
90	Tunisia	0.588	66.7	39.0	130	Yemen	0.242	51.5	21.9
91	Iraq	0.582	65.0	36.3	131	Togo	0.225	54.0	25.8
92	Iran	0.577	66.2	33.0	132	Liberia	0.220	54.2	22.1
93	Maldives	0.534	62.5	63.5	133	Rwanda	0.213	49.5	30.6
94	El Salvador	0.524	64.4	47.0	134	Uganda	0.204	52.0	28.9
95	Botswana	0.524	59.8	47.3	135	Senegal	0.189	48.3	21.6
96	Solomon Is	0.521	69.5	30.3	136	Bangladesh	0.186	51.8	22.1
97	Gabon	0.510	52.5	38.2	137	Equitor Guinea	0.186	47.0	30.2
					138	Malawi	0.179	48.1	28.4
LOW					139	Burundi	0.177	48.5	28.2
98	Indonesia	0.499	61.5	48.9	140	Cambodia	0.175	49.7	19.9
99	Viet Nam	0.498	62.7	57.3	141	Ethiopia	0.166	45.5	33.7
100	Honduras	0.492	64.9	46.3	142	Cent Africa Rep	0.166	49.5	21.3
101	Vanuatu	0.490	69.5	36.6	143	Sudan	0.164	50.8	16.5
102	Algeria	0.490	65.1	32.8	144	Bhutan	0.159	48.9	21.5
103	Guatemala	0.488	63.4	35.9	145	Nepal	0.158	52.2	15.5
104	Swaziland	0.462	56.8	46.3	146	Mozambique	0.155	47.5	18.9
105	Namibia	0.440	57.5	49.2	147	Angola	0.150	45.5	24.3
106	Myanmar	0.437	61.3	52.8	148	Mauritania	0.140	47.0	18.4
107	Lesotho	0.432	57.3	49.3	149	Somalia	0.118	46.1	11.3
108	Morocco	0.431	62.0	28.4	150	Benin	0.114	47.0	12.7
109	Cape Verde	0.428	67.0	32.0	151	Guinea-Bissau	0.088	42.5	20.2
110	Bolivia	0.416	54.5	49.7	152	Chad	0.087	46.5	15.4
111	Zimbabwe	0.413	59.6	42.2	153	Djibouti	0.083	48.0	9.4
112	SaoTome/ Princ	0.399	65.5	39.4	154	Burkina Faso	0.081	48.2	9.7
113	Kenya	0.399	59.7	44.0	155	Niger	0.079	45.5	14.4
114	Egypt	0.394	60.3	30.3	156	Mali	0.072	45.0	15.2
115	Congo	0.374	53.7	35.1	157	Afghanistan	0.069	42.5	16.3
116	Madagascar	0.371	54.5	51.9	158	Guinea	0.066	43.5	11.5
117	Papua N Guin	0.353	54.9	31.4	159	Gambia	0.064	44.0	13.7
118	Zambia	0.351	54.4	45.8	160	Sierra Leone	0.048	42.0	9.1
119	Cameroon	0.328	53.7	32.5					

Figure 19–15

Human development index 1991 is a composite of three factors: life expectancy; education (literacy plus levels of schooling); and real per-capita GDP.
Source: United Nations (4).

References

Asian Development Bank (1) Asian Development Outlook 1990.

Bank for International Settlements (1) International banking and financial market developments, May 1991; (3) Annual report, June 10, 1991; (4) Capital flows in the 1980s: a survey of major trends, April 1991.

Clearing House Interbank Payments System (CHIPS) (1) Yearly volume statistics from 1970 to present, received July 24, 1991.

Deutsche Bank (1) Rebuilding eastern Europe, Mar 1, 1990; (2) The Soviet Union at the crossroads, Oct 1, 1990; (3) The peace dividend — how to pin it down?, Mar 18, 1991.

European Community (1) EC national accounts, 1991; (2) Report on economic and monetary union in the European Community, June 1989; (3) EC commission welcomes pound sterling entry to Exchange Rate Mechanism, News release No. 37/90, Oct 9, 1990.

Eurostat (1) Statistical analysis of extra-Europe trade in hi-tech products, Eurostat CA-54-88-069-2A-C 1989.

General Agreement on Tariffs and Trade (1) GATT international 1988–89, Vol II, Dec 1989; (2) — Vol I, Dec 1989; (3) GATT Newsletter No. 69, Mar 1, 1990; (4) GATT international trade 1989-90, Vol I, Dec 1, 1990; (5) — Vol II, Dec 1990.

Inter-American Development Bank (1) Economic and social progress in Latin America, 1990 report, Oct 1990.

Institute of International Finance (1) Building free market economies in central and eastern Europe: challenges and opportunities, Apr 1990.

International Finance Corporation (1) Trends in private investment in 30 developing countries, Discussion paper #6, Sept 1989; (2) Emerging stock markets factbook 1990, Apr 1990; (3) Emerging stock markets factbook 1991, May 1991.

International Monetary Fund (1) World economic outlook, May 1990; (2) Direction of trade statistics yearbook 1990, May 30, 1990; (3) 1990 annual report, Apr 30, 1990; (4) World economic outlook, Oct 1990; (5) International capital markets, Apr 1990; (6) The economy of the USSR, Dec 19, 1990; (7) International capital markets, May 1991; (8) IMF Survey, May 27, 1991; (9) International financial statistics, Feb 1991; (10) World economic outlook, May 1991; (11) Direction of trade statistics yearbook 1991, Apr 30, 1991; (12) Memorandums to the press, various dates.

J P Morgan and Company (1) World financial markets, Apr 1991.

Organization for Economic Cooperation and Development (1) OECD in figures, supplement to OECD Observer No. 164, June/July 1990; (2) External debt statistics, end–Dec 1989 and end–Dec 1988, published 1990; (3) OECD Observer No. 167, Dec 1990/Jan 1991; (5) OECD in figures, supplement of OECD Observer No. 170, June/July 1991; (6) The Tokyo Roundtable: International direct investment and the new economic environment, 1990; (8) What changes for education? OECD Observer, Feb/Mar 1991; (9) Econonic Outlook, OECD Observer, Aug/Sept 1991.

Stockholm International Peace Research Institution (1) World Armaments and Disarmament Yearbook 1990, reprinted in Deutsche Bank (3).

Twentieth Century Fund (1) The free trade debate, 1989.

United Nations (1) Agricultural trade liberalization in the Uruguay Round, 1990; (3) World economic survey 1991; (4) Human development report 1991.

US Agency for International Development (1).

US Bureau of Labor Statistics (1) International comparisons of manufacturing productivity and unit labor cost trends, 1990, Aug 20, 1991; (2) Output per hour, May 1991.

US Central Intelligence Agency (1) Handbook of economic statistics, 1990, Sept 1990.

US Council of Economic Advisers (1) Economic report of the president, Feb 1991.

US Department of Agriculture (1) Pacific Rim agriculture and trade report, July 1990; (2) Developing economies situation and outlook series, July 1990; (3) Western Europe agriculture and trade report, Nov 1990; (4) US agricultural trade update, Nov 20 and Dec 20, 1990.

US Department of Commerce (1) Survey of current business, June 1991.

US Federal Reserve Bank of Boston (1) New England Economic Review, Sept/Oct 1990.

US Federal Reserve System (1) Country exposure survey, Federal Financial Institutions Examination Council, Apr 10, 1991.

World Bank (1) World development report, 1990; (2) World debt tables, Apr 1990; (3) Textiles trade in the developing countries, 1990; (4) Development issues, Development Committee, May 8, 1990; (5) World debt tables 1990–91, Dec 1990; (6) Global economic prospects and the developing countries 1991, May 1991.